MONTGOMERY COLLEGE LIBRARY -
GERMANTOWN CAMPUS

THE
TROUBLED
REPUBLIC

THE TROUBLED REPUBLIC:
AMERICAN GOVERNMENT, ITS PRINCIPLES AND PROBLEMS

FRED R. MABBUTT
GERALD J. GHELFI

JOHN WILEY & SONS
New York London Sydney Toronto

Copyright © 1974, by John Wiley & Sons, Inc.

All rights reserved. Published simultaneously in Canada.

No part of this book may be reproduced by any means, nor transmitted, nor translated into a machine language without the written permission of the publisher.

Library of Congress Cataloging in Publication Data:

Mabbutt, Fred R 1936–
   The troubled republic.

   1. United States—Politics and government—Handbooks, manuals, etc. I. Ghelfi, Gerald J. II. Title.

JK274.M13   320.4'73   73-19961
ISBN 0-471-55845-1
ISBN 0-471-55846-X (pbk.)

Printed in the United States of America

10 9 8 7 6 5 4 3 2 1

*By education most have been misled;
So they believe, because they so were bred.
The priest continues what the nurse began;
And thus the child imposes on man.*
           John Dryden (1631-1700)

For Carol and Eli
Who nursed a flame.

PREFACE

"I am crammed with one or two hundred dates and one or two thousand particulars about the quarrels of nobody knows who with an obscure governor, for nobody knows what. Just think of all that energy wasted! The only comfort is that this mass of information won't long burden me. I shall forget it with great ease." So commented Woodrow Wilson as a university student, and his lament has been echoed by students of American government into our own time. As the authors of this book, we take it for granted that most college students have been taught (or exposed to) American government before they enter the gates of a university. They have also been exposed to a Niagara of data about their government via television and radio. What we wish to do in this text is to provide the student with the tools to organize that data, and to analyze and evaluate it.

Our purpose has been to identify what were deemed to be just principles of government in 1776, and to test them in terms of their relevance and legitimacy as we approach 1976. We have attempted in particular to examine the experience of the American people from World War II to the present in light of these just principles of government plus the unmistakable fact that American government has undergone a major transformation in that time.

Many of the constitutional and sociological arrangements of power envisioned by the Founders as the cornerstone of republican government now seem unsupportive or even antagonistic to their original intent. Since the dawn of nuclear warfare in 1945, the exigencies of national security have forced the concentration of unparalleled power in the Presidency, but that power itself now poses a challenge to the maintenance of a free people. The affluence of Americans today has been unprecedented, but the prosperity is uneven and undergirded as much by government subsidies to big business, wealthy farmers, and defense contractors as by the initiative of individual citizens. At no time in the past has the nation's economic well-being been under greater direct or indirect governmental control, and there is little prospect in the future for that involvement to diminish. As economics is inextricably linked to political well-being, the viability of historic political principles must be considered in terms of these new socioeconomic conditions.

In 1976 America will celebrate the bicentennial anniversary of its birth. We may expect a whirl of festivities leading up to July 4th, 1976—staged by Madison Avenue admen and presidential commissions alike. But the 200th anniversary of the founding of the republic ought not to be allowed to fizzle to the level of firecrackers and carnivals. The occasion warrants more than the commercial claptrap of commemorative plates, T-shirts, and mugs; it warrants a review of the principles of the Declaration of Independence and a regard for their relevance to the circumstances of 1976. As Jefferson rightly observed, "The earth belongs to the living, not to the dead." Accordingly, we have focused on specific, recent tensions between republican principles and political practice.

The Frenchman Abbé Raynal once posed a question to Jefferson's generation, and that question remains relevant and important today: "Was the discovery of America a curse or blessing to mankind?" Jefferson hoped that it would be a blessing, when he announced in the Declaration of Independence that the goal of America's existence as a separate nation was the creation of a system of government that would ensure the freedom of its people. In 1776 it had yet to be demonstrated that men were not born with saddles on their backs, to be ridden by monarchs or despots. It had yet to be proved that "the people" were capable of self-government. Should the American people fail in their experiment, the hopes of other peoples aspiring to undertake similar experiments would be dashed or severely hobbled, and the general prejudice existent in Jefferson's day (and to some extent in our own), that self-government was unrealistic and freedom impractical, would be confirmed. The discovery of America might then be regarded as a curse for the prospects of democratic government. If, on the other hand, Americans succeeded in vindicating the character of self-government through their example, then the discovery of America would indeed be a blessing to mankind.

Abbé Raynal's question is relevant to us, for every generation of Americans must face the particular dangers unique to its own time that haunt democratic government. While we congratulate ourselves on our democracy in 1976, many foreign observers see us as arrogant, even brutal and contemptuous of the rights of ethnic and racial minorities at home and of smaller nations abroad. We appear to much of the world as Great Britain appeared to us at the time of the Revolution, "professing to stand for the constitutional principles of freedom and liberty contained in the Bill of Rights, to be champions of benevolence and justice, but acting, all too often, very differently." As Professor Page Smith has observed, the more government officials, and particularly the President, insist "on our purity, our virtue, wisdom, charity, and decency, the more many people, especially the young, are turned off America, off its institutions, its values, its 'way of life,' and history."*

The division of responsibility among the two authors is as follows: Fred R. Mabbutt, Chapters 7–14 and the Part introductions; Gerald J. Ghelfi, Chapters 1–6, 15 and 16, and the preface. Many people kindly helped nurture this book. We are grateful to Mrs. Kelley Powell, Assistant Librarian of Santa Ana College, for her many courtesies; to Mr. Thomas Osborne and Mrs. Charmay Allred for reading selected chapters and offering their valuable ideas; to Mr. Robert A. Dodds for his energetic and sage advice throughout the development of the entire manuscript; and to our editors, Mr. Carl Beers and Mr. Wayne Anderson, who steered us through some of the more treacherous academic shoals. We would like to pay tribute to the scholarship of the late Professor Douglass G. Adair and of Professor Martin Diamond whose teachings, both at the Claremont Graduate School and in print, have done much to permit the generation of Founding Fathers to speak within the context of the Founders' own Age of Enlightenment. Finally, we thank our wives, Carol Mabbutt and Eli Ghelfi, for their patience and encouragement during the gestation of the book, and we honor our parents, Morris and Thyra Mabbutt, Aldo and Pat Ghelfi, for their support in years of education that made this endeavor possible.

We have attempted, all in all, to provide a concise, "core" textbook in order to permit college students to use other, selected monographs that individual teachers believe to be particularly worthy of emphasis.

Some omissions exist in such a book, by its very nature. For those omissions that ought not to have been sacrificed, and for all errors, we accept full responsibility.

Santa Ana, California

Fred R. Mabbutt
Gerald J. Ghelfi

*Page Smith, "Too Much Money, Not Enough Spirit: Revival of 1776 Zeal Essential for America's 200th Anniversary," *Los Angeles Times* (July 1, 1973).

Fred Mabbutt would like to express his appreciation to reprint the following articles:

1. Fred R. Mabbutt, "The Constitution and the Nixon Court," *Colorado Quarterly* (Autumn 1973) (Chapter 7, "The Supreme Court") University of Colorado.
2. Fred R. Mabbutt, "Bureaucracy, Democracy, and the Fourth Branch of Government," *Cimarron Review* (July 1973) (Chapter 8, "The Bureaucracy") Oklahoma State University.
3. Fred R. Mabbutt, "The Fiber of Democracy: Equality in America," *Centennial Review* (Fall 1973) (Chapter 11, "The Fiber of Democracy: Equality in America) Michigan State University.
4. Fred R. Mabbutt, "Janus Revisited: Freedom And Conformity In A Technological Age," (April 1972) (Chapter 14, "Politics of a Mass Society) *Cimarron Review,* Oklahoma State University.
5. Fred R. Mabbutt, "Civil Rights in the Twenty-first Century" *Colorado Quarterly* (Spring 1972) (Chapter 12, "Civil Rights in the Twenty-first Century) University of Colorado. This same article was reprinted by *Current* (July/August 1972).

CONTENTS

I
SEEDTIME OF THE REPUBLIC

1. Declaration of Independence: Principles of a Free People 3
2. The Structure of Government: Organization of Power 19
3. A New Sociology: Making Democracy Safe for the World 41
4. The Constitution: Creation of a Federal Republic 63

II
THE FORM OF THE AMERICAN REPUBLIC

5. Congress: Can Americans Keep Their Republic? 85
6. The American Presidency 107
7. The Supreme Court 137
8. The Bureaucracy 159

III

THE REPUBLICAN EXPERIMENT: RIGHTS IN CONFLICT

9.	The Bill of Rights: The Right of Expression	175
10.	The Tides of Justice: Due Process of Law	195
11.	The Fiber of Democracy: Equality in America	217
12.	Civil Rights in the Twenty-first Century	237

IV

GOVERNING THE REPUBLIC: RESOLUTION OF CONFLICTS

13.	The Web of Politics: Struggle for Power	253
14.	Politics of a Mass Society	273
15.	Foreign Policy: Making the World Safe for Democracy	289
16.	Pursuit of Happiness: Resolving Domestic Conflicts	307

Appendices

The Declaration of Independence	327
The Constitution of the United States of America	331
Index	353

THE
TROUBLED
REPUBLIC

SEEDTIME OF THE REPUBLIC

There is no statement more contemporary to Americans, regardless of when they live, than the Declaration of Independence—the document that launched the United States' venture into republican government 200 years ago. Domestic conflicts, whether political or social, are usually justified or condemned in terms of the Declaration's rationale. And a good deal of present-day international politics, especially the arguments of emerging ex-colonial nations in Asia and Africa, are explained within its framework. Yet the Declaration of Independence is generally treated as an antique, limited to the context of American colonial relations with England in 1776. If the original statement of America's reason for existence as a nation is so regarded, it is little wonder that the study of American government in general fades into the realm of the historically interesting, rather than the currently significant, in the minds of many students.

In this text the Declaration of Independence will be regarded in the same manner as was intended by its author, Thomas Jefferson, and later understood by Abraham Lincoln when he worked to preserve the Union. In the midst of civil strife, Lincoln referred to the Declaration of Independence as "a standard maxim for free society." By this, he meant that the Declaration described the requirements for the creation and maintenance of a free people. Lincoln looked to the Constitution as the legitimate organization of power to keep the country united, but he regarded the Declaration of Independence as the benchmark by which the political action of Americans was judged to be right or wrong.

It has frequently been argued that the Declaration of Independence and the Constitution are incompatible documents, that the former is democratic whereas the latter is antidemocratic. This book rejects that view in favor of the analogy Lincoln drew to explain the relationship between them:

> "A word fitly spoken is like apples of gold in pictures of silver."

This analogy, drawn from the Book of Proverbs, means that the word fitly spoken, the apple of gold, is the *ends* of government as defined by the Declaration of Independence—that government exists as a function of the citizens to realize their "life, liberty and the pursuit of happiness." In 1787, when they wrote the Constitution, the Founding Fathers designed a government to put these ends into practice; they placed the apple of gold in the picture of silver. As Professor Harry Jaffa has stated,

> The picture was made, not to conceal, or destroy the apple; but to adorn and preserve it. The picture was made for the apple—not the apple for the picture.

In Part I we will first examine the *ends* of good government as defined by the Declaration of Independence. Then we will look at how the Constitution attempts to provide a picture of silver, or the *means* to put that good government into practice.

DECLARATION OF INDEPENDENCE:
Principles of a Free People

> *The burglars who broke into the headquarters of the Democratic National Committee at the Watergate were in effect breaking into the home of every citizen of the United States. . . . [and] what they were seeking to steal was not the jewels, money, or other property of American citizens, but something much more valuable—their most precious heritage, the right to vote in a free election.*
>
> —*Senator Sam J. Ervin, Jr.*

Senator Ervin, Chairman of the Senate Select Committee on Presidential Campaign Activities, made these remarks in opening the Senate hearings into the "Watergate Scandals" and was speaking about the apparent attempt by the White House to subvert the 1972 election. The Senate hearings revealed how the Committee to Reelect the President, together with some of the White House staff falsified campaign advertisements and letters, rigged polls, spied on opponents, burglarized offices, used electronic eavesdropping, and attempted to use the Central Intelligence Agency (CIA) and the Federal Bureau of Investigation (FBI) to cover up their crimes. Never in the 200-year history of the nation had members of any Administration launched so deliberate and calculated an attack on the very principles of republican government. In the Declaration of Independence Thomas Jefferson justified independence from British tyranny with the argument that governments derive "their just powers from the consent of the governed." But this "truth" was no longer as "self-evident" to the men involved in the Watergate conspiracy in 1972 as it appeared to those who adopted the Declaration in 1776.

The Watergate conspirators did not, of course, intentionally attack the principles of American freedom. Indeed, they thought they were preserving freedom. In the name of national security they used every means available to get Americans to make the "correct" choice in the election of 1972—every means with the exception of reason and honesty, which in fact are the only means by which people can express their own "consent." In a sense the "Watergate Scandals" were symptomatic of the nonrational and frequently deceptive means used to condition Americans to buy what advertisers presumed best for the public. Americans have become too accustomed to having their minds made up for them by public relations men and advertising agents who use sixty-second "spots" on television and radio to sell everything from underarm deodorant—to a President.

The idea of *consent* means at least that people are capable of making up their own minds on public issues. It does not include the use of "dirty tricks." The idea of consent also means that government is limited in what it can legally do. A just government cannot violate those unalienable rights of life, liberty, and the pursuit of happiness Jefferson believed all men possessed. Consent also includes the idea that people have the right to determine largely *how* they should pursue their happiness rather than allow the government or public officials to determine this for them. But governments that exist by the consent of the governed have a built-in tension between the politicians, those who have been elected to formulate public policy, and the people themselves, who claim ultimate sovereignty over these policies. This tension is inherent in the nature of republican government. Politicians do not like the possibility of losing an election, but they ought not to thwart the free-election process because of their anxiety. And the public could help improve the quality of elected representatives if people would respect public offices by giving politicians the searching evaluation they deserve.

Declaration of Independence: Principles of a Free People 5

Americans have historically been suspicious of politicians but they certainly have not been equally vigorous in their demand for excellence in public service. Adlai Stevenson, former governor of Illinois and Democratic presidential candidate in 1952 and 1956, made this observation by contrasting public support for a war and for domestic leadership. In the fall of 1943 Stevenson read in the Army newspaper *Stars and Stripes* that according to a public opinion poll seven out of ten parents declared they would not want a son of theirs to enter into public service as a career. It was fine for them to fight and die in World War II for the principles they believed the United States represented, but they should not work for these principles in peacetime as politicians. "This seemed to me a curious and foolish contradiction. And I suppose one of the problems anybody in public life has is to try to restore respect for politics and politicians. How can you respect, how can young people respect, let alone have any confidence in leadership of politicians, if the word has become a word of contempt, a word of derision. And this, if you please, in the land of Jefferson and Lincoln." Stevenson thought that anyone practicing this profession ought to improve its qualities and maintain the respect and esteem on which the success of politics depends. "We owe this not only to the system which we serve but to the continuity of the society which we fight for and die for."[1]

But the generation following Adlai Stevenson seems less inclined than ever to trust politicians to act within the principles Jefferson described, or in line with what Abraham Lincoln later called government of the people, by the people, and for the people. Having been duped and manipulated for over a decade in the 1960s, many Americans reacted to the political sewage that gushed from the 1972 election with cynicism and contempt for the words "politics" and "politicians." The Fair Campaign Practices Committee, a private, nonpartisan organization, reported that in the twenty years the committee studied elections it had "uncovered no campaign tactics comparable in extent or in potential damage to a free, self-governing society. The sordid scandal called the 'Watergate Horrors' is not simply more of the same tactics which have made 'politics' a dirty word. It is a conscious conspiracy to violate laws, to manipulate voters, and to make a mockery of the democratic system of self-government."[2] Senator Ervin observed that "Our citizens do not know whom to believe and many

---
[1] Quoted from a recorded interview, "A Recorded Portrait of Adlai Stevenson in Conversation with Arnold Michaelis," produced by Arnold Michaelis and made in Stevenson's study at his Libertyville House on June 19, 1956.
[2] *Los Angeles Times* (May 28, 1973).

of them have concluded that all the processes of government have become so compromised that honest governance has been rendered impossible."[3] Public suspicion of the integrity of politicians and particularly of President Nixon caused Americans to discuss, for only the second time in United States history, the possibility of impeaching the President.

Watergate

Before June 17, 1972 "Watergate" was simply a new hotel–office complex in Washington, D.C., which leased space to such prestigious clients as the Federal Reserve Board (eighth floor) and the Democratic National Committee (sixth floor). On the night of June 17th, seven men were arrested for burglarizing the offices of the Democratic National Committee. The investigations resulting from this arrest turned "Watergate" into a synonym for political corruption in Nixon's administration in much the same way as "Teapot Dome" had become a synonym for scandals in the Harding administration fifty years earlier. The defendants had previously entered the Democrats' offices on May 27, 1972, but returned on June 17th to photocopy additional documents and repair one telephone tap that was not working properly.

After the Watergate burglars were arrested, a variety of coverup schemes was developed by members of the White House staff, including former Attorney General John Mitchell, and the Committee to Reelect the President. All seven defendants refused to testify in their burglary trial and pleaded guilty in order to keep the affair from implicating "highest officials" in Washington. Later testimony revealed that funds from the Committee to Reelect the President were used to finance the burglaries by paying salaries and buying expensive cameras and electronic equipment. It was also learned that money from the same source was used to hire the attorneys for the seven defendants and to pay $1000 per month to the families of each man while he was in jail. Testimony revealed also that the defendants were reassured that they would not remain in jail long because the President would shortly grant Executive clemency for them.

To further cover up the White House staff's participation in the Watergate affair, the CIA was asked by White House aides to state publicly that the June 17th burglary was a CIA operation conducted to protect national security. The then-director of the CIA, Richard Helms, refused to compromise the agency and shortly thereafter was relieved

[3] *The New York Times* (May 18, 1973).

of his position because he had been appointed ambassador to Iran. Nevertheless the CIA had other links in the case. Two of the convicted conspirators, James McCord and E. Howard Hunt, were former CIA agents. And the CIA admitted to supplying Hunt with such espionage equipment as false identification papers, a camera, and a disguise kit that Hunt used in burglarizing the office of Pentagon Papers defendant Daniel Ellsberg's psychiatrist. Hunt had served as one of the "plumbers" to plug leaks within the government to newsmen about secret White House operations, and because of his experience Hunt was selected by White House advisors to obtain a psychiatric profile of Ellsberg. When this part of the coverup was eventually exposed the Ellsberg case was thrown out of court by Judge Byrne. In the final sessions of the court, Judge Byrne reported that he had been called to the Western White House in San Clemente, California, while the Ellsberg trial was in progress, and Mr. Nixon's advisor John Ehrlichman suggested President Nixon might name Byrne to be FBI director.

The FBI itself was involved in the illegal activities of the White House. Nixon first nominated a former political supporter, L. Patrick Gray III, to replace the deceased J. Edgar Hoover as FBI director. But as the Watergate scandal unraveled, Gray admitted that while he was serving as Acting Director of the FBI he placed some White House papers in a "burn-bag" and destroyed evidence that "should never see the light of day." Additionally, some FBI agents claimed that the bureau had been seriously compromised by Gray, that Gray tried to make the FBI a political tool of the Nixon Administration. That incident involved attempts by the White House to halt the FBI's investigations of the sources of money for the Committee to Reelect the President. Some of this money was traced through Mexican banks where it had been laundered in an effort to hide the donors' identities. Later investigations linked this money to the funds used to pay the Watergate wiretappers.

The law-and-order rhetoric of President Nixon's political campaigns was not only undermined by these double dealings and crimes, but was also made even more unbelievable when former Attorney General John Mitchell was indicted by a grand jury on charges of conspiracy to defraud the government and six counts of perjury. At issue was the grand jury's charge that Mitchell used his influence as Attorney General to stop the Security and Exchange Commission (SEC) from investigating the financial deals of Robert Vesco, whom the SEC accused of looting $224 million from investors in a mutual fund stock. Vesco reportedly offered $500,000 to the Nixon reelection committee but the Republican Finance chairman, Maurice Stans, who served in Nixon's first cabinet as Secretary of Commerce, assured Vesco only half that amount would be sufficient. It was suggested the money be delivered in cash and given prior to April 7, 1972, the date the new Campaign Practices Act of 1972 came into effect. Gifts prior to that date could be assured of anonymity. Vesco paid $200,000 but the SEC continued probing into his dealings. Nor, according to the grand jury indictment, were the efforts of Mitchell and Stans successful in stopping the SEC's investigations, although the then-director of the SEC resigned. When Mitchell and Stans were indicted on charges of conspiracy and perjury they suffered the possibility of a fate—prison—that has befallen only two other Cabinet members—Warren Harding's Secretary of Interior Albert Fall and his Attorney General Harry Daugherty. Unlike Harding's scandals, however, which involved some schemes to make money as Daugherty's selling illegal liquor permits and pardons, the Watergate affair of 1972–1973 was a deliberate and conscious attempt by powerful, and often arrogant men to subvert the democratic process of American government.

Two of the "highest White House sources" implicated in these various illegalities were two of President Nixon's personal advisors, H. R. Haldeman, White House chief of staff, and presidential assistant John Ehrlichman. President Nixon dismissed both men after newsmen continued to publish findings from their own investigations. It was in John Ehrlichman's White House safe, for example, that the FBI transcripts of seventeen wiretaps ordered by Mitchell were eventually found—after they had mysteriously disappeared from FBI files. Mitchell ordered the taps, thirteen on government employees and four on newsmen, without a court order but on power he presumed to possess as Attorney General. Subsequently the Supreme Court held, 8–0, that the Attorney General in fact does not have that power. The late director of the FBI, J. Edgar Hoover, executed Mitchell's order but reportedly did so reluctantly because taps on newsmen were unprecedented. Later, White House aides became fearful that Hoover might use these transcripts as blackmail to pressure the Administration on some other matters (as Hoover was believed to have done with information the bureau picked up on congressmen). Without Hoover's knowledge these transcripts were moved out of his files and stored in Ehrlichman's safe.

Attorney General Mitchell's statement, "Watch what we do and not what we say" became an ironic prophecy when the Senate investigating committee did indeed watch what he was doing. Senator Ervin's committee learned that in 1970 the White House had organized a secret investigating force, which would have been used much more extensively to gather information about critics of the Nixon administration and political opponents had Hoover not refused to support the plan. The Senate hearings showed also that those who led this conspiracy against the Constitution and Bill of Rights were neither Communists nor Communist dupes, the source of danger Americans had expected since the close of World War II, but former FBI and CIA agents, former policemen, militant Cuban anti-Communists, the Attorney General of the United States, the chief legal counsel to the President, and President Nixon's top personal advisors. These men, who proudly wore emblems of the American flag as lapel pins in their suit coats, justified their activities in the name of national security. One of them, John Caulfield, a former New York policeman, had been involved in a counteraction to prevent the Statue of Liberty from being blown up by radicals.

Thus, while working to save the monuments of the American republic, the Watergate participants trampled upon the principles of free government that the flag and the Statue of Liberty symbolize.

Republican Principles

In 1776 the study of politics, particularly the investigation of how a republic could be created, commanded the attention and respect of politicians and the public alike. The word "republic" is of Latin origin; it combines *res*, thing, affair, or interest, with *publica*, public. In 1755 the English lexicographer Dr. Samuel Johnson defined republic as a "state in which the power is lodged in more than one, a commonwealth" and he defined commonwealth as "the general body of the people; a government in which the supreme power is lodged in the people."[4] Simply stated, a republic, *respublica*, is a government that receives its legitimacy from the consent of the people and responds to the public interest. Two principles are axiomatic to republics: liberty, in order for citizens to choose what they believe is best for themselves; and equality, in order for each citizen to have the same influence upon government.

Liberty

Jefferson's argument for revolution given in the Declaration of Independence is simple: All men are born with certain rights. Jefferson

[4] Samuel Johnson, *A Dictionary of the English Language* (London: Strahan, 1755). See under Republic and Commonwealth.

called them *unalienable rights,* because they are inherent within all human beings by virtue of their humanness and can never be separated from them except by death. Government is necessary to make these rights secure so that men can enjoy the liberties they are born with; if a government double-crosses citizens by obstructing the very liberties it is created to support, then the people have the duty to revolt and establish a new government. This argument was not new, nor did it originate with Jefferson. Englishmen who read the Declaration of Independence were familiar with the logic and probably had read most of the words before.

The Declaration was adopted largely from the earlier revolutionary statement of the Englishman John Locke (1632-1704) who, in his *Second Treatise on Government* (1690), provided the rationale to legitimatize the English revolution of 1688. In 1688, Parliament claimed sovereignty in England on the basis that it was the legislature that truly represented the public interest. Parliament appointed a new monarch, who was required to acknowledge English liberties by signing the Bill of Rights (1689). Because the change to a constitutional monarchy was made without war, the English experience of 1688 is remembered as the Glorious Revolution.

Tyranny, whether in the form of monarchy or dictatorship, at the time of Locke or Jefferson or in our own day, exists on the premise that no man is born free. John Locke taught the opposite: "Men being . . . by nature all free, equal, and independent, no one can be put out of this estate, and subjected to the political power of another, without his own consent."[5] Consent is necessary to make government legitimate. Men must agree with each other to leave their "state of nature"; they must agree to form a political society, and they must agree to have a government rule them. The "state of nature" was an intellectual construction used by Locke to explain that men existed before governments were established. By arguing the prior existence of men, Locke held that government was created deliberately by free men and thus government was the servant of man and not his master.

If men have liberty in this "state of nature," why would they give up their perfect freedom and establish a government to rule them? Locke pointed to two primary motives: reduction of the threat to one's life and preservation of one's property. In the state of nature everyone is perfectly free. There is no superior. No one can tell another what to do. Their guide is reason. "Men living together according to reason, without a common superior on earth with authority to judge between them, is properly the state of nature."[6] Unfortunately all men do not

[5] John Locke, *Of Civil Government, Second Treatise,* Section 95.
[6] *Ibid.* Section 19.

consult reason all the time. Locke noted that conflicts ensue and the state of nature becomes a state of anxiety "full of fears and continual dangers."[7] Without government everyone is responsible for defending themselves as best they can. The weak are at the mercy of the strong; and the strong, who are few, are at the mercy of the weak, who are many, for the majority has the advantage of sheer numbers over the minority.

When do men leave this "state of nature" and establish government? In Locke's view of history this event could happen at any time, whether far in the past or yesterday. Because of the way history is commonly looked at today, this event appears to have occurred only once, a long time ago. Present-day conceptions of evolution and progress, largely framed in the nineteenth century, depict history as a long line of development, and place man's separation from the state of nature in the remote past, when primordial man left his primitive condition once and for all. Locke, of course, lived before the introduction of these nineteenth-century notions of progress and evolution, therefore his references to leaving the state of nature are in the present tense. We miss the significance of Locke's teaching if we project the transition from the state of nature to a civil society as an event occurring in the distant past.[8] As Professor Robert Goldwin notes, a "state of nature" may exist for anyone living today.

---

[7] *Ibid.* Section 123.

[8] These different views of time help account for our different interpretation of the word "revolution." Jefferson's generation thought of revolution in terms of "revolve"; we are more inclined to think of the word "revolt." Isaac Newton's discoveries in astronomy in the 1690s caused his and succeeding generations to emphasize the mechanical characteristic of revolution as returning or revolving to an original position. We use the word in the same way when describing the rotation of engines in revolutions per minute, rpm. Revolution in this sense is harmony and the antithesis of chaos, lawlessness, or anarchy. Newton demonstrated mathematically that the universe was in a continual revolution: stars, planets, suns, moons, all follow a predictable, precise pattern of revolution in which their movements were synchronized by an amazing harmony of their respective energies. The framers of the American Constitution attempted to discover political institutions that would preserve the diversity of free men just as Newton was able to articulate the laws that described the orderly movement of heavenly bodies.

Today, the word "revolution" is associated with a radical departure from the present, often involving violence and anarchy, in which existing institutions are overthrown in a calculated effort to move the nation as far from the past as possible so it can never return to prerevolutionary conditions. We are reminded of the disorderliness of political revolution from the French experience of 1789 down to the present. In science, too, focus has shifted from the mathematical orderliness of Newton's universe and the assumptions of a Creator and purpose, to the evolution of biological and botanical life that Charles Darwin described, in 1859, as emerging from chance in a ceaseless struggle for existence in which the fittest survive and change continually.

Suppose that you are walking alone down an isolated street in any large American city, at night, and off in the distance you see a figure of a man approaching. It is ominously quiet; you see no one else around; you realize that there are no homes on the street; you recall that a police patrol passed five minutes ago and so you have no hope that they will be back for quite a while—not soon enough for you in case you should need help. Now, then, as the two of you approach, there is no common superior to intervene in case of controversy who can intervene in time. For all practical purposes, the two of you are in the state of nature although, in another sense, you are in civil society.

In this state-of-nature situation you obviously have a right to defend yourself if necessary, and even to injure or kill the other if he attacks you. But what if he is bigger? What if he is male and you are female? What if he has a knife? The man approaching may be as frightened of you as you are beginning to be of him, and he may turn and go in the opposite direction; or you may do the same before he does. But suppose the two of you buck up your courage, and stride on toward each other, and then pass with no incident whatever—was that the state of nature? According to Locke's description of it, emphatically yes. The state of nature is not defined by the presence or absence of violence. It is defined only by the presence or absence of someone with authority to settle controversies that might arise.[9]

The state of nature is intolerable because force can be used anytime to intimidate the weak or unsuspecting. When force is used without right the situation changes abruptly to what Locke calls a "state of war." "For instance, if the stranger on the dark street pulled a knife and threatened you with it to steal your wallet, that would be the state of war, for he would be using force without right."[10] Therefore, Locke concluded government is continually necessary for the preservation of the individual and his rights.

Men also establish government to preserve their own property. Locke defined property broadly to include "life, liberty, and estate," which Jefferson restated in the Declaration of Independence as "life, liberty, and the pursuit of happiness." "Every man has a property in his own person," claimed Locke, and when he works picking up apples he extends part of himself to these apples by his labor. By mixing his labor with the apples they become his personal property. Locke observed that this property was an extension of the laborer and therefore he had every right to protect it. He also could gather

---

[9] Robert A. Goldwin, "St. John's College Asks John Locke Some Questions," *The College*, Vol. XXIII, No. 1 (April 1971), p. 4.
[10] *Ibid.*

Declaration of Independence: Principles of a Free People 13

all the apples he wished, as long as he did not deprive someone else of enough apples to preserve their own life. Uneaten apples would rot and thus his effort at hoarding would prove useless.

With the introduction of money, however, Locke noted that one can hoard at will because money, unlike produce, does not deteriorate with age. Money made economic inequality unavoidable, as men have different abilities and some will excel in business. Locke thought the opportunity of increasing goods was advantageous. Nature, left undeveloped by labor, could not produce sufficient goods to provide for the needs of an increased population. The lot of mankind could be improved by labor. But the unequal distribution of money made the absence of government intolerable. Danger of aggression increased with the unequal distribution of possessions, and the accompanying inequality of power. Thus, government was essential to provide "an established, settled, known law"; a "judge with authority to determine all differences according to the established law"; and "power to back and support the sentence when right, and to give it due execution."[11]

Equality

The idea "all men are created equal" is also basic to republican government. Inasmuch as government exists by the free consent of each individual, each citizen must have the same influence upon that government to protect himself. Every citizen should be equal before its laws, all should have equal influence in selecting the men who make and administer those laws, and every citizen should be equal in defining the public interest. Although republican forms of government attempt to translate this goal into reality, in practice the goal is never totally reached.

All men were not equal when Jefferson wrote the Declaration of Independence. Slavery existed on his own farm and slavery is the antithesis of equality. Slavery did not end legally in the United States until the adoption of the Thirteenth Amendment in 1865, eighty-nine lears later. Not until very recently have all minorities insisted on exercising their political equality by voting. Nor were women equal in 1776. Not until the adoption of the Nineteenth Amendment in 1920, 144 years later, did women become politically equal to vote, hold office, own property, and sue in courts. Jefferson was not describing current conditions when he wrote "all men are created equal"; but the experience of the United States has moved—sometimes the country has

---

[11] Locke, *Second Treatise on Government,* Sections 124, 125, 126.

been jerked and pushed—toward making this goal a reality.

Jefferson considered equality "self-evident" on the grounds of man's common origin. As human beings, all men have a common origin; they belong to the same species. No man can grant life, therefore no man can morally take the life of another (with the obvious exception of just punishment), or subjugate another, or make another man his slave. Everyone has an equal right of survival. Everyone has a faculty to reason and choose how to preserve his life. All men everywhere have, or at least potentially could have, the ability to reason and choose. The "self-evident" idea of equality was supported by the philosophy of *natural law,* which held that there was a law that distinguished right from wrong in the world that reasonable men could know. According to natural law, political equality was not the mere invention of men. Neither custom, nor tradition, nor national heritage originated equality. Man was equal by virtue of his existence as a human being. Jefferson, on the eve of his death in 1826, eloquently restated the principle he wrote fifty years earlier in the Declaration of Independence:

> The general spread of the light of science has already laid open to every view the palpable truth that the mass of mankind has not been born with saddles on their backs, nor a favored few booted and spurred, ready to ride them legitimately.[12]

Jefferson addressed the Declaration of Independence to all mankind, not to Parliament or King George III, because he was advocating the rights of humankind, irrespective of time or place.

Despite the virtue of the principle of equality, however, it is exceedingly difficult to put into practice. One reason for this difficulty is that some people deny the principle by declaring their superiority over another race or group. Prejudice, by definition, denies man's equality and thus the discriminated group is reduced to second-class citizenship. Another reason for this difficulty is the fact that even where people openly support the principle of equality there are different talents and abilities in people that give some men more influence on government.

In theory all individuals are equal in shaping the course of government, but in practice those citizens with the advantage of talent, education, money, or family connections will have a greater effect on government than will those people who are limited either by capac-

---

[12] George Sabine, "The Two Democratic Traditions," *The Philosophical Review,* Vol. LXI (Oct. 1952), p. 473.

ity or opportunity. The advantaged citizens can afford the costs of legal proceedings when brought before the law and often escape the consequences of illegalities that poorer people pay for by going to jail; those with advantages will have extraordinary influence in nominating, electing, and influencing the men chosen to legislate and to administer the laws; and those with advantages can exercise greater influence in defining the public interest.

For example, Otto Kerner, a U.S. Court of Appeals judge and twice governor of Illinois, was found guilty in 1973 of taking part in a racetrack stock deal netting him $145,000 in profit. The sixty-four-year-old Kerner could have received up to fifty-eight years in prison but was sentenced to three years and $50,000 in fines. However, he was sentenced under a provision that makes him eligible for immediate parole and therefore he may never serve a day in jail. James R. Hoffa, former Teamsters Union chief, served only part of his thirteen-year sentence due to the commutation of President Nixon. Despite the fact that on three separate occasions the prison parole board refused to grant Hoffa a parole, the then Attorney General Mitchell and the then counsel to President Nixon, Charles W. Colson, recommended Hoffa's term be commuted. Hoffa was released in 1971 and in the 1972 election the Teamsters Union was one of Nixon's strongest supporters among organized labor. Attorney Colson subsequently joined a private Washington law firm and the Teamsters transferred to that firm its legal affairs, estimated to be worth $100,000 a year in fees. And John B. Connally, while Secretary of the Treasury, approved a moratorium on $1.3 million in back taxes owed the federal government by another past president of the Teamsters, Dave Beck. Later Connally became chairman of Democrats for Nixon; his national vice chairman was the current Teamster chief, Frank Fitzsimmons.

Spiro T. Agnew lashed out at "permissive judges" who were "soft on criminals" while on speech circuits as vice president of the United States. But when the Justice Department proceeded with its investigations of Agnew's kickback arrangements with building contractors in Baltimore County, Maryland, the former champion of "law and order" quickly took advantage of judicial leniency by resigning as Vice President on October 10, 1973 and pleading no contest in court to income tax evasion. The Justice Department then agreed to drop evidence allegedly showing that Agnew received at least $88,750 between 1967 and 1972 from engineering firms seeking government business in Maryland; that he received many times that amount in the form of a percentage of costs arising from government contracts he helped secure for individual firms; that he received illegal payments in his vice president's office through December 1972 from at least two individuals who sought more federal contracts. Agnew was given a $10,000 fine and three years' probation. On the day before Agnew's conviction and resignation a draftsman in Sacramento, California was sentenced in municipal court to 70 days in jail for fishing without a license and possessing seven striped bass under the legal size limit; that same week six Mexicans were sentenced in El Paso, Texas to 100 days in jail for illegally coming into this country to find work; on the same day as Agnew's conviction an officer in a Rhode Island electrical-contracting concern pleaded guilty to evading $26,306 in taxes. He was fined $5,000 and sentenced to 4 months in prison.

Turning These Principles into a Viable Government

As long as the United States government is dependent on the consent of American people for its legitimacy, tension will continue between politicians and the electorate. Holding elected officials in reserve and compelling them to face regular elections is healthy, particularly if Americans recognize the importance of politicians to republican government. Certainly Americans will have to break away from the hypnotic sixty-second political commercials on television and critically evaluate candidates for themselves.

Tension between the principles of liberty and equality is also inherent in the nature of republican government. Those citizens with economic, educational, or family advantages tend to emphasize liberty; they wish to exercise their advantages freely and want the role of government narrowly defined. In contrast, those citizens without particular advantages tend to emphasize equality; they want the role of government expanded to ensure that all citizens are treated equally.

These differences are resolved, however imperfectly, by the convention of majority rule. Of necessity we have agreed that a majority must rule. According to John Locke, everyone agrees unanimously to leave the state of nature and join civil society, but it is unreasonable to expect everyone to agree on all policies thereafter. Therefore a legal fiction is created—the majority will speak for the whole. There is no moral reason why the majority should rule. The majority is simply closer to being the whole than the minority. To allow the minority to rule, however, might imply the dangerous proposition that a few are more capable of ruling and thus support the idea that men are not equal.

How these conflicting interests can be resolved, and particularly how the interests of a minority can be protected, is the great desideratum of republican governments. Three requirements, at least, are necessary to turn republican principles into a viable government.

One requirement has to do with the structure of government. Constitutional powers must be arranged in such a way that government can meet its executive, legislative, and judicial functions, but simultaneously checks the tendency of the men who do these jobs from using their power despotically. One significant aspect of the "Watergate Scandals," for example, was the constitutional ability of the Senate to investigate thoroughly the Executive branch. In addition to the importance of the arrangement of powers, however, is the necessity of a Bill of Rights and a free press. It was the free press that eventually brought the White House operations in Watergate to the light of day and, in fact, had done what the Justice Department should have been doing.

Another requirement has to do with the social foundation of government. A large middle class is essential to republics. Ideally all citizens, but at least a large majority, must have sufficient economic security to provide for their subsistence needs of food, shelter, and clothing. A nation composed of half-starved, ill-housed, and poorly clothed citizens cannot support republican government because the miserable condition of the people compels them to place this personal survival ahead of national needs. Such socioeconomic conditions are the seedbed of demagogues and despots.

Finally, people must believe that their government is adhering to democratic processes. Regardless of how wealthy the society or well organized the constitution, the viability of a republic ultimately rests with the people themselves. They must believe their participation in elections will be an honest expression of their consent to have the government govern, and that their participation will have some influence on the direction of the government's policies. If citizens have been manipulated to vote in a particular way, their participation in an election is a sham; they are merely used to confirm policies about which they have no knowledge. This is not government by consent but a form of tyranny wrapped in the appearance of consent. Once citizens realize they are being played for fools they may become cynical about politicians, and, worse, even reject the idea that democratic government is possible.

THE STRUCTURE OF GOVERNMENT:
Organization of Power

Institute new government ... organizing its powers in such form, as to them shall seem likely to effect their Safety and Happiness.
—*Thomas Jefferson*
Declaration of Independence

Can the American Constitution still maintain a viable republic for all 210 million Americans, or should it be laid to rest, as some suggest, with due respect for its past success while a "modern" convention is convened to draw up a new Constitution to deal with twentieth-century problems of governmental power and personal liberty?

Conditions affecting governmental power and individual liberty have changed fundamentally in the nearly 200 years since 1787, particularly within the lifetime of the generation born since the close of World War II in 1945. When the Constitution was written during the hot Philadelphia summer of 1787, Americans lived in a rural, preindustrial society lying east of the Allegheny mountains. The pace of life was slow and the country seemed isolated from foreign conflicts.

Moreover, the problems of the day appeared intelligible to ordinary citizens. Today the United States spans a continent and stretches across 3000 miles of ocean to Hawaii. Its interests encircle the earth and foreign policies are as complicated in their execution as they are to understand.

Before 1945, the two oceans between the Americas and the rest of the world provided the United States with a degree of international security. But now a nuclear warhead contained in the nose of an intercontinental ballistic missile, all set to be fired from a submarine, has wiped out that security. An enemy submarine can lie hidden either in international waters thousands of miles away or just outside the twelve miles of ocean the United States claims along its borders. It can launch the same, devastatingly accurate attack from either position.

Nuclear power has revolutionized political power. Ever since President Harry S Truman ordered the dropping of the first atomic bomb, Americans have been compelled to trust each succeeding President to act secretly, even beyond the normal guidelines of democratic procedure, in order to maintain national security. Presidential power has increased enormously during the lifetimes of those reading this book, and there appears to be little prospect of that power diminishing.

A no less important factor affecting political power relationships has been the changing conditions within the United States. Masses of Americans are now crowded into urban areas, where tensions are rife between differing interests and sections of cities. Public issues are numerous, complex, and beyond the grasp of ordinary citizens. Problems of enormous magnitude and complexity emerge from these social conditions. Technology has created new political crises, such as finding sufficient energy to maintain employment in an industrial economy, or finding means to reduce environmental pollution threatening all forms of life. Such problems are unprecedented in their nature and solution; legislation aimed at reducing pollution often tends to accentuate the energy crisis, and vice versa. And congressmen, who have already been preempted by the President in formulating foreign policies, are often unable to initiate leadership in resolving domestic problems because they find that they are supposed to be representing the interests of opposing factions.

One important consequence of this change is that Americans are left feeling powerless. They are represented by congressmen, but as population increases the constituency of each congressman enlarges also. The size of population alone removes congressmen physically and personally from most of the people they represent. In addition to feeling helpless, many Americans are also frustrated because they cannot influence national policies as republican theory tells them ought to be possible. In the past many Americans at least thought they had control. Abraham Lincoln commented on this belief when he reportedly looked out from his White House window one morning toward a log floating down the Potomac and observed: "There are thousands of ants on that log, and every single one of them thinks he's steering it." Few today would actually claim to be steering.

This frustration and sense of powerlessness helps account for why some Americans feel the Constitution has outlived its usefulness. In the past Americans often used the Constitution as a touchstone in support of whatever position they held. For example, when Americans divided over the legitimacy or illegitimacy of slavery or divided over whether government should or should not pass laws to regulate industry, each group in these controversies would argue the Constitution supported their position. By contrast today some Americans want the Constitution completely rewritten in order to enshrine their own views within it.

How to Update the Constitution

Both conservatives and liberals have recently tried to recreate the Constitution in their own image.

In the 1960s Senator Everett Dirksen of Illinois began a movement among state legislatures to request that Congress call a new Constitutional Convention for the purpose of rewriting the Constitution in order to restrict part of the Bill of Rights and undo the reapportionment decisions of the 1960s. Two issues prompted this request. First was the Supreme Court decision in *Engle v. Vitale* (1962) that held unconstitutional a twenty-one word prayer composed by the New York Board of Regents for use in the New York public schools. "One Southern Senator, jelling his segregationist views with his anguish over the School Prayer decision, lamented, 'They [the Supreme Court Justices] have taken God out of the schools and put the Nigras in.' "[1] The second issue was the Supreme Court's reapportionment decisions in *Baker v. Carr* (1962) followed by *Wesberry v. Sanders* and *Reynolds v. Sims* (1964). In these decisions the Court held that congressional districts for both state and federal legislatures must be drawn so that each district would have approximately the same number of people.

[1] Fred R. Mabbutt, "The Constitution: Has It Outlived Its Usefulness?" *Ball State University Forum*, Vol. XIII, No. 4 (Autumn 1972), p. 37.

Hitherto, for example, one congressional district in Georgia had as few as 272,154 citizens whereas the largest district had 823,680 people. The effect of reapportionment would be the release of the rural–conservative grip on both the state and federal legislatures, and the creation of new districts in urban–liberal areas.

By 1965 conservatives in both political parties were circulating two constitutional amendments; one was the Dirksen amendment, which would allow one legislative chamber to be apportioned on some basis other than population, and the other was the School Prayer Amendment designed to "put God back into the schools." In addition conservatives circulated among the fifty state legislatures a petition to ask Congress to call a new Constitutional Convention for the purpose of writing these two considerations inside the document itself. Article V of the Constitution requires two-thirds of the states to petition Congress before Congress can call a new Constitutional Convention; thirty-three of the necessary thirty-four approved that petition.

Although 1967 was the high-water mark for these efforts, which have since subsided as most states reapportioned their districts to accommodate new population centers, the United States still came within one vote of facing for the first time in its history the possibility of having the Constitution rewritten. Some important questions have been left in the wake of these efforts. Are the petitions still valid? Can states rescind their earlier approval as Utah attempted to do in 1969? What would prevent a convention from "going far beyond the aim of its sponsors and indulging in a wholesale rewriting of the country's basic charter, including a revision of the Bill of Rights?"[2] In 1787 the first Constitutional Convention went beyond *its* original instructions, and wrote a new document entirely instead of revising the old Articles of Confederation.

Liberals have been content to remain within their ivory towers, choosing rather to write models for a new Constitution instead of petitioning for a Second Constitutional Convention. One of their more prominent models was written in the 1960s by Rexford Tugwell and 150 scholars at the Center for the Study of Democratic Institutions in Santa Barbara, California. Tugwell was one of the original members of the New Deal "brain trust" that tried, unsuccessfully, to persuade Franklin D. Roosevelt to centralize control of the national economy. Along with many Americans in the 1930s, Tugwell doubted whether the traditional form of government could cope with the fundamentally changed socioeconomic conditions; his recent "model" attempts to

---

[2] *Ibid.,* p. 38. See also: Theodore C. Sorensen, "The Quiet Campaign to Rewrite the Constitution," *Saturday Review* (July 15, 1967).

correct the apparent weaknesses in the Constitution so the government can deal effectively with twentieth-century problems.

In Tugwell's scheme, the fifty states would disappear in favor of twenty republics, each with about 10 million people, in order to eliminate geographic "distortions" that often obstruct legislation for the common good. "Reflecting his personal experience during the Depression when many of his New Deal farm policies were thwarted by the Supreme Court, Tugwell's Constitution calls for a strengthening of the Presidency and a weakening of the judiciary."[3] Presidents would be allowed one term of nine years, and the judiciary would be fragmented into nine levels, one level of which would give "advisory opinions on the constitutionality of legislation passed by the House of Representatives.

The legislature would change also. The House of Representatives would consist of 400 members, each elected for a three-year term, and senators would be elected for life. A new system of checks and balances would help to ensure that only proper legislation was enacted. The Senate could request the High Court to issue "advisory opinions" on legislation pending in the House and when the House passed a bill both the Senate and the President would have power to veto it. In turn the House could override these vetoes with either a two-thirds or three-quarters majority vote.

There is no Bill of Rights in Tugwell's constitutional model, although most of these rights are scattered throughout the model. Tugwell calls for three additional branches of government, which would plan elections, organize six- and twelve-year economic plans, and supervise the national economy.

Through Article V the Founding Fathers made provision for another Constitutional Convention, but they hoped their efforts in 1787 would produce a Constitution that would continue to be effective long after their deaths. They were motivated to establish a lasting republic out of self-interest as much as public service, for they knew their own fame in history would be tied to the capability of the Constitution to meet changing demands in the future. Perhaps the principles that guided them 200 years ago are still adequate, "needing only to be supplemented by skill in their proper contemporary application." Or perhaps these principles are applicable only to part of our problems, requiring us to find new principles to meet modern needs. Or it may be that the Founders "dealt with bygone problems" and their principles

---

[3] *Ibid.*, p. 39. See also: Rexford G. Tugwell, "Introduction to a Constitution for a United Republics of America: Version XXXVII," *The Center Magazine*, No. 5 (1970).

are now irrelevant. Maybe they were wrong even for their time.[4] Before we accept, modify, or reject the Constitution they offered we ought to consider how they organized power and why they arranged it the way they did.

Classical Forms of Government

Jefferson defined the twin goals of government as securing *safety* and *happiness*. *Safety* meant government must have sufficient power to guard "against dangers from *foreign arms and influence,* as from dangers of the *like kind* arising from domestic causes."[5] What is *happiness?* Like beauty, happiness cannot be defined the same way for everyone. To the classical Greeks happiness was an ideal; men were expected to pursue excellence in whatever station they found themselves. Many of the delegates to the Constitutional Convention in 1787 agreed with this classical definition and were spurred toward excellence in their search for a way to make a viable republican government. Of course, this classical ideal has never become a general principle of all people in any period or nation. Many people live to satisfy their passions and settle with material rewards. However we wish to define the purpose of our lives, the Founding Fathers searched for a way of organizing political power to ensure that people would be free in their pursuit of happiness, regardless of how lofty or mediocre their goals.

Constructing a constitution to secure safety alone is relatively easy; most governments excel in military and police powers. The great task was, and always will be, organizing power to effect safety and happiness *simultaneously.* Although government must have sufficient power to act against foreign or domestic attack, use of that power must be controlled so that government remains a servant of citizens. James Madison summed up the task succinctly: "A good government implies two things: first, fidelity to the object of government, which is the happiness of the people; secondly, a knowledge of the means by which that object can be best attained."[6]

James Madison, and his educated contemporaries on both sides of the Atlantic Ocean, had received a classical education in which the study of politics followed the three types of government Aristotle

---

[4] Martin Diamond, "Democracy and the Federalist: A Reconsideration of the Framers' Intent," *American Political Science Review* (March 1959), p. 52.

[5] Clinton Rossiter, ed., *The Federalist Papers* (New York: The New American Library, 1961), No. 3, p. 42. (All references are to the Rossiter paperback edition.)

[6] Rossiter, ed., *loc. cit.,* No. 62, p. 380.

had first identified: *monarchy,* where power was in one person; *aristocracy,* where power was distributed among a few; and *democracy,* where people had power. Madison became "Father of the American Constitution" as a result of the remedies he discovered to the historic diseases of republics. The means he discovered came from his study of these three simple forms of government and particularly from his teacher at the College of New Jersey (Princeton), John Witherspoon. Witherspoon was a Presbyterian clergyman who emigrated to America after completing his M.A. at the University of Edinburgh, then one of the most scholarly universities in Europe. He was president of Princeton and a signer of the Declaration of Independence; through his articulate teaching, he had had considerable influence on the Founding Fathers.

"There are four things that seem to be requisite in a system of government," Witherspoon taught the young Madison in 1770-1771, "and every form is good in proportion as it possesses or attains them: (1) Wisdom to plan proper measures for the public good. (2) Fidelity to have nothing but the public interest in view. (3) Secrecy, expedition, and dispatch in carrying measures into execution, and (4) Unity and concord, or that one branch of the government may not impede, or be a hindrance to another."[7] Each of the three simple forms of government had characteristics (some valuable, some evil) unique to itself that limited its effectiveness in achieving all four requirements of good government.

"Monarchy," Witherspoon cautioned, "has plainly the advantage in unity, secrecy, and expedition." So, in terms of organizing power for efficient administration and foreign policy, monarchical government surpassed the other two. Why? "Many [as in an aristocracy or a democracy] cannot so easily nor so speedily agree upon proper measures, nor can they expect to keep their designs secret."[8] Witherspoon illustrated the advantage by the command of a ship or army, which requires supreme power entrusted in one man in order to accomplish its purpose. But he pointed to the "vice" of such concentration of power in one man.

> No man can be found who has either skill sufficient or if he had, could give attention to the whole departments of a great empire. Besides, in hereditary monarchies there is no security at all for either wisdom or goodness.[9]

[7] *Works of the Reverend John Witherspoon* (Philadelphia: William W. Woodward, 1800), Vol. III, p. 335 (3 vols.).
[8] *Ibid.*
[9] *Ibid.*, pp. 335-336.

Nor would an elected monarch reduce the danger of tyranny, but rather "has been always found in experience worse than the other, because there is no reason to expect that an elected monarch will have the public good at heart, he will probably mind only private or family interest."[10]

Thus while the concentration of power in one man gave government the essential requirement of efficient administration and ability to develop foreign relations secretly for the nation's advantage, such concentration failed utterly to protect the public interest or to provide wisdom.

The second simple form of government, aristocracy, appeared superior to the other two forms in securing the requirement of wisdom. Aristocracy outdid "all the others for *wisdom* in deliberation, that is to say, a number of persons of the first rank must be supposed by their consultations to be able to discover the public interest."[11] Conversely, there was no guarantee that an aristocracy would be faithful to this public interest and it was not efficient in either administration or foreign relations. "The most ambitious projects, and the most violent and implacable factions often prevail in such states."[12]

The third simple form, democracy, "has the advantage of both the others for fidelity; the multitude collectively always are true in intention to the interest of the public, because it is their own."[13] Of the four requirements for good government, democracy had the single advantage over the other two forms in giving the people the ability to protect their interest. But it had little to offer in the way of "wisdom, or union, and none at all for secrecy, and expedition." A simple democracy, by its very nature, ruled by majority vote rather than by wisdom. It could not unite everyone through a powerful administration nor could it capture diplomatic initiative because foreign policies made up in public were not secret. Furthermore, the well-intentioned people in a democracy were always in danger of being duped. "The multitude are exceeding apt to be deceived by demagogues and ambitious persons. They are very apt to trust a man who serves them well, with such power as that he is able to make them serve him."[14] Pure democracies had been traditionally the seedbed of dictatorships and tyrannies.

Thus, regardless of which form of government Madison and his colleagues in the Constitutional Convention turned to in evaluating

[10] *Ibid.*, p. 336.
[11] *Ibid.*
[12] *Ibid.*
[13] *Ibid.*
[14] *Ibid.*

how political power should be organized, they found an anomaly. Each pure form was remarkably successful in fulfilling one or two functional demands of good government, but none met all four requirements. Each had inherent defects serious enough to destroy itself. Witherspoon's summary of these evils is the standard judgment of all educated men of his generation in both Europe and America:

> Monarch every one knows is but another name for tyranny.
> Aristocracy always makes vassals of the inferior ranks.
> Pure democracy cannot subsist long . . . it is very subject to caprice and the madness of popular rage. They are very apt to chuse [sic] a favorite and vest him with such power as overthrows their own liberty—examples, Athens and Rome.[15]

From this analysis of political power Witherspoon drew three conclusions about the means of attaining good government. First, none of the simple forms could provide wisdom, fidelity, expedition, and unity together. To secure all four essential requirements a constitution must be a complex mixture of the functions of a monarchy, aristocracy, and democracy. Although sufficient power must be given a government to fulfill all these responsibilities, that power must somehow also be controlled to avoid the peculiar vice inherent in each form. Without such restraint a monarchy could degenerate into tyranny, aristocracy into a corrupt oligarchy, and democracy first into anarchy and then dictatorship.

Second, the three branches must have a common connection so they will function together interdependently as one government. He called for a *nexus imperii,* or joining of power. This vortex could be created by dividing the powers as "in the British government, the king has the power of making war and peace . . . but the parliament have the levying and distribution of money, which is a sufficient restraint."[16]

"The third observation is that the ruling part of any state must always have considerable property." Witherspoon offered two reasons: (1) "Property has such an invariable influence, that whoever possesses property must have power," and (2) property "is also some security for fidelity, because interest then is concerned in the public welfare."[17] If the wealth of a nation were more widely held so that most of the citizens were economically secure, the public could be expected to participate in a republic more reasonably or with greater restraint than if they were impoverished.

[15] *Ibid.,* p. 337.
[16] *Ibid.*
[17] *Ibid.*

Diagram of Witherspoon's Analysis of the Advantages and Disadvantages of the Three Classical, Simple Forms of Government

Form of Government	Government of	Advantage	Disadvantage	Corrupt Form
Monarchy	one	Secrecy, expedition and dispatch. As a government of one, a king can make quick decisions in national emergencies.	He rules by personal whim. There is no protection for the people's liberty. There is no certainty he will be wise. Because of the inter-marriage of royal families, kings often have been dull and spoiled.	Tyranny
Aristocracy	few	Wisdom to plan proper measures for the public good. By definition an aristocracy is composed of men of talent.	Acting as a group the aristocracy cannot make quick decisions. Nor will they necessarily be faithful to the public interest. They might use their power to advance their own, selfish interests.	Oligarchy
Democracy	many	Fidelity to the public interest. The people are the government so the government is inclined to protect the people. At least people think they are protecting their interest.	It cannot conduct foreign policy in secrecy because everyone must know the policies in public debate. Nor can a simple democracy administer needs of government quickly or respond to danger with expedition. Nor is there any advantage for wisdom. The people are apt to be duped.	Anarchy & Dictatorship

The Structure of Government: Organization of Power 29

Although Madison and other delegates to the Constitutional Convention in 1787 understood this and other theories of government, they could not establish a new government for the United States from theory alone. They were astute politicians in addition to careful students of republican principles. The delegates were not agreed on how government powers should be organized. They advanced their differing opinions as skillful politicians by arguing, persuading, and compromising their points in order to retain as much of their position as a majority would support. In discussing the functions of each major office in the Constitution it should be remembered the Founders acted as politicians, "not metaphysicians, disembodied conservatives or Agents of History." What they did in convention "was to hammer out a pragmatic compromise."[18]

Functions of Power

The President

The Presidency drew more debate in the Constitutional Convention than did any other office because the delegates were caught on the horns of a dilemma. Having just revolted against King George III they were reluctant to invest the executive branch with enough power to permit a President to transform himself into a tyrant. Yet they were anxious about the consequence of not entrusting the President with sufficient power to permit him to act for the nation's security. The Republic of Poland, then the largest republic in Europe, was being partitioned by Russia and Prussia at the same time Americans were trying to create their own republic. The explanation for Poland's disorders was the absence of a strong, national government powerful enough to defend its national integrity. "Equally unfit for self-government and self-defense," observed Alexander Hamilton, "it [Poland] has long been at the mercy of its powerful neighbors, who have lately had the mercy to disburden it of one-third of its people and territories."[19] Poland's experience was also cited by Madison as an example of the corruption that resulted when legislatures rather than the people selected the chief executive.

Eventually the convention agreed with Hamilton that "Energy in the Executive is a leading character in the definition of good government" and created the office of President for a single, powerful Execu-

---

[18] John P. Roche, "The Founding Fathers: A Reform Caucus in Action," *American Political Science Review,* Vol. LV (December 1961), p. 799.
[19] Rossiter, ed., *op. cit.,* No. 19, p. 132.

tive to be elected by the people. He was to be Commander in Chief, and his specific powers were to include "Power, by and with the Advice and Consent of the Senate" to make treaties "provided two-thirds of the Senators present concur"; power to nominate and appoint ambassadors, consuls, judges of the Supreme Court also "by and with the Advice and Consent of the Senate." Four important checks were imposed on presidential power: (1) the President was indirectly elected via the electoral college; (2) the term in office was limited to four years (although since 1951 the Twenty-second Amendment limits the number of terms to two, or a maximum of ten years); (3) he must rely on Congress for money to pay for his policies; (4) consent of the Senate is required for approval of treaties and certain of his appointees.

Echoing Witherspoon's observation that "secrecy, expedition, and dispatch" could best function in a single Executive, John Jay praised the new Constitution because the President could negotiate in "perfect *secrecy.*" But in 1973 the Nixon Administration believed the government did not have enough secrecy and proposed a revision of a federal criminal code to make it a crime to communicate information, "regardless of its origin" relating to the military capability of the United States "or of an associate nation." In addition, the disclosure of classified documents by present or former government employees would be a crime, even if the information were unnecessarily classified. Unauthorized persons who had such documents, such as newsmen or broadcasters, would be guilty of an offense if they failed to return the information. The net effect of such a proposal would permit any President to conduct foreign affairs with as much secrecy as he might choose.

Secrecy is an elastic term that can be stretched to cover anything a President wishes. Report of the My Lai massacre in Vietnam could be interpreted by Nixon's proposal as detrimental to the morale of the nation; exposure of waste and inefficiency in the military-industrial complex could also be squashed in the name of national security. However important secrecy is to the conduct of foreign relations, particularly in this nuclear age, government by secrecy is the antithesis of government by public consent. The threats to republican principles in the twentieth century exist as much from the misuse of secrecy within the country by Presidents who today wield unprecedented power as from foreign attack. National security requires we look for dangers coming from both directions.

Coupled to this rise of secrecy is the peculiar nature of presidential power. One of the ironies of power in the twentieth century is that the number of Executive agencies is so large and their activities so extensive that no President can be kept fully informed about their work so they can personally control these activities. This is particularly true of the CIA, the Central Intelligence Agency, the most highly secret of all federal institutions. In theory the President controls the CIA because it is a function of Executive power. In practice we are warned that the CIA "can become a kind of law unto itself, operating independently even of the President" and even when fulfilling a presidential order "may perform acts which would otherwise not be authorized or approved."[20] The CIA participation in the illegal Watergate activities, as requested by presidential assistants, is a recent and familiar example. In 1967 the CIA spied on groups within the United States through its subsidy to the National Student Association. In 1961 the CIA reportedly "had its own political desks, and military staffs; it had in effect its own foreign service, its own air force, even, on occasion, its own combat forces."[21] A President cannot know everything that is done by the CIA and Congress is kept ignorant of the agency's budget. Thus power slips into the hands of agents who may interpret their authority for gathering information into authority for actually formulating policy. Recent studies in fact indicate that on occasion the CIA has made policy, directed foreign relations, and interfered with internal affairs of other countries. Has it become "an invisible government?"[22]

The Senate

At the Constitutional Convention James Madison argued that the Senate should have two important functions. "First to protect the people ag[ain]st their rulers" by creating two branches within the legislature so each could check the other to ensure legislation was being passed for public rather than for private interest. One precaution against the danger of the legislature betraying its public trust would "be to divide the trust between different bodies of men, who might watch & check each other."[23]

[20] Eugene J. McCarthy, *The Limits of Power* (New York: Holt, Rinehart and Winston, 1967), p. 77. See also David Wise and Thomas B. Ross, *The Invisible Government* (New York: Random House, 1964); David Wise and Thomas B. Ross, *The Espionage Establishment* (New York: Random House, 1967); David Wise, *The Politics of Lying: Government, Deception, Secrecy and Power* (New York: Random House, 1973).
[21] Arthur J. Schlesinger, Jr., *A Thousand Days* (New York: Houghton Mifflin, 1965), p. 427.
[22] See: David Wise and Thomas B. Ross, *The Invisible Government* (New York: Random House, 1964).
[23] Max Farrand, ed., *The Records of the Federal Convention of 1787* (New Haven: Yale University Press, 1911–1937), Vol. I, p. 421 (4 vols).

The second function of the Senate was "to protect [the people] ag[ain]st the transient impressions into which they themselves might be led." People "were liable to temporary errors, thro' want of information as to their true interest" or "from fickleness and passion." Members of the House of Representatives could not be expected to protect the people from momentary misjudgments of the people; the House "might err in the same cause" because they stood for election every two years and thus would probably champion these opinions in order to be reelected.[24]

Of the four requirements Witherspoon listed for good government, the Senate and the judiciary were designed to secure wisdom. Although the President and members of the House might act wisely, it would more likely be the consequence of their personal character rather than an inherent function of their office. The President, exercising power as one man, had the advantage of efficient administration; the House, as we shall see, had the advantage of securing the public interest; and the Senate and judiciary were expected to have the advantage over the President or House for wisdom.

Because federal justices were selected rather than elected, selection could be based on ability, merit, or wisdom. But how could senators, who were elected indirectly or directly by the people, be expected to be any different from candidates for President or the House? Madison and other delegates suffered under no illusion that politicians campaigning for Senate offices would necessarily be wise people. But they did design the office with the hope of eliciting this quality from whomever was elected.

One encouragement for senators to act wisely was the limited number of members in the Senate. With only two senators from each state, each might be inclined to regard his vote as having important consequence and therefore might consider issues carefully. Another encouragement for wisdom was the six-year term, the longest term of any elected official. Time could give senators familiarity with long-range policy and thus provide continuity to government even if different Presidents were elected who wished immediate and abrupt change. Continuity within the Senate was also ensured by the staggered method of Senate elections; only one-third of the senators come up for election every two years. Because they were not so frequently answerable to the public, they could react to legislation on the basis of merit rather than popularity. But the fact that they had to stand for reelection at the end of six years was thought to be a check on

[24] *Ibid.*, p. 422.

any tendency of senators to degenerate into a corrupt oligarchy that held the public interest in contempt.

The function of the Senate was carefully planned, although the final decision for six-year terms, method of election, and specific responsibilities were worked out through debate and compromise. It was by the deliberate intention to give government the advantage of wise counsel that Presidents were charged to obtain advice and consent from the Senate on foreign policies and treaties and to submit names of appointees to the Supreme Court and ambassadorships to the Senate for approval. Despite these efforts to have the Senate provide "wisdom to plan proper measures for the public good" there are glaring exceptions to the intended function.

For example, in the 1950s the demagogy of Senator Joe McCarthy's charges of "Communism" was as much an example of "fickleness and passion" as ever could be expected from the House or among citizens. Moreover, a system of seniority rather than personal ability is the basis by which senators receive chairmanships of powerful committees. Seniority is a form of government by tollgate, in which senators must pay the price of being reelected a number of times before passing through the gates to power. Most senators who are reelected time after time usually come from rural states, particularly from the South, where population is not as complex nor the number of interests so numerous as in the more populated states. Thus power in the Senate often goes to men who have no incentive from their constituencies to press for imaginative leadership.

One glaring example of the Senate acting as a selfish oligarchy occurred in the decades following the Civil War when a few Americans were becoming phenomenally rich by exploiting their opportunities and sometimes their fellowmen as well. Instead of acting wisely to protect the public interest, the Senate became indifferent and aligned itself with private interests. As great economic power mushroomed in corporations and trusts so did political power concentrate in these economic interests; senators became faithful, obedient servants of the trusts. Writer Frederick T. Martin laid bare the twisted perversion of politics, "We are rich; we own America; we got it, God knows how, but we intend to keep it."[25]

Own America they did. They even owned the United States Senate. In the 1880s and 1890s there were Standard Oil senators, sugar trust senators, railroad senators, brewery senators—men whose political careers were created and financed by the trusts. In return senators would champion legislation favorable to their respective interest. The

[25] Frederick Townsend Martin, *Passing of the Idle Rich* (Garden City, New York: Doubleday, Page and Co., 1911), p. 149.

trusts kept their power for decades by "throwing all the tremendous weight of our support, our influence, our money, our political connections, our purchased senators, our hungry congressmen, and our public-speaking demagogues, into the scale against any legislation, any political platform, any presidential campaign, that threatens the integrity of our estate."[26]

Women's suffrage in 1918 was an example of one such piece of legislation that "threatens . . . our estate." Afraid that nondrinking women might support prohibition laws against the sale of alcoholic beverages, brewers organized to crush statewide referendums for women suffrage, and then sent lobbyists to Washington to "sit in the gallery of the Senate and tell his men with his hands how to vote."[27] Industrial employers of women workers also opposed female suffrage because they were afraid women would use their vote to support legislation that would improve their working conditions. Thus senators from Northern states, which employed many women in factories, joined in their opposition to woman suffrage with senators from Southern states, where there was fear that women's suffrage would open the door to equal rights for blacks.

For example, Senator Smith of South Carolina assailed the few Southern supporters of women's suffrage with the warning "that when the test comes, as it will come, when the clamor for Negro rights shall have come, that you senators from the South voting for it [women's suffrage] have started it [Negro rights] here this day."[28] Besides, argued Senator Smith, the Senate had no business discussing women's suffrage in the first place, because that was a question for local government to consider. State legislatures should determine if women can vote so states can "frame their laws as to preserve our civilization without entangling legislation involving women of the black race."[29]

The House of Representatives

The purpose of republican government, and the object of the delegates at the Constitutional Convention, was to keep the politicians who exercised political power faithful to the public interest. To help ensure that "fidelity to have nothing but the public interest in view" the Founding Fathers employed a dual strategy. First, by granting citizens the ability to vote for their own representatives, the Framers of the

---
[26] Ibid.
[27] Quoted in Eleanor Flexner, *Century of Struggle: The Women's Rights Movement in the United States* (New York: Atheneum, 1970), p. 298.
[28] *Congressional Record*, 66th Congress, 1st Session, Vol. 58, Part I, p. 619.
[29] Ibid.

The Structure of Government: Organiz

Constitution were ensuring the right of the peop
or indirectly through elections, the President ev
tor every six years, and all members of the Ho
every two years. Of these three popularly e
the House was designed specifically to secure
all requirements of good government, fidelity to the pe,
ought to be most aware of the changing sentiments of t
because representatives must face frequent elections; all memb
stand for reelection at the same time (which gives the people opportunity to change the entire composition of this branch of the legislature in two years); and by making congressmen represent a particular group of people located in a relatively small district it was hoped both the congressman and the constituents could become familiar with each other.

The second strategy had to do with the particular function of power given to the House. Just as the English Parliament had power to control some policies of the king through its ability to cut off financial support for programs considered to be in the private (king's) interest rather than the public interest, so the House was given the "power of the purse" to control the power of the President and the Senate. All taxes and appropriations must originate in the House, thus enabling the branch of government theoretically closest to the people to ensure that the policies of the government are supported by the public. Inasmuch as representatives spend the money their constituents must pay in taxes, the public's interest in their own personal taxes would theoretically cause them to consider carefully actions of their congressmen. And since congressmen stand for elections every two years, it was believed they would have a personal interest in following their constituents' wishes.

This strategy appears to have broken down recently. Studies reveal that Americans are more critical in their selection of Presidents and senators than they are of representatives. It is estimated that 75% of congressional seats are "safe," i.e. the same men are reelected over and over again. Only ninety of the 435 House seats shifted from one party to another in the five years from 1965 to 1970. "Only seven of the thirty-eight seats in California have changed parties during this period, four of the eleven in Indiana, two of the twelve in Massachusetts, three of the fifteen in New Jersey, two of the twenty-seven in Pennsylvania, and two of the ten in Wisconsin." Fifty-one House seats were "so securely nailed down" in the election of 1968 that incumbents in seventeen states had no opposition at all.[30]

[30] *U.S. Politics—Inside and Out* (Washington, D.C.: U.S. News and World Report, 1970), p. 131.

...time of the Republic

...t of the explanation for this is that as a consequence of the ...al government's involvement in creating and maintaining pros...y, congressmen have become quasi-employment agents by mak...g certain their constituents receive appropriate amounts of federal ...id, whether farm subsidies, construction projects, defense contracts, or whatever. Instead of controlling policies by restricting appropriations, many congressmen are not even informed how the money they are approving will be used and thus vote billions of dollars for items that they are told are classified as too important for "national security" for them to know.

Congressman Mendel Rivers, chairman of the powerful House Armed Services Committee from 1965 to his death in 1970, made a practice of keeping information away from members of his committee, which was responsible for studying the expenditures of every dollar requested for defense. Military and industrial facilities were frequently built in the districts of members of this committee to help ensure that funding would continue, not only for a particular program but also to maintain employment among a congressman's constituents. Frequently the committee appeared more interested in increasing the appropriation than investigating how efficiently the money was being used. For example, Marshall Frady, a member of the House Armed Services Committee, complained bitterly that although "we are dealing with the largest agency of government," one that is fantastically complex and for which "we hear all this testimony for weeks," the committee did not draw up the bill or even discuss it. "The chairman gets his little group together . . . and they draw up the bill, and we walk in and sit down and here it is already printed up and semi-accomplished—around a billion and a half dollars—and we have fifteen minutes to discuss it."[31]

"Father, I Cannot Tell a Lie"

Those who exercise political power in a republic are answerable to the people in whose name actions are taken, for unlike a monarchy or dictatorship, a republic is founded on the principle of consent—people choose to invest someone of equal rank as themselves with power to act for their interest. Honesty is a prerequisite to consent. This important linkage between honesty and those who hold political power as a public trust was recognized by George Washington's first biographer, Reverend Mason L. Weems, who invented the "cherry

[31] Marshall Frady, "The Sweetest Finger This Side of Midas," Life (February 27, 1970), p. 58.

tree story" in which young George confesses to his father that he whacked down the tree with his ax. The tragedy of Weem's story is not so much the fact that he uses a lie to support the virtue of honesty, but the implication that Washington's reputation was so insufficient of itself to merit remembrance that Washington needed the crutch of a lie to hobble through history. Nothing can be more insulting than to have his reputation remembered by future generations on the basis of such emptiness. Washington followed a code of ethics that was tied to an eighteenth-century concept of honor. That concept of honor, which required men to be honest if they were to be remembered well in history, has since been forgotten and replaced by a cherry tree.[32] But the importance of honesty in the affairs of republican government needs continued emphasis now that the power of government, in particular the power of Presidents, has increased so phenomenally.

Being honest with Americans has become particularly difficult for politicians because of the increase in secrecy that has accompanied the country's rise as a superpower. Consider, for example, the circumstances surrounding our involvement in World War I and the sinking of the British passenger liner *Lusitania* by a German submarine on May 7, 1915. Official papers that have been kept secret these fifty years now reveal that the British Admiralty deliberately set up the *Lusitania* and its passengers, including 158 Americans, to be sunk by the Germans in order to whip up American sentiment and involve the United States in the war on the Allied side. President Wilson knew the ship was packed with ammunition before it set sail, although he did not know of the British intent to allow the ship to be torpedoed. Unwittingly, Wilson played into the British trap by choosing rather to denounce Germany's attack on 1959 lives instead of warning Americans not to sail on a ship carrying ammunition to a wartime belligerent.[33]

The *Lusitania* was a Cunard-owned passenger ship that made monthly round-trip voyages from Liverpool to New York when World War I started in 1914. It was armed with twelve six-inch guns; before the war portions of the mail rooms and coal bunkers were secretly converted into large cargo-carrying areas, and the entire length of the ship was double-plated with steel. Before leaving on her last voyage

---

[32] For a superb study of the motives of the Founding Fathers, see Douglass G. Adair, "Fame and the Founding Fathers," in Edmund P. Willis, ed., *Fame and the Founding Fathers* (Bethlehem, Pennsylvania: Moravian College, 1967), pp. 27–52.
[33] This information is based on Colin Simpson, *The Lusitania* (Boston: Little, Brown, 1973). For a synopsis see: Colin Simpson, "Lusitania," *Life* (October 13, 1972), pp. 60–80.

to Liverpool the *Lusitania* was loaded in New York with 173 tons of ammunition, including 4927 boxes of cartridges (each containing 1000 rounds), 1248 cases of three-inch shells (all of which were stamped "nonexplosive in bulk"), which totaled 10.5 tons in explosives alone. In addition, there were seventy-four barrels of fuel oil and 2000 cases of small-arms ammunition loaded near the No. 1 boiler. The actual manifest identifying everything on board numbered twenty-four pages of closely written details; the manifest submitted for clearance to sail filled one page. The ammunition was disguised, with official American knowledge, and was listed on the manifest to be such innocent transactions as "sporting cartridges" and stamped "not liable to explode in bulk."

The New York City German community tried to run an ad a week in advance of the *Lusitania*'s departure in fifty American newspapers, warning passengers of the risk of traveling on the *Lusitania*. The State Department intercepted the ad, with the result that it was published in only one newspaper. One leader of the New York German community, George Viereck, met with Secretary of State William Jennings Bryan, warned him that the ship carried 6 million rounds of ammunition, and received a promise that Bryan would try to persuade Wilson to warn Americans not to travel on board. Bryan's opinions carried less weight with Wilson than did the more belligerent deputy in the State Department, Robert M. Lansing. No such warning was given by Wilson.

The captain of the *Lusitania,* Captain William Thomas Turner, was ordered to rendezvous with the British cruiser *Juno* south of Ireland for protection against German submarines known to be active in the Irish Sea. Specifically, the British Admiralty knew the German submarine U-20 was lying in wait for the *Lusitania* off the southern coast of Ireland. Not only did the Admiralty know that the U-20 attacked other British ships in the vicinity, sinking several, within the week of May 7th, but Admiralty personnel had deciphered the German radio code months earlier. On May 5th the Admiralty ordered *Juno* to abandon her escort mission, leaving the *Lusitania* uninformed that she was now alone and closing every minute on the U-20.

On the morning of May 7th, while the *Lusitania* was less than 100 miles from the trap, President Wilson's personal representative, Colonel House, called on the British Foreign Secretary in London and was shortly asked, "What will America do if the Germans sink an ocean liner with American passengers on board?" House replied carefully that the flame of indignation would sweep Americans and "that by itself would be sufficient to carry us into the war." A couple of hours later, around noon, when House was then visiting the royal palace, House was asked by King George V, "Colonel, what will America do if the Germans sink the *Lusitania?*" At 2:10 that afternoon the U-20's Captain Schweiger fired one torpedo at the *Lusitania,* and the internal explosion from the cargo of ammunition blew out the bottom of the ship. It sunk within a few minutes.[34] Along with the Cunard liner and its crew were sacrificed 1198 passengers, including 128 American citizens.

President Wilson knew that the *Lusitania's* cargo included vast quantities of ammunition; he had sealed a copy of the accurate manifest in an envelope marked "Only to be opened by the President of the United States." Wilson did not reveal this information to the American people, and the public reacted as indignantly against Germany as Colonel House had predicted. Senator Robert LaFollette of Wisconsin did make a speech in Minnesota reporting that the *Lusitania* carried mostly ammunition for cargo, and that President Wilson knew this all along. The Senate tried to censor him, but when a customs agent in New York offered to support LaFollette's testimony, the matter was quickly dropped.

Perhaps the most succinct statement about the use of political power was made by the British Admiral of the Fleet, Winston Churchill, who participated in the decision to let the *Lusitania* be sunk: "At the summit true politics and strategy are one. The maneuver which brings an ally into the field is as serviceable as that which wins a great battle."

This rationalization of the use of power helps explain why President Eisenhower thought it necessary to lie about the U-2 incident, although when the Russians produced the pilot he was compelled to admit that the United States had sent spy planes over Russia; or why President Kennedy lied about the United States' involvement in the Bay of Pigs invasion of Cuba; or why President Lyndon Johnson took advantage of a highly questionable incident in the Gulf of Tonkin (where North Vietnamese boats were alleged to have attacked American ships) and use the public outcry over the incident to get congressional approval of a resolution he had prepared weeks in advance that would permit him a free hand in waging war in Vietnam; or why President Nixon, Vice President Agnew, and Nixon's news secretary Ronald Ziegler denied that there was anything of substance to the

---

[34] One torpedo could not sink the *Lusitania.* Captain Schweiger noted that torpedoes were next to useless against a ship that had her bulkhead watertight hatches properly secured. On May 6, 1915, the day before the *Lusitania* was sunk, it took an hour and 20 minutes for the British *Centurion* to sink and it went down only after Schweiger surfaced and fired a second torpedo at point-blank range. Evidence from underwater research on the *Lusitania* confirms that the bottom blew out from an explosion inside.

Watergate reports and even castigated the newsmen who persisted in their research. When the truth eventually oozed out of the coverup attempts, Ziegler declared that all his previous denials were now "inoperative."

The way power is organized can be decided in a constitution, but honesty in the use of that power cannot be contained in the document. It may be that presidential power has expanded now too far to be contained or controlled adequately by any constitution, be it the Constitution of 1787 or a new one. It may be that we are compelled to trust that the public judgment and the judgment of the men the people elect will be sound and honest.

A NEW SOCIOLOGY: Making Democracy Safe for the World

What is the American, this new man? The rich and the poor are not so far removed from each other as they are in Europe. We are a people of cultivators, scattered over an immense territory. We are all animated with the spirit of an industry which is unfettered and unrestrained, because each person works for himself. We have no princes, for whom we toil, starve and bleed: we are the most perfect society now existing in the world.
—*J. Hector St. John de Crèvecoeur*

Americans often project miraculous qualities to the Constitution, as though the document is capable of pulling them out of any political crisis. However, despite all its advantages, it cannot ensure the success of this republican experiment, which depends as much upon the existence of particular social conditions as upon the proper organization of political power. Although the Constitution remains fundamentally as it was written 200 years ago, the social foundation upon which the government rests has changed markedly, especially since the middle of the twentieth century, and any serious examination of American government demands an examination of these social conditions.

James Madison, whose fame as "Father of the Constitution" is tied to his brilliant insight into the social conditions that could preserve or threaten the safety of a democracy, cited violence from hostile factions as the principal vice of democratic government. "So strong is this propensity of mankind to fall into mutual animosities," that Madison believed people would deliberately create hostilities even when there was no substantial cause for disagreement. "The most frivolous and fanciful distinctions have been sufficient to kindle their unfriendly passions, and excite their most violent conflicts." The most common source of factions, however, "has been the various and unequal distribution of property, those who hold, and those who are without property, have ever formed distinct interests in society" and divided a nation between a rich minority and an impoverished majority. "A landed interest, a manufacturing interest, a mercantile interest, a monied interest, with many lesser interests, grow up of necessity in civilized nations, and divide them into different classes, actuated by different sentiments and views."[1]

To eliminate the cause of factions requires either (1) destroying of liberty "which is essential to its [faction's] existence," or (2) giving every citizen the same opinion. The first remedy "is worse than the disease" and the second "is as impractical, as the first would be unwise."[2] Because the *causes* of faction cannot be removed without either losing liberty or transforming human nature, Madison looked for a solution that would control the *effects* of faction. He discovered that a solution might be possible if a society were composed of a large number of different factions; each would compete against the other on such limited and localized issues that the effect of their conflicts would not envelop the whole nation.

If a majority were threatened by a selfish minority, then the democratic principle of majority rule would defeat the efforts of a clique. But how could minority interests be protected from a hostile majority? If a way could be found to protect a minority within a democratic

[1] Clinton Rossiter, ed., *Federalist Papers* (New York: The New American Library, 1961), No. 10, p. 79.
[2] *Ibid.*, p. 78.

A New Sociology: Making Democracy Safe for the World 43

government, then democracy would "be recommended to the esteem and adoption of mankind."

Madison thought he had found such a way. His solution depended upon the existence of social and economic conditions that would permit and encourage the growth of many interests. A multiplicity of factions would make it difficult for a majority to be formed, or at least a majority that singled out a particular minority for vengeance and repression. Increasing the number of religions and nationalities, kinds of laborers and varieties of employment opportunities would create numerous factions that would make less probable the rise of a common motive to unite these diverse groups into one powerful clique.

> The smaller the society, the fewer probably will be the distinct parties and interests composing it; the fewer the distinct parties and interests, the more frequently will a majority be found of the same party; and the smaller the number of individuals composing a majority, and the smaller the compass within which they are placed, the more easily will they concert and execute their plans of oppression.[3]

Should by chance a common motive manage to emerge through such divisions "it [would] be more difficult for all who feel it to discover their own strength, and to act in unison with each other."

But how can democracy be made safe in the twentieth century? Our affluence has reversed the social conditions to which Madison directed his solution. The poor, not the wealthy, are the minority today. This new minority is in double danger from a majority that is not only more numerous but also more powerful economically. Nor do as many countervailing factions exist in the twentieth century to make Madison's solution applicable. Economist John Kenneth Galbraith suggests that there are three factions facing each other today—huge labor unions and mammoth corporations, sparring under the eye of a government turned behemoth.

Projecting Madison's idea of "faction checking faction" to contemporary conditions may appear reassuring but it hardly describes reality. Instead of "checking" each other these giants are now cooperating to such an extent that their interests, particularly huge corporations and vast government agencies that award contracts, are blended into one. And the middle class—the consumer, the independent worker, the small businessman, and the farmer, all of whom pay a higher percentage of taxes relative to their income than do other groups—is caught in the cross fire.

[3] *Ibid.*, p. 83.

Power Elites

In his farewell address, in 1961, President Eisenhower called public attention to two examples of this concentration of economic and political power. First, "the potential for the disastrous rise of misplaced power exists and will persist" because of the rise of the military-industrial complex. This "conjunction of an immense military establishment and a large arms industry is new in the American experience," and although its development is imperative for national security, Eisenhower noted, its implications are grave. "In the councils of government, we must guard against the acquisition of unwarranted influence, whether sought or unsought, by the military-industrial complex."[4]

Second, "in holding scientific research and discovery in respect, we must also be alert to the equal and opposite danger that public policy could itself become the captive of a scientific-technological elite." Technology rests upon a "formalized, complex, and costly" research. Historically, the free university was the "fountainhead" of new ideas but now the university is dependent upon government to finance research. "Partly because of the huge costs involved, a government contract becomes virtually a substitute for intellectual curiosity." Thus, "the prospect of domination of the nation's scholars by federal employment, project allocations, and the power of money is ever present—and is gravely to be regarded."[5]

In 1963, sociologist C. Wright Mills pointed out that most power now resides in economic, political, and military domains rather than with the American people. His analysis has proven disturbingly prophetic. The economy is no longer "a great scatter of small productive units," each balancing the other, but is dominated by two or three hundred corporations that are so politically and administratively interrelated that together they hold the keys to economic decisions in the country. Nor is the political order a weak mixture of national and state authorities; it has become "a centralized, executive establishment which has taken up into itself many powers previously scattered, and now enters into each and every cranny of the social structure." And the military is not held in distrust and kept weak, but as one of the most expensive establishments of the government, it combines

---

[4] Dwight D. Eisenhower, "Farewell Address to the American People, January 17, 1961," in *Public Papers of the Presidents of the United States, Dwight D. Eisenhower, 1960-1961* (Washington, D.C.: Government Printing Office, 1961), pp. 1036-1040.
[5] *Ibid.*

A New Sociology: Making Democracy Safe for the World

"smiling public relations" with "all the grim and clumsy efficiency of a sprawling bureaucratic domain."[6]

There is nothing conspiratorial about this concentration of economic and political power. Everyone knows somebody must make these decisions and somebody does. Many people do not care to make the decisions anyhow, nor do they know how to. "So the gap between the people and the experts gets wider." Americans may assume they determine governmental policies but in fact this gap between the people and those who make decisions in the name of the people has increased so much that often decisions of enormous public consequence are made without the people knowing they are being made. The *Pentagon Papers* reveal the profound extent of this gap. While Americans were being assured in the 1964 presidential campaign that the war in Vietnam would not escalate, that the 190 Americans who had died in Vietnam as of the summer of 1964 were a sufficient American sacrifice, the Lyndon Johnson Administration was in fact laying plans to commit over a half-million Americans to the war.

Whereas James Madison searched for ways to protect a minority from the tyranny of the majority, oddly enough today, in recent presidential campaigns, it is the majority of the electorate that need protection from a clique of advertising agents-turned-campaign organizers who delineate the "issues" and try to tell the people how to vote. The ratio between givers of opinion and receivers has increased with the development of mass communication. By hooking up to a national radio or television network, one person can speak "to a million people he never saw and never will see. Entire brackets of professions and industries are in the "opinion business, impersonally manipulating the public for hire."[7]

This consolidation of interests into a few powerful groups, plus the emergence of an affluent majority living in urban centers, has fundamentally altered the social Foundation of the American republic. Yet it is important that we review the Founding Fathers' understanding of the relationship between social conditions and political institutions, not only to appreciate the past success of Madison's "multiple-factions" solution to political stability in a republic, but to identify some of the problems the American republic faces in the twentieth century, when the number of factions is being reduced.

---

[6] C. Wright Mills, *The Power Elite* (New York: Oxford University Press, 1963), p. 7.
[7] *Ibid.*, p. 305.

Social Foundation of Government

In the Declaration of Independence Jefferson linked political sociology—the study of society's peculiar habits, manners, and attitudes—with the organization of political power as two equally important bases for the building of free government. In establishing new government Jefferson advised Americans to proceed by "laying its foundation on such principles" and by "organizing its powers in such form" as seems most likely to secure safety and happiness.

"Principles" referred not only to such fundamentals as liberty and equality, but also to the characteristics of society. Those who planned a new government for the United States had to consider the social peculiarities of American people in order to be sure that society was stable enough to support democratic government. Since sovereignty is distributed among all citizens in a democracy, the success of democratic government is particularly dependent upon conditions that nurtured friendship so that citizens would be inclined to support the needs of each other. The French political theorist Montesquieu, whose ideas were universally known in the 1780s, made this point when he distinguished between the form, or organization, of power, and the principles of government. "Its nature is that by which it is constituted, and its principles that by which it is made to act." Principles were "the human passions which set it [government] in motion."[8]

Setting equality as one of its goals, democratic government arouses the enormous expectation that people can advance themselves socially or economically if they have basic abilities and are willing to use them. If such opportunities exist, or at least if people *believe* opportunities exist, for them to translate their expectations into reality, then citizens are motivated to improve themselves and participate in the political process. Society in general shares the optimistic belief that the promise of democratic government can be fulfilled. If such opportunities do not exist, however, or if many citizens believe opportunities do not exist for them to advance themselves, then the goal of equality can become a mockery, a false hope that breeds despair and contempt. This sociological disillusionment can undermine government just as seriously as can an improperly organized constitution.

The interrelationships of social conditions to politics had been as carefully and rationally explored by Jefferson's generation as had the relationships of heavenly bodies been studied by Isaac Newton

---

[8] Baron de la Brède et de Montesquieu, *The Spirit of Laws,* 10th ed. (London: Crowder, Ware and Payne, 1773), Vol. I, p. 22.

(1642-1727). It was believed politics could likewise be subject to rational inquiry. After Newton's discovery of the principles of gravity, mankind could no longer wallow in ignorance and superstition about the nature of the universe; similar rational inquiry into politics could, it was believed, enlighten men about the principles of free government. So enlightened, men could create their own government based upon intelligent research, instead of continuing in the ignorance and tyranny of traditional monarchies. Because of today's explosion of scientific knowledge, which makes moon walks and space labs commonplace, it is difficult for men today to comprehend and feel the hope in man's ability to improve his condition that permeated the generation that followed Newton. Never had confidence in human ability been so high. As English poet Alexander Pope put it,

> Nature and nature's laws lay hid in night;
> God said, "Let Newton be," and all was light.

Part of this light came from a renewed study of Aristotle, who had advised founders of democratic governments against speculating on an ideal constitution for ideal people living in ideal circumstances. If a democratic government is to be practical, taught Aristotle, it must adjust to imperfect men living in the imperfect conditions they find themselves. Nevertheless, a democratic government would have the best chance to succeed under conditions where people had enough wealth, health, and material resources to enjoy "a truly happy life," one free of poverty or disorderliness. Without sufficient resources for most citizens a society would divide between the rich few and the impoverished mass, causing such jealousy that hatred would replace friendship.[9]

> A state aims at being, as far as it can be, a society composed of equals and peers; and the middle class, more than any other, has this sort of composition. . . . The middle class enjoy a greater security themselves than any other class. They do not, like the poor, covet the goods of others; nor do others covet their possessions, as the poor covet those of the rich. Neither plotting against others, nor plotted against themselves, they live in freedom from danger. . . .
> It is clear from our argument, first, that the best form of political society is one where power is vested in the middle class, and, secondly, that good government is attainable in those states where there is a large middle class.[10]

---
[9] Aristotle, *Politics,* trans. by Ernest Barker (New York: Oxford University Press, 1958), Book IV, Chapter XL, Section 1, p. 180.
[10] *Ibid.,* Book IX, Chapter XL, Sections 8-10, pp. 181-182.

Aristotle's teaching about the socioeconomic bases of government was neglected during the Middle Ages, when most Europeans were peasant farmers. Not until the rise of commercial enterprise began to affect social relationships and political power in the 1600s were the social foundations of government reexamined.

In studying the causes for the desperate Civil War that wracked England for eight miserable years, 1641-1649, Englishman James Harrington examined changes in England's society resulting from a shift of economic wealth away from the king and into the hands of a larger public represented in Parliament. Ownership of land was no longer concentrated in the king as it had been in feudal times. A larger public owned land and held commercial economic resources, and the king was now dependent upon them, through Parliament, for adequate revenue to finance the government. Although this economic shift was slow in development, some adjustment of the king's power was inevitable, claimed Harrington, to permit Parliament to advance the different interests of the men who now held considerable wealth. Harrington's conclusion, published in *Oceana* (1656), was based on his discovery that political power gravitates to those who have economic power.

King Charles I went to war against Parliament to defend his traditional prerogatives, but his efforts appeared doomed from the beginning to Harrington, who explained that the socioeconomic foundation of England would no longer support such concentration of power in one man. Yet in the midst of its victory over Charles I, Parliament seemed destined to wreck England's chance at republican government. The members of Parliament, the new leaders of the country, had not developed habits of leadership much better than the king's. Parliament and the autocratic Oliver Cromwell, Lord Protector of England, duplicated the autocratic habits of their defeated enemies and used their newly acquired power to clamp their own narrow and selfish religious views on all Englishmen. Harrington lamented that the absence of a reformation in attitudes toward power "should render them incapable of a commonwealth." "Of necessity they must thereby contract such reformation of manners as will bear no other kind of government."[11] England's only republican experiment failed.

Harrington distinguished monarchy, aristocracy, and democracy as three different class structures in which wealth was distributed to the one, the few, and the many. "For as much as he who wants bread is his servant that will feed him, if a man thus feed a whole

---

[11] James Harrington, *The Commonwealth of Oceana*, Charles Blitzer, ed. (New York: The Liberal Arts Press, 1955), p. 103.

people, they are under his empire." If people "hold the land . . . the empire is a commonwealth."[12] In studying the impact of this expanding commercial wealth on different classes, he saw a dynamic relationship between the "goods of the mind" and the "goods of fortune," or between public attitudes and the way people make their living. Wisdom, prudence, and courage were goods of the mind. These were the psychological characteristics of society that shaped public attitude. Goods of fortune related to how citizens made their living, which influenced a country's wealth, size, and strength. How people made their living, the amount of wealth in the nation, and the distribution of that wealth, all combined to influence both the disposition of citizens and the internal strength of the nation. Economics touched every citizen for "men are hung upon these . . . of necessity and by the teeth" since men must eat. How men earn their living and how well they are fed is as important to political stability as a well-regulated constitution.

Some of the Founding Fathers of the United States understood the connections between social conditions and free government that Harrington propounded. More of them, however, were familiar with the social–political analysis of Montesquieu's *Spirit of Laws* (1748), which expanded Harrington's study. Montesquieu made the distinction between form, or organization of constitutional power, and principle, or social foundation of government, which Jefferson later incorporated in the Declaration of Independence. Montesquieu reasoned that society could be "corrupted" just as individuals: every monarchy tended to become a tyranny; every aristocracy degenerated into a corrupt and unjust oligarchy; and every simple democracy, as history demonstrated, inevitably promoted class conflict, social disorder, and anarchy. The cause behind this corruption of society was different in each type of government because the holders of power were different in each case, yet the source of the corruption in each case lay within society.

Montesquieu identified a particular social principle that must exist to preserve each form of government from its peculiar kind of corruption. The principle of a monarchy was *honor*. Honor, which one could achieve by using power in such a way to cause future generations to remember and honor one's reputation, could keep a king from using his power for selfish, tyrannical ends. But society itself would have to act on this definition of honor by giving public recognition to a king for acting for the future, and not merely on the basis of his title or the office he holds. The Founders hoped the principle of honor,

[12] *Ibid.*, p. 44–45.

the sense of using power to achieve future glory rather than acting expediently for the moment, would be active in the office of President.

The principle of an aristocracy was *moderation*. Where each member of an aristocracy had an adequate amount of wealth, held in moderation, there seemed to be less inclination for particular members of the aristocracy to use their power to advance their own selfish interests. Moderation could inclide an aristocracy to advance the general interest of the public by reducing the temptation of using power for personal interest.

The principle of a democracy was *virtue*. A sense of public spirit, friendship, could act as social cement to keep the people in a democracy from following their own selfish purposes, which invariably led to anarchy and dictatorship. The principle used by a dictator to keep people under his power was *fear*.

Virtue was not thought of in its ideal or perfect quality. Virtue was the highest state of friendship that could be expected to exist among human beings. Because in a democracy sovereignty would be distributed among all citizens, the success of a democratic government depended upon social conditions that encouraged men to treat each other with common decency. Even though men were not perfect, they could be virtuous if they lived where there were adequate resources for each citizen to advance his condition.

Economic Abundance and Political Democracy

One of the most succinct twentieth-century restatements of this analysis has been made by Professor David Potter, who echoes today what the Founders knew well, that

> in every country, the system of government is a by-product of the general conditions of life, including, of course, the economic conditions, and that democracy, like any other system, is appropriate for countries where these conditions are suited to it and inappropriate for others with unsuitable conditions. Viewed in these terms, there is a strong case for believing that democracy is clearly most appropriate for countries which enjoy an economic surplus and least appropriate for countries where there is economic insufficiency. In short, economic abundance is conducive to political democracy.[13]

[13] David M. Potter, *People of Plenty: Economic Abundance and the American Character* (Chicago: University of Chicago Press, 1963), p. 112.

A New Sociology: Making Democracy Safe for the World 51

This is not abject determinism. Countries are not destined to be nondemocratic merely on chance of poor climate or absence of natural resources any more than nations endowed with resources will automatically establish democratic government. The relationship of economic plenty to political democracy exists because the promise of democracy has a better chance of being fulfilled in an economy of abundance. Men derive a personal satisfaction when they are able to advance themselves socially or economically, and are thereby satisfied that their self-interest can be fulfilled within a democratic government.

"Our democratic system," continues Professor Potter, "which, like other systems, can survive only when its ideals are realized, survived because an economic surplus was available to pay democracy's promisory notes."[14] Nowhere have the expectations of democracy been higher and the accompanying abundance greater than in the United States. By applying economic organization, science, technology, and sheer hard work to vast natural resources for nearly two centuries, Americans have produced a cornucopia of industrial and agricultural products. This economic and political success has resulted from conditions over which man had no control, such as natural resources, a favorable climate, and fertile land, as well as "the ventures and struggles of the pioneer, the exertions of the workmen, the ingenuity of the inventor, the drive of the enterpriser, and the economic efficiency of all kinds of Americans, who shared a notorious addiction to hard work."[15] The history of the United States is one of optimism because its wealth tends to fulfill the promise of success.

In a sense perhaps, the nation has been too successful, for in the midst of plenty economic abundance is taken for granted as though prosperity was inherent within America. Many fail to see why the study of American government should go beyond memorizing the functions of the three branches of government or the arrows in some diagram showing "how a bill becomes a law." They thus ignore the study of social principles, as some of the blunders in foreign policy since World War II tragically testify. For example, the investment of over 50,000 lives and $120 billion tax dollars in an effort to export democracy to Vietnam (or preserve "freedom" there), only to have that investment spurned by many South Vietnamese leaders who are as indifferent to democratic processes as are their Communist enemies to the north, is a terrible tuition to pay for the elementary knowledge that particular

[14] *Ibid.*, p. 93.
[15] *Ibid.*, p. 89.

social conditions must exist before a nation can venture into the uncertain experiment of popular government.

The American tendency in foreign policy since World War II to divide the world between "freedom-loving nations" and nations that do not love freedom, makes the success of democracy appear to be merely an exercise in emotional attachment or a decision of free choice. Much of our foreign policy has assumed that all people in the world were "presented with a choice between a right principle of government and a wrong one, and we, more than any others had been unequivocal in choosing the right." [16]

In contrast to the view commonly held today, the Founding Fathers did not take economic abundance for granted in the United States, nor did they imagine a free government could be wished into existence. They worried about finding an economic "mean" that was attainable by almost every citizen so the United States could avoid the social disorders caused by extremes of poverty and wealth. They took Aristotle seriously when he observed that people living under social extremes "find it hard to follow the lead of reason." The extremely poor are filled with envy and jealousy; the extremely rich are "nurtured in luxury" and often become so selfish that they "never acquire a habit of discipline." [17] Without economic abundance it was feared American society would be squeezed in a vise from the discontent of the poor on one side and the selfish indifference of the rich on the other.

"Be afraid of too unequal a distribution of riches, which shows a small number of citizens in wealth, and a great number in misery; whence arise the influence of the one, and the disgrace of the other," advised Abbé Raynal. "The rich and the poor, the men of property and the hirelings . . . form two classes of citizens, unfortunately, in opposition to one another." [18] Another European sounded the same warning in 1785. "This is the incurable disease of all free states where riches are unequally divided, [for] the sentiment of liberty, enfeebled and almost destroyed, cannot subsist for any length of time . . . and the republic will experience those shocks and violent commotions which, necessarily must drive it to destruction." [19]

---

[16] *Ibid.*, p. 111.
[17] Aristotle, *Politics,* Book IV, Chapter XI, Section 5, p. 181.
[18] Abbé Raynal, "An Address to the Independent Citizens of America," in *Lloyd's Evening Post and British Chronicle* (December 22–28, 1785), pp. 619–620.
[19] Abbé Mably, *Remarks Concerning the Government and the Laws of the United States of America: In Four Letters Addressed to Mr. Adams* (Dublin: Printed for Mongrieffe, et al., 1785), pp. 166–167.

In addition to civil war, the Founders were worried about the threat to public virtue that occurred when people were so consumed with accumulating wealth that honesty was no longer a ruling principle. "Virtue, like everything else, becomes a subject of speculation," observed another European friend of America. "From that moment, adieu to morality, adieu to patriotism, adieu to public spirit."[20] If the public honor men who possess no other merit than the ability to obtain money, thought Frederick II of Germany, then people are confirmed "in the vulgar prejudice that wealth only is necessary to gain respect." Dishonesty becomes commonplace, "corruption increases, takes root, and becomes general. Men of abilities and virtue are despised, and the public honor none but the bastards of Midas, who dazzle by their excessive dissipation and their pomp."[21]

"In the Sweat of Thy Face Shalt Thou Eat Bread" (Genesis 3:19)

The one great hope that American society could indeed support republican government rested on the abundance of land in the United States and the fact that most Americans could support themselves by agriculture. "Cultivate, Cultivate, I will repeat to them," was the candid advice of another European.[22] "I assure you that the Americans are and will be for a long time free; it is because nine-tenths of them live by agriculture."[23] Benjamin Franklin was especially heartened that Americans might succeed in their republican experiment when he compared the independent farmers in the United States with Europe's "abject, rack-rented, tythe-paying tenants, and half-paid, and half-starved ragged laborers." Franklin would agree with Crèvecoeur that "we are the most perfect society now existing in the world" because adequate economic opportunities existed to support a free government "where the cultivator works for himself, and supports his family in decent plenty."[24]

[20] Gabriel Riqueti, Comte de Mirabeau, *Considerations on the Order of Cincinnatus* (London: J. Johnson, 1785), p. 214.
[21] *Posthumous Works of Frederick II, King of Prussia*, trans. by Thomas Holcroft (London: G.G.J. and J. Robinson, 1789), Vol. V, p. 30 (15 vols.).
[22] Jacques Pierre Brissot de Warville, *New Travels in the United States of America, Performed in 1788*, 2nd ed. (London: J. S. Jordan, 1789), Vol. I, p. 10 (2 vols.).
[23] Étienne Clavière, *Considerations on the Relative Situation of France and the United States*, trans. by J. P. Brissot de Warville (London: Rodson and Clarke, 1788), p. 59.
[24] Benjamin Franklin, *European Magazine* Vol. X (August 1786), p. 114.

This appeal for Americans to invest their political future in the earthy simplicity of a farming society, coupled with a serious suspicion of social conditions spilling out of urban centers and commercial enterprise, cannot instill similar conviction today. Fewer than 6 million Americans, or about 3% of the total population, now feed approximately 210 million people; the remaining 97% of the population make their living in some form of enterprise. Since the first census in 1790, when 95% lived in rural areas, Americans have made such an exodus from farms to cities that by 1970 over 70% of Americans lived on about 1% of the land. Moreover, agriculture has become a huge commercial business.

Yet Franklin's attitude must not be dismissed as mere antiquated sentimentality, for to do so would ignore the relevance of poverty to the workings of democratic government in the urban slums of today or the eighteenth century. This country's founders had good reason to believe a commercial society would not support democratic government. In England, industrialization combined with the inhuman practices toward laborers encouraged by the prevailing wage theory of mercantilism, created such wretched social conditions that no reasonable person, living then or today, could expect popular government to function in such a situation.

Mercantilism may call to mind the international trade rivalry that characterized European states' search for and competition over colonies. What is often overlooked is the impact of mercantilism on the life conditions of the impoverished laborer, his position in society, and his rights.

Mercantilists defined wealth only in terms of gold and silver. There was nothing in this definition to force attention to the distribution of money among people or to call attention to the well-being of citizens. The American concept of national prosperity, which holds that the sum of goods and services produced by individuals equals national wealth, relates national prosperity to the prosperity of individual citizens. That the majority of workers in Europe were hungry and existed in hovels and rags was irrelevant to those mercantilists who calculated national wealth. Indeed, it was assumed laborers must be impoverished in order for England to be wealthy.

Consistent with defining wealth in terms of bullion, mercantilists pursued a policy of selling manufactured goods to foreign countries that paid for them in gold. Concurrently, wages had to be kept low in order for the nation to be rich because increased wages would only add to product cost, thereby reducing the profit England could receive. Higher wages, moreover, might enable workers to purchase some of these goods, thus diverting products otherwise destined for gold-paying foreign countries. Because domestic spending did not generate wealth in a mercantilist system, there was no interest in making it possible for laborers to improve themselves.

Finally, wages had to be kept low in order to keep workers on their job. As there was little opportunity for social or economic mobility, employers could not rely upon the laborer's personal incentive to keep him coming to work. Under such a wage theory laborers could have no incentive. By holding wages down to a bare subsistence level—just enough money to pay for daily bread, gin, and housing—employers could force workers to return to the job everyday by the ever-present threat of starvation.

Because workers could not improve their lives, it is understandable that they would have no personal incentive to work, but this disinterest was interpreted as a natural inclination to laziness, "sloth," and "indolence." "Every one but an idiot knows that the lower classes must be kept poor or they will never be industrious . . . [that] they must be in poverty or they will not work," claimed one English observer.[25] This belief was repeated over and over. "The lowest orders should endure a state bordering on want in order that a necessity may exist for their labor."[26] Employers theorized that if they paid workers slightly more than a subsistent wage, the workers would abandon their jobs, squander their few pennies on gin, remain drunk for two or three days, and thus leave their machines idle for the period of their debauchery. Low wages could thus be justified on the presumption employers were protecting the morals of their workers.

This wage theory had a built-in assumption that the majority of laborers were incapable of moral judgment. Employers predicted workers would use an increased salary to sink deeper into the mire of social disgrace rather than to improve themselves, and the social conditions produced as a consequence of this low opinion of laborers led them to gin in order to drown out their misery. The prophecy is self-fulfilling. The expected antisocial behavior came to pass, though as a consequence of employers' policies rather than as a consequence

---

[25] Arthur Young, *Farmer's Tour Through the East of England* (London, 1771), Vol. IV, p. 361.

[26] John Weyland, *Observations on Mr. Whitebread's Bill* (London, 1808), p. 62. For an analysis of the social conditions arising from this wage theory see: Edgar S. Furniss, *The Position of the Laborer in a System of Nationalism* (Boston: Houghton Mifflin Company, 1920), reprinted in 1965 by Augustus M. Kelley, New York. See also: Michael T. Wermel, *The Evolution of the Classical Wage Theory* (New York: Columbia University Press, 1939).

of a particular defect in the workers' human nature. The majority of eighteenth-century Englishmen were sickly, dwarfed, rickety paupers who were neither psychologically nor sociologically capable of participating in democratic government. Riots were not infrequent, particularly during periods of unemployment, and often occurred in the summer months. Farmers, by contrast, generally could subsist easier; and the demands of plowing, planting, and harvesting made the summer months their busiest time.

This same moral judgment is used today to describe the character of welfare recipients living in the ghettos of large American cities or in rural America. In Chicago during the racial conflicts of the 1960s, for example, politicians "spent most of their time in empty-headed debate over the number of black babies being born to sex-crazed welfare mothers and able-bodied, sex-crazed black men who chose a life of idleness. To hear the politicians tell it, life in the ghetto was a whirl of passion, welfare checks, and liquor."[27] These predictions about social action of the poor are as self-fulfilling now as they were in Madison's and Jefferson's day. The poor are often presumed to be in their condition because of moral inferiority and often various welfare programs intended by different governmental agencies to improve these social conditions are judged to have the opposite effect of confirming habits of idleness and sloth. The want of good education, adequate jobs, or an environment conducive to incentive can hardly inspire hope and help those who do wish to help themselves.

Today, education is critically important as a means to advance one's position, because technology has increased the degree of skill necessary to obtain a job. But the unequal distribution of educational opportunities contributes to the inequality of employment opportunities. A four-year, $2 million study of school financing conducted by the United States Office of Education concluded, in 1971, that the ideal of equal educational opportunity is a myth. Over 50% of educational costs are met by local property taxes; the study showed that wealthier districts spent up to $5.50 a child for every $1 spent by the poorest districts. "While we give lip service to equality," concluded study chairman Dr. Roe L. Johns, "our school systems are not functioning as they should to give every child a share in the American dream."[28]

Technology has also altered the kinds of jobs available by reduc-

---

[27] From the book *Boss: Richard J. Daley of Chicago* by Mike Royko, p. 135. Copyright © 1971 by Mike Royko. Published by E. P. Dutton & Co., Inc. and used with their permission.

[28] *Los Angeles Times* (November 5, 1971).

ing the number of needed low-skilled or semiskilled jobs. At one time agriculture employed most Americans, but technology has reduced the number of low-skilled farm jobs by a factor of 200,000 jobs every year for the twenty-two years from 1947 to 1969. Agriculture is now at the bottom of the list of job opportunities. Since 1956 white-collar jobs have continued to exceed blue-collar jobs in number in the United States. This transition has made the occupational profile of the United States unique in the world; in most other countries the majority, like many of the poor in America, need low-skilled to semiskilled jobs.

The reduction of certain kinds of jobs together with the unprecedented number of young people looking for work is hitting the decade of the 1970s with a one–two punch. The largest number of employees are in the twenty to thirty-four age bracket. These are the "war babies" who are engulfing the job market with an impact similar to that which befell the elementary and secondary schools in the 1960s. This age group accounts for 65% of the increase in American labor force between 1965 and 1975, calculates Professor Seymour Wolfbein, whereas in the previous decade this age group accounted for only 13% of the work force.[29] Wolfbein suggests that the prospect of finding enough jobs is dim, and the effect will be greater on nonwhites, if for no other reason than the fact that their birthrate has been higher than that of whites. "For example, the number of nonwhites in their early twenties is now in the process of going up by 55%. The number of nonwhite teenagers is going up by 35% in the period 1965–1975, almost double the rate of upturn among their white counterparts."[30]

If jobs will not increase in proportion to demand then the traditional pattern of men supporting themselves by their own employment may have to give way to the totally new concept of a guaranteed annual income. The concept of work itself will have to be redefined, along with the moral values attached to the work ethic. For thousands of years man has made a living in the manner prescribed for Adam: "In the sweat of thy face shalt thou eat bread." Technology may have changed that forever.

The March to Washington

"In 1776 the nation signed a huge promissory note," but the promise of opportunity in America excluded Negroes, observed civil rights

[29] Seymour Wolfbein, *Work in American Society* (Glenview: Scott, Foresman and Company, 1971), p. 116.
[30] *Ibid.*, p. 114.

leader Martin Luther King in April 1968, shortly before his assassination. In preparing to lead a Poor People's Campaign to Washington, D.C., that year to get legislation improving the economic plight of the nation's poor, King described the economic help the United States government made available to white poor in the past. The government refused to give Negroes any land following the Civil War, but at the same time through an act of Congress the United States government "was giving away millions of acres in the West and Midwest, which meant that it was willing to undergird its white peasants from Europe with an economic floor. But not only did they give the land but they built land-grant colleges, with government money, to teach them how to farm." In addition the government provided county agents to help further expertise in farming; it provided low-interest-rate loans so they could mechanize their farms. "Today millions of these people are receiving millions of dollars in government subsidies not to farm and these are the very people telling the black man that he ought to raise himself by his own boot straps."[31] "We are coming to Washington," King explained, "to get our check."

The rich had already been to Washington to get theirs. The "soil bank" provides milllions of tax dollars for wealthy farmers. It had been initiated in the 1930s, when the number of farmers was large and their farms were small, to give money to individual farmers not to raise crops in order for food prices to rise high enough for farmers to make a profit. Through the soil bank the government became involved in helping farmers as the government for years had been involved in helping business by the high protective tariffs that excluded cheaper European manufactures. Since the 1930s the number of farms and farmers have been reduced and consolidated into huge agribusinesses but the payments have continued in the form of welfare checks for the rich. Curiously, some of the most outspoken critics of socialism are the very ones whose fortunes are increased by these payments. John Wayne, a self-proclaimed defender of free enterprise, collects over $200,000 annually as his part of the soil bank "welfare."[32] And Senator James Eastland (Democrat, Mississippi), who is Chairman of the Senate Judiciary Committee and thereby responsible for guarding the moral integrity of the federal judiciary, voted against a bill that would limit soil bank payments to $55,000 per person. CBS news reported in 1972 that when the bill passed despite his opposition, it was reported he divided his land holdings among members of his

[31] Quoted from the film, "Martin Luther King, The Man and the March," produced by N.E.T.: Indiana University Audio-Visual Center.
[32] Santa Ana *Register* (July 7, 1971).

family so that each person could collect $55,000, thereby returning him his regular $330,000 per year.

The middle class has been caught in the cross fire. Its members pay more in taxes relative to their incomes than do the rich because they do not earn enough to invest in tax loopholes, and they earn too much to qualify for the welfare benefits that go to the poor. Instead of marching to Washington, they try to improve their condition by hard work and initiative. Yet many of their paychecks are indirectly coming from Washington because of the large contracts various government agencies grant to private corporations. The dependence of the American economy upon government contracts is usually obscure until the near collapse of some private corporation—such as Lockheed Aircraft of California in 1971, which received large government-sponsored loans—reveals how dependent our free enterprise is upon tax dollars.

Unlike the social conditions in the eighteenth century, when James Madison suggested the creation of numerous interests as a remedy to the danger of factions dividing society, today the promise of opportunity in America has been reached by a majority of people. We have been so successful in transplanting the goals of democracy into practical success that for the first time in the history of any nation, whether ancient or modern, the poor rather than the rich are a political minority. The social foundation of American government shifted in the mid 1950s, although not until the 1960s did writers force us to turn our critical attention away from studying the affluent majority to consider the social implications of the invisible poor. The poor have been "invisible" partly because the cost of apparel has been reduced, so that the poor could not always be distinguished by their dress; they were also out of sight since freeways went over urban ghettos and major highways bypassed areas of rural poverty.

If the poor were out of sight to the majority they were out of mind to the politicians. At the bottom of the social heap the "other American" was politically invisible: he had no lobbies pushing forward special legislation for his interest. The poor could not afford to hire lobbyists, as could wealthy special-interest groups; nor did they have numerical power at the polls to press their claims. "They have no face; they have no votes," observed critic Michael Harrington, whose studies helped inspire Lyndon Johnson's War on Poverty.[33] An example of the powerlessness of the poor minority occurred when Chicago's Mayor Richard Daley reviewed the election pattern to determine the

[33] Michael Harrington, *The Other America: Poverty in the United States* (Baltimore: Penguin Books, 1969), p. 13.

key to his third-term victory as mayor in 1962. He discovered his opponent received 51% of the vote cast by white citizens. The large black vote gave him his victory:

> The people who were trapped in the ghetto slums and the nightmarish public housing projects, the people who had the worst school system and were most often degraded by the Police Department, the people who received the fewest campaign promises and who were ignored as part of the campaign trail, had given him his third term. They had done it quietly, asking for nothing in return. Exactly what they got.[34]

When the poor were a political majority they could nudge government to respond to their needs by the force of their numbers. Even cynical politicians who had no interest in their plight were compelled to pay lip service to the poor out of political necessity. Today there is little political necessity for politicians, whether cynical or not, to articulate the needs of a poor that has little political muscle. The poor have the power of neither the purse nor the polls to keep their interests in national focus, and it is this very fact of powerlessness that creates an enormous and unusual problem for republican government in the twentieth century.

It is essential that a sense of equality be preserved, for the success of free government depends on the belief that democracy can work for all. "So long as these beliefs can be maintained intact—so long as they approximate reality closely enough to be convincing—they exercise an immense moral power," observes Professor Potter. This belief promotes friendship and decency.

> The optimism with which Americans have confronted the future; the confidence with which they have grappled with difficult problems; their conviction that merit will be rewarded and that honest work is the only means to attain success; their integrity in social relations; and their respect for human dignity of any man or woman, regardless of that person's social credentials, are all by-products of the ideal of full equality in a classless society.[35]

Whether members of a majority or a minority, Americans increasingly look to Washington to make the promise of equality a working reality. Black Americans were left out of the government spending-game until they organized and their relative success inspired others.

---

[34] From the book *Boss: Richard J. Daley of Chicago* by Mike Royko, pp. 127-128. Copyright © 1971 by Mike Royko. Published by E. P. Dutton & Co., Inc., and used with their permission.
[35] Potter, *loc. cit.,* p. 98-99.

White workingmen of European descent also organized in major American cities because they felt ignored by an officialdom more interested in the problems of blacks or Puerto Ricans. However, this failure of national policies to advance all groups equally out of a motive of moral obligation rather than political pressure tends to divide Americans into racial or ethnic parts. Such division is the reversal of the social characteristics Crèvecoeur saw in 1782: "Here individuals of all nations are melted into a new race of men, whose labors and posterity will one day cause great changes in the world."[36]

[36] J. Hector St. John de Crèvecoeur, *Letters from an American Farmer* (New York: E. P. Dutton Co., 1957), p. 39.

THE CONSTITUTION:
Creation of a Federal Republic

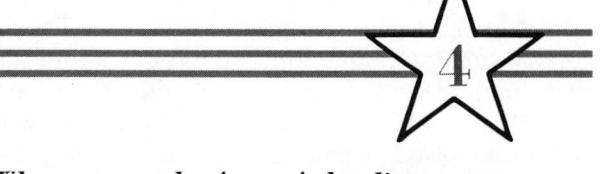

> *When we speak of . . . federalism, we are concerned, as were the founders, [with] the means by which we organize our common efforts [to] adapt to the new and larger challenges which we face.*
> —*Senator Edmund S. Muskie,*
> *Chairman of the Senate Subcommittee*
> *on Intergovernmental Relations*

Nigeria and more recently Malaysia are contemporary examples of republics where federalism failed to prevent the centripetal pull of power inward to the central government. In the eighteenth century, Poland and the Dutch Republic were examples of countries where federalism failed to curb the centrifugal thrust of power away from the center to concentrate in the member provinces. Since the eighteenth century, republicanism has been linked with a federal system in which political powers were given to both the national and the state governments. Despite the separation of 200 years, the inability of all these republics to keep the tension between central and local governments in balance makes the study of federalism as relevant today as it was to the Americans who declared the United States independent in 1776.

Regardless of how carefully the Founders considered the forms and principles of government when writing the American Constitution, the test of their theory came when the new government was put into practice. Could it govern a large territory? Could it unite a variety of people into one nation without smothering their individuality? Combining a central government that possesses national sovereignty with state governments that retain sovereignty in their own spheres, the Founders created what twentieth-century political scientists describe as "a new and better thing to which is given the name 'federalism.' "[1]

Federalism is an American invention designed to make republican government practical in a large and populous country. American federalism differs from the traditional federal system. Federal and confederal, from which comes the term "confederation," were synonymous in eighteenth-century dictionaries. They described an association of small, independent, sovereign states loosely linked together as a league for the purpose of mutual defense. By combining the federal principle of individual states together with the unitary principle of a national government that was sovereign over all citizens in all states, the Founders created a new concept of federalism. James Madison described the new invention simply: "The proposed Constitution, therefore, is, in strictness, neither a national nor a federal constitution, but a composition of both."[2]

Lying somewhere between national and federal, the new system did not settle precisely what functions each partner was responsible for. The tension between centripetal pull of power to Washington and centrifugal thrust of power to the states has characterized our history. Although, as in the cases of Nigeria and Malaysia, the direction of power in twentieth-century United States has been toward the central government.

Federalism Was Born in Controversy

Prior to the Philadelphia Convention, the idea of federalism as a weak association of independent states was regarded "as the sole way in which some of the advantages of great size could be obtained by

[1] See: K. C. Wheare, *Federal Government,* 4th ed. (New York: Oxford University Press, 1963).
[2] Clinton Rossiter, ed., *Federalist Papers* (New York: The New American Library, 1961), No. 39, p. 246.

those who wanted to enjoy the blessings of republicanism."[3] Only a small republic would stop the natural inclination of a nation to become warlike, and only a small country would keep the political issues few and simple so citizens could remain alert to vote intelligently. Poland, the Dutch Republic, and even Switzerland were examples of federal republics, in which each province retained its local sovereignty but joined a league to secure some of the advantages of larger size.

The Articles of Confederation created just such a league of thirteen colonies-turned-states, or independent nations. Each of the thirteen states was sovereign in all matters but joined in a confederation for mutual defense against their common enemy, England. (The word "state" is often ambiguous to Americans because it has a dual meaning: Under the Articles of Confederation such member states as Massachusetts regarded themselves as separate nations; with the adoption of the Constitution of 1787 the United States became a new nation and member states could no longer exercise exclusive sovereignty over citizens.)

When the delegates met in Philadelphia there was not one among them who claimed to be an academic expert on federalism, not one among them who had preconceived notions as to its "true" nature.[4] Relations between national and state governments were worked out as a compromise in a protracted struggle between two dominant factions in the Convention of 1787. Nationalists, who championed the Virginia Plan of Union, were prepared to give the new government limitless superiority, even entrusting it with power to interpret the Constitution at will. In opposition were the traditional federalists who countered with the New Jersey Plan of Union. They wanted to keep the new government weak in order to protect the autonomy of the several states. The Constitution emerged as a compromise, although the national government was given sovereignty over all citizens in all states.

James Madison studied the tortured history of republics and was convinced that small size was the source of their fatality. Not only were small republics in constant danger of being gobbled up by larger, more powerful monarchies, as was happening in Poland before Madison's very eyes, but their smallness reduced the number of different

---

[3] Martin Diamond, "What the Framers Meant by Federalism," in Robert A. Goldwin, ed., *A Nation of States: Essays on the American Federal System* (Chicago: Rand McNally, 1963), p. 35.
[4] Clinton Rossiter, *1787: The Grand Convention* (New York: Macmillan, 1966), pp. 193–194.

social interests. This made it easier for a majority to tyrannize a minority. Petty bickering and even civil war were the lot of these small republics.

Madison carefully noted that the threat to liberty in a republic came from a different source than it did in a monarchy. Because kings were sovereign, the threat to liberty in a monarchy came from the central government. But in a republic, where sovereignty was distributed among the people, liberty was particularly vulnerable at the local level where a majority could readily identify a minority and use its greater number of votes to tyrannize the minority. He concluded that only a large country could provide a safe dwelling place for republicanism, and thus turned the small-republic idea upside down.

To keep American federalism alive it was essential that both elements of the compound be preserved. The delegates made sure that each partner, the state government and the national government, would have political powers. They enumerated the powers of the national government in Article 1, Section 8 of the Constitution, and stated in the Tenth Amendment that nondelegated powers "are reserved to the States respectively, or to the people." In addition to guaranteeing each partner political power, the Founders made it impossible for either to vote the other out of existence. The process of amending the Constitution perpetuates federalism because both the states and the national government must participate before an amendment is valid. States can initiate an amendment, but they cannot change the Constitution by themselves. Two-thirds of the states must petition Congress to call a convention for the purpose of revising the Constitution.[5] Nor can the national government change the Constitution by itself. Congress may propose amendments but two-thirds of the states must ratify each proposal. Thus the Founders attempted to build federalism into the Constitution, but since they did not include a final statement declaring where the jurisdiction of one begins and that of the other ends, they also included in the Constitution the tensions that exist between national and state governments.

Both the states and the national government appeal to the Constitution whenever the two are in conflict over jurisdiction. And conflicts over jurisdiction are inevitable, because both claim the right to act directly upon citizens without being hampered by the other. Some final point of reference is essential to the operations of any federal

---

[5] Although the Constitution has never been amended in this manner the states are only one vote shy of the two-thirds needed before requesting a new Constitutional Convention to meet. For a discussion of the consequences of such a request see: Fred R. Mabbutt, "The Constitution: Has It Outlived Its Usefulness?" *Ball State University Forum*, Vol. 13 (Autumn 1972), p. 36ff.

system. Usually it is the judiciary. But when the Supreme Court ruling is unacceptable to some, as when the Supreme Court struck down school segregation, the Supreme Court is denounced and states' rights are proclaimed, all in the name of the Constitution.

"When I go to stand in the door, it is to raise dramatically the question of sovereignty of the state."

In his 1962 campaign for governor of Alabama, George Wallace promised to refuse "any order to mix races in our schools" and if necessary he offered to "stand in the schoolhouse door." Unlike many politicians, Governor Wallace fulfilled his campaign promise. When the all-white University of Alabama was ordered by a federal court to admit two Negroes a year later, Wallace was present "to bar the entrance of any Negro who attempts to enroll at the University of Alabama." Before being compelled by the national government to obey the law, Wallace used his opportunity to remind Americans that "strong local government is the foundation of our system and must be continually guarded and maintained."[6] In citing the legitimate importance of local government to dignify segregation, Governor Wallace fulfilled Madison's prophecy, made nearly two centuries earlier, that in a republic the greatest threat to individual liberty would come from local government where a majority could identify and then persecute a minority.

By the Civil Rights Act of 1964 the national government became empowered to do what local governments ought to have done on their own. The act forbade distributing federal aid to school districts that practiced racial discrimination. Although initially the threat of removing all federal support to education affected only states in the South, where segregation was practiced by law, after 1968 the Federal Office of Education extended the requirement to school districts in the north. Local boards, of course, remained free to choose whether or not they wished to comply with the Civil Rights Act. For example, the school board for Jeff Davis County, Georgia, chose not to comply. But the loss of federal money means a shift of the costs to the already overburdened local property-tax payer, and usually elected school-board members have chosen to comply with the law rather than force their constituents to pay for the luxury of discrimination out of their own pockets.

Racism, of course, is inconsistent with the principles of republican government. As the recent examples of Malaysia and Nigeria demonstrate, federalism is also incompatible with long-term racial conflict.

[6] As quoted in *The New York Times* (June 12, 1963), p. 20.

When local or national governments are used to support racial inequalities, then social division is institutionalized into political conflict and the government can no longer remain a republic.

Federalism is the sharing of political power at the local, county, state, and national levels by all social, economic, and racial groups. With 210 million people in the United States today, the challenge to federalism is one of equality of participation in all levels of government by all groups in American society. Federalism must provide the basis for social tranquility in the twentieth century, as it was able to provide the administrative machinery to govern a large area in the eighteenth century.

Despite Governor Wallace's objection to the new role of the national government, its acting as a kind of guardian of the national conscience in educational matters, support from the national government for education is not new. Education has become the nation's second-largest business, second only to national defense in terms of total expenditures, and a substantial part of the defense budget is spent on education. The Department of Defense is the "world's largest educator of highly skilled men," observed former Defense Secretary Robert S. McNamara, and from its immense educational complexes "the services return over a half-a-million personnel annually to the country's skilled-manpower pool."[7] Providing educational opportunities to military dependents around the world would make the Defense Department the ninth largest school district in the United States. The involvement of the national government with local and state governments in supporting education offers an insight into the nature of American federalism and how it works.

Federalism in Action: Who Supports Education?

Contrary to the traditional American view that education is purely a local responsibility, state and national governments have been involved in the process for a long time. Lincoln set federal land aside in the new western states for future colleges and in so doing he continued a practice begun in 1789. Federal vocational-aid programs in agriculture, home economics, and industrial arts developed in 1917; federal surplus of food, property, and equipment have long been distributed to schools; and since World War II the national government has made special grants to school districts that experience an un-

[7] Robert S. McNamara, *The Essence of Security, Reflections in Office* (New York: Harper and Row, 1968), p. 132–133.

usually high influx of military families. In reality, all levels of government have supported education. Professor Morton Grodzins points to this reality. In all states "local districts are dependent upon state financial aid, state teacher certification, state prescription of textbooks, and state inspection of performance in areas as diverse as building maintenance and the caliber of Latin instruction."[8]

So many different governments have their fingers in the pie, in fact, that American education has grown into a hodgepodge of overlapping jurisdictions that defy simple analysis. In a variety of different ways local school districts are dependent on city and county governments, on tax-levying and tax-collecting agencies, on health departments, on state educational departments, and recently on new programs the national government has superimposed on this maze. In spite of all of this government, the quality of education in the United States is very uneven. Educational resources and opportunities vary widely from state to state and among districts within states. There are no uniform, minimum educational standards in the United States. The quality of a student's education depends solely on where he happens to live.

Not until President Johnson's Elementary and Secondary Education Act of 1965 was enacted did the national government achieve full partnership with state and local districts in supporting education. This was the first national aid-to-education bill ever passed by Congress, and from it emerged a host of programs for school districts serving low-income families. The national government was limited to giving emergency assistance rather than initiating nationwide reforms, but since 1965 greater responsibility for education in the United States has been pushed on the national government's shoulders. Not only have local districts been unable to raise sufficient money to pay the increased costs of education, but state supreme courts have ruled that the existing tax basis supporting public schools is unconstitutional because property taxes do not yield an equal amount of money to give all children within a state an equal educational opportunity.

In 1963-1964, for example, local districts supplied 56.3% of school revenues, states provided 39.3%, and the national government contributed 4.4%. Four years later, in 1967-1968 "the local share had fallen to 52% and the national share had risen to nearly 8%, but the state share remained right at 40%."[9] Inner-city schools particularly are in a financial crisis. Wealthier citizens and factories move out

[8] Morton Grodzins, *The American System*, by Daniel J. Elazar, ed. (Chicago: Rand McNally, 1966), p. 4.
[9] Richard H. Leach, *American Federalism* (New York: Norton, 1970), p. 87.

of the city, taking their higher tax assessments with them; then school districts do not have sufficient revenue to support existing programs at the very time new demands are made to provide skills for students who want to obtain jobs. Ironically, the allocation of national and state aid is not relieving this crisis because under existing formulas more money goes to the areas least in need. Federal and state aid represents only 27% of the cost of city schools, 29% in the suburbs, and 37% of all expenditures in the rest of the nation.[10]

The chairman of President Nixon's Task Force on Education described the future involvement of the national government in supporting higher education as inevitable. "Whether public or private, most U.S. colleges are in such desperate financial straits that by the year 2000 they will be almost totally dependent on the federal government for support." He believes the trend is irreversible. In 1967 one-fourth of the $16.8 billion all colleges spent came from the national government, but, by 1975, the amount "may climb to 50%."[11] First, however, must come a clear definition of the federal government's role in education. President Nixon's commission reported that existing effort is "characterized by a multiplicity of uncoordinated, and sometimes conflicting, initiatives from many different departments and agencies of the Executive branch and from Congress."[12]

Education is representative of the way federalism functions in other areas of American life. Just as education is supported "through the joint efforts of many governments" so are "virtually all functions performed by the governments of the United States" likewise supported.[13] American federalism is not a simple, efficient system of government. Contrary to popular belief, the areas of political responsibility for different governments are not clearly drawn, nor do the various partners in federalism have exclusive jurisdiction over major political functions. Instead of describing American federalism as a division of local, state, or national "levels" of government, a more realistic description is a swirl of authority in which powers are diffused and touch each other at various points like chocolate in a marble cake.[14] This imprecision of authority, in fact, gives federalism its vitality, and accounts for the changing relationship between state and national governments in American history.

[10] Alan K. Campbell, "Inequities of School Finances," *Saturday Review* (January 11, 1969), p. 44.
[11] Alan Pifer, as quoted in *Time* (January 26, 1968), p. 75.
[12] Quoted in Leach, *op. cit.*, p. 98.
[13] Grodzins, *loc. cit.*, p. 5.
[14] Morton Grodzins, "The Federal System," in *Goals for Americans. The Report on the President's Commission on National Goals* (Englewood-Cliffs, New Jersey: Prentice-Hall, 1965), p. 265.

Federalism Before the Civil War: Dual Federalism

By its nature federalism requires a final point of reference to determine where the jurisdiction of states end and the national government begins. Except for the Civil War, that final point has been the Supreme Court. When Maryland attempted to tax a federal bank, for example, Chief Justice John Marshall made one of the most comprehensive expositions on national sovereignty in *McCulloch v. Maryland* (1819). Marshall held that because the national government derived its existence from all citizens of the United States and not from the individual states, the national government was supreme in its sphere of action and therefore could not be taxed by a state. "The power to tax is the power to destroy," he argued; the Founders "did not design to make their government dependent on the states." Marshall recognized that the states, like the national government, had legitimate functions, but when the two came in conflict the national government must be supreme. He admitted that the extent of the powers granted to the national government would always come into question. This was the nature of federalism. "The question respecting the extent of powers actually granted is perpetually arising, and will probably continue to arise, as long as our system shall exist."[15]

South Carolina's John C. Calhoun, one of Marshall's equally articulate contemporaries, disagreed with Marshall's conclusion that the national government was supreme. Calhoun referred to the United States as a "democratic federal republic," by which he meant "a community of states, and not the government of a single state or nation." Falling back on the doctrine that sovereignty was indivisible, "like a woman's chastity," Calhoun claimed the states must be the judges of their own power.[16] South Carolina's secession from the Union in 1860 was based on this interpretation of federalism.

When the Department of Interior was organized in 1849 this controversy was renewed. Although this new department relieved the workload of older Executive agencies and thereby made the national government more efficient, its birth was cause for alarm to some Americans. Dire predictions were made about the sinister effect the Department of Interior would have on the integrity of the states. "The whole tendency of this government is to increase patronage, to foster and enlarge the Executive power, which is becoming a maelstrom to swallow up all the powers of this government," warned one senator.[17]

---

[15] McCulloch v. Maryland, 4 Wheat. (U.S.) 316 (1819).
[16] See John C. Calhoun, *A Disquisition on Government*, C. Gordon Post, ed., (New York: The Liberal Arts Press, 1953).
[17] *Congressional Globe*, 30th Congress, 2nd Session, p. 671.

"There is something ominous in the expression, 'the Secretary of the Interior,' " cautioned the anxious Calhoun.[18] In fact, however, not the Department of Interior but the practice of slavery eventually led to the Civil War and to the very shift in national-state relations that some expected to result from the new Department of Interior. As has been the case throughout American history, many of the people concerned with states' rights would ignore slavery or the rights of other men, and it has been this neglect that has prompted more national involvement in federal relations.

The Post-Civil War Era, and the March of Power to Washington

Before the Civil War states and the national government were on almost equal terms. The national government depended upon the state militias for its army; the amount of money in circulation was determined largely by state-chartered banks, and the states were usually economically independent from the national government. After the war these relations changed.

National Army

From their precolonial background in England, settlers in America believed a national, standing army was an immediate threat to their liberties. When Americans fought the Revolution and even after the new Constitution was adopted, Americans retained the ancient prejudice toward a powerful, established military system. Citizens organized locally controlled, state militia to protect the new republic. But the petty jealousies and divisions of command never gave the state militias an impressive military record either during the War of 1812 or the War with Mexico, 1845. Military necessities during the Civil War forced state militias to merge into a national Army that was capable of providing national defense. "The substantial disappearance of the state militia forces, except as social organizations, until the national guard was established under federal guidance and federal standards was an inevitable consequence."[19]

National Economy

Before the war each state bank printed its own money, sometimes with jealous abandon, and despite the confusion this created for

[18] *Ibid.*, p. 673.
[19] Leonard D. White, *The States and the Nation* (Baton Rouge: Louisiana State University Press, 1953), pp. 14-15.

industry, states refused to permit the national government to nationalize money. Not until the necessity of financing the Civil War was the national government able, in 1863, to issue national currency and tax the currency of state banks out of existence.

The taxing power of the national government did not change substantially, however, until 1913 when the Sixteenth Amendment gave the national government access to the pocketbooks of Americans through the income tax. Political power follows economic power, observed Englishman James Harrington in 1659, and the truth of his observation has become embarrassingly obvious in the expanding power of the national government in the twentieth century.[20] Before 1913 there was relative balance between the income of the national government and the income of the states: the national government raised money from customs duties and land sales, whereas states depended upon real-estate taxes and such excise taxes as those on alcohol and tobacco. But there has been no competition between the tax-gathering abilities of the two governments since the national government got access to private and corporate incomes.

The Depression of 1929 proved the efficiency of the income tax and proved state and local governments did not have adequate fiscal procedures of their own to meet the necessities of the hour. In fact, states contributed to the catastrophe of the Depression by long denying power to counties and cities to tax and borrow so that local government could obtain local revenue to meet local needs. This inflexibility of state governments has contributed to the radical shift of financial power to the national government. Hesitantly at first, even apologetically, the national government stepped in to fill the breach. "But when under Franklin Roosevelt and subsequent Presidents it became evident that national programs of recovery and reform could be achieved only by a large degree of nationalization of financial direction and control, the national government acted overtly and directly," observes Professor Richard Leach. "One of the most impressive changes in the United States' history is the shift in fiscal balance thus brought about."[21]

National Constitution

With the adoption of the Thirteenth, Fourteenth, and Fifteenth Amendments to the Constitution, states were compelled to protect a citizen's civil rights just as the national government had been required when

[20] "The Congress shall have power to lay and collect taxes on incomes, from whatever source derived, without apportionment among the several states, and without regard to any census or enumeration." (Amendment XVI, February 25, 1913).
[21] Leach, *op. cit.*, p. 197.

the Bill of Rights were originally adopted. "Nor shall any State deprive any person of life, liberty, or property, without due process of law," states Section 1 of the Fourteenth Amendment. The "due process" clause was interpreted variously by the Supreme Court to distinguish jurisdictions between the states and the national government. For example, when Utah prohibited employment of workers in mines, smelters, or ore refineries for more than eight hours a day except in emergencies, the Supreme Court upheld the state law as constitutional in *Holden v. Hardy* (1898). Seven years later, in 1905, the court reversed itself by declaring unconstitutional a New York statute limiting the number of hours a baker could be employed to sixty hours a week and ten hours a day, *Lochner v. New York* (1905). "We think that a law like the one before us involves neither the safety, the morals, nor the welfare, of the public, and that the interest of the public is not in the slightest degree affected by such an act," argued the majority of justices in striking down New York's Ten-Hour Act.

Despite the ambiguity the Supreme Court created, states continued to initiate legislation to resolve some of the social problems created by the impact of industrialization. The Oregon state legislature passed a statute prohibiting employment of women in factories and laundries for more than ten hours in one day, but the law was challenged by employers. The Supreme Court acted from a new concept of law and upheld Oregon's statute in *Mueller v. Oregon* (1908). In his brief supporting Oregon's law, Louis Brandeis convinced the justices that the onset of major economic changes required a readjustment in the relative position of various interest groups, and the advent of industrialization in America necessitated new laws to protect society from the effects of these changes. As a result of the "Brandeis brief" the Supreme Court began to consider social legislation in terms of the welfare of society rather than in terms of whether the issue was a state or a national function.

Despite the trend of the court to consider state legislation in light of its reasonable and plausible relation to social welfare, the court did not grant national legislation the same flexibility. The attempt by Congress in 1916 to set uniform, minimum standards for child labor throughout the United States was ruled unconstitutional.

In *The Bitter Cry of the Children,* written in 1906, author John Spargo despaired at the way industry was using American children. Although conditions were not as wretched in the United States as they were in Europe, Spargo thought that a picture he saw in a French paper might describe some conditions in America at the turn of the twentieth century:

The Constitution: Creation of a Federal Republic   75

A woman, haggard and fierce of visage, representing France, was seated upon a heap of child skulls and bones. In her gnarled and knotted hands she held the writhing form of a helpless babe whose flesh she was gnawing with her teeth. Underneath, in red ink, was written in rude characters, 'The wretch! She devours her own children!' "[22]

Up to 2.25 million children between four and sixteen years of age were estimated, in 1906, to be employed in American industry. They worked in the textile mills of the South, where their number increased by more than 160% in the 1890s; they suffered ammonia burns in the oyster and shrimp canneries of New England; older children dug and sorted coal in Pennsylvania and West Virginia while younger ones worked as "trappers" by standing just inside the drafty mines pulling a string for ten or twelve hours a day to open and shut the door so haulers could push their carts back and forth; four-year-olds earned nineteen cents an afternoon stringing beans in New York canning factories, while anonymous thousands did menial tasks in the factories of urban America.[23] The hours were long and the work demanding. Whistles at the oyster factories blew at 4 A.M., the factory opened a half-hour later, and company watchmen "knock the kids off—that is, waken them—at 3:30 or so" said one mother describing the daily routine.[24] Industrial accidents, callous abuse, illiteracy, poverty, and no industrial compensation were the conditions many Amer-

[22] John Spargo, *The Bitter Cry of Children* (Chicago: Quadrangle Books, 1968), p. 147. Conditions in England were equally grim. Child-labor was so extensive in nineteenth-century England that men went into business transporting stolen, bought, or deserted children from one section of England to another in much the same way slave traders in the United States transported Negroes. One young apprentice remembered children were kept in the same area as pigs and described the competition for food between the pigs and children. For fattening, pigs were often given meatballs and dumplings in their swill. The apprentices would "slip away and slyly steal as many of these dumplings from the pigs as possible, hastening away with them to a hiding-place, where they were greedily devoured." But the pigs "learned from experience to guard their food by various expedients. Made wise by repeated losses, they kept a sharp lookout, and the moment they ascertained the approach of the half-famished apprentices, they set up so loud a chorus of snorts and grunts, it was heard in the kitchen, when out rushed the swineherd, armed with a whip, from which combined means of protection for the swine this accidental source of obtaining a good dinner was soon lost. Such was the contest carried on for some time at Litton Mill between the half-famished apprentices and the well-fed swine." (*Ibid.*, 133.)
[23] See: Bureau of Labor. *Report on Condition of Woman and Child Wage Earners in the United States* (Washington, D.C.: Government Printing Office, 1910–1913), Vol. I (19 vols).
[24] Grace Abbott, *The Child and the State* (Chicago: University of Chicago Press, 1938), Vol. I, p. 373 (2 vols.).

ican children faced sixty years ago. An effort was made to obtain uniform, minimum standards for all child laborers in 1916, through the Keating–Owen Child Bill.

"We think this committee ought to be encouraged to leave this matter to the states themselves," argued Southern cotton manufacturers in opposition to the bill during congressional hearings.[25] When passed, the act merely prohibited interstate shipment of goods produced in factories or mines that employed children under fourteen years of age (sixteen years for work mines), and prohibited children from working more than eight hours a day or night. Although opposition to the act came exclusively from textile interests, the National Association of Manufacturers joined them in warning Congress that the act infringed upon states' rights.

Of course, in the very states that needed laws to protect children there was little chance for legislation to pass. By 1914 only nine states had adopted three reasonable standards that had been recommended ten years earlier: An eight-hour day, no night work, and documentary proof of age. Twenty-two states still permitted children under fourteen to work in factories; sixteen states did not require documentary proof of age (either prompted by their parents or their own necessity, children often lied about their age, claiming they were older in order to work); twenty-eight states permitted children to work more than eight hours; and twenty-three states failed to adopt adequate restrictions on night work. "Between states specializing in the same industries—Massachusetts and North Carolina, for example—there remained in child-labor standards wide differences that gave an unwholesome competitive advantage to those with the lower legal requirement."[26]

The Keating–Owen Child Labor Act received overwhelming support (52–12 in the Senate; 337–46 in the House), and Congressmen from only two states, North and South Carolina, voted unanimously against it. The action of the Congressmen from the Carolinas was soon supported by the United States Supreme Court.

Three days before the law was to go into effect, a federal district judge in North Carolina challenged its constitutionality because it infringed upon the rights of Reuben and John Dagenhart, aged fourteen and twelve, to work more than eight hours a day. Within nine months the Supreme Court ruled that America's first child-labor law was unconstitutional in *Hammer v. Dagenhart* (1918), on the ground

---

[25] Quoted in Elizabeth Sands Johnson, "Child Labor Legislation," in John R. Commons, and others, *History of Labor in the United States, 1896–1932* (New York: Macmillan, 1938), Vol. III, p. 440 (4 vols).
[26] Robert H. Bremner, *From the Depths: The Discovery of Poverty in the United States* (New York: New York University Press, 1956), pp. 224–225.

that Congress must not "control the States in their exercise of the police power over local trade and manufacture." The logic was curious when compared with earlier court decisions prohibiting from interstate commerce the white-slave trade (women taken across state lines and forced into prostitution), impure foods, and lotteries. But in its 5-4 decision the Supreme Court held that Congress overreached its authority when it legislated for children.

In his enthusiasm to uphold states' rights, Supreme Court Justice Day misquoted the Tenth Amendment, which guarantees state powers. To the states and the people the "powers not *expressly* delegated to the national government are reserved." The word "expressly" is not in the Tenth Amendment, and in fact was specifically rejected by the framers of the amendment.

Falling back on states' rights arguments, American federalism failed to remedy child-labor abuses until the Dagenhart case was reversed in 1941. Nor did American federalism secure the civil rights of Black Americans as long as states were not compelled to treat all Americans equally. During Congressional hearings on child labor legislation in 1914 Southern textile manufacturers were asked how many employees were white. One manufacturer, Mr. Parker, testified, "They are all white. The only work given to the Negroes at all in the cotton mills is what we call the menial work, cleaning the floors, hauling the heavy bales of cotton, work which is simply menial in character." Then, when asked if it was not a fact "insofar as the schooling is concerned, that the Negro children are getting it, while the white children are in the mills," the question of educational opportunity in the South was raised momentarily.[27] This relationship of education to child labor had been drawn six years earlier by Senator Albert J. Beveridge of Indiana: "Whereas the children of the white working people of the South are going to the mill and to decay, the Negro children are going to school and improvement."[28] This strange paradox of white children receiving jobs and some black children receiving an education in the South was drawn to national attention again in 1914. Mr. Parker continued his testimony on the child labor bill by suggesting the need of a compulsory education law in order to maintain white supremacy.

> That is why I am advocating compulsory education, because I recognize the fact that the Negro believes that his salvation lies in

---

[27] *Child Labor Bill. Hearings Before the Committee on Labor, House of Representatives, Sixty-third Congress, Second Session, on HR 12292, A Bill to Prevent Interstate Commerce in the Products of Child Labor, and for Other Purposes,* May 22, 1914 (Washington: U.S. Government Printing Office, 1914), p. 90.
[28] Bremner, *op. cit.*, p. 224.

education, and we have not yet impressed upon our white people the fact that his superiority must continue only through intelligence and through superior education. . . .[29]

Not until 1954 would local school districts be challenged by the national government to provide equal educational opportunities for all Americans. At the end of World War II, school segregation existed throughout the South by law. Eighteen states made segregation mandatory by statute, and six states permitted segregation at the discretion of local school districts in the name of "local control." Segregated schools were supposed to be "separate but equal" but in fact schools for Blacks were notoriously *un*equal. In *Brown v. Board of Education* (1954), the Supreme Court ruled unanimously that school segregation violated the Constitution, and in the following year the Courts implemented its decision by ordering lower courts to work out equitable educational opportunities "with all deliberate speed."

The social revolution this decision triggered continues to reverberate in the 1970s, testing the ability of American federalism to make the republic viable for all citizens. In order to stop this march of power to Washington, local, county, and state governments must take the initiative to resolve this and other social problems. Recently politicians have made deliberate efforts to use the national government as a greater stimulus for local governments to become full partners in American federalism.

Ferment of Federalism in the 1970s

Lyndon Johnson and Richard Nixon used the word "federalism" to identify the domestic programs of their administrations. "Creative Federalism" was coined by President Johnson at Michigan State University in 1964 to launch the Great Society legislation of 1964–1968. Here, federalism meant the national government would lay out general policy guidelines, but the states were to develop creative ideas. If the idea was attractive enough the national government literally bought it. An example is the Model Cities Program, in which resources from all governments are concentrated to reduce blight and decay and to encourage local leadership to participate in city improvement. In contrast to the older grants-in-aid programs, in which national money was given to those states that cried help, Creative Federalism turned the states' approach for money away from "see how poor we are"

---

[29] *Hearings Before the Committee on Labor, loc. cit.,* p. 90.

The Constitution: Creation of a Federal Republic 79

to "see how bright our future is and what a good investment we are."

President Nixon's New Federalism was discovered in 1969. The thrust of New Federalism was to deemphasize the national government: "Washington will no longer dictate. We can only toss the ball; the states and localities will have to carry it," Nixon promised in terms that described federalism in the language of a football game.[30] President Nixon never developed the specifics of how New Federalism worked, leading *The New York Times* to comment editorially that without substance the term will be "little more than a rhetorical phrase."[31] Generally, New Federalism may be described as an attempt to have the national government give blocks of money with no strings attached. Whereas Creative Federalism had a carrot and very mild stick, New Federalism seems to be all carrot.

Both Presidents could talk about "creative ideas" and "throwing the ball" without unleashing public wrath, because the national government is so well bankrolled through the income tax that it does not have to raise taxes to support new programs. The flair of Madison Avenue jingles such as "Creative Federalism" or "New Federalism" often obscures the realities of how the various partners work or cannot work together.

Disproportionate income for the federal government and the state is one important economic reality. The income tax has been Alladin's Lamp to Washington. Rubbed every April 15th, it automatically gives the national government an amount of revenue directly proportionate to current business activity. Because personal incomes have increased faster than have other values, the national government has a built-in economic advantage over local and state governments, which raise most of their money from property taxes. And property taxes have not increased nearly as fast as has personal income. The economic initiative is thus with Washington. The national government enjoys what Professor John Kenneth Galbraith calls "the pleasant privilege of underwriting its own loans," whereas state and local governments must ask a reluctant public to increase taxes before they can start or even maintain programs.[32]

Another difficulty of American federalism is that many local governments are not functionally able to do the jobs they claim are their own responsibility. "Local control" is often more sentiment than reality. For one thing, state constitutions are generally not concise but huge,

---

[30] As quoted in *The New York Times* (Sept. 3, 1969), p. 1.
[31] *Ibid.*, p. 46.
[32] John Kenneth Galbraith, *The Affluent Society* (New York: New American Library, 1958), p. 207.

clumsy documents that encumber state governments with administrative trivia, making efficient government at the local level almost impossible. In comparison with the national Constitution's 6000 words, the constitution of Louisiana has 253,830 words, Alabama's has 106,000, California's has 82,570, and Texas' has 52,270.[33] Not only did authors of state constitutions approach their task with a telephone book in mind, but they did not display the same competence as the Founding Fathers. They confused constitutional procedures with administrative matters. Many state constitutions institutionalize administrative detail that is not only irrelevant but obsolete. In order to adapt to current needs, state constitutions have been forced to undergo numerous amendment changes: Louisiana's constitution was amended 460 times; Alabama's, 260; California's, 350 times; and Texas', 178 times.[34] "In earlier years, when life moved more slowly and there was less need for government involvement at every turn, a cumbersome state constitution made little difference," observes Professor Leach, "but today it is one of the prime reasons why the national government has been called on so often when action has been necessary." Instead of assisting local control, "state constitutions hinder and obstruct it and thereby provide justification for national action."[35]

Nor have most states invested their governors with sufficient power to initiate policy or plan budgets. The healthy suspicion of government has often exceeded prudence to the point where states are incapacitated. In states where governors are weak, the state legislatures are often invested with Executive functions in addition to their regular legislative responsibilities. The purpose, ostensibly, is to keep state policies closer to the will of the people. In reality, however, state legislatures often have not represented a majority of the state's electorate. Until the Supreme Court forced state legislatures to draw up legislative districts according to population, state capitols have been the happy hunting grounds for special interests. Railroad and utility companies ran many state legislatures for decades. Today Anaconda Copper exercises disproportionate influence in Montana, race track operators influence the legislatures in Illinois and Florida, cattlemen's associations have special influence in Wyoming, oil companies in Louisiana, and insurance and drug companies in Connecticut.[36] As a result of the "one-man, one-vote" decision in *Wesberry v. Sanders,* perhaps local control will assert itself in state governments.

[33] Leach, *op. cit.,* p. 118.
[34] *Ibid.,* p. 119.
[35] *Ibid.,* p. 120.
[36] Terry Sanford, *Storm Over the States* (New York: McGraw-Hill, 1967), p. 33.

The Constitution: Creation of a Federal Republic 81

Governing the American city is supposed to be local control in action, but state and national governments often hinder rather than help cities govern themselves. Too often what cities can do, and how they can do it, is written into state constitutions. Thus city governments have the impossible task of administering contemporary urban problems through institutions that were written over 100 years ago. Once inscribed in the state constitution, only major crises are able to pry revisions out of the legislature or the public. Some state constitutions dictate how many men should be on a city council, what their salaries should be, and even describe methods of personnel administration. Although states complain of the national government controlling state activities, in fact states have been notorious in treating cities as petty fiefs or neglecting reforms that will permit cities to govern themselves. Such inflexibility takes control away from locally elected officials. "We are convinced that the American federal system in general, and the initiative and self-reliance of local government in particular, would be greatly strengthened by loosening many of the existing bonds upon local government," concluded the Advisory Commission on Intergovernmental Relations in 1962. Even in the early 1960s "the adequate and sound development of local government functions [is] retarded and repressed;" by now they may be killed.[37]

Efficient city government, in which all members of the public participate, is imperative, not only to keep federalism vital but to handle the impending crunch of the cities. Eighty percent of the population increase between now and the twenty-first century is expected to be in the cities. This will increase the importance of solving the current list of already critical problems: mass transit and highway congestion; water supply and sewage disposal; educational and recreational facilities; ugliness; violence and crime; housing shortage and slum clearance; labor relations with such public service employees as teachers, firemen, policemen, sanitation workers, and public health officers; and the concentration of racial minorities. Given some of the realities of local government, it is not surprising that already the national government is bypassing states by giving direct financial aid to cities. The traditional state–national relationships may be changing into a new city–national federalism in which American cities will enjoy political independence from states like certain cities in Europe.

What is the future of American federalism? In the years ahead

---

[37] Quoted in Leach, *op. cit.*, p. 136. The Advisory Committee was created in 1959 by Congress as a twenty-six-member, bipartisan body representing governors, mayors, county officials, state legislatures, Congress, the President, and the public—all of the parties involved in American federalism.

federalism will depend on what the American people define as their needs and to what degree governments will be expected to help meet these needs. The national government seems destined to increase its involvement in meeting some of these needs, such as initiating national health insurance, but this does not mean state and local governments will be dwarfed. Vigorous state and local governments are needed to provide the greater services urban Americans will demand. All levels of federalism must remain strong in order to prevent the shift of power toward either Washington or city hall. Finding means to bridge rather than widen the gaps between local, state, and national governments is essential if we are to "organize our common efforts to adapt to the new and larger challenges which we face."

THE FORM OF THE AMERICAN REPUBLIC

In the Declaration of Independence, the institution of government was regarded as a necessity to secure or preserve the rights that individuals were regarded to have in the state of nature, viz. life, liberty, and the pursuit of happiness. Unlike the marxist view that government is evil and will wither because of the eventual perfectibility of human nature, the Founding Fathers viewed human nature as having *both* good and selfish potentialities, and therefore, never considered a time when government would not be needed. Madison stated this succinctly in *The Federalist # 51* when he said:

> But what is government itself but the greatest of all reflections on human nature? If men were angels no government would be necessary. If angels were to govern men, neither external nor internal controls on government would be neces-

sary. In framing a government which is to be administered by men over men, the great difficulty lies in this: you must first enable the government to control the governed and in the next place oblige it to control itself. A dependence on the people is, no doubt, the primary control on government; but experience has taught mankind the necessity of *auxiliary precautions*.

In Part II we will consider the "necessity of auxiliary precautions" of the organization and the use of power in the American government. We are not merely concerned here with human nature and the separation of powers—this has been detailed and memorized before—but rather in *why* these powers were granted to particular branches of government, and whether or not this division of power has any applicability to today.

CONGRESS: Can Americans Keep Their Republic?

> [Two] *things that seem to be requisite in a system of government and every form is good in proportion as it possesses or attains them, (1) Wisdom to plan proper measures for the public good, (2) Fidelity to have nothing but the public interest in view.*
>
> —*John Witherspoon*
> **Lectures on Political Philosophy**

When the Constitution was framed in 1787, Congress was regarded as an essential power to make republican government a viable, practical reality for the United States. Congress was also expected to be the most powerful branch of government. In Article I of the Constitution, congressmen were given a job description longer and more detailed than that for the President (Article II) or the judiciary (Article III). In Article I are listed most of the powers of the Congress (Section 8), its limitations (Section 9), and its relations with state governments

(Section 10). To protect the United States from external danger, Congress must provide and regulate an army and navy; it must tax and borrow "to provide for the common defense"; and it may declare war. To provide for national affairs within the United States, Congress was given a variety of powers, including authority to regulate commerce between states, "fix the standard of weights and measures," coin money and regulate its value, and "establish a uniform Rules of Naturalization, and uniform Laws on the subject of Bankruptcies throughout the United States."

In practice Congress has seldom approached its high calling. Congress's relationship with the President is now just the opposite of what the Founding Fathers expected. Instead of the office of President needing protection from an ambitious, powerful legislature, Congress has become so subordinate to the Chief Executive that some Americans now wonder if Congress is not an unnecessary relic of the eighteenth century. Critics charge that Congress's chief function now is serving as a rubber stamp to approve Executive decisions, a routine that makes the national government appear to be functioning according to the Constitution. Senator Joseph Clark called Congress "The Sapless Branch" after noting that since the republic was founded Congress rarely initiates anything, rarely faces up to current problems, even more rarely resolves them.[1]

One historic exception to this indictment occurred in the decade of the 1870s when Congress initiated reconstruction of the South following the Civil War. Then the fear of the Founding Fathers was supported for Congress did assert its influence over the Executive far beyond constitutional intent. Congress's irregular powers were turning the American government into a quasi-Parliament wherein both executive and legislative powers were exercised by legislators. Today, a century later, the relationship between Congress and the President is reversed.

In the decade of the 1970s, following both "hot" and "cold" wars and even greater economic change than the industrialization of the 1870s, the President exercises unprecedented power and Congress is dwarfed by its own acquiescence and apparent public indifference. The Americans who will celebrate the second centennial of the nation's birth in 1976 will like their predecessors be obligated to make the republic viable, but unlike their predecessors in 1876, who had to elect a strong President to restore Executive independence, today Americans have the more difficult task of demanding that their 535 congressmen—100 senators and 435 representatives—do the job the

[1] Joseph Clark, *Congress: The Sapless Branch* (New York: Harper and Row, 1964).

Constitution requires of them. This assumes, of course, Congress is worth restoring, that the national legislature is vital to the survival of republican government in the United States.

Relationship of Congress to Republican Principles

Professor Witherspoon's conclusion, "that every good form of government must be complex, so that the one principle may check the other," was the *modus operandi* of the delegates to the Constitutional Convention in 1787. To obtain efficient administration, they sought the advantage of a monarch in a one-man President; to obtain wisdom they created an independent judiciary and also designed the Senate to provide the peculiar advantage of a wise aristocracy; and to obtain fidelity they made selection of the President and congressmen dependent on public elections and also designed the House of Representatives to enhance democracy.

Although the job descriptions of each branch were worked out in a series of compromises and made by delegates who bargained with each other as pragmatic politicians as much as supporters of republicanism, each office was created to maximize the peculiar advantage it could provide to make republican government a reality in the United States. Checks and balances were incorporated to reduce the particular defect peculiar to each office—so the President could not become an abject tyrant, or the Senate a corrupt and selfish oligarchy; and should all members of the House of Representatives suddenly be elected by an unreasoning, vengeful public, the checks and balances would help to prevent the degeneration of the nation into anarchy or dictatorship.

As practical politicians the delegates recognized the source of corruption lay within human nature and therefore beyond the power of mortal man to remove. "As long as the reason of man continues fallible, and he is at liberty to exercise it, different opinions will be formed," observed James Madison. "Men of factious tempers, of local prejudices, or of sinister designs, may, by intrigue, by corruption, or by other means, first obtain the suffrages, and then betray the interests, of the people."[2] As practical politicians the delegates were suspicious of those who claimed man must be made perfect before republican government could exist, because those who wished to change human nature were, themselves, corrupt. Historically, when

[2] Clinton Rossiter, ed., *Federalist Papers* (New York: The New American Library, 1961), No. 10, pp. 78, 82.

such men held power they succeeded only in destroying liberty by compelling everyone to hold the same opinion. Unable to remove the cause of corruption, the delegates did try hard to design a Constitution that would control the effects of corruption.

For example, the six-year term of senators was a compromise between various suggestions. This length of time seemed long enough for the senators to gain knowledge from experience, yet short enough to prevent senators from ignoring the public. A six-year term provided time for them to act on knowledge gained, and would even enable them to support legislation that might for the moment be unpopular but still in the public's best interest, without the fear of immediately standing for reelection. The six-year term also brought some continuity to national policy because the terms of at least one-third of the senators would overlap two presidential terms. Because the Senate was expected to have the advantage of wisdom, it was from the Senate, not the House, that the President was directed to seek "advice and consent" on matters requiring careful deliberation, such as appointments of Supreme Court Justices and foreign policies.

The two-year term for House members was also a compromise. It seemed a short enough period to permit the changing views of the people to be represented in the national government. All members of the House of Representatives, but only one-third of the Senate, stand for election every two years. To secure the democratic principle in the House, the Founders also modified the nature of representation between the two groups in Congress. Unlike senators, who represent geographical areas with no regard at all to the number of people in each state, each representative, in theory, is responsible to an equal proportion of Americans. For the purpose of electing representatives, the United States is now divided into 435 districts composed of differing and often competing socioeconomic interests.

Recently the Supreme Court has had to compel representatives to remain faithful to the democratic principle of equal representation. In theory the number of congressmen from a state is adjusted after each ten-year census to accommodate the shifting population patterns both between and within states. In practice during the 1960s this adjustment was not made, for although the average congressional district had a population of 410,000 the actual population varied significantly. It was the disparity of representation in Georgia (one rural congressional district had 272,000 people, while the Fifth Congressional District around Atlanta had 823,000 citizens), that caused the Court to rule in *Wesberry v. Sanders* that all Americans should have equal representation.

Congress: Can Americans Keep Their Republic? 89

Measured against the two requirements for good government Congress was created to secure—"wisdom to plan proper measures for the public good," and "fidelity to have nothing but the public interest in view"—Congress is clearly in need of even greater improvement than removing the disparity of population between congressional districts. The Senate, for example, gives little advice and less consent to the direction of foreign affairs, largely because senators are ignorant of the policies—out of presidential secrecy or from some senators' own disinterest. Secrecy and ignorance dominate the method of appropriating budgets. Thirteen subcommittees, "isolated from everyone else inside and outside of Congress," cut up the $200 billion budget in 1971. Ignorance, rather than wisdom, is particularly revealed when the Senate acts on defense spending. Critic Robert Sherrill cites an incident in mid-July of 1970, when Senator Barry Goldwater of Arizona accused Senator William Proxmire of Wisconsin of revealing secret Pentagon plans for an "electronic battlefield." Senator Goldwater called Proxmire's action a dangerous leak of such highly classified material that "even the Armed Services Committee has not been able to hold hearings on it." Yet Senator Goldwater himself inserted into the *Congressional Record* on October 16, 1969, a speech by General Westmoreland that covered the upcoming electronic "automated battlefield," in detail. "Furthermore, in the January 31, 1970, issue of *Business Week* magazine and in the February 16, 1970, issue of *Product Engineering,* and in the November 1969, issue of McGraw-Hill's *DMS Market Intelligence Reports* not only were the details of the new computerized battlefield systems spelled out but the names of the contractors were given as well."[3] Thus the information available to businessmen and defense contractors was not available to members of Congress who had already spent $2 billion without any careful deliberation.

Congressmen are usually keenly knowledgeable about bills for projects that pump money back into their home districts and enable them to get reelected easier. Because of the internal organization of the House and Senate—those parliamentary procedures adopted out of convenience and custom, not from the Constitution—the only way a congressman can rise to power within a committee is by the seniority that comes from being reelected repeatedly. Most representatives are so successful in getting public works money funneled to their home districts—"the simplest way to tell whether a district is rich or poor in government projects is to see how long its repre-

[3] Robert Sherrill, *Why They Call It Politics* (New York: Harcourt, Brace, Jovanovich, 1972), pp. 109–110.

sentative has been in Congress"[4]—that nearly 75% of congressmen are returned to Washington every two years.

Yet the very repetition of most congressmen's reelection time after time works against the principle of representation. The House of Representatives does not reflect the public's changing moods as much as does the President. One important reason for this contradiction to the Founders' expectation is that the problems in need of solution today are more national in scope, causing Americans to express their opinions most forcefully in the elections of Presidents and even senators. Because economic livelihood depends increasingly on decisions in Washington, congressmen are also functioning as employment agents; so long as there are sufficient jobs in a congressman's district the public appears less inclined to replace him.

Congressmen, however, cannot begin to secure the two fundamental requirements of republican government intended by the Founders until they act on the two powers they have, the power to tax and the power to spend. Giving Congress control of the nation's purse strings was the Founding Fathers' linchpin in turning, as far as was possible, the ideal of republican government into a practical reality. They made Congress the cornerstone of the American republic.

Unlike other governments, which permit rulers to make their own private opinions appear to be public policy, a republic by definition is a government that responds to public matters. Because money is the grease that supports all policies, whether private or public in origin, the Founders hoped to give Americans control over their government's policies by following the English parliament's example of linking taxation to representation. By requiring congressional approval to finance new policies the Founders tried to ensure that these policies were truly in the public's interest rather than in the private interest of one man or a clique. In giving control of the purse to the most democratic branch, the delegates to the Constitutional Convention in 1787 attempted to compel the government to remain faithful by forcing it to rely on Congress for money. In turn, they attempted to keep congressmen faithful by forcing them to face their constituents at frequent and regular elections.

But Congress no longer controls the nation's purse despite its constitutional obligation. Congressmen have become mere spectators, going through the form of approving budgets that in fact have already been worked out by the President's Office of Budget and Management. Since the Budget and Accounting Act of 1921, which permitted the President to draw up a national budget for the whole government,

[4] Mark J. Green, James M. Fallows, and David R. Zwick, *Who Runs Congress? The President, Big Business, or You?* (New York: Bantam Books, 1972), p. 111.

Congress has steadily given up its control of the purse strings until now it is the President, not Congress, who appropriates money. The fault for this serious distortion lies primarily with Congress, not the President.

The House Ways and Means Committee: Fidelity to Whom?

If the love of money is the root of most evil, control of the nation's taxes was best placed in the hands of congressmen in order for the people to protect themselves from the evils of political tyranny. England furnished Americans with this concept. When King John signed the Magna Charta in 1215, he agreed he would levy no extraordinary taxes without the nobles' consent. For five centuries after that, the controversy between king and Parliament over which had power to levy taxes and appropriate funds continued, until the issue was finally resolved in Parliament's favor in 1689. Then Parliament asserted its supremacy by appointing a new king, compelling future kings to protect certain rights of Englishmen, and, most important, assuming complete domination over the power to tax and the power to spend—the powers that make all others pale into insignificance. The English Bill of Rights specified "That levying money for or to the use of the crown by pretense or prerogative, without grant of Parliament for longer time or in other manner than the same is or shall be granted, is illegal."

This principle was extended to Congress in the American Constitution. Only congressmen can order the government to spend money, and they take their power seriously. Of the twenty-one standing committees through which the House does its work of legislation, overseeing government operations, and representation, the two most powerful committees deal with finance. These two are the twenty-five-member House Ways and Means Committee and the fifty-five-member House Appropriations Committee. Of the Senate's nineteen standing committees, two are responsible for finance. These four are regarded by congressmen as the most powerful, prestigious, and important, of all committee assignments. "The Appropriations Committee is the most powerful committee in the House. It's the most powerful committee in the Congress," reported one member. "This is where all the money starts rolling." One congressman commented proudly on his Ways and Means assignment, "It's the top committee in the House of Representatives. The entire revenue system is locked into the committee."[5]

All hope to become members of these committees, but rarely do

[5] *Ibid.*, p. 55.

freshmen get placed on one, because, claimed one veteran, "It would be too risky to put on a person whose views and nature the leadership has no opportunity to assess."[6] No member enters these committees without careful screening to determine his views on a particular interest of some faction. For example, former Speakers Sam Rayburn and Lyndon Johnson refused to permit anyone to sit on the House Ways and Means Committee or the Senate Finance Committee without first determining what he thought about oil depletion allowance.[7]

Having spent over thirty of his sixty-two years in the House of Representatives, and having served as chairman of the House Ways and Means Committee since 1958, Wilbur Mills of tiny Kensett, Arkansas surprised his colleagues when he announced his candidacy for the Democratic presidential nomination in 1971. "Wilbur, why do you want to run for President and give up your grip on the country?" asked Congressman Sam Gibbons of Florida, whose question was based as much on fact as rhetoric.[8] Not only does Mills hold the reins on Presidents, congressmen, and businessmen, but he is remarkably influential with foreign heads of government as well, because his committee covers all parts of the national government that relate to money—taxes, revenue sharing, tarriffs, and foreign trade quotas. Chairman Mills holds the keys to special tax breaks at home and import restrictions on foreign countries, which helps explain why Japanese textile manufacturers yielded in 1971 to Mills' rather than President Nixon's persuasions to restrict their exports to the United States. It also helps explain why businessmen help provide for his needs, as did Sears, Roebuck and Company by lending him one of their private jet planes in 1971, or as did the American dairymen in providing $45,000 for his presidential primary campaigns in 1972, and why in his New Hampshire primary he received top-notch professional support from high-level Washington lobbyists for oil, banking, and beer.

Recent studies of Congress do more than suggest that such favors were expressions of gratitude on the part of businessmen for tax loopholes and other advantages Mills' committee has permitted. The House Ways and Means Committee enabled 1300 Americans with incomes over $50,000 a year to escape paying any taxes in 1971; helped Gulf Oil pay only 1.2% on its $990 million income; buried reform proposals, and passed measures to redistribute income *to* corporations; arranged the Revenue Act of 1971 to cut federal income taxes by $9 billion, "with over $7.5 billion of that cut going to corporations,

[6] *Ibid.*
[7] *Ibid.*
[8] *Ibid.*, p. 71.

a $70 million tax cut for banks, sponsored by Chairman Mills himself, and numerous other, similarly inclined, bills."[9]

Wilbur Mills rose to power by becoming a technical expert on the labyrinth of federal tax codes. He studied the complicated and detailed tax laws so well that few could compete with his knowledge or interpretation of the impact of new legislation on revenue. Mills abolished subcommittees when he became chairman of the House Ways and Means Committee in 1958 and so concentrated power in his own hands that during congressional hearings on new legislation he has often been the only congressman in attendance who can comment in detail on the tax impact of the proposal. Because of his power few congressmen dare challenge his interpretation. Some members have accused him of keeping junior committee members ignorant of information by not revealing the time when special hearings are scheduled and by "prohibiting committee members from bringing professional staff into secret sessions, although he occasionally lets dozens of Treasury Department staff sit in and participate."[10]

Those Democrats who question his personal ways and means may find their careers so blunted as to make them incapable of achieving legislation that will be useful both for their own district and their own reelection. Those Democrats on the House Ways and Means Committee also serve as the Committee on Committees, which serves as a clearinghouse for appointing Democrats to various other committees. Chairman Mills can make certain committees are filled with the "right" Democrats. Even the former Democratic Majority Leader Hale Boggs was compelled to reconsider a criticism of Mills' request to have interest rates raised on the national debt, which was a bonus for the nation's largest banks. "Hale," Mills said, "I wouldn't make that speech if I were you. I made you leader and I can unmake you just as easily."[11] Boggs never made the speech.

As a yearly bonus to the Ways and Means Committee's hard work there is a "Members' Day," when each committee member, seated around a large green felt-covered table, submits the tax bills especially written for favored constituents. "Each member is given a chance to offer a bill for consideration. After it is accepted the next member presents his bill—and so on around the table until everyone is satisfied," writes Tom Stanton. "Depending on the appetites of the members, the process may stop after one round, but may go on for two or three. Sometimes members use the occasion to correct minor

[9] *Ibid.*, p. 72.
[10] *Ibid.*, p. 73.
[11] *Ibid.*, p. 75.

inequities in past laws; or to 'deliver' favors to other congressmen for reciprocal favors at a politically opportune time."[12]

Once reported out of committee Mills' creations have little chance of being repudiated by the full House because of the rule requiring members accept in total every bill affecting taxation or reject the bill entirely. To avoid even potential controversy some bills are carefully scheduled to escape criticism on the House floor. Such scheduling occurred "during lunch when only thirty congressmen were present" for the 1971 Revenue Act, which sheared corporate taxes by $7.5 billion (more than the combined 1972 budget for the Environmental Protection Agency, Department of State, and the whole federal court system combined). Mills had the bill voted by voice rather than roll call because, he explained, "where there is a questionable gain politically, I do not ask for one (a roll-call vote)."[13]

Despite public criticism of Mills' techniques in 1972, the "Members' Bills" of 1972 were no different than those passed previously. In 1972 House Majority Leader Hale Boggs, who came from the offshore-drilling state of Louisiana, sponsored a five-year tariff rebate worth $250,000 to owners of offshore oil-drilling and oceanographic vessels, shrimp boats, and barges. This rebate would have been retroactive to 1967. One bill that particularly stimulated opposition provided for a reduction of the excise tax on cigars by $120 million between 1972 and 1979, and by $21 million per year thereafter. This bill was sponsored by Congressman James A. Burke, whose Boston district includes some cigar-making firms. Blocked in February, Burke's tax bonanza for cigar manufacturers reappeared in April in a different form, leading Congressman Les Aspin of Wisconsin to write, "I find it incredible that we are being asked to approve a blatant $12 million tax break for the cigar industry without the benefit of committee hearings and without the right to offer amendments to the bill on the floor."[14] Other bills headed off but not killed in 1972 included a grant of $70 million in tax breaks to banks, a $25 million tax cut to four large timber companies, a $3 million tariff benefit to the olive industry, and a $500,000 benefit to private foundations.

Attack on the "Members' Bills" was led by Wilbur Mills' equally powerful colleague, Wright Patman, chairman of the House Banking Committee. Patman objected to the nondemocratic procedure of having these bills sail through the House with no hearings, no floor debate, and no detailed information about their economic impact. He also

---
[12] *Ibid.*, pp. 73-74.
[13] *Ibid.*, p. 74.
[14] *Los Angeles Times* (Oct. 10, 1972).

criticized these round-robin adventures for turning the nation's tax and tariff laws into Swiss cheese by providing loopholes that give sizable benefits to private interests. Patman claimed ignorance of "Members' Bills" during his forty-four years in Congress because they came up only once a year and then at an off time such as at Christmas or on New Year's Eve. In those final few minutes of the calendar year Congress moves with uncommon speed, spending many millions of dollars on projects few congressmen understand and even fewer study. Such an occurrence took place on Christmas Eve in 1966, when congressmen voted millions in tax exemptions for, among others, aluminum companies, oil companies, tobacco companies, hearse-manufacturing companies, investment funds, and persons earning more than $25,000 a year. For good reason it was called the "Christmas Tree Bill" of 1966.

The speed by which Congress indulges special interests contrasts with the snail's pace Congress follows in enacting legislation for the national interest. "The pattern is clear," observes critic Robert Sherrill. "When the action benefits friends in the party, or indulges special interests to whom the lawmakers are indebted (or hope to become indebted), or helps somebody make money on a grand scale—speed is not out of the question. But there is not much money to be made from giving food stamps to the poor, or building clean housing for migrant laborers," or financing bilingual education, Teacher Corps for slums, or rehabilitation of handicapped children.[15] Medical care for the aged has been proposed in every session of Congress for a generation before it was passed, and still nothing has been done to relieve the middle-class American from the shadow of frightening medical costs. Mills reported in 1972 that a nationalized medical-insurance program for all Americans could not be worked into his committee's schedule for at least two years. In the meantime congressmen remain protected by their own medical-insurance scheme paid for by tax dollars.

Congressional Representation in a National Welfare Economy

Although the method of enacting "Members' Bills" and special legislation in midnight sessions is undemocratic, congressmen can claim they are doing their job to help people in the local districts whom

[15] Sherrill, *op. cit.*, p. 96.

they were elected to represent. Congressmen are bound to give special attention to parochial needs of their own districts because their political futures are determined by local rather than national constituencies. Congressman Richard Bolling of Missouri admits that "the mortar that binds the system consists largely of what has been called inelegantly but properly 'boodle.' " The need for each congressman to help the other obtain economic advantages for his district is the cement that binds Congress.

> Boodle includes the location of a military installation, with a construction payroll followed by a steady payroll of civilian and military employees who live and spend and pay taxes in a member's district. It also includes a wide variety of public works—dams, rivers, and harbor projects, federal post office and office buildings, conservation and reclamation projects. The boodle in itself is legitimate and productive. The hitch is in the way it is distributed. Generally, the stay-in-line orthodox member will come away with the fuller plate.[16]

Although congressmen have been consistently piping "pork" and "boodle" back home ever since the Constitution was adopted in 1788, the practice is more noticeable today because the economic livelihood of almost all Americans depends on the policies of the national government. As a consequence of our foreign commitments and domestic economy Congress is pumping money out of Washington on a scale unparalleled in American history. Moreover, more Americans than ever have a personal interest in this money because local boodle directly affects the majority of Americans for the first time. The image of Americans earning their livelihood strictly on their own initiative, independent of government assistance, is a memory, not a reality. Although the national government made the exercise of "rugged individualism" a little easier for nineteenth-century frontiersmen by passing the Homestead Act, in the past these special favors from Washington were largely reserved for the Carnegies, Rockefellers, Morgans, and Mellons in the form of high protective tariffs or railway and banking subsidies.

Although certain interests today receive a larger amount of welfare from the national government than do others, the majority of Americans now live by the grace of Congress. There are few Americans whose jobs are not significantly supported by federal appropriations. Defense contracts, space program, Social Security payments, veter-

---

[16] From the book *House Out of Order* by Richard Bolling, p. 109. Copyright © 1964, 1965, 1966 by Richard Bolling. Published by E. P. Dutton & Co., Inc., and used with their permission.

ans' benefits, federal home mortgage guarantees, "Members' Bills," tax loopholes, business subsidies, and the more recently approved programs of federally guaranteed annual income and federal assistance to cities and states—these and other conduits of money from Washington may be described collectively as "revenue sharing." Our welfare economy seems destined to be national. When the Ninety-second Congress ended in 1972, President Nixon had his revenue sharing bill approved, permitting the treasury to send $30.2 billion to states, counties, and cities by 1977, so local governments could balance their budgets. Also approved then was Nixon's request for the first federally guaranteed minimum income of $195 per month per retired couple on Social Security, which, when it began on January 1,1974, affected more than 5 million elderly or handicapped Americans. Although the Ninety-second Congress did not approve Nixon's welfare recommendation for a family assistance plan to guarantee incomes for poor families with children, the principle of nationalizing welfare was less in question than the methods of its finance.

Even the rhetoric of "free enterprise" is obsolete. Many Americans once believed all social and political solutions were contained within that magic phrase, but, as political scientist V. O. Key, Jr., observed in 1961, "If by some miracle we should overnight establish a free-enterprise system by wiping from the statute books all interferences with common liberty, it would be regarded tomorrow as a catastrophe." Against free enterprise would march lobbyists for the "airlines, the steamship conferences, the investment trusts, the chambers of commerce, the banks, the truckers, the petroleum industry, the real estate developers, the cosmetologists, and the Nevada gamblers."[17]

Research by a special project team of Associated Press reporters ten years later in August 1971 documented Key's observation on the involvement of the national government in our economy. Although the reporters could not be absolutely certain of the exact figures, they were convinced that subsidies to private corporations totaled at least $28 billion and "may run as high as $38 billion" annually. "Private enterprise in America collects roughly $30 billion a year in government subsidies and subsidy-like aid, much of it hidden or disguised."[18] Up to $15 billion annually was granted in the form of tax breaks, incentives, and exemptions; "farm subsidies total between $6 billion and $9 billion; loans to business (direct, guaranteed, and insured) come to $250 billion, 'six times the outstanding credit advanced

---

[17] V. O. Key, Jr., "Public Opinion and the Decay of Democracy," *The Virginia Quarterly Review* (Autumn 1961), p. 492.
[18] Sherrill, *op. cit.*, p. 96–97.

by all commercial banks'; the maritime industry gets $450 million a year; the airlines $63 million (including $10.5 million to multimillionaire Howard Hughes' Air West Airlines), and the railroads receive $172 million over a five-year period; defense contractors get to use $14.6 billion worth of government property for profit-making purposes; United States companies doing business overseas receive over $6 billion in loans and insurance."[19]

The welfare benefits Congress provides for big farmers is second only to those given defense industrialists. For example, W. R. Poage, chairman of the House Agriculture Committee, protects his Texas constituents and his own grain and cotton farms as well. Texas receives nearly one-third of the total subsidies paid by the government to the nation's cotton farmers and Texas gets the fifth largest handout for feed grains. Senator Allen Ellender, chairman of the Senate farm group, and his fellow Louisiana sugar farmers receive millions from the Sugar Act Program. Senator James O. Eastland, the third ranking member of Ellender's farm committee, receives well over $250,000 annually from the taxpayers for his 5000-acre plantation in Mississippi.

Although the farm-subsidy total increases annually, the number of farmers receiving money continually decreases. Despite the fact that the Department of Agriculture's budget has quadrupled since 1940 there are less than half as many farms today, and about 150,000 small farmers sell out each year to the agribusinessmen.[20]

The significance of this and other documentation, as we must recognize, is that today Congress provides the magic for high employment, high profits, and economic prosperity. So, in a sense, today's congressmen have really become local employment agents and welfare distributors. Despite the traditional American view that government and business are separate and distinct, and never do (or should) the twain meet, in reality the national government and business have always been interrelated. Never has this reality been more obvious than today. In August 1971, for example, Congress voted to bail out Lockheed Aircraft Corporation from certain bankruptcy by guaranteeing private loans with taxpayers' dollars. In 1973 New York's senators began to initiate some economic assistance to the Grumman Aircraft Company to keep the company solvent and to preserve jobs. In 1973 the Pennsylvania Railroad appeared to need massive federal assistance to save it from bankruptcy.

The interrelationship between economic interests and government

[19] *Ibid.*
[20] *Ibid.*

policy has long been recognized. Aristotle taught that the study of politics must include both the structure of political organization and the peculiar socioeconomic principles of the citizens of that government. Englishman James Harrington rediscovered Aristotle's dual approach when he explained, in 1656, the cause for England's recent civil war between Parliament and king. The war was related to the fact that the feudal principles on which absolute monarchy rested were no longer as viable as they once were. Recent expansion of land ownership and commercial profits created a new and larger economic interest, and therefore, observed Harrington, some adjustment in constitutional powers was necessary to permit those who held property and were represented in Parliament to exercise more political power. The American Founding Fathers understood these relationships. By making Congress responsive to new and ever-changing interests they hoped the new Constitution would enable the United States to escape the violent adjustment that plagued England in the 1640s.

James Madison, for example, hoped the United States would have many independent interest groups that would compromise their positions during local congressional elections, and then he hoped a national consensus would come when the representatives compromised their positions within Congress. Not only would a general public interest be identified, but the national government would self-adjust to changing views. Now, 200 years later, with an industrial-technological society in which the economy is increasingly centralized, the source of these different interests is reversed. It is the national government through its boodle, "pork," defense contracts, job opportunities, Social Security payments, farm subsidies, veterans' benefits, home mortgage loans, revenue sharing, etc., that is shaping the interests of particular congressional districts. Moreover, the problems requiring solution are national rather than local in scope—such as pollution control, national defense, economic policy, civil rights, clean air, and even mass transportation. Because Congress traditionally responds more quickly to special interests "back home" than to national problems, it is to the President rather than to congressmen that Americans have been accustomed to turn for leadership.

Unless congressmen begin to think of themselves as national legislators and pursue national legislation with the same vigor they yield favors to local interests, Congress will continue to defer leadership to the President and fail to fulfill its constitutional obligation to check and balance the Executive office.

No Checks, No Balances

Congress was given control over taxation and appropriation so the American legislature, like the English parliament, could check irregular Executive power. However, in October 1972 the House of Representatives voted to give their power over expenditures to President Nixon. The Senate refused to confirm the House's action, which nearly turned away the one power that has kept Congress an existing institution. Except for the Senate's action the supposedly most democratic branch of government would have abandoned the very power which Englishmen died to keep in Parliament instead of in the hands of the king.

President Nixon asked for the legislation to cut all federal expenditures over $250 billion whenever he wanted to cut them, a request made partly in response to Congress's irresponsibility in refusing either to expand revenue to cover new programs or to trim expenses. Rather than discipline themselves the House took what appeared to be the easy way out by throwing away their power over the budget to the President. "The problem was not that the Executive was trying to steal our powers," explained Oregon's Senator Bob Packwood. "The graver problem was that we were prepared to give them away. Congressional power is rather like chastity: seldom lost by force, it is usually yielded voluntarily."[21]

The reactions of others were equally sober. As one concerned citizen wrote, the House's vote "is chilling evidence of the deterioration of checks and balances in our government. We should not ever forget that Hitler came to power essentially because the German parliament recognized that it could not cope with the problems of Germany."[22]

Perhaps checks and balances never did exist adequately in American government, but if so the absence of such balances is more obvious today. It was Congress's inability to check the flow of money in and out of the government that led it to give the President authority to prepare an annual budget for the national government in the Budget and Accounting Act of 1921. Until then the President had little if any voice in the entire budget; budgeting followed a haphazard procedure in which Executive departments submitted their requests to twenty-four different congressional committees. There was virtually no overall view of the nation's financial picture. In the fifty years since 1921 Congress has steadily deferred to the President and the Office of

---

[21] Bob Packwood, "Congress Nearly Abdicates Its Chief Power," *Los Angeles Times* (October 24, 1972), Part 2, p. 11

[22] *Los Angeles Times* (October 31, 1972), Part 2, p. 10.

Management and Budget (OMB) responsibility for estimating various costs of the ever-increasing yearly budget. Today, the newly created OMB attempts to prepare budgets and manage the government. For a year the OMB receives reports from all Executive agencies and in rounds of "haggling and calculation" the various departments are forced to compromise their estimates with the OMB. At the beginning of each calendar year Congress receives these adjusted figures from the OMB and then the various congressional committees have six months to complete their own study of the requests before approving a new national budget by July 1st.

Congress has neither the time, the staff, or the internal organization to create a national budget by itself or to investigate adequately the figures presented to it by the President's OMB. Although various appropriations committees attempt to review budget requests, their efforts are enfeebled by inadequate information and by undemocratic procedures within the committees. Further, Congress makes little use of modern computers or efficient accounting procedures. Congressman Bolling described the inefficiency by noting that as many as eighteen committees have jurisdiction over different aid programs for education. Between one-third and one-half of all education bills are referred to the Education and Labor Committee, the remaining bills are scattered elsewhere. For example, the Interstate and Foreign Commerce Committee has jurisdiction over education bills affecting physicians and dentists; the Committee on Veterans' Affairs hears bills affecting education programs for veterans; the Armed Services Committee has jurisdiction over programs for servicemen and women; the House Ways and Means Committee guides legislation affecting tax credits to parents with children in college; bills relating to college classroom construction are forwarded to the Banking and Currency committee; and science scholarships are handled by the Science and Astronautics committee.[23]

Even when Congress manages to create its own programs there is no assurance its initiative will be carried out. Through the use of such instruments as "impoundment," "reprograming," and "transfers," the President is able to fund programs Congress refuses to refinance and he can postpone forever laws Congress funded and presumed were in effect. By a provision in the Budget Act of 1950, Presidents do not need to spend the money Congress grants; they can impound money "to provide for contingencies or to effect sav-

[23] From the book *House Out of Order* by Richard Bolling, pp. 31ff. Copyright © 1964, 1965, 1966 by Richard Bolling. Published by E. P. Dutton & Co., Inc., and used with their permission.

ings." For example: Congressman Paul Rogers, Chairman of the Public Health Subcommittee, reported the Nixon Administration spent only half the money Congress appropriated for cancer research; the same Administration requested less money for the Environmental Protection Agency than was authorized when Congress created the agency in the Clean Air Act of 1970, but even some of this reduced money was impounded; for water-pollution control only $262 million of Congress's $880 million appropriation for 1970 was spent, and but $475 million of the $1 billion appropriation for 1971. To meet the crisis in urban transportation, Congress passed a second mass transit bill authorizing, in 1970, $3.1 billion over five years. Of this sum, the $2 billion appropriated for 1971 and 1972 was frozen while the 42,500-mile interstate highway budget was left untouched at $68.3 billion.

Political scientist Louis Fisher notes that the use of impounds for purely political reasons is a unique development "under the Nixon Administration, where funds have been withheld from domestic programs because the President considers those programs incompatible with his own set of budget priorities." Using his power to impound as a lever to pry money for his own bills is a new departure from the Budget Act of 1950. "Impoundment is not being used to avoid deficiencies, or to effect savings, or even to fight inflation, but rather to shift the scale of priorities from one Administration to the next, prior to congressional action."[24] Whether Congress can manage to unite behind the defense of its constitutional prerogative and challenge the President's use of impounds in the Supreme Court remains as important a question as the outcome of any litigation that congressmen talked about in 1973.

Not only are checks and balances undermined by the President's ability to withhold funds, but he can *spend* money with the same freedom. By reprograming and transfers the Chief Executive can almost run the country the way he wishes. For example: In order to avoid going to Congress to get $52 million for military aid to Cambodia in August 1971, Secretary of Defense Melvin Laird was told by the Joint Chiefs of Staff not to fret for he could transfer that amount from the economic aid account to the military aid account on his own authority. Other options were also available: he could increase the Army's request from Congress by $52 million and then "loan" the money to Cambodia, or declare "some of the Army's equipment obsolete, and then (sell) it at bargain rates to Cambodia."[25] It is estimated the Pentagon has $50 billion in approved appropriations

[24] Green, Fallows, and Zwick, *op. cit.*, p. 115.
[25] *Ibid.*, p. 117.

which, not yet spent, would have been enough to run the Vietnam war without congressional approval. The amount of unspent money in the "pipeline" explains why the Pentagon spent more money in recent fiscal years than Congress approved during those years.

"He who makes the budget sends the money on its way. Those who 'approve' the budget are spectators."[26] Yet Congress need not remain a rubber stamp. Since Congress still has potential power over the purse, it can become an active branch in the government as the Founders intended, and as the Constitution outlines. Only by such an assertion can the republic be viable.

Do Americans Want a Strong Congress?

Although Congress has a long history of reforming itself only when forced to do so, the status of Congress's power or weakness is generally a reflection of the American citizen's expectations. Congressional reform, like redemption from sin, is hard work and almost invariably comes after public pressure. In the past, Congress passed a reform act only once in a generation, but since the last effort was the Legislative Reorganization Act of 1970, we have had our quota of reform until the year 2000 unless Americans demand more.

One consequence of the 1970 Act was the limitation of members of the House to no more than one chairmanship of a legislating subcommittee. Previously, the old returnees—those reelected time and time again—rose to chairmanships of standing committees and also four or five subcommittees, a condition that left Congress in the hands of approximately forty senior citizens. The act also ended the House's practice of taking nonrecord votes when sitting as a "committee of the whole"; this practice had permitted a congressman to take one position publicly and the opposite when he voted without anyone not present on the floor of the House being the wiser. These and other reforms were originally passed overwhelmingly by the Senate in 1967, but the House Rules Committee let them get lost for three years, until finally, in 1970, the House enacted a few of the Senate's original reforms. Not touched was the near-sacred seniority system. The House beat down two reasonable and modest reforms, i.e. that the age ceiling for committee chairmen be set at 70, and the number of years for a chairman be limited to eight in order for the position to rotate. Because up to 90% of a congressman's work is done in committees, any significant reform requires some adjustment to the seniority sys-

[26] *Ibid.*, p. 108.

tem—a system Congressman Henry Reuss of Wisconsin termed "seniority, senility, secrecy, and satrapy."

In a democratic republic the people usually get the quality of national government that they deserve. Except for recent efforts to organize public opinion for congressional reform by the lobby group Common Cause, Ralph Nader's profiles of the Ninety-second Congress, and improved news coverage of Congress's activities, the public in general has not taken Congress as seriously as it ought. The public in general must be criticized for permitting congressmen to neglect their constitutional obligations, and for reelecting the same men repeatedly. Despite these criticisms of Congress, it may be that congressmen are performing in general at a superior level than the people have the right to expect. One of the strange ironies of democracy is that people themselves must be nudged to respect and protect their own interests.

What is needed is more discernment on the part of the people, so they may recognize and then honor the many representatives who make a decent contribution to government, and reject the popinjays—those talkative coxcombs who play continually to the grandstand. They would also do well to respect congressmen's time and expect them to use their tenure for weightier matters than acting as public-relations men who must insert local trivia in the *Congressional Record*. All congressmen are expected to spend part of their time reporting nationally such local gossip as, for example, did Representative Thomas Ashley:

> Mr. Speaker, it is with great pride that I take this opportunity to congratulate the Whitmer High School debate team of Toledo, Ohio, for winning its second consecutive national debate championship in the National Forensic League tournament held at Wake Forest University in Winston-Salem, N.C., from June 19 to June 22.[27]

Congressmen are frustrated with the menial demands made on them by the people, but they have little chance to criticize their constituents. "I came here to write laws and what do I do?" asked Congressman Jim Wright. "I send out baby books to young mothers, listen to every maladjusted kid who wants out of the service . . . and give tours of the Capitol to visitors who are just as worn out as I am."[28] For constituents who demand a little extra dab of government Congress has hired two men whose daily work consists only in raising and lowering flags over the Capitol in order for congressmen to send

[27] *Ibid.*, p. 184.
[28] *Ibid.*, pp. 203–204.

a genuine "United States flag flown over the Capitol" to special constituents. Unlike the slower pace of an earlier generation when flags flopped in the breeze a few hours or days, today's instant momentos have only a few seconds at the top before they are quickly hauled down to make way for the next. Working fast in 1971 these two men got 27,649 flags ready for congressmen to distribute. Apparently not all flags were actually "genuine," however, since one observer saw, on August 9, 1972, only eighty-six flags proceed up and down the flagpole, of which only eight hit the top. Yet the Capitol Architect's office reported that 128 flags were ready to distribute for that day.[29]

Answering mail is much more a part of congressmen's daily routine and all letters must be answered seriously no matter how crank or foolish. One congressman was able to tell his constituent the truth and the example of Congressman John Steven McGroarity of California probably remains the classic response by other congressmen who feel the same but dare not express the sentiment. In 1934 he wrote, "One of the countless drawbacks of being in Congress is that I am compelled to receive impertinent letters from a jackass like you in which you say I promised to have the Sierra Madre mountains reforested and I have been in Congress two months and haven't done it. Will you please take two running jumps and go to hell."[30]

We could also improve the quality of Congress by being less impressed with the name of a congressman on a large federal building than with his career in the national legislature. For example, by 1972 there were thirty-four federal buildings, some still on the drawing board, that would be named or renamed to honor former, or soon-to-be-former, congressmen. Two nameplates were decreed in a last-minute deal for two votes needed to salvage a bill creating a $65 million civic center in Washington. One nameplate came for retiring Mississippi Democrat William M. Colmer who got the William M. Colmer Building; the other was for California's departing Republican H. Allen Smith whose name was to grace the Jet Propulsion Laboratory in Pasadena.[31] In marked contrast Congressman William McCulloch of Ohio did not need a building to support his ego upon retiring in 1972 after twenty-five years of service. He had a distinguished record as senior Republican on the House Judiciary Committee, where he proved tough as leather in defending civil rights out of principle rather than expediency. Upon entering Congress he vowed his constituents would

---

[29] *Ibid.*, p. 182.
[30] *Ibid.*, p. 201.
[31] Subsequently, students at California Institute of Technology blocked Smith's name from being added to the Jet Propulsion Laboratory.

not evalute his work by the amount of federal dollars he brought back to his district, and he held to his conviction to his retirement. When the Public Works Committee reported in 1972, "Bill, we want to name some federal installation in your district after you," he reported there was none but a tank depot that was being dismantled.[32]

To become the vital branch of government the Founding Fathers intended, Congress needs a larger staff, more time, less parliamentary encumbrances, reform of the seniority system, and more use of such twentieth-century innovations as computers. More than these, however, Congress needs a reasonable and alert public who have the common sense that makes a republic worth having in the first place. We, the people, along with congressmen, make the republic viable. Benjamin Franklin made the point 200 years ago when he emerged from the Constitutional Convention in Independence Hall. A woman, Mrs. Powell, anxiously asked him, "Well, doctor, what have we got—a republic or a monarchy?" "A republic," replied Franklin, "if you can keep it."

[32] *Los Angeles Times* (November 9, 1972).

THE AMERICAN PRESIDENCY

> *No other generation in our history produced a galaxy of statesmen comparable to that which provided the leadership for revolutionary America. A nation of fewer than 3 million whites [fewer than 1 million adult males] gave us in one generation a Franklin, a Washington, a Jefferson, a Madison, a John Adams, a Hamilton, a George Mason, a John Marshall, a James Wilson, a Tom Paine....*
>
> *Why is it that the United States today—a vast, modern, urbanized country with over 200 million people—has nothing to show that is remotely comparable to this record?*
>
> —*Henry Steele Commager*[1]

The most obvious characteristic of American government is the escalation of power and responsibility of the President, which makes him the most powerful man in the world. What has been obscured is that the framers of the Constitution intended Congress rather than the President to have greater power, for in Article I of the Constitution they allocated to Congress most of those powers that now have been

---

[1] Henry Steele Commager, "U.S. Needs Renewed Sense of Disinterested Service," *Los Angeles Times* (July 1, 1973).

assumed by Presidents. This transformation, caused as much by Congress's willing surrender of its authority as by the Presidents' assumptions that they needed such powers in order to respond quickly to crises, began early in our history. But this shift of power from Congress to the President has accelerated with uncommon speed in the lifetime of Americans living today.

While despotism has always been a danger to republics, the framers of the Constitution expected the threat to come from Congress rather than from the President. Now that the powers have been distorted from their original arrangement, a greater potential for *presidential tyranny* exists. This danger is now inherent in our politics because Presidents must remain powerful to cope with the complexity of twentieth-century foreign and domestic events.

Since the end of World War II, and the dawn of the nuclear age in 1945, the United States has been thrust into world leadership by the magnitude of its economic and military dominance. Consequently the President must be empowered to decide quickly when to use nuclear weapons for national defense. Moreover, because the consequences of his decisions affect many other nations, not just the United States and its enemies, the American President now has a worldwide role. As long as the United States retains its military and economic superiority, no President, not even a Barry Goldwater who campaigned in 1964 against the ever-swelling powers of the office, can succeed in reducing the awesome position of modern Presidents.

Although responsibility for foreign affairs alone is a sufficient cause to account for this increase in presidential power, even before the President had become "policeman of the world," he had become chief problem solver of America's domestic difficulties.

The Great Depression of the 1930s, by which the rich became enormously rich and the poor only slightly less poor, resulted in the inability of most Americans to buy the goods they needed. As the whole economy collapsed, so did the hopes of millions of men who searched in vain for any work to support their families. No longer primarily self-sufficient farmers, the majority of Americans lived in the 1930s as they have come to live increasingly since then—in urban centers where they have been dependent upon the complexity of an industrial economy to earn money with which to buy even food. This dependency has increased in the succeeding decades until now almost everyone receives his daily bread from a check. Because the Depression was caused in part by governmental policies, it was to the President that desperate Americans turned for help. The economic crisis created opportunities for such extremes as Nazism or Communism. Feeding on the popular discontent of the unemployed a group of Communists staged a National Hunger Strike on Washington in December 1931. President Hoover and the Capitol were protected by policemen and machine-gun nests in the stonework above the steps; the marchers were armed with angry banners, calling for violence that never came. With the election of Franklin Roosevelt in 1932, the office of President represented a way out of the tragedy that remained within the framework of the American Constitution.

Since the 1930s modern Presidents have accepted "the idea that government should be active and reformist, rather than simply protective of the established order of things." [2] Americans continue to look to the President for solutions to desperate problems. Furthermore, he is blamed personally for not resolving problems as varied as pollution, race relations, and mass transit.

Whether as world leaders or chief problem solvers at home, recent Presidents have been expected to perform near-miracles, and, in contrast to their predecessors, they have been granted nearly enough power to do the impossible. For example, where President Richard Nixon needed a White House Staff of 548 at an annual budget of $9.1 million to give him needed assistance in administering his office, Herbert Hoover needed but forty-two assistants in 1928, and George Washington employed his nephew at his own expense to assist with clerical duties.

Presidents Nixon, Johnson, and Kennedy could manage only "working vacations" in retreats preequipped with elaborate electronic apparatus connecting them with the various "hot lines" to Moscow and emergency centers both abroad and at home, and were always accompanied by the "football," that locked briefcase containing cryptographic orders to military chiefs to send nuclear weapons in case of attack; whereas President Grover Cleveland could take an extended vacation without even a secretary to answer his mail.

With the death of President Kennedy in Dallas, Texas in 1962, when the "football" was rushed down the Parkland Hospital corridor to Vice President Johnson, Americans took new interest in the increased importance of the office of Vice President. Now that the chain of presidential authority must be absolutely certain at all times, the public dares not continue to disregard the office or personality of the Vice President. Goaded by this public concern, Congress added the Twenty-fifth Amendment (1967) to the Constitution to clarify the procedure of transferring presidential powers to the Vice President

[2] Edward S. Corwin, *The President: Office and Powers* (New York: New York University Press, 1957), p. 311.

in emergencies. Provision now exists for the Vice President to become Acting President in case the President is disabled physically or mentally.[3]

The importance of the psychological stability of Vice Presidents was thrown into dramatic and embarrassing focus during the Nixon–McGovern presidential campaign in 1972. Senator McGovern's running mate, Senator Thomas Eagleton of Missouri, admitted to being hospitalized three times for nervous exhaustion and having twice undergone electric-shock treatment. Americans and Europeans alike immediately questioned Senator Eagleton's ability to handle the stresses of the Presidency, should circumstances ever force him into the office. He resigned from the campaign in a few days, but the incident again directed public attention to the vital importance of an office that is "only a heartbeat away" from the Presidency.

Democrats extended the question of emotional stability to President Nixon's Vice President, Spiro Agnew, whose attacks on the press and intemperate speeches, such as calling leaders of the protest against the Vietnam War an "effete corps of impudent snobs," led the International Press Institute meeting in Zurich in January 1970 to name him "the most serious threat to the freedom of information in the Western world in 1969."[4] To news of Senator Eagleton's shock therapy, Democrat Congressman Julian Bond of Georgia retorted that "At least we know ours had treatment. What about theirs?"[5]

The Eagleton Affair of 1972, together with the disability provision of the Twenty-fifth Amendment, demonstrate the importance attached to the psychological fitness of the man who seeks or who already has the world's most powerful office. Now that the President has been elevated to such extraordinary heights of power, we seem to expect to find men of equally extraordinary temperament and judgment to

---

[3] In case of death or resignation of the President, the Vice President becomes President.

In case of physical or mental disability of the President, the Vice President becomes Acting President with full powers and duties of the President. This transfer of power can originate in two ways:

(a) The President can send to the President Pro Tempore of the Senate and Speaker of the House a written statement that he is unable to discharge his office.

(b) The Vice President and a majority of the Cabinet can send a written declaration to the Senate and House that the President is unable to discharge his office.

The President may regain his position under provision (a) merely by declaring he is able to discharge his duties. Under provision (b) the President can write his declaration of ability also, but if the Vice President and a majority of the Cabinet write, within four days, to the contrary, then both Houses of Congress must decide within twenty-one days. See Appendix for a full statement of the Twenty-fifth Amendment.

[4] *Los Angeles Times* (October 1, 1972), Section G, p. 1.

[5] *Time* (August 7, 1972), p. 6.

fill the office, men who are somehow untouched by the infirmities of the ordinary human beings who have held the job in the past.

Obviously Americans had no such exalted expectations of our past Presidents. As a young man Rutherford B. Hayes wandered the streets of Sandusky, Ohio, crying uncontrollably; Abraham Lincoln had recurring periods of suicidal depression; Franklin Pierce's drinking habit may have approached alcoholism, and John Adams had a number of nervous breakdowns. Alabama's Governor George Wallace, who won 13.5% of the popular vote for the Presidency in 1968, continues to receive a 10% veteran's disability for "psychoneurosis" incurred from World War II."[6]

Along with our expectations of a President's personality, we must consider the age-old practical problem of giving the government, including the President, enough power to do the job of governing while retaining safeguards against the ever-present danger that these powers will be abused. Many wonder today if the expansion of the powers of the President has not seriously increased the chance of despotism. Others, looking at the problems that remain unsolved, wonder if the President has been invested with enough power, at least so he can initiate action in domestic crises as forthrightly as he has in international relations.

The question of how much political power to invest in the office of President every generation must decide for itself. Thomas Jefferson speaks to each new generation as he did to his own when, in the Declaration of Independence, he called for Americans to institute government on such principles and powers "as to them shall seem most likely to effect their Safety and Happiness."

Creation of the President

This question of power was at the heart of the debate on the office of President in the Federal Convention of 1787. Delegates spent more time discussing that office than they did analyzing any other branch of government. Basically, they held the same two opposing views as exist today; those delegates wanting a strong Executive branch stressed the necessity of giving government power to do the job of governing; those delegates seeking to limit Executive powers were afraid that recently won liberties would be subverted by a new, American-made George III.

[6] *Ibid.,* p. 10.

Madison, Wilson, and Morris, for example, favored a single Executive, independent of the legislature, with specific powers to act on his own initiative. They looked back specifically to the absence of efficient administration under the Articles of Confederation, particularly the inability of the national government to function during the critical years of the Revolutionary War and to formulate a single foreign policy for all thirteen states after the war was over.

Other delegates were afraid an investment of such power in one man would make the President a "foetus of monarchy." After looking back to the threats of personal liberties that such power created when invested in royal governors and King George III, they suggested the President be an appointee of the legislature. "The person or persons ought to be appointed by and accountable to the Legislature only, which has the depository of the supreme will of the Society."[7]

Both groups of delegates realized tyranny could come from either direction. Histories of ancient and contemporary republics taught them that dictators could usurp Executive powers and that legislatures could degenerate into popular tyranny. Although the source of tyrannical impulses differed between a monarchy and a republic, the consequence was similar. In contrast to monarchies, where the power of the king was the seedbed for dictatorship, in republics the particular danger to liberty came from the legislature where demagogues could use their oratorical skills to create a popular tyranny. A weak Executive was found to be no more security for liberty than was a powerful legislature.

Since the Convention delegates were obligated to safeguard liberty *and* empower a government so it could work, they gradually concluded they could not fulfill their responsibility by making government weak but safe. In that apparent safety there would be no functional government at all. In the course of debates a majority of delegates gradually replaced the notion "that a vigorous Executive is inconsistent with the genius of republican government," with the idea that "energy in the Executive is a leading character in the definition of good government."[8] Thus the Convention created and the public ratified the concept of a vigorous Executive.

No offspring of a legislature nor stepchild of a ruling council, the President was to be his own man, elected from his own national constituency to a fixed term of four years that, like his salary, could

---

[7] Adrienne Koch, ed., *Notes on Debates in the Federal Convention of 1787 Reported by James Madison* (New York: W. W. Norton, 1966), p. 46.

[8] Clinton Rossiter, ed., *Federalist Papers* (New York: The New American Library, 1961), No. 70.

not be reduced by the whim of a legislature. As a separate branch of the government the President was given broad Executive responsibilities, both domestic and foreign. How these powers would be used has changed according to the personalities of the men elected and the crises the thirty-seven different Presidents had to face.

Role of Personality and Crisis in Shaping the Presidency

Although George Washington immediately set precedents for Executive independence from Congress during his two terms, his major contribution to the office was made before he was President. The prevailing assumption of delegates to both the Philadelphia Convention and later state ratifying conventions was that Washington would be the first President. Because of Washington's personality, this assumption helped calm most of the fears that the office was a "squint" toward monarchy. Even those most apprehensive about the tendency of ambitious men to become petty despots recognized in Washington that it was possible to find men who could be trusted with power.

Washington's refusal to accept military and political powers immediately after the Revolution, when his generals were pressing him to accept and the public would have showered him with any position he desired, won for him the reputation of being an American Cincinnatus—that legendary Roman hero who was called to lead the republic in war but then retired to the obscurity of his farm rather than yield to the temptation of exploiting his momentary popularity and accepting extensive military and political powers. The appreciative but fickle public would have thus undermined the Roman republic by creating a potential dictator at the very moment they were celebrating the defeat of their foreign enemy.

Washington also returned to the farm. In pursuing his self-interest Washington knew his fame would also be tied to the success of this American republic.[9] In him many Americans pinned their hope that the United States would not repeat England's sad, recent experience with the autocratic Oliver Cromwell who, in accepting political powers after defeating King Charles I (1649), was believed to have ruined England's chance of becoming a republic. Washington's honor had enormous influence in the creating of a powerful Executive position in American government.

[9] See: Douglass G. Adair, "Fame and the Founding Fathers," Edmund P. Willis, ed., *Fame and the Founding Fathers* (Bethlehem, Pennsylvania: Moravian College, 1967), pp. 27–52.

Thomas Jefferson's character was also a major determinant in expanding the powers of the Presidency. Like many Americans, Jefferson wished to diffuse power rather than have it concentrated in the national government, but like many Presidents who succeeded him, President Jefferson extended the powers of the Presidency to meet responsibilities he never anticipated. Although a stalwart champion of the "literal" interpretation of the Constitution, which held that the national government should obey the letter of the Constitution and do nothing beyond those things specifically mentioned in it, as President, Jefferson went beyond the letter of the Constitution when he doubled the size of the United States by seizing Napoleon's offer to sell the Louisiana Territory (1803), and later took extraordinary control of the nation's economy by placing an embargo (1807) on all American shipping with England and France. Both of these actions were early testimonies to the impracticality of the literal interpretation of the powers of the President in times of national emergency or crisis.

During the twenty years between Jefferson's term of office and the election of Andrew Jackson (1828), the Executive office degenerated into a quasi-council system in which the opinions of the President were regarded as equal to those of the members of his Cabinet or influential senators. Every four years these men formed a "Congressional Caucus" to nominate a new presidential candidate and, like the political bosses who selected Warren G. Harding in their "smoke-filled rooms" a century later, these few men dominated the Presidency. Neither Madison, Monroe, nor Adams could afford to offend their "makers," and each carried a number of his predecessor's Cabinet members into office. Although the framers of the Constitution rejected the plan of having Congress select the President, this mutant procedure operated until Andrew Jackson combined his dominating personality with leadership of his political party to restore the enfeebled office to its separate position as an equal with Congress.

In addition to defending the autonomy of his powers, Jackson established the Presidency on a broader and more democratic basis than before. By exploiting the political potentialities of the office, Jackson made the President chief politician in addition to Chief Executive. For the first time a national nominating convention replaced the Congressional Caucus as the means for selecting presidential candidates. With Jackson's "spoils system," employment in government offices was opened to a large public, usually to the party faithful, rather than automatically remaining in the hands of families who viewed their public jobs as a private inheritance. Although civil service examinations would later replace the "spoils system" in the selection of most governmental employees, since the time of Jackson the President's role as chief politician has remained a principal characteristic of the office.

As a former military commander who was accustomed to giving orders and having them obeyed, Jackson had a personality that gave his critics the opportunity to picture him "as a detestable, ignorant, reckless, vain, and malignant tyrant." But as chief politician in a democratic government Jackson actually widened public support for the office. Those afraid he was turning the office into an "elective monarchy" attacked him for establishing the office of President on what appeared to them to be such "frightening" principles as "universal suffrage and our unfettered press." But popular support and freedom of the press are the tools of democracy. Instead of leading the United States toward tyranny, in expanding the political powers of the Presidency Jackson supported the very democratic principles his critics thought of "too violent a nature for our excitable people." [10]

It is Abraham Lincoln more than any other President before or after who can most accurately be charged with possessing the powers of a dictator. His understanding of the powers available to the President to meet the crisis of the Civil War caused him to assume more authority over the lives of Americans than has been exercised by such twentieth-century wartime Presidents as Woodrow Wilson, Franklin D. Roosevelt, Harry Truman, Lyndon Johnson, or Richard Nixon. In order to preserve the Union, President Lincoln searched for authority that would permit him to act immediately. He claimed to find that authorization in his power as "Commander in Chief," and in the order of his oath of office to "take care that the laws shall be faithfully executed." By uniting these two clauses he actually created new, and what have become today unlimited, powers. Lincoln called these "war powers."

Within a few weeks after becoming President, Lincoln took a series of extraordinary measures that placed him beyond constitutional restraint. Without the approval of Congress, which he had not bothered to assemble immediately because their factional bickering would retard action, Lincoln summoned troops and organized a navy, spent $2 million in unappropriated funds, proclaimed a blockade on Southern ports, and suspended the writ of habeas corpus (that basic protection of individual rights that compels arresting authorities to bring a prisoner to court to show why he is being detained); this right, according to the Constitution, could only be suspended by Congress. He also caused men to be arrested who, in his judgment, acted or even

[10] Corwin, *op. cit.*, pp. 21–22.

contemplated "treasonable practices." Lincoln's exercise of war powers clearly implies that in times of crisis a President may determine that the emergency is serious enough to suspend the Constitution.

As a person Lincoln's magnanimity set him apart from the petty, doctrinaire politicians—those exploiters of public fear who are ever-present but become nationally visible in times of crisis—who would turn the Presidency into a self-righteous dictatorship if given a chance. Although he bequeathed these war powers permanently to the Presidency, Lincoln's fidelity to republican government throughout his career helps to explain why Americans have accepted these war powers as a necessary part of the office of President. In addition to being remembered for the Gettysburg Address and Emancipation Proclamation, Lincoln should be remembered for his important contribution to the public acceptance of the Presidency as a legitimate instrument for resolving national crises. In the words of Professor Winston Fisk, "It was part of Lincoln's genius that he employed dangerous power without being corrupted by it, and it is part of the genius of the American political system that it has always been able to recover its constitutional balance after crisis—at least so far." [11]

Public acceptance of the presidential war powers was essential to Teddy Roosevelt when he first used the Presidency to influence the domestic economy by pitting his prestige against the monopolies. Public acceptance of Woodrow Wilson's leadership in World War I and of Franklin D. Roosevelt's leadership in both the Depression of the 1930s and World War II was essential to the resolution of those crises. But since 1945 and the dawn of the nuclear age, with the awesome possibility of war beginning with less than thirty minutes warning, the necessity for a President to act quickly for national defense removes any question of his ultimate war power today. Should he exercise his war powers to plunge the country into nonnuclear war at his own discretion? Our experience with the war in Southeast Asia again raises the age-old question of finding a balance between delegating sufficient power to fulfill the purpose of government, and yet checking that power to prevent its abuse.

Striking a balance on the use and control of presidential power has been made difficult because of the increase in number of crises and the speed of events. Crises have become so commonplace that Americans have come to expect Presidents to resolve crises on their own initiative. Now there is no time for the public to respond to the

[11] Martin Diamond, Winston Fisk, and Herbert Garfinkel, *The Democratic Republic* (Chicago: Rand McNally, 1966), p. 184.

call for a general consensus about a particular crisis. By contrast, during the 1930s and 1940s, FDR had time to lead and to follow public opinion in dealing first with the Depression and later with World War II. Americans are now told what policy must be instead of participating in the creation of such policy.

Another reason that Americans are now less able to participate in the formulation of policy is because it is so difficult to distinguish between foreign and domestic matters. The economy has become so inexorably enmeshed in foreign policies through defense contracts that foreign and domestic policies are not entirely separate. Small adjustments in defense budgets can mean boom or bust to many cities. Such small towns as Igloo, South Dakota (population 1700 a few years ago) disappear "as the result of a scratch through some line in a military-appropriations bill." In fourteen states more than 10% of personal income comes from Pentagon contracts, and in three states (Alaska, Connecticut, and Idaho) plus the District of Columbia, "more than 20% of the personal income is from defense payrolls."[12]

It is also difficult to control presidential power today because recent elections have focused on personality rather than political party or issues and Americans have selected Presidents by how well they claim to be able to resolve crises. Professor Richard Neustadt argues that our politics have become crisis-oriented, a phenomenon that came into existence after World War II and has become the political way of life. "The weakening of party ties, the emphasis on personality, the close approach of world events, the changeability of public moods, and above all the ticket-splitting, none of this was 'usual' before the Second World War."[13]

This emphasis on personality encourages campaign organizers to employ advertising agents who are skilled masters at creating and projecting an image and then selling the candidate as convincingly over television as they sell mouthwash. Advertising techniques are more concerned with creating an illusion than revealing truth, appealing to emotion rather than reason, offering impossible dreams and unfulfilled promises. The criterion of effective advertising is not hon-

---

[12] Robert Sherrill, *Why They Call it Politics* (New York: Harcourt, Brace, Jovanovich, 1972), p. 44. The fourteen states are: Alabama, Arizona, California, Colorado, Georgia, Hawaii, Maryland, Mississippi, Missouri, New Hampshire, New Mexico, Texas, Utah, and Virginia. One of every three manufacturing employees in Utah looks to the Pentagon for his paycheck (p. 44).

[13] Richard E. Neustadt, *Presidential Power: The Politics of Leadership* (New York: John Wiley, 1960), p. 4.

esty but "will it sell?"[14] The application of advertising techniques to presidential campaigns has resulted in disaster.

President Lyndon Johnson, who accepted the largest mandate in history partly on the promise to end the war in Southeast Asia, turned around and escalated the Vietnam war beyond even what his opponent said he would do. The result was a bitter public revulsion and an unparalleled credibility crisis between the public and the government. President Richard Nixon experienced a bit of this revulsion when the National Guard killed four Kent State University (Ohio) students in 1970 in the course of student protests against his sending troops into Cambodia at the same time he was winding down the war in Vietnam.

The public's fear of being duped again by presidential candidates serves to intensify the existing focus on personality while political issues are seriously neglected. This confluence of personality and crisis has contributed both to the rise in presidential power and to the blurring in the public's mind of precisely what the President should do with his newfound powers.

Responsibilities of the President

The Oath of Office (Article II, Section 1) requires that the President "faithfully execute the Office of President of the United States" and "preserve, protect, and defend the Constitution of the United States." To do this the Constitution appoints the President Commander in Chief; empowers him to fill vacancies in the Senate, and, with the Senate, enables him to make treaties, appoint ambassadors, Supreme Court Justices, and other officers to courts and departments; it requires him periodically to give Congress information on the state of the Union, recommend legislation for Congress's consideration, and "take Care that the Laws be faithfully executed." For convenience these responsibilities may be reduced to three: administration of government and execution of laws as Chief Executive; initiation of legislation as Chief Legislator; and management of foreign and military affairs as Chief of State.

Chief Executive

Interpreting their Executive responsibilities differently, Presidents have exercised degrees of power ranging from that of a clerk to that of

[14] See: John Philip Cohane, "The American Predicament: Truth No Longer Counts," *Los Angeles Times* (October 1, 1972), Section G, p. 1.

a national leader. For example, in the face of deepening economic depression President Hoover believed he had no other power than what was necessary to carry out the legislation of Congress. Obviously Lincoln took a much broader view, as did Teddy Roosevelt who looked at the Presidency as the office of a "steward of the people." "The Buck Stops Here" insisted President Truman, and his popularity bounced like a yo-yo as a result of such decisions as his ordering the use of the atomic bomb, involving the United States in the Korean War and the Marshall Plan, dismissing General MacArthur, and nationalizing the steel industry in 1952.

Every President in the twentieth century since Franklin D. Roosevelt has taken the broad view of the Presidency, with the possible exception of Dwight Eisenhower, who preferred to let Cabinet members administer government. He took action when forced, however, such as supporting the Supreme Court's declaration of 1954 that segregation in public schools was unconstitutional. Defied by Arkansas' Governor Faubus, Eisenhower sent troops to Little Rock to enforce a federal court order permitting Negroes to attend a newly desegregated school.

Both Presidents Kennedy and Nixon agreed that the Presidency must be an active office but differed in identifying which function they thought demanded their principal attention. As a candidate in 1960, John F. Kennedy thought principally of domestic problems when he declared that a President must "place himself in the very thick of the fight."[15] Richard M. Nixon, as a candidate in 1968, looked primarily at the problems of foreign policy in declaring "the days of a passive Presidency belong to a simpler past. The next President must take an activist view of the office. . . . He must lead."[16]

Leading the various Executive offices to assist the President in his obligation "to take Care that the Laws be faithfully executed" is difficult if not nearly impossible. Before becoming President, Nixon had declared "I've always thought this country could run itself domestically, without a President. All you need is a competent Cabinet to run the country at home."[17] President Nixon had yet to recognize that "an old-line government agency is a hissing, clanking machine without an off switch. It has a comfortable sense of its own permanence, knowing it was here before the President arrived and will be here when he is gone, still doing precisely what it was doing before

[15] *Congressional Record* (January 18, 1960), p. 711.
[16] Richard Nixon, "The Nature of the Presidency," speech broadcast on NBC radio for September 19, 1968.
[17] Theodore H. White, *The Making of the President 1968* (New York: Atheneum, 1969), p. 147.

he came."[18] After his election President Nixon shortly discovered the country could not "run itself" domestically by a Cabinet. Within a year he asked, and received, Congressional approval to reorganize the Executive Office, the umbrella that covers all those "hissing, clanking" agencies that are responsible for giving him advice so he can fulfill his obligation to administer government. Despite his increased powers, there is serious question of how much the President can control even his own house. Consider the number and variety of these agencies: Office of Management and Budget, the White House Office, National Security Council, Council of Economic Advisers, National Aeronautics and Space Council, Office of Economic Opportunity, Office of Emergency Preparedness, Office of Science and Technology, Domestic Council, Council on Environmental Quality, and special offices concerned with trade policy, telecommunications policy, international economic policy, consumer affairs, intergovernmental relations, and drug abuse.

This reorganization is the third major attempt to bring efficiency to federal administration in as many decades: President Franklin D. Roosevelt created the Executive Office to manage the mushrooming agencies in 1939, and President Truman's Hoover Commission made further recommendations in 1947–1949. As the responsibilities of the President increase, the Executive Office will grow in importance because it is on this staff that Presidents must rely to carry out their extensive and complex tasks.

Nor is the Cabinet able to administer the great departments, with their legion of civil servants, even in those rare instances where a Cabinet member is a capable administrator. For example, only 100 of the 60,000 employees of the Interior Department are presidential appointees. The 108,000 employees in the Department of Health, Education, and Welfare are so divided over money and ideology among conflicting and competing agencies that one of its best administrators, Secretary Robert Finch, was forced to resign from physical exhaustion after a year and a half. Ideas ossify with the bureaucrats. Irrelevant attitudes remain encased in the bureaucratic cocoon as Presidents come and go. Whether it is a ten-year-old "position paper" in the State Department or blatant racism in the Southern-dominated Department of Agriculture, the President inherits them all—ideas and men— when he takes his oath to faithfully execute the laws.

But the President, himself, has the major responsibility for setting the tone of his Administration, for it is he who selects which laws

[18] David Brinkley, "Leading from Strength: LBJ in Action," *The Atlantic Monthly* (February 1965), p. 52.

to enforce and which to ignore. Professor Edward S. Corwin correctly states "the President's very obligation to the law becomes at times an authorization to *dispense with* the law" for he can avoid pressing those laws that may be politically unpopular. Presidents Cleveland, Harrison, and McKinley were not disposed to enforcing the Sherman Antitrust Act of 1890. Their attitude is best summed up by the then Attorney General Richard Olney, who freely admitted to "not prosecuting under a law I believed to be no good."

The Refuse Act of 1899 is another example of a law ignored for political convenience, although many Americans today are paying for that indifference with their health and perhaps their lives. The Refuse Act prohibits a person or corporation from dumping refuse into navigable streams without permission from the Army Corps of Engineers; it imposes fines ranging from $500 to $2500, authorizes half of the fine be given to the person reporting the violation, and requires the Justice Department to enforce the law vigorously. The act was obviously not faithfully executed, as is evidenced by the death of Lake Erie from its current daily pollution of nearly 52 billion gallons of household and industrial waste, and by the hazards to health for swimmers along Long Island Sound, the Potomac River, and according to the Illinois Department of Health, in every river in that state.

The forty-odd environmental laws passed since the federal Water Pollution Control Act of 1948, up to the Water Quality Improvement Act of 1970 are further evidence of the grim problem of pollution. This legislation is also evidence that the public, along with the President, must share the blame for indifference in law enforcement. Crises not only widen powers of Presidents; crises seem necessary to arouse Americans out of lethargy or cynicism to insist that Presidents use their power for the public interest.

Chief Legislator

Although the President has extraordinary powers, there is no certainty that he will be able to obtain results from his orders. Authority is no guarantee of action, nor is his prestige sufficient of itself to achieve results. "Despite his status he does not get action without argument," observes Professor Neustadt. What, then, is the power of Presidents? Neustadt's classic answer is "Presidential *power* is the power to persuade." [19]

President Truman understood that the essence of his power was persuasion. "I sit here all day trying to persuade people to do things

---

[19] Neustadt, *op. cit.,* p. 10.

they ought to have sense enough to do without my persuading them. . . . That's all the powers of the President amount to."[20] Truman thought Eisenhower would be especially surprised to see the different kind of power he would have as President than he had formerly as General. "He'll sit here and he'll say, 'Do this! Do that!' *And nothing will happen.* Poor Ike—it won't be a bit like the Army. He'll find it very frustrating."[21] And one of President Eisenhower's aides reported in 1958 that Eisenhower was frustrated in getting things done. "The President still feels that when he's decided something, that *ought* to be the end of it . . . and when it bounces back undone or done wrong, he tends to react with shocked surprise."[22]

Persuasion is the heart of the President's power and nowhere is this more obvious than in winning support from Congress for his legislative proposals.

Presidents have always shared the legislative process with Congress. Neither has a separate, exclusive jurisdiction in lawmaking despite the assumption that our "three separate branches of government" balance each other like jewels in a clock. The location of legislative power is ambiguous in the Constitution. Whether the President or Congress dominate the legislative process—or, more likely, whether the two fend each other on relatively equal terms—depends on a number of changing factors including personalities, events, and the parties in control of Congress and the President. All have to do with the power of persuasion.

An important advantage a President has in influencing legislation is his ability to command national publicity. He is one person. He is elected from a national constituency. Congress is 570 men and women elected from fifty states and 476 Congressional Districts. It is the President who can command the attention of most Americans at one time, which is exactly what he tries to do every January when he delivers his State of the Union Message to a joint Congress and to millions of Americans clustered around his picture on their television sets. Since Harry Truman and the television tube, Presidents have used the annual address as a national announcement of the legislative proposals they will send Congress in the following year. For the next twelve months we hear reports on the contest between President and Congress, periodically receive the number of "victories" and "defeats" of legislation passed or rejected, and then by the following January, when the President is ready to deliver another State of the

[20] *Ibid.*
[21] *Ibid.*, p. 9.
[22] *Ibid.*

Union Message, we receive the final tally of the year's total "wins" and "losses" and then measure the President's effectiveness.

In addition to obtaining national publicity when he wishes, the President has other political vantage points he can use to persuade a congressman that his personal interest can be furthered by the President's help if the congressman will support particular legislation. "With hardly an exception, the men who share in governing this country are aware that at some time, in some degree, the doing of *their* jobs, the furthering of *their* ambitions, may depend upon the President of the United States." Professor Neustadt summarizes the President's advantage over Congress well: "Their need for presidential action, or their fear of it, is bound to be recurrent if not actually continuous. Their need or fear is his advantage." [23]

Presidents' use of these vantage points varies with their personalities and experience. Although President Kennedy was a good politician, his relations with Congress were cold; he was unable to obtain quick or lasting Congressional responses. His narrow victory robbed him of the effective influence his successor, Lyndon Johnson, would relish. Congressmen still remembered Kennedy as a former junior colleague while he, in turn, respected his former "congressional elders." Furthermore, his urban, New England manners made it difficult for the many "country-boy" congressmen to relate to him. As one such congressman from Tennessee stated in 1962: "All that Mozart string music and ballet dancing down there and all that fox hunting and London clothes. He's too elegant for me. I can't talk to him." [24]

Country-boy congressmen could talk to LBJ. Under pressure to avert a national railroad strike in April 1964, President Johnson had management and union leaders meet daily and into the night, alternating from the Cabinet Room, Oval Room, and the Executive Office Building—anywhere close enough for the President to apply his considerable persuasive powers. When the president of Illinois Central stood up in one meeting and began speaking "Mister President, I'm just a country boy. . . ." David Brinkley described Johnson immediately getting up, placing both hands over his hip pocket and saying "Hold on, now. I've dealt with country boys before, and I'm holding on to my pocket book. Now what was it you wanted to say?" [25] President Johnson used his influence successfully: the strike was averted.

[23] *Ibid.*, p. 35.
[24] Brinkley, *op. cit.*, p. 51.
[25] *Ibid.*

Knowing from long experience in Congress how important it was for a President to assert his leadership early, Lyndon Johnson carefully chose as his target Congressman Otto Passman of Louisiana, to remind congressmen of his influence yet not challenge their power. As chairman of the House Subcommittee on Foreign Aid Otto Passman devoted his energies to an annual routine of cutting foreign-aid budgets by approximately 20% in order to trumpet his reputation as a saver of taxpayer"s dollars. The foreign-aid administration was forced to play along with Passman's game by padding the budget an extra 20% so the congressman could get his annual publicity back home and the foreign-aid department could get its needed money. But President Johnson wanted credit for an initial low budget, so by a series of quiet telephone calls he was able to persuade a majority of the subcommittee not to approve their chairman's routine request for a reduction. When the subcommittee refused Passman's request, the chairman was shocked to see his power collapse and "went raging out of the room in a burbling and screaming incoherence."[26]

Deals and favors are also important vantage points for Presidents to persuade Congress. Kennedy had to make a deal with Democrat Senator James O. Eastland of Sunflower County, Mississippi, chairman of the Senate Judiciary Committee, in order to get Thurgood Marshall, a Negro and counsel for the NAACP, appointed to the Second Circuit Court of Appeals. Eastland, who wanted his old college roommate appointed as judge in the federal courts that heard civil rights cases in the South, informed Attorney General Robert Kennedy one day in a Senate corridor, "Tell your brother that if he will give me Harold Cox I will give him the nigger."[27] Later Thurgood Marshall was appointed to the Supreme Court, the first black American to receive such an appointment.

President Nixon had less success with his favors in getting the Senate to approve either Harold Carswell or Clement Haynsworth, Jr., to the Supreme Court. Nixon had no difficulty getting James Eastland's approval for the Southern conservatives, despite charges that Carswell had shown racial bias and did not have a distinguished legal career. On the eve of the Senate vote Senator Margaret Chase Smith, Republican of Maine, received a "Dear Maggie" note assuring her that a defense contract had just been approved for her state. She voted against the Carswell nomination anyhow.

The President does have specific power over legislation, however, in the veto. Presidential threats of veto can be as effective as actually

[26] *Ibid.*
[27] Sherrill, *op. cit.*, p. 78.

exercising the power as a means of persuading Congress to examine impending legislation along the lines he suggested earlier. If he vetoes a bill by signature, the issues receive national publicity because he can return the bill to Congress with his reason for veto attached. Although in earlier history Presidents believed they could veto only certain measures, today Presidents feel free to veto any bill they choose. It is rare that Congress is able to muster a two-thirds majority to override a President's veto.

Chief of State

The American President combines the eminence of a king with the powers of a prime minister; he is at once the symbolic head of the nation and the principal representative of the people. Where other countries have divided these jobs into two separate offices, such as England's monarch and prime minister, we have combined them into one. As representative of the United States to foreign nations, a President receives dignitaries from other countries, awards national honors, and symbolizes American values; as representative of the people, he is a politician elected to fulfill Executive responsibilities in governing the United States. This combination left the nation's founders in a bit of a quandary in selecting an appropriate title for the position. From his diplomatic experience in Europe, John Adams understood the importance of having foreign nations recognize these dual functions in the new office and therefore was pleased when the Senate suggested the President be known officially as "His Highness, the President of the United States of America, and Protector of their Liberties."

The House of Representatives left Adams dismayed by deciding on the simpler title of "President of the United States." Adams, of course, was concerned about foreign rather than domestic respect for the new office. But he could not know then that the powers of the President as Commander in Chief and as Chief Diplomat would establish the reputation of the Presidency and the nation on a more formidable foundation than the "protective coloration" of John Adam's title: "His Highness the President."

Commander in Chief

The President is the highest military authority in the country. By putting a civilian in charge of the military the Founders intended to protect the republic from succumbing to a military coup, the fate of most free governments in history. While the necessity of military power for national defense was never questioned by the authors of the Constitution, neither was the ever-present potential of military despotism ever doubted. This problem has always worried free men: How can a necessary but dangerous military establishment be made capable of providing defense yet remain safe for free government? The solution was to make the military an integral part of the government and, by recognizing it within the Constitution, thus establish its legitimate functions.

By making the military dependent on the more popular House of Representatives for its funds, and on the popularly elected President for its commands, the founders hoped the public would have sufficient control over its operations so that the civil government would never be directly overthrown by a military coup. Their solution has worked remarkably well considering the fate of other countries. There has never been a direct attack on civilian government in the tradition of Latin America. Nor has a clique of officers presumed to be "better patriots" than their civilian masters and thereby transfered their allegiance *from* the government *to* the flag, the people, or the Constitution in order to take their own initiative in plunging the United States into war. Such was the terrible experience of Japan and Germany in World War II. Japanese officers claimed their allegiance to the Emperor, not to the government, and the German High Command pledged its allegiance to the State, not the citizens. Hence the Japanese and German civilians in Nagasaki, Hiroshima, or Dresden had no control over the military leaders who steadfastly refused to surrender, a decision that sealed the fate of thousands of civilians in dreadful annihilation.

The Founders could not have anticipated the conditions the republic finds itself in today. The civilian leaders are so fused with the military in budgets and policy that the two are partners instead of antagonists. The necessity of the House of Representative's approval of military budgets is not a major control now that defense contracts have been spread throughout congressional districts. Any major cutback in military spending is politically dangerous for congressmen because of probable increase in unemployment in their districts. The peculiar nature of nuclear war requires instant decisions by a President. Although national defense in this nuclear age does not permit the luxury of time-consuming, thoughtful decisions on war by the Senate, most Presidents in our history have not felt constrained to get congressional approval, much less Congress's opinion, before ordering military action.

In its brief history the United States has been involved in 125 military adventures, including six undeclared wars, and the President's actions have never been held unconstitutional. "There is nothing in the Constitution that says that the President may not wage war abroad at his discretion," explains Saul K. Padover. "The Constitution merely states that only Congress can 'declare' war. But it does not say that a war has to be 'declared' before it can be waged."[28]

For example, acting as Commander in Chief and without congressional declaration of war, Thomas Jefferson sent three small frigates into the Mediterranean Sea in 1801 to stop the Barbary pirates from plundering American merchant ships. In the past thirteen years Presidents have involved the United States in five military engagements without consulting Congress: President Kennedy approved the abortive Bay of Pigs invasion of Cuba, and, in 1962, blockaded Cuba in the missile crisis; President Johnson sent 23,000 troops into the Dominican Republic in 1966 while committing a half-million Americans to war in Southeast Asia; President Nixon sent troops into Cambodia in 1970 and ordered continuous bombing of North Vietnam to "bomb 'em back into the Stone Age" as one air general described the order—all without prior consultation or approval of Congress.

The constitutional right of Presidents to wage war remains substantially the same as it was for Thomas Jefferson, but the consequence of this warmaking ability today is incomparably more grave. Because Presidents now behave as though only they can make war decisions in both nuclear and nonnuclear situations there is serious question whether the office of President is still capable of exercising the intended civilian restraint on military operations. President Truman's dramatic assertion of civilian authority over the military in 1951, when he dismissed General Douglas MacArthur for insubordination and accepted the consequence of the public's initial outrage, contrasts with what the *Pentagon Papers* suggest as a joint effort by President Johnson and the military to use an emotional incident to increase public support for the war in Vietnam. "For six months before the Tonkin Gulf incident in August 1964," commented *The New York Times* on the *Pentagon Papers,* "the United States had been mounting clandestine military attacks against North Vietnam while planning to obtain a congressional resolution that the Administration regarded as the equivalent of a declaration of war."[29]

Nor can a President always know what his military officers are doing, as was the case of General John D. Lavelle, Commander of the Seventh Air Force attacks on North Vietnam between November 1971 and March 1972. Ignoring President Nixon's strict orders, on

[28] Saul K. Padover, "The Power of the President," *Commonweal* (August 9, 1968), p. 524.
[29] *The Pentagon Papers* (New York: Bantam Books, 1971), p. 234.

his own authority General Lavelle sent planes to attack targets President Nixon prohibited, and then the General had the reports deliberately falsified.

Whether from civilian collusion with the military or civilian ignorance of military actions, these incidents make Professor Henry Steele Commager's warning serious: civilian control has largely been circumnavigated by recent Presidents who have acquiesced what was formerly regarded as their own authority to the Pentagon and the CIA.

Much of the emergence of military power has been the consequence of drift rather than of calculation. When Washington became President, the United States Army consisted of fewer than 1000 men and officers. Now ours is the largest and most powerful military establishment in the world. It absorbs almost half the budget, it maintains its own foreign affairs policy, it even instigates wars and supports revolutions without the knowledge of the Congress to whom, presumably, is assigned the authority to declare war. There has been no formal repudiation of the principle of the supremacy of the civilian over the military, but we delude ourselves if we think the principle means what the Founding Fathers supposed it to mean.[30]

Chief Diplomat

"You need a President for foreign policy," explained Richard Nixon in 1968 after assuring Theodore White the country could run itself domestically without a President. "No Secretary of State is really important; the President makes foreign policy."[31] The Constitution, however, is not that specific in designating who should conduct the nation's foreign affairs, the President or the Senate.

Presidents must share responsibility with the Senate for appointing ambassadors and recognizing new nations by receiving their ambassadors, and the Senate must confirm international treaties with the United States by two-thirds majority. Thus the Constitution invites a struggle between the President and the Senate over the conduct of foreign relations, although in fact Presidents have advantages in taking the initiative.

As a single individual the President has the advantage of making relatively quick decisions, taking immediate action, and negotiating from secret information funneled to him from his vast network of information-gathering services in the Pentagon, the CIA, and the State Department. He can also appoint special assistants in foreign policy,

[30] Henry Steele Commager, "The Defeat of America," *New York Review of Books* (October 5, 1972), p. 7.
[31] White, *op. cit.*, p. 147

as President Nixon did with Henry Kissinger or Woodrow Wilson did with Colonel House, to travel, negotiate, and compile information for the President exclusively. The Senate cannot compel an Executive assistant to testify before it, as it can a Cabinet member, such as the Secretary of State, whom it has confirmed in office.

Another advantage Presidents enjoy is their ability to sign "Executive agreements" with other foreign heads of state, thus bypassing the Constitutional requirement of two-thirds majority for Senate approval for treaties. Often these Executive agreements arrange trade and commercial matters, but they have been extended to include military and other policy arrangements by the President's discretion or by specific authority granted him by Congress. Because the Constitution makes no explicit provision for Executive agreements, they do not need Senate approval, yet they have as much legal standing as treaties. Since President Wilson's disastrous experience with the Treaty of Versailles to end World War I, which the Senate refused to ratify, Presidents have resorted to Executive agreements with increasing frequency instead of formal treaties in binding the United States to foreign commitments. In 1939 there were 10 treaties as compared to 26 agreements; in 1940 the ratio was 12 to 20; in 1941, 15 to 39; in 1942, 6 to 52; in 1943, 4 to 71. Twenty years later, the ratio jumped in 1963 to 9 to 248; in 1964, 13 to 231; in 1965, 5 to 197; in 1966, 10 to 242; in 1967, 10 to 218; and in 1968, 57 to 226.[32]

These advantages do not permit a President to conduct foreign policies without congressional knowledge or support, however. Although the President may have more specific information in world affairs, much of this is conflicting, and there is no certainty that the reports he receives are correct or unknown to members of the legislature. Congress has considerable power over budget requests and legislation, which it can use to pry information and obtain particular concessions. And much of the strength of an Executive agreement is the belief by foreign heads of state that the President does have sufficient congressional support to be able to fulfill the obligations he has committed the United States to meet.

But although the Senate's power is essentially a negative one of probing, checking, correcting, or discouraging policies, the President can initiate action, negotiate, and lead. One dramatic recent example of this positive advantage was President Nixon's visit to China in 1972. Even the London *Times* was struck by President Nixon quoting the thoughts of Chairman Mao: "So many deeds cry out to be done

[32] Hans J. Morgenthau, "Congress and Foreign Policy," *New Republic* (June 14, 1969), p. 18.

and always urgently. The world rolls on. Time passes. Ten thousand years are too long. Seize the day. Seize the hour."[33] Nixon did seize the initiative in foreign policy and thereby not only altered foreign relations for the United States but reshaped the relations of other countries to an extent no other elected official in American government, or in the world, could have duplicated.

Administering the Office: Can a President Lead and Still Be a Clerk?

A crucial problem facing all Presidents today, in the midst of their unprecedented power, is retaining the ability to lead the nation for the future while attending clerkship duties over programs accumulated from the past. If the powers of the office have expanded with the administrative bureaucracy, so have the expectations of the people. Everyone expects the President to do something about everything. Actions that once identified a President as being "strong" or showing "leadership," however, are now part of the daily operation of government. What was once exceptional has become mere routine. The increased responsibilities have so transformed the office that Presidents are no longer easily identified as "great" or "exceptional" leaders.

Professor Neustadt points out that where Teddy Roosevelt assumed the unusual responsibility for assisting the settlement of the critical coal strike of 1902, legislation now makes such intervention mandatory upon Presidents; where FDR asserted personal responsibility for guiding the American economy, legislation "binds his successors to that task;" where Wilson and FDR became world spokesmen in times of war, our alliances and national power prescribe that role for Presidents "continually in times termed 'peace;' " and where Harry Truman made the first decision to use the atomic bomb, "the Atomic Energy Act now puts a comparable burden on the back of every President."[34]

As a result of these accumulated responsibilities, all Presidents may now appear as leaders although in fact they may be mere clerks managing existing programs. But, notes Professor Neustadt, the public expectation that the Presidents will be the Great Initiator does give him the opportunity to be a leader in fact as well as in appearance. His leadership today consists primarily in persuading other men in

[33] London *Times* (February 22, 1972), p. 6.
[34] Neustadt, *op. cit.,* pp. 5–6.

government to look to him for guidance in doing their jobs. If the *public* expects the President to lead so, often, will government workers. As long as he is capable of persuading men that their interests can best be served by following his lead, then a President can administer the government and become a leader at the same time. The principal avenues through which he can exercise this leadership are: his political office as head of his party, his Cabinet, and his special councils.

The Presidency is primarily a political office; he is the nation's leading politician and usually the chief of his political party. A President will use his power to as much political advantage as possible in filling offices with men who will contribute to the success of his policies. Often many of the men who organized his election campaign will be appointed to key Executive positions, where their campaign skills will be tested in the more formidable crucible of gaining approval of the public and Congress for the President's programs. Thus the President is the Chief Politician, for he alone is answerable directly to the whole nation and therefore must be sensitive to public opinion to know the limits of what is politically possible.

The Cabinet is an informal advisory group selected by the President to assist him in making decisions, helping him in managing the federal bureaucracy, and aid him in winning congressional approval for his legislation. He is "not required by law to form a Cabinet or to keep one," notes Richard F. Fenno; it has become "institutionalized by usage alone."[35] Following George Washington's example of assembling the heads of departments for consultation, succeeding Presidents continued to form Cabinets from these secretaries. (Now: State; Treasury; Defense; Justice; Interior; Agriculture; Commerce; Labor; Health, Education and Welfare; Housing and Urban Development; and Transportation). Use of the Cabinet meetings has varied among Presidents. Eisenhower relied on his Cabinet much more than did Kennedy, and Johnson dominated his.

In appointing Cabinet secretaries a President gives special consideration to the political advantage of uniting his party by selecting representatives from different factions. Sometimes it is to his advantage to appoint a member of the opposite party, as did FDR in appointing two Republicans during World War II and more recently as did President Nixon in selecting conservative Democrat John Connally of Texas as Treasurer, in order to obtain wider, national support. But the Cabinet is his to do with as he pleases. One or two secretaries often have more influence than does the Cabinet as a whole, depend-

---

[35] Richard F. Fenno, Jr., *The President's Cabinet: An Analysis in the Period from Wilson to Eisenhower* (Harvard University Press: Boston, 1959), p. 19.

ing on personality, the political influence of a secretary with Congress, and the role a President chooses to give his appointees.

Two Executive offices through which Presidents can exert considerable leadership are the National Security Council and the Office of Management and Budget. Created in 1947 to coordinate national defense and military policies out of the disarray after World War II, the National Security Council has been called with varying degrees of regularity by different Presidents, but the council's opinion is taken seriously. Recently Presidents have appeared to lead the council while in fact they have acquiesced to the military, intelligence, and foreign policy experts.

The Office of Management and Budget, re-created in 1970 out of the older Bureau of Budget, is responsible for the conduct of government services and budget preparation and administration. Since 1921, when Congress relinquished to the President the power to draw up an annual budget to replace the confusion of money bills that had financed government before, Presidents have gradually turned the budget into a major management tool to compel different agencies and departments to support their programs. The budget has also been an important source of presidential leadership in Congress, because the budget director draws up the various expenditures, divides the monies in a variety of different categories, and then apportions isolated parts of the budget to different House committees where no one in Congress can review the budget as a whole for general evaluation or criticism. The budget has become one of the most important sources of power for the President, giving him direct control where persuasion may not work.

"The Rarity of Lofty Ambition"

The English ambassador to the United States, Lord Bryce, explained in 1888 "why great men are not elected President" by suggesting that in democracies the majority elect Presidents who have the ordinary abilities of the "common man." Although it is true the United States has had mediocre Presidents, it is also true that some Presidents, and other politicians as well, have exercised extraordinary ability. Never have so many capable politicians come out of such a small population pool as those who wrote the Constitution in 1787. They recognized the democratic tendency Lord Bryce described but hoped the office might spur even mediocre men to good performance.

By right Americans have become skeptical of the acclaim that makes the Founders appear superhuman, as though they were not touched with the infirmities of character that beset the rest of human flesh. But in countering this tendency to exaggerate their virtues, it cannot be denied that the generation that produced a John Adams, Alexander Hamilton, James Wilson, John Rutledge, and a galaxy of Virginians including George Washington, James Madison, Thomas Jefferson, and Edmund Randolph "must be set down as a remarkable one, for this, or any other country."[36] Considering how Americans today complain about the difficulty of finding two capable candidates for President out of 210 million people, the generation of Founders is all the more remarkable because of the tiny population pool of 3,600,000 people out of which these men rose to leadership.[37]

In researching the cause for this amazing concentration of political ability in one generation, Professor Douglass Adair discovered that prior to the Revolution of 1776 these men had no greater aims than those Alexis de Tocqueville discovered among Americans in the 1830s. The first thing that strikes a traveler to the United States, commented the young Frenchman, was the democratic urge of everyone to better himself; the second striking characteristic of Americans was

> the *rarity* of *lofty* ambition to be observed in the midst of the universally ambitious stir of society. No Americans are devoid of a yearning desire to rise; but hardly any appear to entertain hopes of *great* magnitude, or to pursue very *lofty* aims. All are certainly seeking to acquire property, power, reputation; few contemplate these things on a great scale. . . . Ambitious men in democracies are [little] . . . engrossed . . . with the interests and judgments of posterity; the present moment alone engages and absorbs them. They are more apt to complete a number of undertakings with rapidity, than to raise lasting monuments of their achievements; and they care much more for success than for fame.[38]

Not only does this description fit twentieth-century politicians but it also describes the generation of Founding Fathers before the Revolution. John Adams listed the trivial ambitions of his generation before 1776: "[to be] worth ten thousand pounds Sterling, ride in a Chariot, be a Colonel of a Regiment of Militia and hold a seat in his Majesty's Council. No Man's Imagination aspired to anything higher beneath the skies."[39] George Washington lusted after land and by "setting his sights low—though in terms of success not fame—his 'Summum

---

[36] Adair, *op. cit.*, p. 27.
[37] The census of 1790 was 3,600,000 people including women and children and black Americans. The population of Virginia in 1790 was just over 700,000 counting the slaves and free inhabitants.
[38] Adair, *op. cit.*, p. 29.
[39] *Ibid.*, p. 30.

Bonum' was to obtain a Colonel's commission in the British regular army."[40]

The redefinition of their life goals occurred after the crisis of 1776 when their provincial stage of action gave way to a world theater and provided them with the opportunity of creating a lasting monument to their honor. Their self-interest was tied to the interest of the new republic because only by its success would they be remembered honorably. But the simple cause–response explanation is insufficient to account for this explosion of talent. The challenge of the Revolution "evoked along with patriotism, self-sacrifice, and splendid performance in defense of liberty, a sordid picture of many Americans trying selfishly to cash in on the crisis, treating the war as an excuse to get rich quick, to scramble for place and profit."[41] Alexander Hamilton claimed the Revolution exhibited "human nature" in its "blackest colors" as well as "its brightest."

Professor Adair discovered that it was their reading of the men in classical history who became famous and honorable as the founders of states, and especially founders of commonwealths where individual liberty was protected, that spurred these Americans to immortalize their names to future generations by discovering laws that could make republican government work in the United States. Of course they were motivated by patriotism; but they were also pursuing their self-interest. Their study of history taught them that the pursuit of fame "was a way of transforming egotism and self-aggrandizing impulses into public service; they had been taught that public service nobly (and selfishly) performed was the surest way to build 'lasting monuments' and earn the perpetual remembrance of posterity."[42] This desire was a dynamic element in shaping the historical process. It urged man "to become a person and force in history larger than the ordinary. The love of fame encourages a man to make history, to leave the mark of his deeds and his ideals on the world; it incites a man to refuse to be the victim of events and to become an 'event-making' personality—a being never to be forgotten by those later generations that will be born into a world his action helped to shape."[43]

This love of fame is ethically neutral: the Founders acted for an audience of descendents that was wise, who could discriminate between virtue and vice and "recognize egotism transmuted gloriously

[40] *Ibid.*
[41] *Ibid.,* p. 29.
[42] *Ibid.,* p. 31.
[43] *Ibid.,* p. 35.

into public service." This passion can also become terribly perverted, causing a person to take actions that are remembered because of their superlative wickedness. Such perversion is an important reason why Presidents become like lightning rods in attracting assassins.

An assassin also shapes history, and the more renowned his victim, the greater potential he has for altering the course of events. The assassin of President Garfield in 1881 was a pitifully empty man, Charles Guiteau, in search for recognition he could never achieve on his own merit. The same was true of the murder of President John Kennedy in 1962 by the paranoid and jealous Lee Harvey Oswald, and of the fantasying, deranged Arthur H. Bremer who stalked President Nixon in Canada in 1972 and considered killing Senator George McGovern. He admitted to himself his life was a failure, "I have to kill somebody, that's how far gone I am." He shot Alabama's Governor George Wallace but only as a third choice. Bremer did not think a governor could command enough publicity to make him internationally famous. To his diary Bremer wrote, "They never heard of Wallace in Russia or anyplace. . . . If something big in [Viet] Nam flares up, it'll end up at the bottom of the first page. He won't get more than three minutes on the network TV news."[44]

However, as a spur to noble action today, the words "fame" and "honor" and the concept of "the love of fame" as a "ruling passion" for magnanimous conduct has for us "but a faint and tattered remnant of its eighteenth-century meaning." Fame is now synonymous with great mass popularity, and it calls to mind the approval and acclaim of the populace for a famous sports hero, or for a Miss America contest winner; to some it is inseparable from the dazzle of lights and tinsel at a ceremony in Hollywood celebrating movie actors. Such judgment is, "to quote Milton, of 'a herd confused; a miscellaneous rabble, who extol things vulgar' [meaning, "commonplace," "general," or "popular"]."[45] The politicians who look for the mere popularity of ticker-tape parades and aim their actions solely for the exhilaration of the moment, the Founders would mock with Goldsmith's couplet "Of praise a mere glutton he swallowed what came, and the puff of a dunce, he mistook it for fame."[46]

It was in the office of President that the Founding Fathers hoped to preserve the love of fame as a *noble* passion "because it can transform ambition and self-interest into dedicated effort for the com-

[44] *Time* (August 14, 1972), p. 23.
[45] Adair, *op. cit.*, p. 32.
[46] *Ibid.*

munity, because it can spur individuals to spend themselves to provide for the common defense, or to promote the general welfare; and even on occasion to establish justice in a world where justice is extremely rare."[47]

[47] *Ibid.*, pp. 35-36. This article was reprinted in 1974 by W. W. Norton, Co., edited by H. Trevor Colbourn.

THE SUPREME COURT

We are very quiet there, but it is the quiet of a storm center, as we all know.[1]

So spoke Justice Oliver Wendell Holmes as he sat on the bench of the United States Supreme Court in 1913, and his assertion has drawn little disagreement. Indeed, since the founding of the republic, the winds of controversy have swirled about the Court and its legitimate place in a democratic republic. From Thomas Jefferson to Richard Nixon the Court has been disavowed, Nixon going so far as to indict it for "weakening the peace forces as against the criminal forces in our society."

Pundits, as well as politicians, have railed against the "judicial despotism" of the Court as it exercises its power of judicial review to void acts of other more democratic branches of the national government, or of local majorities at the state or local level. Thus, liberal scholars like Henry Steele Commager and David Spitz have condemned the philosophical basis of judicial review as undemocratic, wrong in theory and dangerous in practice.[2] More recently, however,

[1] "Law and the Court," in Mark De Wolfe Howe, ed., *The Occasional Speeches of Justice Oliver Wendell Holmes* (Cambridge, Mass.: The Belknap Press of Harvard University Press, 1962), p. 168.
[2] Henry Steele Commager, *Majority Rule and Minority Rights* (Gloucester, Mass.: Peter Smith, 1958), p. 80; David Spitz, *Democracy and the Challenge of Power* (New York: Columbia University Press, 1958), p. 85.

it has been conservatives like President Nixon who have led the attack on the Court, though their vituperation has been less enthusiastic and more directed at judges and not at the Court as such, "on abuse of the power of judicial review, not on judicial review itself."[3]

Of all the allegations against the Court, however, the most enduring and damning is the charge that judicial review is undemocratic in that basic policy decisions are placed in the hands of a nonelected, lifetime judiciary that is not responsible to the popular or common weal for its decisions. As Professer Commager put it,

> The philosophical basis of judicial review is undemocratic. The purpose of judicial review is to restrain majorities. The assumption behind judicial review is that the people either do not understand the Constitution or will not respect it and that the courts do understand the Constitution and will respect it.[4]

Thus, while the history and theory of judicial review are banal subjects, the controversy over whether judicial policymaking is compatible with democracy remains unsettled. Though the charge that judicial review is undemocratic may be directed at any national court, it is the exemplar of that power—the United States Supreme Court—that shall be the concern of this chapter.

Democracy and Judicial Review

At the heart of the controversy regarding judicial review and its compatibility with democracy lies confusion and disagreement over the meaning of the word "democracy." As George Orwell once pointed out, "the English language is in a bad way." This is particularly true of political language, which is too frequently "designed to make lies sound truthful and murder respectable."

> In the case of a word like "democracy," not only is there no agreed definition, but the attempt to make one is resisted from all sides. It is almost universally felt that when we call a country democratic we are praising it: consequently the defenders of every kind of regime claim that it is a democracy. . . .[5]

---
[3] Martin Diamond, "Conservatives, Liberals, and the Constitution," in Robert A. Goldwin, ed., *Left, Right and Center* (Chicago: Rand McNally, 1967), p. 75.
[4] Commager, *op. cit.*, pp. 79–80.
[5] George Orwell, "Politics and the English Language," in Richard H. Rovere, ed., *The Orwell Reader* (New York: Harcourt Brace Jovanovich, 1956), pp. 359–360.

One scholar has estimated that there may be as many as 200 definitions of democracy,[6] and people as diverse as Hitler, Stalin, and Nixon have claimed to lead what they termed "democratic" regimes. No doubt this "disorderly conduct of words"[7] explains why some scholars like Stuart Chase have come near pronouncing that all abstract words like "democracy" are meaningless. But if words like "democracy" are meaningless, how can one judge a practice like judicial review to be undemocratic? Or for that matter how can one justify expending American blood and treasure to "make the world safe for democracy" against the threats of Nazism or Communism? To accept the judgment that all abstract words are meaningless is to accept chaos over order, and the Orwellian Newspeak of *1984* whereby

> WAR IS PEACE
> FREEDOM IS SLAVERY
> IGNORANCE IS STRENGTH

There is no strength in ignorance. It is this fact that forces one to seek more precision in the word "democracy." And the knowledgeable man, as Aristotle asserts, seeks only such precision in each class of things as the nature of his subject allows: to demand mathematical proof of political oratory is as unreasonable as accepting guesses from mathematics.[8]

Words like "democracy" have been used with such imprecision that elastic and stipulative definitions have become commonplace. Yet, it is possible within the bounds that this subject allows to arrive at a definition of democracy that will conform to its earliest usage as well as the understanding of the Founders when they framed the Constitution.

Of course the word "democracy" never appears in the Constitution. Rather, Article IV of the Constitution guarantees to the states "a Republican Form of Government." This fact has led some to insist that the United States is a republic, not a democracy. Certainly, James Madison's definitions and discussion of "democracy" and "republic" in *Federalist* #10 can leave no doubt that he was aware of the differences between those two forms of government: one being small

---

[6] Massimo Salvadori, *Liberal Democracy* (Garden City: Doubleday, 1957), p. 20.
[7] The phrase is from Zechariah Chafee, Jr., "The Disorderly Conduct of Words," *Columbia Law Review*, Vol. 41 (1941), p. 381.
[8] For an expanded discussion of this problem, see Harry V. Jaffa, "The Conditions of Freedom," *Claremont Journal of Public Affairs*, Vol. I, No. 1 (Spring 1972), pp. 41–56.

and having direct representation, while the other is large and necessarily must have indirect representation. What is too often forgotten, however, is that Madison was even more aware of their similarities in that both have as their sheet anchor the principle that the people are sovereign and that their will is reflected in the form of a majority. The word "republic" itself derives from the Latin *respublica,* meaning the business of the people, and for over 2000 years it was applied to any government that regarded politics as the business of the people rather than the private preserve of a king or set of oligarchs. It was what Alexander Hamilton called *representative government.*[9]

Thus, the essence of democracy and its surrogate republic is majority rule, a finding which a 1951 UNESCO survey on democracy revealed constituted a core area of broad agreement among countries of the Western world.[10] The word "democracy" is derived from the Greek word *demos* and when linked to *kratein* (meaning to rule) is usually translated as rule by "the people." But that translation, as Professor Martin Diamond observes, is "soft" and obscures the fact that "rule means rule by some over others." In the case of democracy, it means "that the greater number of consenting equals rules the lesser."[11]

The great problem lies in the fact that the will of the many is not always compatible or even noninjurious to the interests of the few. As Tocqueville noted in *Democracy in America,* "Men do not change their characters by uniting with one another."[12] They do not suddenly become angels. In fact, if they did, as Madison observed in *Federalist* #51, there would be no need for government. The problem has nowhere been more succinctly stated than by Thomas Jefferson in his First Inaugural Address:

> All, too, will bear in mind this sacred principle, that though the will of the majority is in all cases to prevail, that will to be rightful must be reasonable; that the minority possess their equal rights, which equal law must protect, and to violate would be oppression.

In essence the problem raised is primarily philosophical, for it involves the discernment on the part of the majority as to what is rightful and reasonable. As Madison said earlier in *Federalist* #51:

---

[9] Alexander Hamilton, *Writings,* H. C. Lodge, ed. (New York: Putnam, 1904), Vol. II, p. 92.
[10] Richard McKeon, ed., *Democracy in a World of Tensions: A Symposium prepared by UNESCO* (Chicago: University of Chicago Press, 1951), p. 303.
[11] Martin Diamond, Winston Mills Fisk, and Herbert Garfinkel, *The Democratic Republic* (Chicago: Rand McNally, 1966), p. 71.
[12] Alexis de Tocqueville, *Democracy in America* (New York: Vintage Books, 1945), Vol. I, p. 269.

"Justice is the end of government. It is the end of civil society." And majority rule is a *means*—though sometimes a very imperfect means—to that end.

Although the legal or conventional right to rule devolves to a majority in a democratic regime, the inalienable right to life and liberty remains with all individuals, including those in the minority. Yet, may not a foolish or vicious majority attack such inalienable rights? And although it is true that an organized minority may be every bit as vicious as any majority, it is, nonetheless, true that in a democratic republic it is the majority alone that may "execute and mask its violence under the forms of the Constitution." [13]

For 2500 years preceding the American experiment democracies had "been spectacles of turbulence and contention;" had "ever been found incompatible with personal security or the rights of property;" and had "in general been as short in their lives as they [had] been violent in their deaths." [14] Indeed, in our own time did not Hitler's rise to power in the Weimar Republic of Germany have something to do with majority rule? Or for that matter, does not the schema of Marx and Engels have a great deal to do with majority rule, albeit an unbridled proletarianized majority, which is bent upon establishing its dictatorship through domestic and international convulsion?

That the framers of the Constitution were aware and critical of the dangerous propensities of democracy has in large measure contributed to the success of this, the now-oldest republic in the world. It was correctly not their desire, nor the *telos* of this polity, to create a merely democratic regime. Nations, like people, do not have to strive to simply be a nation or a person. The real task is to assume the best form, rather than the worst. Thus, while Woodrow Wilson correctly understood the necessity of making the world safe for democracy, the Founders fathomed the importance of making "democracy safe for the world" [15] as well. It is the challenge of this double necessity that each new generation of Americans must meet lest they lose their republic.

It should now be apparent that the term "democracy" has been rescued from its ancient meaning wherein all philosophers agreed that it represented rule by a mob that was either hopelessly foolish

---

[13] Clinton Rossiter, ed., *Federalist Papers* (New York: Mentor Books, 1961), No. 10, p. 80.
[14] *Ibid.*, p. 81.
[15] This phrase was one which Professor G. L. Pierson of Yale University applied to Alexis de Tocqueville. See Martin Diamond, "The Federalist," in Leo Strauss and Joseph Cropsey, eds., *History of Political Philosophy* (Chicago: Rand McNally, 1964), p. 580.

or vicious in terms of respecting the rights of minorities. As the term has evolved in usage into the twentieth century, it has taken on a *qualitative* as well as quantitative dimension, for the word today is endowed with the strong implication that the majority is both "rightful" and "reasonable" in exercising its will.

It is by no means axiomatic, however, that majorities will automatically be rightful or reasonable, for consent does not require enlightenment or wisdom. To know what wisdom is or how to obtain it remains one of mankind's unresolved mysteries. It is not very comforting to the 70,000 Americans of Japanese descent who were placed in American concentration camps and stripped of their property during World War II by an inflamed majority to be assured that experience will teach the people to correct their mistakes in law by remedial legislation.[16]

"A dependence on the people," Madison said, "is, no doubt the primary control on government; but experience has taught mankind the necessity of auxiliary precautions."[17] Foremost among those auxiliary precautions, of course, is the concept of limited government that *binds* the rule of men to law through a written Constitution. "[As] men are neither beasts or gods, they ought not to play God to other men, nor ought they to treat other men as beasts."[18] In recognition of this principle, the Founders "replaced the sway of a king with that of a document."[19]

The majority, which acts for the whole nation, is obliged to act within the limits of power delineated by the Constitution, for Article VI holds that "This Constitution, and the Laws of the United States which shall be made in Pursuance thereof . . . shall be the Supreme Law of the Land. . . ." But who is to judge if the majority, acting through its elected representatives in the national or state governments, is overstepping its bounds? Who is to interpret the meaning of the highly generalized wording of the Constitution?

To these questions the Constitution provided no final answer, but since the time of the *Marbury v. Madison* decision in 1803 it has been the Supreme Court that has become the interpreter of the supreme law of the land as well as the judge of when governmental policy

---

[16] The sentiment is Professor Commager's in *Majority Rule and Minority Rights*, p. 72; for an incisive discussion of the problem of majority rule in respect to the relocation of the Japanese-American during World War II, see Eugene V. Rostow, "The Japanese American Cases—A Disaster," *Yale Law Review*, Vol. LIV (1945), p. 489.
[17] Rossiter, *op. cit.*, No. 51, p. 322.
[18] Harry V. Jaffa, "What Is Equality," paper presented to The Center of Constructive Alternatives (Hillsdale, Mich.: Hillsdale College), p. 8.
[19] Edward S. Corwin, *The "Higher Law," Background of American Constitutional Law* (Ithaca, New York: Cornell University Press, 1971), p. 1.

has exceeded its bounds. As Charles Evans Hughes bluntly put it in 1907: "We are under a Constitution, but the Constitution is what the judges say it is."

Concurring with Benjamin Hoadly's comment that whoever "hath an absolute authority to interpret any written or spoken laws, it is he who is truly the lawgiver, to all intents and purposes, and not the person who first wrote or spoke them,"[20] some scholars like Professors Commager and Spitz have held that an appointive Supreme Court, holding office for life, and wielding the power of judicial review, is undemocratic. Indeed, Supreme Court Justice Felix Frankfurter himself considered it to be "a limitation of popular government" and thus "an undemocratic aspect of our system."[21]

There is little profit in trying to establish whether or not judicial review is a power intended by the Framers. That is largely a historical question, and as Professor Leonard Levy has noted "decisive evidence cannot be marshalled to prove what the Framers had in mind."[22] More important is the question regarding the alleged undemocratic nature of judicial review.

Much of the charge rests on the assumption that the Supreme Court is itself undemocratic because members of that Court are not elected and remain on the bench for life "during good Behaviour." Is this not a nonpopular element in our government, designed to act as a brake on rash or barbarous majorities?

Although it is true that the Court was intended by the Framers to be one of the important devices for remedying the defects of democracy, it must be emphasized that, true to the claim of *Federalist* #10, it represents a *republican* remedy. Majorities may do anything it is not humanly impossible to do. That includes determining through a Constitution the mode of selecting justices for the Supreme Court. A major device settled upon to rescue democracy from its dangerous propensities was the federal principle. By integrating this principle into the mode of selecting judges, the Founders hoped to avoid the natural tendency of democracies to divide into irreconcilable ideological majorities and minorities, thus proscribing them to be "spectacles

[20] Quoted in James Bradley Thayer, "The Origin and Scope of the American Doctrine of Constitutional Law," *Harvard Law Review,* Vol. VII (October 1893), p. 152. A reprint of this article may be found in Leonard W. Levy, ed. *Judicial Review and the Supreme Court* (New York: Harper Torchbooks, 1967), pp. 43–63.
[21] Minersville School District v. Gobitis, 310 U.S. 586, 600 (1940); West Virginia State Board of Education v. Barnette, 319 U.S. 624, 650, 666 (1943); A.F. of L. v. American Sash and Door Co., 335 U.S. 538, 555 (1949). Cited in Leonard W. Levy, "Judicial Review, History, & Democracy," *Judicial Review and the Supreme Court,* p. 14.
[22] Levy, *op. cit.,* p. 2.

of turbulence and contention" which were "as short in their lives as
. . . violent in their deaths." By fragmenting the majority through this
principle, the Framers hoped to create a moderate majority of shifting
coalitions, one which would reflect the spirit of compromise rather
than follow the strata of class, residence, or religion. Thus the Founders hoped to allow the majority to rule on the one hand, yet deflect
it from potential "schemes of oppression" on the other.

Reflecting this federal principle, justices of the Supreme Court
receive their appointment by sharing the political philosophy of *both*
the national majority as represented by the nominating power of the
President as well as the more parochial state majorities as represented
by the power of confirmation resting with the Senate. Forgetting this
momentarily, President Nixon witnessed the Senate veto of Judges
Clement Haynsworth and G. Harrold Carswell, his two Southern
nominees to the Supreme Court in 1970.

Moreover, as Robert Dahl has indicated, this mixed majority has
had frequent opportunities to exercise its joint power of appointment,
averaging one new justice every twenty-one months over the whole
history of the Court.[23] Thus, Hoover had three appointments; Roosevelt, nine; Truman, four; Eisenhower, five; Kennedy, two; Johnson,
two; and Nixon has had four in his first four years of office, with a
possible two more in the offing during his second administration.

The agonies that Franklin Roosevelt experienced with a "horse
and buggy" Supreme Court[24] that stood in the way of his and Congress' New Deal legislative efforts to cope with the Depression was
most unusual. Bad luck forced him to wait for four years for his first
Supreme Court appointment. In spite of this, and the defeat of his
"court-packing" bill in 1937, he had made five appointments by the
end of his second term, and as he entered his third term Justice
Owen Roberts was the only justice remaining from the Hoover era.
All of this points to the fact, as Dahl has put it, "that the policy views
dominant on the Court are never for long out of line with the policy
views dominant among the lawmaking majorities of the United
States." [25]

Related to the allegation that the Supreme Court is an undemocratic body is the complaint that its power of judicial review results in
judicial legislation, and that this amounts to "judicial supremacy"

---

[23] Robert A. Dahl, "Decision-Making In A Democracy: The Supreme Court As A National Policy-Maker," *Journal of Public Law,* Vol. 6 (1958), p. 284.
[24] Franklin D. Roosevelt, Press Conference #209, May 31, 1935, *Press Conferences of Franklin D. Roosevelt* (Hyde Park, N.Y.: 1956), Vol. V, pp. 322–323.
[25] Dahl, *op. cit.,* p. 285.

inasmuch as the Supreme Court has "the last word"[26] in a chronological sense to decide on the constitutionality of an act passed by Congress and signed by the President. Though in days past justices of the Supreme Court may have claimed that it was their duty to "find" the law, rather than make it, by laying "the article of the Constitution which is invoked beside the statute which is challenged and to decide whether the latter squares with the former,"[27] this so-called "slot-machine" explanation of the judicial function has been disproved by numerous studies of the judicial process. As Paul Freund noted,

> Old Jeremiah Smith, who began the teaching of law at Harvard after a career on the New Hampshire Supreme Court, properly deflated the issue. "Do judges make law?" he repeated. " 'Course they do. Made some myself."[28]

To admit the legislative function of the Court is not, however, proof of judicial supremacy or the undemocratic nature of judicial review. Far from it. The Constitution is, as Chief Justice Marshall stated in *Gibbons v. Ogden,* "one of enumeration, and not of definition...."[29] The Framers provided a statement of general principles, but left it to the living majority to designate its meaning. As Edward S. Corwin once put it,

> As a *document* the Constitution came from its framers, and its elaboration was an event of the greatest historical interest, but as a *law* the Constitution comes from and derives all its force from the people of the United States of this day and hour. In the words of the preamble, "We the people of the United States, *do* ordain and establish this Constitution"—not did ordain and establish. The Constitution is ... a living statute, to be interpreted in the light of living conditions.[30]

Most of the interpretation of our living conditions comes from the President and Congress, not from the Supreme Court. That the Supreme Court should share in this admixture of legislative power is hardly shocking when one recalls Madison's concern in *Federalist* #51 for "contriving the interior structure of government" so that "its

[26] Charles L. Black, *The People and the Court: Judicial Review in a Democracy* (New York: Macmillan, 1960), pp. 167–168.
[27] United States v. Butler, 297 U.S. 1 (1936).
[28] Paul A. Freund, *The Supreme Court of the United States* (Cleveland: Meridian, 1962), p. 28.
[29] Gibbons v. Ogden, 9 Wheaton (22 U.S.) 1 (p. 24).
[30] Edward S. Corwin, "Constitution v. Constitutional Theory," in Alpheus T. Mason and Gerald Garvey, eds., *American Constitutional History: Essays by Edward S. Corwin* (New York: Harper Torchbooks, 1964), p. 107.

several constituent parts may, by their mutual relations, be the means of keeping each other in their proper places." Thus, it is not to be contested that the Supreme Court, along with its sister branches, is a political body rather than Yankees from Olympus."[31]

In interpreting the metes and bounds of such terms as "liberty" and "due process of law," or what Justice Robert Jackson once termed the "great silences of the Constitution,"[32] the Supreme Court must inevitably legislate. Moreover, it must be admitted that the jurisdiction of the Court's legislative activity may expand from time to time, depending on the political risks involved and the rewards to be harvested. Demonstrative of this point, Justice Joseph Story used to tell a story about the Marshall Court that is still told at the Supreme Court. On rainy days it was the custom of the justices of the Marshall Court to brighten their conferences with wine. On other days Marshall might remark, "Brother Story, step to the window and see if it doesn't look like rain." If the sun was shining and the Chief Justice wanted wine, Marshall would order the wine nonetheless, since "our jurisdiction is so vast that it must be raining somewhere."[33] Thus, while the Court refused to enter the "political thicket" in *Luther v. Borden* to order reapportionment in 1894, rain turned to sunshine in 1962 when the Court ruled in *Baker v. Carr* that reapportionment was a justiciable question.[34]

At the extreme, cases like *Hammer v. Dagenhart*[35] may be cited to demonstrate that the Court, through tortured construction and misquotation of the Constitution, legislates in whatever direction it chooses. But in an age when Spencerian ideology was in vogue and faith in the myth of laissez faire went hand in hand with the simplistic dogmatism of "survival of the fittest,"[36] who is to say that the *Dagenhart* decision to void a congressional act designed to protect children from exploitation by businessmen in the labor market did not reflect

[31] Typical of the view that members of the Court represent a latter-day collection of Delphic Oracles is Catherine Drinker Sowen's *Yankee from Olympus: Justice Holmes and His Family.*
[32] H. P. Hood & Sons v. DuMond, 336 U.S. 525 (1949).
[33] Mary Ann Harrell and Stuart E. Jones, *Equal Justice Under Law: The Supreme Court in American Life* (Washington, D.C.: The Foundation of the Federal Bar Association, 1965), p. 29.
[34] Luther v. Borden, 7 Howard (U.S.) 1 (1894); Baker v. Carr, 369 U.S. 186 (1962).
[35] Hammer v. Dagenhart, 247 U.S. 251 (1918). In this case Justice William R. Day actually inserted a word into the Tenth Amendment—"expressly"—which had been debated and rejected by the Framers as it changed the entire meaning of that amendment.
[36] Richard Hofstadter, *Social Darwinism in American Thought* (Boston: Beacon Press, 1960), pp. 201-204.

popular opinion? After all, if children were no longer profitable to employ, they would be discharged; and since the father of the household could not expect his own wage to be raised to a level necessary to support his family, how would that family now be able to make ends meet? Such an opinion may not have been wise, but it may have been popular. Certainly it could not have been sustained in the presence of popular opposition to it.

A case like *Dagenhart,* which involves the Supreme Court literally rewriting the Constitution to suit its own legislative predisposition, is misleading and exceptional. Although the Court does legislate, we should not lose sight of Paul Freund's reminder that it does so at retail, whereas legislatures make it wholesale.[37] Even retail judicial legislation must be employed with public opinion in mind, for public displeasure with the Court could easily lead to the loss of its independence. The partial eclipse of the Supreme Court after the judicial imperium of the *Dred Scott* case in 1857 and the fright engendered by the "court-packing plan" of 1937 occasioned by judicial myopia during the Great Depression demonstrate clearly how carefully the Court must concern itself with the effects of popular opinion on the other political branches of government.

It is well to remember that popular opinion overturned the first truly unpopular decision rendered by the Supreme Court in *Chisholm v. Georgia* (1793),[38] which involved the return of confiscated Tory property by American patriots as a result of the provisions of the Treaty of Paris that ended the American Revolutionary War. Popular opinion easily produced the passage of the Eleventh Amendment (1795) to the Constitution, which forbids suits against states by citizens of other states or nations. One hundred and twenty years later, popular reaction against the income-tax cases of 1895 (which had been subsequently narrowed by the Supreme Court itself)[39] resulted in the ratification of the Sixteenth Amendment providing for such a tax.

Much less is needed to circumvent a Supreme Court decision that is intensely unpopular with the "more representative" branches of government. Professor Leonard Levy has observed that "Judicial review . . . exists by tacit consent of the governed," but that consent may be withdrawn at any time. Not only might a constitutional amend-

---

[37] Howard E. Dean, *Judicial Review and Democracy* (New York: Random House, 1967), pp. 150–151.
[38] Chisholm v. Georgia, 2 Dallas 419 (1793).
[39] Nicol v. Ames, 173 U.S. 509 (1899); Knowlton v. Moore, 178 U.S. 41 (1900); Patton v. Brady, 184 U.S. 608 (1902); Flint v. Stone Tracy Co., 220 U.S. 107 (1911).

ment be added to the Constitution[40] forbidding any future exercise of judicial review by the Court, but those other political branches, the President and Congress, can "bring the Court to heel" by simple legislation that could restrict its jurisdiction, funds, and procedures as well as neutralize its decisions by denying them enforcement. As Hamilton noted in *Federalist* #78, the power of the purse belongs to Congress, the sword belongs to the President, and the Supreme Court has "neither FORCE nor WILL but merely judgment."

Beyond this the Supreme Court cannot compel lower courts, state or national, to respect its decisions if they choose to pervert or circumvent the rulings of the high tribunal."[41] Thus, directly flying in the face of the school segregation cases' ruling that segregation be ended "with all deliberate speed," Federal District Judge William H. Atwell refused to order Dallas, Texas to set a date for integration because he felt this would cause "civil wrongs."[42]

What is, then, left to the Court in fulfilling its role as judicial legislator? And given the fact that, in the last analysis, the finality of its judicial judgment rests on public opinion, how does judicial review serve as an "auxiliary precaution" to ensure that majorities in this country are both reasonable and rightful in formulating public policy?

The role of judicial legislator was aptly summed up by Justice Holmes, when he averred that "judges do and must legislate, but they can do so only interstitially; they are confined from molar to molecular motion."[43] By legislating "interstitially" Holmes, of course, was drawing attention to the fact that the high tribunal's legislative scope is much smaller than that of the President and Congress, and that it is largely restricted to filling in the gaps of meaning in our 3500-odd word Constitution occasioned by such indistinct phrases as "unreasonable searches and seizures," "probable cause," "due process of law," and "cruel and unusual punishments." As Justice William J. Brennan, Jr. has put it, "the Founding Fathers knew better than to pin down

---

[40] While it has been pointed out that a minority (consisting of bare majorities in the thirteen least populous states) could prevent the passage of an amendment, Professor Martin Diamond has demonstrated that our political system is so responsive to majorities that even a small (though *nationally* distributed) minority in the thirty-seven least populous states can pass amendments over the opposition of overwhelming majorities in the twelve most populous states. See "Democracy And *The Federalist,*" *American Political Science Review*, Vol. LIII (1959), p. 57.

[41] Walter F. Murphy, "Lower Court Checks On Supreme Court Power," *American Political Science Review*, Vol. LIII (1959), pp. 1017–1031.

[42] *Ibid.*, p. 1028.

[43] Southern Pacific Co. v. Jensen, 224 U.S. 205, 221 (1917).

their descendants too closely. Enduring principles rather than petty details were what they sought to write down."[44] Thus, the Court's task is to interpret the Constitution "as a living statute, palpitating with the purpose of the hour, reenacted with every waking breath of the American people. . . ."[45] They sit, said Woodrow Wilson, as "a kind of Constitutional Convention in continuous session."[46]

In respect to protecting the rights of the minority against majority foolishness or violence, there is precious little evidence "to demonstrate that any particular Court decisions have or have not been at odds with the preference of a 'national majority.' "[47] Indeed, the record indicates that the Court is an unreliable champion of minority rights when protection is most needed. Thus, the Court at various times has put its stamp of approval on slavery, racial segregation, and the relocation of over 70,000 Americans of Japanese descent in concentration camps.[48] As John P. Frank has observed, "The dominant lesson of our history in the relation of the judiciary to repression is that courts love liberty most when it is under pressure least."[49]

Thus, in supplying the *qualitative* dimension to the modern meaning of democracy the Court has been "a sunshine defender" of individual liberties. Only since the time of the Hughes Court—and especially during the years of the Warren Court (1954-1971)[50]—did civil rights decisions extend constitutional protection to the rights of the individual in any significant manner.[51]

Justice Jackson once observed that the Constitution casts the Supreme Court in the role of our most philosophic branch of government, charged with the responsibility of engaging the nation in a vital seminar regarding the formation of the character of our citizenry.[52] No doubt this is true, but it does not necessarily follow that the national seminar will light the way for a more enlightened and tolerant view

[44] Harrell and Jones, *Equal Justice Under Law*, p. 10.
[45] Edward S. Corwin, *The Constitution and What It Means Today*, 3rd ed. (Princeton: Princeton University Press, 1924), p. 2.
[46] Harrell and Jones, *op. cit.*, p. 10.
[47] Dahl, *op. cit.*, p. 283.
[48] Dred Scott v. Sanford, 19 Howard (U.S.) 393 (1857); Plessy v. Ferguson, 163 U.S. 537 (1896); Korematsu v. United States, 323 U.S. 214 (1944).
[49] John P. Frank, "Review and Basic Liberties," Edmond Cahn, ed., in *Supreme Court and Supreme Law* (Bloomington, Indiana: Indiana University Press, 1954), p. 114.
[50] Paul C. Bartholomew sets the "watershed" point between the "Warren Court" and the "Burger Court" at the 1971-1972 term. See Paul C. Bartholomew, "The Supreme Court of the United States, 1971-1972," *Western Political Quarterly* (December 1972), p. 761.
[51] Levy, *op. cit.*, p. 20. So rarely has the high court cast itself as a defender of civil liberties that Professor Levy terms the Warren years "a golden age."

150   The Form of the American Republic

of the rights of man. For good or for ill, however, the Court takes the whole nation to school.

That ill-contrived judicial teaching that sanctions governmental action that unjustly suppresses the rights of a minority can undermine the rights of all has recently been demonstrated by Eugene Rostow in his examination of the internment of Japanese–American citizens during World War II.[53] He noted that the *Korematsu* decision that sanctioned the imprisonment of American citizens "with as little as one-sixteenth Japanese blood" set the "precedent for the proposal that concentration camps be established [in the United States] for citizens suspected of believing in revolutionary ideas."[54] Thus, during the 1950s, when Senator Joseph McCarthy, through tactics of fear, hatred, and prejudice, was conducting his popularly supported reign of terror against critics whom *he* deemed "subversive," Congress passed the Walter McCarran–Richard Nixon Internal Security Act of 1950 over the veto of President Truman who disavowed it as "worse than the Sedition Acts of 1798."[55] Title II of the "Emergency Detention" provisions of that act authorized the President to arrest all persons whom he believed would "probably" engage or conspire in espionage. In the event that the President should exercise this power, the government held in readiness six concentration camps left over from World War II.[56] Although the United States is most assuredly not a garrison state, there is little doubt that it could become one.[57]

From this it may be discerned that judicial review is a tool that may either be the nation's transcendent teacher, instructing the governing majority to be reasonable and rightful in its legislation, or it may abdicate its power of judicial statesmanship in favor of sanctioning, and thus encouraging, the passions of the public when it occasionally voices intolerance. In its best form, judicial review "undoubtedly means . . . some slowing down of the process of gov-

[52] Robert H. Jackson, *The Struggle for Judicial Supremacy* (New York: Knopf, 1941), pp. 312–313.
[53] Rostow, "The Japanese–American Cases—A Disaster," *Yale Law Review*, Vol. LIV (1945).
[54] Eugene Rostow, "The Democratic Character of Judicial Review," *Harvard Law Review*, LXVI, p. 207.
[55] Samuel Eliot Morison and Henry Steele Commager, *The Growth Of The American Republic* (New York: Oxford University Press, 1962), Vol. II, p. 868.
[56] *The New York Times* (December 27, 1955); see also Levy, *op. cit.*, p. 41.
[57] Writing twenty-seven years after publication of his celebrated book, *Majority Rule and Minority Rights,* Professor Commager appears to have second thoughts about majorities correcting their mistakes by remedial legislation. In a 1970 article, he states, "It would be an exaggeration to say that the United States is a garrison state, but none to say that it is in danger of becoming one." Henry Steele Commager, "Is Freedom Dying in America?" *Look* (July 14, 1970), p. 19

ernment," for it was intended to insert into the democratic process "one further, final step in the discussion, clarification, [and] rationalization of public opinion."[58] To do this, as Hamilton noted in *Federalist* #78, "would require an uncommon portion of fortitude in the judges to do their duty as faithful guardians of the Constitution, where legislative invasions of it had been instigated by the major voice of the community."

Judicial Review and the Nixon Court

Though the Warren Court (1954-1971) has been condemned by President Nixon for "weakening the peace forces as against the criminal forces in our society," one may be reasonably certain that neither he nor anyone else would charge it with a lack of fortitude. Was its fortitude that of a gangster or the fortitude required to protect the weak from the strong as envisioned by Hamilton in *Federalist* #78?

No criticism of the Warren Court evoked more emotion than the charge that it was "coddling criminals," and no case produced more apprehension than the case of *Miranda v. Arizona*.[59] For that reason the *Miranda* decision may be taken as a gauge of the validity of the "coddling" charge; it may also serve as a useful foil for evaluating the performance of the new Nixon Court.

In March of 1963 a Mexican-American indigent by the name of Ernesto Miranda was arrested on suspicion of kidnapping and raping an eighteen-year-old girl near Phoenix, Arizona. After being picked out of a police lineup by the girl, Miranda was interrogated—without being warned of his constitutional right to an attorney and his right against self-incrimination—and he confessed after two hours of questioning. The Warren Court struck down his conviction in a 5-4 decision on the grounds that the Fifth Amendment required that suspects be informed of their constitutional rights before they are asked any questions by police authorities.

To many here was a clear case of the Court coddling criminals. Crime is not good for society, so why should the Court be good to crime? At the heart of this question rests the nature of our political regime and the relationship of the individual to it. A closer inspection of the *Miranda* decision will reveal how the Warren Court viewed that relationship.

---

[58] Edward S. Corwin, *Court Over Constitution* (Princeton: Princeton University Press, 1938), pp. 208-209.
[59] Miranda v. Arizona, 384 U.S. 436 (1966).

Need the police advise the rich of such rights? Of course not. The police would not transgress the rights of the rich because they know that lawyers will soon appear and their work will be undone to the peril of the case and perhaps their own careers. Need the police advise the mobster or the hardened criminal of such rights? Of course not—he knows them. So, too, the educated man and the plain person with common sense know, however frightened they may be at the moment, that they can remain silent. Who then is left but the poor, the ignorant, the sick, and the weak. Have we so little sense of justice that we would take advantage of these?[60]

The question, while rhetorical, is not simply a matter of "Whose ox is gored?" by the constitutional interpretation rendered by the Warren Court of the Fifth Amendment.[61] The question goes to the very heart of human dignity, for rights are a necessary protection of that dignity. Democracy rests upon the recognition of that human dignity, and the rights enshrined in the Constitution protect the freedom without which human beings cannot fully be human.

It should not be deemed a violation of the canons of good political science to judge the performance of its political agents in terms of such a normative criteria, for as Professor Martin Diamond has noted, "the scientific study of politics . . . requires the hypothesis that reason can teach men something about how they *ought* to live politically."[62] Do not political scientists and laymen alike presuppose knowledge of what is "rightful" political behavior when they analyze such things as violence and categorize it as "ghetto riot" or "resistance against oppression"? Without such a "normative score card," no political behavior is intelligible.

The irony of the *Miranda* decision, which merely extended to "the poor, the ignorant, the sick, and the weak" the rights hitherto enjoyed by the rich, the educated, and the strong, in that J. Edgar Hoover's FBI, on its own initiative, "in the interest of effective investigation, began giving the essentials of the Miranda warning in 1948, eighteen years before the Supreme Court pronounced its rule. No one has criticized the FBI for being soft on crime because of this; nor has its conviction rate suffered."[63] A final irony is that Miranda was sub-

---

[60] Ramsey Clark, in Stephen Gillers, *Getting Justice* (New York: Basic Books, 1971), pp. vi–vii.
[61] According to John Roche, "The basic canon of constitutional interpretation has always been 'Whose ox is gored?' " John P. Roche, *Courts and Rights* (New York: Random House, 1961), p. 20.
[62] Martin Diamond, "The Dependence Of Fact Upon 'Value' ", *Interpretation: A Journal of Political Philosophy* (Spring 1972), Vol 2/3, p. 226
[63] Clark, *op. cit.,* p. vii.

The Supreme Court 153

sequently *convicted* on the same indictment without the use of illegally obtained evidence.

In 1968, during the spring preceding the Presidential election of that year, the Gallup Poll revealed that "crime" was ranked by most Americans as "the most important domestic problem" in the United States. Campaigning in August of 1968 and knowing the potency of the crime issue, Nixon spoke of "sirens in the night" and "cities enveloped in smoke and flame."[64] Linking the Warren Court to black militancy, rising crime, and urban riots, Nixon promised to change all of that by reversing the trend of the Warren Court by appointing "strict constructionists" to the Court.[65]

The resignations of Abe Fortas and Earl Warren, coupled with the deaths of Hugo Black and John Harlan, provided the new President with four appointments and the opportunity to create a "Nixon Court" during his first four years in office.[66] Though the Nixon nominations of Judges Clement Haynsworth and G. Harrold Carswell were turned down by the Senate on the grounds of conflict of interest in decision making (Haynsworth) and advocating segregation in judicial decisions (Carswell), the President finally secured the appointment of Warren Burger as chief justice and Harry Blackmun, Lewis Powell, and William Renquist as associate justices of the Supreme Court. Thus, the old Warren majority has been shrunk to three: Justices William Brennan, Jr., Thurgood Marshall, and William O. Douglas, with the balance of power being exercised by Potter Stewart and Byron White.

Although Nixon's appointments reflected his conviction that the balance between the rights of society and the individual needed to be tipped toward society, the question remains as to whether his appointees have fulfilled his expectations. At brief glance it would appear that the so-called Nixon Court is much more liberal than "judicial conservative," as Nixon envisioned. Since the 1969 appointment

[64] Richard M. Scammon and Ben J. Wattenberg, *The Real Majority* (New York: Coward, McCann & Geoghegan, 1971), p. 41. Nixon publicly charged the Warren Court with "a large measure of responsibility for some of the bitterness in American life today over the administration of criminal justice." See *Congressional Quarterly, Weekly Report* (May 30, 1969), p. 844.
[65] Robert Sherrill adroitly points out that members of the Warren Court were "strict constructionists," especially in regard to the First Amendment. Justices Black and Douglas, for example, in interpreting the First Amendment prohibition that "Congress shall make no laws . . . abridging freedom of speech, or of the press," interpreted it to mean just that—*no* law, including laws against pornography. Rhetorically, Sherrill asks, "Is this what Nixon meant, too?" Robert Sherrill, *Why They Call It Politics* (New York: Harcourt Brace Jovanovich, 1972), p. 137.
[66] Nixon was also able to get Congress to create sixty-one new federal judgeships during the first two years of his first administration.

of Chief Justice Burger, the Court has struck down almost every death penalty statute in the country as a violation of the constitutional prohibition against cruel and unusual punishments.[67] Later, in 1973, the new Nixon Court ruled that every woman in the United States has a right to an abortion during the first six months of pregnancy.[68] Rooting the abortion decision on the Court's view of the right to privacy, Blackman held that such a right was a part of every American's "liberty," which is protected by the Fourteenth Amendment.

Yet, in spite of these few decisions—which found from one-half to all of the Nixon appointees dissenting—the Nixon Court has not only voted consistently together, but, as Professor Paul Bender has noted, has "quietly begun to extol the state at the expense of the individual."[69]

Of the ninety-odd decisions that the Nixon appointees had participated in up to the 1973 session, Burger and Renquist split in eight, and Powell and Renquist in only nine decisions. In all other cases the four Nixon appointees voted together.[70] In light of this, one may well be justified in referring to the present court as the Nixon Court.

What have been the major decisions rendered by that Court to date? And what has been its general philosophy? Thus far the important decisions of the Warren Court, which knocked down racial segregation and malapportionment, as well as extending the protection of the Bill of Rights to the states and into the police station, have not been frontally assaulted. Some, however, have been modified and the thrust of the Court appears to be in the direction of strengthening the power of the government at the expense of the individual.

Where many of the Warren decisions exhibited a deep skepticism about whether government officials, if left to themselves, would be sensitive to individual constitutional rights in exercising their far-reaching powers over a person's life, liberty, or pursuit of happiness, the Nixon Court has been more willing to assume that the majority, acting through the government, will act reasonably and rightfully toward the individual citizen. This, of course, leads to enormous burdens placed upon the individual to demonstrate that the government violated his or her constitutional rights. As Professor Bender notes,

[67] Furman v. Georgia, 408 U.S. 238; dissenting opinions were filed by *all* four of Nixon's appointees.
[68] *Roe v. Wade*, U.S. Law Week, Vol. 41, p. 4213; *Doe v. Bolton*, U.S. Law Week, Vol. 41, p. 4233.
[69] Paul Bender, "The Techniques of Subtle Erosion," *Harpers Magazine* (December 1972), p. 18.
[70] *Ibid.*, p. 30.

The Supreme Court   155

"The new justices tend to see the Warren Court's safeguards as unwarranted intrusions into the activities of other branches of government."[71]

Thus, in 1971 the Nixon Court modified the *Miranda* decision and opened the way for the police under certain circumstances to introduce into the courts certain kinds of illegally obtained evidence. Chief Justice Burger, writing the opinion held that a statement of confession inadmissible as evidence in court because the suspect had not been warned of his rights could nevertheless be used in court to counteract any evidence the suspect gives on the stand.[2] In dissent, Justice Douglas wrote, "It is monstrous that courts should aid or abet the lawbreaking police officers."

The importance of the *Harris* decision is that it will encourage law-enforcement agencies to use Nixon's 1968 Omnibus Crime Control and Safe Streets Act, which overruled the *Miranda* ruling by returning to the old standard of "voluntariness." That same act permitted government wiretapping on an unprecedented scale as well as preventive detention before trial of certain defendants and "no-knock" search warrants allowing the police to enter private homes without announcement under certain circumstances in Washington, D.C. President Nixon called the law a "model anticrime package"; North Carolina Senator Sam Ervin described it as "a blueprint for a police state."[73] Until the *Harris* decision, law-enforcement officers had been reluctant to use the Omnibus legislation for fear it would not survive the test of constitutionality with the Supreme Court. Needless to say, there is no more need for timidity.

So far the Nixon appointees have won twice as often as they have lost. When the Court splits into "liberal" and "conservative" blocs, the Nixon judges need only one of the swing-votes of Stewart and White to prevail, while Douglas, Marshall, and Brennan need them both. Thus far the Nixon Court scoreboard demonstrates that the Supreme Court is moving back to its historical role as a "sunshine defender" of civil liberty. A brief review of its record tends to confirm Professor Bender's conclusion that the Nixon Court has extolled the state at the expense of the individual.

1. All four Nixon appointees have voted to allow nonunanimous jury verdicts in state criminal trials and all except Powell would

[71] *Ibid.*, p. 26.
[72] Harris v. New York, 401 U.S. 222 (1971).
[73] Congressional Quarterly, *Nixon: The Second Year of His Presidency* (Washington, D.C.: Congressional Quarterly, Inc., 1971), pp. 63–64.

seemingly extend the ruling to federal trials. This decision weakens the presumption of innocence and gives added power to an already powerful government.[74]

2. All of the Nixon appointees (Justice Renquist did not participate in this case) voted to weaken the Fifth Amendment's protection against self-incrimination by granting only narrow testimonial immunity, rather than broader contractual immunity. This means that a witness can be convicted of a crime he has been forced to testify about unless *he* can prove that the government used his own testimony against him. Again, given the power of the government, this is a heavy burden for an individual to bear.[75]

3. All four Nixon appointees voted to curtail the right to counsel at lineups and provided that an anonymous tip would be sufficient cause for the police to stop and frisk any citizen on the street.[76]

4. All four Nixon appointees dissented from the historic decision that stipulated that the death penalty or its haphazard application equaled cruel and unusual punishment. They would also have permitted a state to use prior unconstitutional convictions against an individual who is on trial for a different charge.[77]

5. All four Nixon appointees agreed that a citizen's charge that the Army's electronic surveillance of lawful citizen activity in politics was not a complaint that the Supreme Court would consider because there was no evidence of "specific present objective harm or a threat of specific future harm" resulting from the Army's surveillance. In his dissenting opinion Justice Douglas protested that "The present controversy is not a remote, imaginary conflict. Respondents were targets of the Army's surveillance. . . . Army surveillance . . . is at war with the principles of the First Amendment."[78]

Conclusion

So, too, may democracy be at war with its own raison d'être. The genius of a democratic system lies in its recognition that the passen-

---

[74] Johnson v. Louisiana, 406 U.S. 356 (1972); Apodaca v. Oregon, 406 U.S. 404 (1972).
[75] Kastigar v. United States, 406 U.S. 441 (1972).
[76] Kirby v. Illinois, 406 U.S. 682 (1972); Adams v. Williams, 407 U.S. 143 (1972).
[77] Furman v. Georgia, 408 U.S. 238 (1972).
[78] Laird v. Tatum, 408 U.S. 1 (1972).

gers do not exist for the sake of the ship of state, but rather the other way around. Democracy is a means to an end, and that end is the preservation of the freedom necessary to the development of the human personality.

In an age where economics, politics, and social structure have become enmeshed by technology, the private and public sectors are no longer distinct and the most important component of democracy—the individual—seems to be imperiled by overbearing majorities acting through an omnipresent government.

Recognizing that democracy should entail more than mere headcounting, and that reason is unreliable and often distorted by passion, our Framers undertook to provide auxiliary precautions against unreasonable government. As one of those auxiliary precautions, the Supreme Court has historically been disappointing in its record of balancing minority rights with majority rule. With the brief exception of the Warren Court, Finley Peter Dunne's wry comment about the Supreme Court following the election returns does not seem too far off the mark.

At its best the Supreme Court can contribute to the formation of *enlightened* consent by engaging the nation in a dialogue of the controversial issues of the day. At its worst it can validate and give legitimacy to heedless public opinion, paying more attention to the passions and the whims of the majority than to the dignity of the individual, which philosophically underpins the very justification of majority rule itself.

Given the fact that a Purdue University study of teenagers revealed that 83% favor wiretapping; 58% support the use of third-degree methods by the police; 60% find no fault in the censorship of books, periodicals, and newspapers; 25% thought that the police should be permitted to enter a home without a search warrant; and that there is reason to believe that adults would be even more enthusiastic in sharing these views—one may wonder how the Nixon Court will exercise its power in the future.[79]

[79] H. H. Remmers and D. H. Radler, *The American Teenager* (Indianapolis: Bobbs-Merrill, 1957), Chap. 8, pp. 16–17. See also Judge Sidney H. Asch, *Civil Rights & Responsibilities Under the Constitution* (New York: Arco, 1970), p. 184.

THE BUREAUCRACY

... the true test of a good government is its aptitude and tendency to produce a good administration.[1]

—*Publius*

Without a bureaucracy, lawmakers and politicians are generals without armies. Certainly, no one understood this fact of political life more clearly than did America's greatest general as he prepared to meet his new responsibilities as the first President of the United States. In a letter to his Secretary of War, President Washington lamented the "ocean of difficulties" that he faced in respect to the task of organizing his new administration. Who in America knew anything about the nature of administration or bureaucracy, let alone had the necessary experience to run it?

Washington's concern was well-founded since he had inherited from the defunct Articles of Confederation "government" no more than a dozen of its clerks with their pay in arrears, an empty treasury, and a burden of debt. Not only did he have no taxes coming in, but worse, there was no machinery for collecting taxes—or for enforcing the law for that matter.

[1] Clinton Rossiter, ed., *The Federalist Papers* (New York: Mentor Books, 1961), No. 68, p. 414.

Contrast this circumstance to that of America's thirty-sixth President, Richard Nixon, who inherited a bureaucracy of over 3 million civilian employees who possessed no less than 15,000 different job skills.[2] Ironically, the hue and cry among conservatives and liberals alike is now that the federal government possesses too much bureaucracy. From Senator Barry Goldwater, Americans are warned that "the spread of federal bureaucracy must be arrested—before it cannibalizes us all."[3] At the same time many liberals agree with the late Senator Robert Kennedy that America suffers from "an inefficient, overstructured, often tyrannical bureaucracy."[4]

It is clear from the experience of both George Washington and his modern counterparts that the art of governing the American people will be bogged in an "ocean of difficulties" without a proper bureaucracy. Therefore, an understanding of the nature of bureaucracy as well as the problems it faces and poses is essential if one is to comprehend the reasons why a democratic government may or may not be responsive or responsible to the public.

The Anatomy of the Federal Bureaucracy

Like most bureaucracies in the world, the American federal bureaucracy is depicted in the organizational charts as forming a pyramid, the peak of which is made up of a relatively small number of Cabinet secretaries, chairmen of independent regulatory agencies, and executive bureaus. According to one estimate, the base of this pyramid includes "twelve Cabinet appointees; 300 sub-Cabinet officials and agency heads; 124 ambassadors; and 1700 aides, assistants, and confidential secretaries."[5]

It must be emphasized, however, that the organizational charts are more often clear than accurate. For one thing, there is more *pluribus* than *unum* in this pyramid of bureaucratic authority. The federal bureaucracy is not monolithic, but rather is polycentric and consists of many centers of autonomous and often overlapping power that are often inadequately controlled by either the President or Con-

[2] United States Civil Service Commission, *Challenge and Change,* Annual Report, 1968, p. 66.
[3] Barry Goldwater, *New York Herald Tribune* (October 1, 1964), Goldwater's development of his thesis may be found in *Vital Speeches,* August 15, 1970.
[4] Robert F. Kennedy's address at Brigham Young University (Provo, Utah), March 27, 1968.
[5] Max Frankel, "Priorities for the Nixon Team," *The New York Times* (November 15, 1968).

gress. The mere size of the federal bureaucracy makes it impossible for the President or Congress to know or influence more than a modicum of administrators whose day-to-day activities determine whether or not a governmental program will succeed or fail.

A second characteristic of the federal bureaucracy is that, strictly speaking, it is *not* sharply differentiated from the state and local bureaucracies throughout the nation. Indeed, the very word "federal" signifies the joint enterprise of nation *and* state. It is erroneous to visualize the American form of government as a layer cake, with the state and national bureaucracies having diffeerent jurisdictions of power. As Professor Morton Grodzins put it:

> The American form of government is often, but erroneously, symbolized by a layer cake. A far more accurate image is the . . . marble cake, characterized by an inseparable mingling of differently colored ingredients, the colors appearing in vertical and diagonal strands and unexpected whirls. As colors are mixed in the marble cake, so functions are mixed in the American federal system. . . .[6]

One of the more frequently overlooked aspects of the federal bureaucracy is that the officials who work in such areas as welfare or budgeting *interact* in their professional capacities with their counterparts on the state and local level. When they meet in such organizations as the National Association of State Budget Officers or the American Public Welfare Association, these bureaucratic officials are bound to influence one another and take each level of government into account when administering or creating a program. In other words, the federal bureaucracy is but one interrelated part of a single bureaucratic system that views itself as the dynamic wheelhorse of a 101-flavored marble cake.

A fourth feature of the federal bureaucratic anatomy relates to its political impact due to its expanded scope and professional expertise. In terms of sheer numbers, the scope of the bureaucracy has increased at a phenomenal rate since the beginning of the twentieth century. From a force of 200,000 in 1900, it has multiplied fifteen-fold to its present size of over 3 million civil servants, excluding those in the military service.[7] Most of this increase can be dated to the Great Depression of the 1930s, when the government responded to the challenge of that crisis by initiating the New Deal and the Welfare State. There is nothing sinister in this fact, for as people demand more services from their government, new agencies or bureaus will be created. However, this is not without political consequences. As

[6] Morton Grodzins, *The American System* (Chicago: Rand McNally, 1966), pp. 8–9.
[7] Civil Service Commission, *op. cit.,* p. 66.

Kenneth Boulding has pointed out, large bureaucracies invariably suffer from *red tape,* i.e. internal communication breakdowns wherein the right hand of the bureaucracy does not know—or even care—what the left hand is doing because of overlapping jurisdictions and the mountains of paperwork that are the hallmark of bureaucratic activity.[8]

Not infrequently, bureaucratic agencies have so little coordination that they will even work *against* one another. One post-World War II example of this resulted from the overlapping bureaucratic jurisdiction and agency confusion regarding the right of an attempted merger of the El Paso Natural Gas Company with one of its competitors, the Pacific Northwest Pipe Line Corporation. Both the Federal Power Commission (FPC) and the Justice Department claimed jurisdiction in this controversy, which involved the legitimacy of the move in respect to the statutory prohibition against business monopolies which are in restraint of trade.

Regulatory agencies like the FPC tend to become promoters of the businesses under their jurisdiction, and hence it was no surprise that the FPC approved the merger. The Justice Department, on the other hand, is institutionally oriented to oppose such mergers. This, of course, often plays into the hands of powerful interest groups who can play the bureaucratic agencies against one another for their own interests.[9]

The lack of coordination and clear jurisdiction is not the only cost of maintaining a leviathanlike administrative system. Unlike the spoilsmen of the Jacksonian era, today's civil servants are specialists and experts in their given field, in contrast to the heads of their departments who are most often political appointees with a much higher turnover. By comparison, Presidents, congressmen, and even Cabinet secretaries—the men responsible for direction and control of the Administration—are amateurs who frequently find it difficult, if not impossible, to master their own departments. No doubt many have shared the frustration of Secretary of State William McAdoo as he accepted his responsibilities during the Wilson Administration:

> I was like a sea captain who finds himself on the deck of a ship he has never seen before. I did not know the mechanism of my ship; I did not know my officers—even by sight—and I had no acquaintance with the crew.[10]

Not only may the person entrusted with administrative responsibility and accountability become lost in the sea of souls he has to

---

[8] Kenneth E. Boulding, "The Jungle of Hugeness," *Saturday Review* (March 1, 1968).
[9] Peter Woll, *American Bureaucracy* (New York: W. W. Norton, 1963), pp. 75-80.
[10] Richard Fenno, Jr., *The President's Cabinet* (Cambridge: Harvard University Press, 1959), p. 225.

direct, but he may easily become lost in the maze of data offered by bureaucratic specialists. This is true not only of the heads of departments, but also of the *elected* officials to whom they are responsible. The following dialogue between a member of a legislative committee attempting to learn what legislation would be needed to build a proper naval defense system and the Secretary of Defense is illustrative of this problem:

> SECRETARY MCNAMARA: It is a question of antisubmarine emphasis versus antiaircraft plus antisubmarines. The three DE's are almost exclusively for antisubmarine warfare. The two DEG's had some desirable capability beyond antisubmarine warfare.
> Our chief problem is antisubmarine warfare, and it seemed to me wise to consider putting in three antisubmarine warfare ships instead of two that had some antiaircraft capability.
> MR. HARDY: I can't disagree with any of these things—they are completely over my head—but I am trying to explore how we arrive at the specific things we have.[11]

Thus the expansive scope, coupled with the professional expertise, of the bureaucracy have raised serious questions as to whether they or our elected officials are running the country. Have they, at the expense of our elective branches, become a Fourth Branch of government?

Bureaucracy and Democratic Theory

In *Federalist* #47 James Madison noted that "the accumulation of all powers, legislative, executive, and judiciary, in the same hands, whether of one, a few, or many, and whether hereditary, self-appointed, or elective, may justly be pronounced the very definition of tyranny."[12] Moreover, as is made clear in The Declaration of Independence, government may exist legitimately only by consent of the governed, and it is expected to be both responsive and responsible to the public interest.

Today, the powers exercised by the administrative branch of government does not conform either to the theory or the practice

[8] Kenneth E. Boulding, "The Jungle of Hugeness," *Saturday Review* (March 1, 1968).
[9] Peter Woll, *American Bureaucracy* (New York: W. W. Norton, 1963), pp. 75–80.
[10] Richard Fenno, Jr., *The President's Cabinet* (Cambridge: Harvard University Press, 1959), p. 225.
[11] Charles E. Jacob, ed., *Policy and Bureaucracy* (Princeton, N.J.: Van Nostrand Reinhold Co., 1966); reproduced in Ronald Moe and William A. Schultze, eds., *American Government and Politics* (Columbus, Ohio: Charles E. Merrill, 1971), p. 231.
[12] Rossiter, *op. cit.*, p. 301.

of separation of powers in that bureaucratic agencies make and enforce laws, as well as adjudicate controversies surrounding them.[13] Because of the broad and often ambiguous legislative responsibility given to the agencies by Congress, not only do they have leadway to make policy or to legislate, but they also have the power to enforce and adjudicate their own policies. Moreover, it is a familiar finding to learn that bureaucratic agencies are often more responsive to a particular interest group than to the public interest. Was Madison wrong in his definition of tyranny, or does this development represent a challenge to the maintenance of our democratic republic?

First, let us remember that there *is* a price that has to be paid for the benefits of having a modern government that provides the public with as many services as our bureaucracy does. As Professor John Vieg once observed:

> Assembly-line techniques offer marked advantages over those of custom craftsmanship. They also have their price. They entail the imposition of an order of progression, the fixing of a rate or rhythm of operation, and the discipline of a regular routine. Set order, fixed price, and adherence to routine—these are the very stuff of which red tape is made. Yet they are the essence of system, too.[14]

One may, however, reasonably ask whether or not the price is too high or whether this order and routine—which has its cost in red tape—has kept in mind the *end* and justification of its very existence, namely to serve the individual and enhance human dignity.

Bureaucracy, on the whole, has been overly preoccupied with its internal organization and the *means* or procedures of bureaucratic efficiency and competence. Considering the fact that no citizen, from the moment of birth to the moment of death, is outside the jurisdiction of the administrative process, it would seem fundamentally important to have a bureaucracy that is vitally concerned with the ends of good government as they are stated in the Declaration of Independence, namely the enhancement of human dignity by nurturing as best it may each individual's "life, liberty, and the pursuit of happiness." As with technology, the civil servant must remain just that—a *servant* of the people rather than their master—and must be ordered toward constructive rather than demeaning ends.

On a more sinister level, there is the question of bureaucratic loyalty. To whom does the bureaucrat owe his ultimate responsibility? To the people? Or the state? If the FBI should indulge in the electronic

---

[13] Woll, *op. cit.,* p. 13.
[14] Alvin W. Goulder, "Metaphysical Pathos and the Theory of Bureaucracy," *American Political Science Review* Vol. 49 (June 1955), pp. 496–507.

surveillance of people like Martin Luther King or Senator Adlai Stevenson III simply because they are critical of governmental policies, to whom does the agent owe his allegiance? To J. Edgar Hoover? Or to the First and Fourth Amendments of the Constitution, which forbid the suppression of speech or the unreasonable invasion of privacy? To whom does the bureaucrat owe responsibility in reporting the success or failure of the war in Vietnam? That the answer to this question has all too often been one wholly inconsistent with democratic principles has been tragicomically demonstrated by Richard Goodwin's analysis of bureaucratic flimflam and deception in reporting the military progress of American forces in Vietnam.

> If we take the number of enemy we are supposed to be killing, add to that the defectors, along with a number of wounded much less than our own ratio of wounded-to-killed, we find we are wiping out the entire North Vietnamese force every year. This truly makes their continued resistance one of the marvels of the world.[15]

One might add that it also makes for a crisis of credibility wherein the American people become more and more cynical about their government with each disclosure of government duplicity. This ebbing away of belief in the American government may well be the most serious cost the American people must bear for bureaucratic irresponsibility, for a government that loses its legitimacy in the eyes of its citizenry will not last long.

Max Weber long ago posited that an administrative system would extend its loyalty to whatever political regime took over the reigns of government. That there is some truth to this statement was borne out in Germany during the 1930s and 1940s when the *Beamte* or German civil service served Hitler so well.[16] America cannot afford such a valuefree bureaucracy. Lacking a basic commitment to democratic values, bureaucracy can undermine a democratic government. At its best the bureaucracy is a collection of nonpartisan or small "d" democratic civil servants faithfully applying the law equitably to all. At its worst, it is a Gordian knot of red tape or even a threat to democratic government as the Nixon administration's Watergate crimes remind us.

Many argue, however, that the real threat bureaucracy poses to a democratic government comes not from its mistaken loyalties or

---

[15] Richard Goodwin, "Triumph or Tragedy: Reflections on Vietnam," in Arthur M. Schlesinger, Jr., *The Bitter Heritage* (New York: Fawcett Crest Book, 1967), p. 74.
[16] Frederic S. Burin, "Bureaucracy and National Socialism: A Reconsideration of Weberian Theory," in Robert Merton et al. *Bureaucracy* (New York: The Free Press, 1952), pp. 33–47.

even from a boundless appetite for power so much as from its inertia. Like judges on the lower benches, bureaucrats often live in fear of being wrong and subsequently overruled by their superiors. Rather than risk this, they often prefer to ignore problems and decision making that rank high in terms of public concern or else to deal with such matters without vigor and imagination. This capacity for nondecision frustrates or emasculates the ability of a President or a congressman to be responsive and responsible to the public interest, thus further widening the credibility gap between the government and the people. No man knew the limits that bureaucracy may put on governmental action better than did Franklin D. Roosevelt:

> The Treasury is so large and far-flung and ingrained in its practices that I find it is almost impossible to get the action and results I want—even with Henry [Morgenthau] there. But the Treasury is not to be compared with the State Department. You should go through the experience of trying to get any changes in the thinking, policy, and action of the career diplomats and then you'd know what a real problem was. But the Treasury and the State Department put together are nothing compared with the Na-a-vy. The admirals are really something to cope with—and I should know. To change anything in the Na-a-vy is like punching a feather bed. You punch it with your right and you punch it with your left until you are finally exhausted, and then you find the damn bed just as it was before you started punching.[17]

Much of this inertia comes from the fact that Presidents and congressmen come and go, but the federal bureaucrat is relatively permanent either because he has special skills that makes him hard to replace or because he is protected from dismissal by civil-service laws. At one time the public administration was so much of the spoils system, and rotation of office so frequent that President Lincoln is said to have remarked while disabled with smallpox: "Tell all the office-seekers to come at once, for now I have something I can give them."[18]

The political corruption and inefficiency attending the "rotation of office" of the spoils system is well known. Less obvious is the cost to democratic principles in maintaining a "nonpolitical" and relatively permanent civil service. Indeed, "nonpolitical" is a misnomer, for it is far easier to take the civil service out of politics than to take the politics out of the civil service. If the spoils system may be symbolized as a carrousel in its style of recruitment, the bureaucracy

---

[17] Clinton Rossiter, *The American Presidency* (New York: Time Inc., 1963), p. 54.
[18] Martin Diamond, Winston Fisk, and Herbert Garfinkel, *The Democratic Republic* (Chicago: Rand McNally, 1966), p. 272.

based upon technical competence might be characterized as a cemetery, for while new personnel are constantly being added with a fixed tenure, precious few are displaced or "rotated."

It has been estimated that out of the over 3 million civilian employees in the federal administration a President may appoint 2200 people, and his own appointees will be outnumbered 1000 to one in the federal establishment.[19] And like the "midnight" judges whom Jefferson inherited from his Federalist opponents, today's President inherits "hangovers" from previous Administrations who well may be of a different political persuasion and disinclined to carry out Presidential policy.

Moreover, agencies designed to regulate industries, like the Interstate Commerce Commission (ICC), soon become the industry's spokesmen and act as "transmission belts" through which private-interest groups may pursue their goals in other governmental offices like the legislature and the White House itself.

In essence, an agency becomes a front organization for translating private interest into public policy. Once an agency establishes the support of an interest group, it can become virtually autonomous of the elected branches of government, a fact most amply demonstrated by J. Edgar Hoover and the FBI. It becomes what Douglas Cater calls the "Fourth Branch of Government" and exercises a powerful voice in the determination and implementation of public policy.[20]

Administrative agencies also gain autonomy because they operate with low visibility in areas like public welfare and housing, which serve a relatively poor and powerless clientele. Professors Cloward and Piven have described the effects of this in the area of public welfare:

> Public welfare systems are under the constant stress of conflict and opposition made . . . by the rising costs to localities of public aid. And, to accommodate this pressure, welfare practice everywhere has become more restrictive than welfare statute; *much of the time it verges on lawlessness.* Thus, public welfare systems try to keep their budgets down and their rolls low by failing to inform people of rights available to them; by intimidating and shaming them to the degree that they are reluctant either to apply or to press claims, and by arbitrarily denying benefits to those who are eligible.[21]

In other words, public welfare agencies adapt themselves so well to the monetary frugality and skepticism of the public that they take punitive action against their clients to balance their budgets, even

---

[19] "Dug In Bureaucrats Await New President," *U.S. News and World Report* (December 30, 1968), pp. 40–41.
[20] See Douglas Cater, *The Fourth Branch of Government* (Boston: Houghton Mifflin, 1959).
[21] Richard Cloward and Francis Fox Piven, "Poverty, Injustice, and the Welfare State," *The Nation* (February 28, 1966).

at the cost of perverting the welfare law and the Constitution itself. Midnight raids on welfare mothers to search for evidence of a "man in the house" in order to cancel public assistance is not only demeaning but illegal. Customarily, the welfare worker's demand for entry into the home is not accompanied by a search warrant, but is presented with the threat of automatic cancelation of welfare benefits should the individual not "cooperate."

In the area of public housing, not only have bureaucratic managers used their wide discretionary powers over their tenants to create de facto racial segregation, but they have also used the almost unlimited power of eviction either to control the behavior of their tenants or to evict "problem" families. One housing manager, for example, attempted to evict two Puerto Rican brothers under the age of twenty-one on the ground that since they had recently been orphaned by their mother's death they were minors and therefore not entitled to enter into a lease with the government.[22]

Bureaucratic low visibility not only results in this kind of administrative high-handedness, but more often than not makes the bureaucracy a kind of cloistered sanctuary that insulates it from public scrutiny so that its mistakes—and even its deceptions—may be kept secret, all in the name of national interest. As the *Pentagon Papers* demonstrated in its exposure of bureaucratic and political double-talk regarding the escalation of the war in Vietnam, government officials have gotten into the habit of labeling documents secret whenever they feel that their activities would prove embarrassing or would make bad publicity for the Administration.

In hearings conducted by the House Foreign Operations and Government Information Subcommittee in June 1971, William G. Florence, a former security-classification expert for the Defense Department, estimated that of some 20 million classified documents only 0.5% should be kept from public view.[23] Needless to say, this is hardly the case.

So powerful is the bureaucratic tendency to keep information from public view that the Army once classified as a military secret a modern version of the bow and arrow, while the Air Force labeled as secret pictures of the interior of some of its planes that had been luxuriously remodeled with expensive lounges for the comfort of its top brass. Bureaucratic secrecy, however, is not limited to the Defense Department. The General Services Administration has refused to release

---

[22] Lawrence M. Friedman, "Public Housing and the Poor," *California Law Review*, Vol. 54, No. 2 (May 1966).
[23] "The U.S. Mania for Classification," *Time* (July 5, 1971), pp. 14–15.

figures on what it is paying to lease office space, the Forest Service has kept secret the list of names of persons it has permitted to graze cattle in a national forest, and the Department of Health, Education, and Welfare has refused to release a study of problems in human reproduction.[24] In light of this, one is tempted to surmise that the bureaucratic tendency upon discovering Newton's First Law of Motion would be to classify it.

Given the concentration of power in the bureaucracy, its lack of coordination and accountability, its mistaken loyalties, secrecy, and sometimes illegality, one is led to wonder what constraints on the bureaucracy exist and whether or not they are adequate.

Bureaucracy and the Stewardship of Power

All modern governments require extensive bureaucracies. The problem in a democratic government is to keep the administrative system responsive and responsible to the elected officials and the public interest. Yet, as Peter Drucker has noted:

> There is no government today that can claim control of its bureaucracy and of its various agencies. Government agencies are all becoming autonomous, ends in themselves, and directed by their own desire for power, their own rationale, their own narrow vision rather than by national policy.[25]

While there is no doubt much truth in this assessment, it must be noted that some rather effective constraints on bureaucratic power do exist.

Most obvious are the institutional checks on bureaucratic power. Although it is true that no one can rule without a bureaucracy, it is equally true that the bureaucracy cannot rule alone. Congress not only creates, organizes, and funds bureaucratic agencies, but it regulates the Administration by virtue of these powers as well as its power to investigate. Yet, as we have seen, this control is incomplete because of the vastness and expertise of the bureaucracy.

Less extensive, but nevertheless significant, is the judicial check on bureaucratic action, which delimits the boundaries and constitutionality of bureaucratic power. Presidential control exists, but it is not far-reaching because of the fact that the bureaucracy is not simply part of the Executive or presidential branch of government.

---
[24] *Ibid.*
[25] Peter Drucker, *The Age of Discontinuity* (New York: Harper & Row, 1969), p. 226.

170   The Form of the American Republic

Although the Constitution makes the President the focal point of leadership in the American system, the separation of powers makes it virtually impossible for any branch of government to maintain continuous and effective control over the bureaucracy. Ironically, the specter of a powerful and relatively autonomous Fourth Branch of government in the form of a bureaucracy is the result of the Founders' fear of unrestrained power. For it is the very constitutional fragmentation of power designed by the Founders to prevent tyranny that has made the bureaucracy incompletely controlled by any of the traditional branches of government.

Yet, as Carl Friedrich has argued, it is unrealistic to think that the cure for the ills of bureaucracy can be overcome by the reduction of bureaucracy.[26] The complexities of modern government present societies with no alternative but to rely on the expertise of bureaucrats to deal with the problems of a nuclear-space age. The problem remains as Madison understood it in *Federalist* #51.

> If men were angels, no government would be necessary. If angels were to govern men, neither external nor internal controls on government would be necessary. In framing a government which is to be administered by men over men, the great difficulty lies in this: you must first enable the government to control the governed; and in the next place oblige it to control itself.[27]

Even though the institutional or external checks on bureaucratic power are inadequate, bureaucratic power cannot be reduced. Greater reliance upon the internal checks thus becomes paramount.

Of all the internal checks upon bureaucratic power, dependence upon the development of "a moral basis for bureaucratic power" or a commitment to the ideals of human dignity as embodied in the Declaration of Independence is wishful thinking or, at best, risky business. If bureaucrats forget their proper role as servant rather than master, something besides their political values must be relied upon for corrective action.

A more dependable base upon which to restrain power is self-interest. This was not unfamiliar to the Founders of this nation, for as they observed in *The Federalist Papers:* "the constant aim is to [provide] that the private interest of every individual may be a sentinel over the public rights."[28]

One such set of interests that helps to restrain a bureaucratic misuse of power is that of the news media. As the publication of the

[26] Carl Friedrich, "Public Policy and the Nature of Administrative Responsibility," *Public Policy* (Cambridge: Harvard University Press, 1940), pp. 3–24.
[27] Rossiter, *The Federalist Papers,* No. 51, p. 322
[28] *Ibid.*

Pentagon Papers showed, American journalists do not view themselves to be servants of the government as in a totalitarian state, but rather esteem themselves as the watchdogs of government. The *independence* of our newspapers ensures this. Because the news media comprises an interest group committed at times to goals incompatible with those of the government, there is no more effective instrument for providing the public with information that bureaucratic agencies would like to conceal.

A second check built upon the principle of self-interest and counteracting ambition with ambition is the competition for power among the bureaucratic agencies themselves, which makes them much more susceptible to control. As Francis E. Rourke has demonstrated, this prevents the bureaucracy from becoming a monolithic voice in government. His analysis of the competition within the armed forces is illustrative of the consequences of this principle.

> In the United States ... the various branches of the armed forces have long engaged in vigorous competition for financial support as well as jurisdiction over various weapons systems and combat missions. Somewhat unexpectedly, this competition has played an important role in facilitating civilian control over the military, primarily because it has forced each branch of the service into searching criticism of the defense policies advocated by the others, thus preventing the emergence of a monolithic military point of view on national security matters.[29]

The inconstant nature of power, too, sets limits to the political influence a bureaucratic agency may wield. As the use of "the Pill" becomes controversial, or the public apathy is jogged by the discovery of rat dung in food, or cancerous beef in the marketplace, the influence of the Food and Drug Administration may surge, only to ebb as the sense of crisis diminishes.

Though the aforementioned devices to secure a responsive and responsible bureaucracy no doubt are imperfect, one can expect the bureaucracy to continue its growth and enlarge its power in the future. In a very real sense, this is a consequence of the fact that government *is* responsive to the public demand for new services to help it cope with the complexities and needs of a rapidly changing technological society. The real task in dealing with the problems of bureaucracy is not to dismantle it, but rather to find realistic devices by which to harness it to the public interest. As Madison put it in *Federalist* #10, we must be sure that the cure is not worse than the disease.

---

[29] Francis E. Rourke, *Bureaucracy, Politics, and Public Policy* (Boston: Little, Brown, 1969), p. 144.

THE REPUBLICAN EXPERIMENT: RIGHTS IN CONFLICT

Just government is more than merely the correct arrangement of constitutional powers. Government may be described as "just" only when it secures man's unalienable rights as outlined in the Declaration of Independence, viz. "life, liberty and the pursuit of happiness" to all citizens whether they constitute a majority or a minority.

The Founders rightly understood the problem of blending majority rule with the protection of minority rights. Because only the majority may legitimately rule in a democratic republic, only that majority can cloak its violence and self-interest in the aura of law. But as Patrick Dollard observed in the *Anti-Federalist Papers*, "Lust of dominion is natural in every soil, and the love of power and superiority is as prevailing in the United States . . . as in any part of the earth." Thus the problem of maintaining a just government becomes: How can the majority be permitted to rule and yet be forced to respect the rights of people even though they are in a minority?

In Part II, we described the proper constitutional arrangement of power as the Founders conceived it, and its contemporary applicability. We noted that as novel as the Constitution was, it was deemed insufficient to check the "lust of dominion."

Equally important was a Bill of Rights that institutionalized man's political equality and limited the power of the majority. Although the Bill of Rights protects all men, the Founders expected that the minority would most need this protection. Otherwise the republic might become a "spectacle of turbulence and contention" that would be as short in its life as it had been violent in its death.

In many ways the Bill of Rights is the most important institutionalization of man's equality. However, these rights are not static. In a technological age, we can readily discern new rights and freedoms unknown before, but presumed to exist by our eighteenth-century Founders, i.e. the right to use or not to use contraceptive devices in birth control *(Griswold v. Connecticut)*, the right to privacy and protection against wiretapping.

In Part III, we will look at those rights in their contemporary meaning by examining the written Bill of Rights in its current interpretation as well as examining the "forgotten" Ninth Amendment to discern what new rights may lie on the horizon.

THE BILL OF RIGHTS:
The Right of Expression

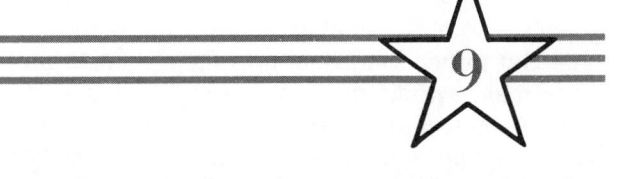

I disagree heartily with every word you say; but I will defend to the death your right to say it.
—*Voltaire*

It is difficult to imagine a more forceful commitment to the right of expression than this famous apocryphal statement by Voltaire. No doubt it may surprise many Americans to learn that Voltaire actually held little hope for freedom of speech in a democracy, especially in a large democratic nation of the proportions of the United States. After all, classical philosophy as well as historical experience had demonstrated that freedom and tolerance emerged only through education, which in turn was dependent upon the possession of a degree of wealth and leisure. (The word "school" is derived from the Greek *schole*, which means leisure.) Since it appeared that there existed a kind of natural scarcity of wealth and free time, society would divide into a minority of well-to-do and educated people and a majority of poor, uneducated, and intolerant people. For this reason, democracy was shunned by Voltaire and most of his contemporaries as being synonymous with "mobocracy." Had not an Athenian democracy killed Socrates for his insistence upon his right of expression? Voltaire shared the belief held by most intellectuals before the American experience that the best hope for freedom and tolerance lay in *despotisme éclairé*—an enlightened monarchy that understood the value of freedom of speech both to the individual expressing an opinion and to the larger society, which may not like what it hears. The essence of this was captured by John Stuart Mill in his book *On Liberty*.

> . . . the peculiar evil of silencing the expression of an opinion is, that it is robbing the human race: posterity as well as the existing generation. . . . If the opinion is right, they are deprived of the opportunity of exchanging error for truth: if wrong, they lose, what is almost as great a benefit, the clearer perception and livelier impression of truth, produced by its collision with error.[1]

On the whole the Founders of the United States accepted the validity of the classical view that rule by the uneducated was dangerous. But rather than rejecting majority rule and democracy, as some have maintained,[2] they attempted to make democracy safe for the world by creating an economically prosperous nation. Prosperity was seen as a necessary precondition to universal education and a democracy controlled and ruled by the educated. As Professor Leo Strauss has noted, "The difference between the classics and us with regard to democracy consists exclusively in a different estimate of the virtues of technology."[3] This is not to say, however, that the democracy of the United States has solved the problem of ensuring freedom of expression through universal education. What the Founders meant by education was the formation of character rather than institutional training, and there is a good deal of doubt as to whether the United States has achieved this kind of "universal education." Moreover, American education has characteristically placed heavy emphasis on producing "the cooperative fellow." This emphasis has fostered a "creeping conformism," which has not been conducive to the type of freedom of expression that *needs* protection in a democracy—the view of the unpopular minority.

A less dependable, though important, precaution was taken by

---

[1] John Stuart Mill, *On Liberty* (Chicago: Henry Regnery, 1955), p. 24.
[2] See Charles A. Beard, *An Economic Interpretation of the Constitution of the United States* (Free Press, 1913) and John Hope Franklin, "The Bitter Years of Slavery," *Life* (November 22, 1968), pp. 90–95. An opposing point of view may be found in Fred R. Mabbutt's "The Bitter Years of Slavery," University of Houston *Forum* (Fall–Winter, 1970), pp. 13–18.
[3] Leo Strauss, "What Is Political Philosophy," *The Journal of Politics* (August 1957), p. 366.

The Bill of Rights: The Right of Expression 177

the Founders by adding a Bill of Rights to the original Constitution. Here again, however, "universal education" overlaps in importance in the protection of rights, including the right of expression. After all a Bill of Rights is only parchment—as the Soviet Union's Bill of Rights demonstrates—and in a democratic nation this will mean no more than the public will allow it to mean. As Ivor Jennings put it, "Liberty is the consequence of an attitude of mind rather than of precise rules. . . . The source of our liberty is not in laws or institutions, but in the spirit of free people."[4]

History has demonstrated that "the spirit of free people" may vacillate, and that such a spirit is not a gift from heaven. In times of insecurity, freedom may easily be abandoned in favor of what *appears* to be safety. And as the American experience during the 1950s demonstrates, legitimate American fears regarding Communism may be parlayed into personal power for demagogues like Senator Joseph McCarthy. McCarthy fed the flames of insecurity so successfully that not only did the American people "suspend" a significant portion of the Bill of Rights, but even the President of the United States was not sure that his power and prestige were sufficient to directly confront the Senator.[5]

With the dawn of the atomic age and the introduction of missiles that can carry nuclear warheads to any part of the world in a matter of minutes, America's historic geographic security has yielded to a state of insecurity it has never known before. Whereas, at one time Americans could view their history as one of permanent peace with brief interruptions of war, many now view their present historical situation as one of permanent war—a "cold" war—with brief interruptions of peace. All of this cannot but help create a climate of insecurity that could easily erode the freedoms so long enshrined in the Bill of Rights. Benjamin Franklin cautioned the American people against this two centuries ago, when he said: "Those, who would give up essential liberty to purchase a little temporary safety deserve neither liberty nor safety."[6] Today, many scholars like Henry Steele

---

[4] Herbert Agar, *The Perils of Democracy* (New York: Capricorn Books, 1965), p. 23.
[5] Emmet John Hughes, *The Ordeal of Power* (New York: Atheneum, 1963), p. 92. Mr. Hughes, a personal advisor to President Eisenhower, records that "As for countering McCarthy, the President—along with Dulles—believed the most effective retort could never be a political or forensic thrust across the line between the Executive and Legislative. The Wisconsin senator's power would have to be rolled back gradually *within* the Legislature . . . until, at last, he would be left to stand alone."
[6] A convenient and readable edition of Benjamin Franklin's writings may be found in Frank Donovan, ed., *The Benjamin Franklin Papers* (New York: Dodd, Mead and Co., 1962).

Commager fear that Benjamin Franklin's warning has gone unheeded. Professor Commager asserts that

> Today we are busy doing what Franklin warned us against. Animated by impatience, anger, and fear, we are giving up essential liberties, not for safety, but for the appearance of safety. We are corroding due process and the rule of law not for order, but for the semblance of order. We will find that when we have given up liberty, we will not have safety, and that when we have given up justice, we will not have order.[7]

Whether or not Professor Commager's fears are justified will be left to the judgment of future historians. What may be appreciated now, however, is the accuracy of his understanding that a Bill of Rights is meaningless without the popular support of an informed American people. The fundamental rights first enunciated in the Declaration of Independence acquired "no greater moral sanctity" by being made part of a Bill of Rights, but, as Alpheus Mason has noted, "individuals could thereafter look to the courts for their protection. Rights formerly natural became civil."[8]

The Bill of Rights and Sociological Jurisprudence

In a masterful analysis of the Bill of Rights, one of America's foremost judges, Judge Learned Hand, undermines the popular misconception that the Bill of Rights is the first ten amendments to the Constitution. As he correctly notes, the Bill of Rights is "the first eight and the Fourteenth amendments of the Constitution of the United States."[9] The Ninth and Tenth Amendments do not list or present a bill of rights that must be respected by government. The Fourteenth Amendment is included as part of the Bill of Rights because it has been the vehicle by which the Supreme Court has applied these rights to the state level of government, a level not originally affected by the first eight amendments. The Bill of Rights, Judge Hand continues, was

> ... generally regarded as embodying the same political postulates that had been foreshadowed though not fully articulated in the exordium of the Declaration of Independence: "self-evident" and "unalienable rights" with which all men "are endowed by their Creator" and among which are "life, liberty, and the pursuit of happiness."[10]

[7] Henry Steele Commager, "Is Freedom Dying," *Look* (July 14, 1970), p. 16.
[8] Alpheus Mason, *The Supreme Court: Palladium of Freedom* (Ann Arbor, Michigan: University of Michigan Press, 1962), p. 46.
[9] Learned Hand, *The Bill of Rights* (New York: Atheneum, 1968), p. 1. Other rights are sprinkled throughout the original body of the Constitution as well. See Robert Allen Rutland, *The Birth of the Bill of Rights, 1776-1791* (New York: Collier Books, 1962).
[10] *Ibid.*, pp. 1-2.

When articulating these rights, the Founders wisely limited their work to enunciating the rights to be protected and left the definition and scope of those rights to the judgment of future American generations. As a document the Bill of Rights is a product of the eighteenth century, but as *law* it "derives all its force from the people of the United States of *this day and hour.*"[11]

Frequently Americans have regarded freedom as a gift of the eighteenth-century American. In a sense, this is true. However, the preservation of this gift depends on our own effort, and the continual reassessment and interpretation of freedom in the context of the contemporary American needs. As Edward S. Corwin put it:

> The proper point of view from which to approach the task of interpreting the Constitution is that of regarding it as a living statute, palpitating with the purpose of the hour, reenacted with every waking breath of the American people. . . .[12]

This process of interpreting rights in light of the needs and desires of contemporary America—a philosophy of law known as sociological jurisprudence—was first formally introduced to the Supreme Court in 1908, when Louis Brandeis submitted his famous brief to demonstrate the need to uphold an Oregon law that prohibited women from working more than ten hours a day in factories and laundries.[13] This brief, three pages of which were statements of traditional legal points, contained 113 pages devoted to the presentation of facts and statistics to demonstrate that Oregon needed to protect overworked women because they often fell ill, turned to drink, gave birth to weak or sickly children, and then neglected them.

The unanimous acceptance of the validity of the philosophy of sociological jurisprudence by the Supreme Court in this case (*Muller v. Oregon*) gradually paved the way to make it the main business of the judiciary to adjust the Constitution to the advancing needs of the time. In other words, the meaning of the Constitution and the rights of the American people are not static, but are elastically adapting to the changing experiences of the day. Good law is not a finished thing, but always in the making—adjusting and changing according to the needs of each particular age. Oliver Wendell Holmes captured the essence of sociological jurisprudence when he concluded, "Our Constitution . . . is an experiment as all life is an experiment."

---

[11] Edward S. Corwin, "Constitution v. Constitutional Theory," *American Political Science Review*, Vol. 19 (May 1925), p. 290.
[12] Benjamin N. Cardozo, *The Nature of the Judicial Process* (New Haven, Conn.: Yale University Press, 1921), p. 71.
[13] Muller v. Oregon, 208 U.S. 412 (1908).

The Right of Expression: Seditious Speech

With this understanding it is now possible to consider the most fundamental of American freedoms, the freedom upon which the entire American political process is based, namely freedom of speech and press. This freedom is enshrined in the First Amendment, which reads in part: "Congress shall make no law . . . abridging the freedom of speech, or of the press." We know that this amendment protects freedom of spech, but what *is* speech? And what are the limits of it?

Is David Paul O'Brien's quiet burning of his draft card in protest against the war in Vietnam a *new* form of speech protected by the First Amendment?[14] Topless-bottomless dancers during the 1970s have claimed that their work was protected from police interference because it was a form of expression protected by the First Amendment—a form of expression, it might be added, that clearly *was* saying something!

Because nothing is stable, because times change, the Supreme Court, through experience and study, but with few guidelines, must fill in the answers to these questions. The Court acts as a *legislator,* filling in the current meaning to the great principles uttered in 1791. As Justice Cardozo noted, however, "the limits for the judge are narrower [than for the legislature]. He legislates only between gaps. He fills the open spaces in the law."[15] Thus, the Court has ruled that draft-card burning is not a new form of "symbolic speech," although a silent protest against government policy by the wearing of black armbands is.[16]

Life is not orderly, however. Frequently rights deemed desirable are in conflict with each other, and, instead of life being a bowl of cherries, it may deteriorate to being one of pits. A dramatic case in point is the story of Dr. Sam Sheppard, a Cleveland osteopath, who was convicted by a jury of bludgeoning his wife to death. Convicted in an atmosphere termed by the Supreme Court as a "Roman holiday" for the news media, Sheppard spent twelve years in an Ohio penitentiary fighting off roaches and homosexual attacks before the Supreme Court reversed the conviction on the grounds that his trial had been

---

[14] United States v. O'Brien, 391 U.S. 367 (1968). Chief Justice Warren, writing the majority opinion for the Court, stated: "We cannot accept the view that an apparently limitless variety of conduct can be labeled speech whenever the person engaging in the conduct intends thereby to express an idea."
[15] Cardozo, *op. cit.,* p. 113.
[16] Tinker v. Des Moines School District *et al,* 393 U.S. 503 (1969).

so influenced by "massive, pervasive, and prejudicial publicity," that Sheppard had been denied his right to a fair trial.[17]

Thus, the right of the Cleveland *Plain Dealer,* Cleveland *News,* and Cleveland *Press* to exercise their freedom of speech and press denied to Dr. Sheppard his right to an impartial and fair trial by jury. Rights are not absolute. One man's rights leave off where another man's begin. Much of the work of the Court is concerned with balancing such individual rights in conflict, as well as balancing the *freedom of the individual* against the *security of the state.* It is no accident that the balance—the scale—is the emblem of justice in the United States.

The interpretation of free speech in the United States properly begins, according to Robert G. McCloskey in *The American Supreme Court,* in 1919 when the Court was called upon to construe security legislation passed during World War I in the light of the First Amendment right to freedom of speech.

A few months after Congress declared war on Germany in April 1917, it passed an Espionage Act, which punished attempts to interfere with military enlistment or discipline in the armed forces. In the next year a Sedition Act was passed that was "so broadly worded that almost any critical comment on the war or the government might incur a fine of $10,000, or twenty years in prison, or both." [18]

Speech that is critical of the government is particularly valuable and worth protecting. Without it, there can be no orderly change in government. After all, Mr. Nixon did not gain his office in 1968 by traveling about the country praising the policies of the government. Justice William O. Douglas has summed up the reasons why this form of speech must be maintained:

> The vitality of civil and political institutions in our society depends on free discussion . . . it is only through free debate and free exchange of ideas that government remains responsive to the will of the people and peaceful change is effected. The right to speak freely and to promote diversity of ideas and programs is therefore one of the chief distinctions that sets us apart from totalitarian regimes.[19]

Because it is difficult to tell legitimate criticism of the government from lies, the Court has generally subscribed to the belief that the

---

[17] Sheppard v. Maxwell, 384 U.S. 333 (1966). A vivid narrative of Sheppard's ordeal may be found in his autobiography, *Endure and Conquer* (Cleveland: World, 1966).
[18] The Foundation of the Federal Bar Association, *Equal Justice Under Law* (Washington, D.C.: The Foundation of the Federal Bar Association, 1965), p. 67.
[19] Terminiello v. Chicago, 337 U.S. 1 (1949).

best remedy for unpopular speech is not censorship, but rather *more speech*. In other words, let the government answer its critics. Yet, there are certain limits to any freedom and the Court felt that Charles T. Schenck had exceeded them when he mailed circulars to drafted men during World War I urging them not to submit to conscription.

Speaking for a unanimous Court, Oliver Wendell Holmes wrote that "in many places and in ordinary times" Schenck would have been within his constitutional right. But the Bill of Rights does not protect speech that creates a "clear and present danger" of "evils that Congress has a right to prevent." Schenck spent six months in jail and the Supreme Court had defined the scope of freedom of speech for the first time.

The significance of this decision is not so much the "clear and present danger" formula itself. It is not an absolute and therefore changes to meet the needs of the changing times. Indeed, Mr. Holmes himself had little respect for formulization and more than once acknowledged that "No generalization is wholly true, not even this one." Rather the significance of this case rests upon the recognition of the Court that the broad principles of the Constitution must be enunciated. As Justice Benjamin N. Cardozo observed in *The Nature of the Judicial Process:*

> It is the function of our courts . . . to keep the doctrines up to date with the *mores* by continual restatement and by giving them a continually new content. This is judicial legislation, and the judge legislates at his peril. Nevertheless, it is the necessity and duty of such legislation that gives to judicial office its highest honor.[20]

Later, in *Gitlow v. New York* (1925), the Court ruled that freedom of speech and press, subject to its continuing interpretation, could not be abridged by *state* governments. Until this time states were not bound by the First Amendment. The clear language of the Bill of Rights had been to prohibit *Congress* (*i.e.* the national government) from interference with this right. However, the Fourteenth Amendment, which was passed three-quarters of a century later, addresses itself to the state governments rather than the national, and says that no state may deprive any person of "life, liberty, or property, without due process of law." Speaking for the Court in the *Gitlow* case, Justice Sanford made a decision of paramount significance. He declared that "freedom of speech and of the press—which are protected by the First Amendment from abridgment by Congress—are among the fundamental personal rights and 'liberties' protected by the due-process

[20] Cardozo, *op. cit.*

clause of the Fourteenth Amendment from impairment by the States."[21]

Through what has come to be known as the *doctrine of incorporation,* the Supreme Court has assumed that most of the liberties or rights enunciated in the Bill of Rights are contained or incorporated into the word "liberty" in the Fourteenth Amendment and thus apply to *both* the state and the national governments.

The incorporation, however, has not been total, for the Court adopted what is known as the *Palko test,* which is a doctrine of selective incorporation.[22] The test of incorporation has been to include only those rights that are "of the very essence of a scheme of ordered liberty" or are related to "a principle of justice so rooted in the traditions and conscience of our people as to be ranked as fundamental."[23] Thus, the Court has not deemed fundamental the right to bear arms, security against the quartering of troops in private homes, grand jury indictments for serious crimes, the guarantee against double jeopardy, and the guarantee of trial by jury in civil cases involving more than a $20 settlement.

Gitlow won his point that states had to refrain from interference with freedom of speech, but he nonetheless went to jail for three years for violating New York's criminal anarchy law. The Court, elaborating on the "clear" test handed down in the *Schenck* case, stated its *bad-tendency doctrine,* which held that the government did not have to allow speech that had a tendency to produce a *substantive* evil. Gitlow's publication of his "Left Wing Manifesto" calling workers to rise against capitalism was deemed by a majority on the Court as "a direct incitement." Holmes dissented calmly, saying "Every idea is an incitement." Many constitutional scholars have felt since that the Court overreacted to the "Red Scare" of the 1920s and that Gitlow's speech did not present a "clear and present danger" that had a tendency toward producing a "substantive evil" to the larger society. Indeed, one reader of his "Left Wing Manifesto" said:

> Any agitator who read these thirty-four pages to a mob would not stir them to violence, except possibly against himself.[24]

During the 1950s the concern of most Americans shifted to the cold war that developed between the Soviet Union and the United States. This was an age of fear—the Korean War had broken out and

---

[21] Gitlow v. New York, 268 U.S. 652 (1925).
[22] Palko v. Connecticut, 302 U.S. 319 (1937).
[23] *Ibid.*
[24] *Equal Justice Under Law,* p. 68.

there were revelations about Alger Hiss and Communists infiltrating the State Department. It was not an easy time for the Court to decide questions of free expression against national security.

In 1951 Eugene Dennis and ten other members of the Communist Party were convicted for violating the Smith Act, which made it a crime to teach or advocate the overthrow of the government by force or violence.

Every society needs protection against the overthrow of government by force. The right of revolution can never be a constitutional right and can exist only as a natural right. Yet, where does legitimate political dissent end and sedition begin? Although the Court has held as a rule that limitation of speech is allowable only when national security is quite clearly threatened, it went as far as it has ever gone in setting those limits in *Dennis v. U.S.*

Although the defendants were not charged with actually advocating to overthrow the government, the Supreme Court upheld their convictions, explaining that the mere advocacy of overthrow of the government as an abstract doctrine is protected speech; however, advocacy aimed at facilitating violence is not protected and Dennis and the others were guilty of the latter. Accepting the decision of Appellate Court Judge Learned Hand, the Supreme Court held that before speech may be abridged it must consider "whether the gravity of the evil, discounted by its probability" warranted it. In other words, speech must not only present a "clear and present danger" that is substantial, but the danger must be immediate.

Clearly, one can see sociological jurisprudence at work here as the Supreme Court interpreted the First Amendment in light of what it perceived to be the needs of the time. Yet, this does not mean that its perceptions will necessarily coincide with reality. Again, with the hindsight of a Monday-morning quarterback, some scholars have felt that the Court did precisely what it warned against, i.e. judge an abstract doctrine rather than consider the particular evidence of the particular case. In view of the actual strength of the Soviet Union, which had lost almost half of its male population as a result of World War II, some scholars like Isaac Deutscher have felt that the United States overreacted with "irrational panic" to the Red Scare of the 1950s.[25]

In later cases, the Supreme Court returned to quieter times and decided several cases involving freedom of expression in *favor* of

---

[25] Isaac Deutscher, "Myths of the Cold War," in David Horowitz, ed., *Containment and Revolution* (Boston: Beacon Press, 1967), pp. 13–26.

The Bill of Rights: The Right of Expression   185

Communist litigants.[26] At this point, one may wonder why it should even be necessary to consider the constitutional rights of Americans who have subscribed to the doctrines of Communism. Why not just send them packing to the penitentiary? In protecting the speech of Communists in the *Yates* case (1957) and the *Scales* case (1961), had the Court become feebleminded?

Herein lies one of the greatest dangers for a democratic society. Society must protect itself from seditious conspiracies, but it is all too easy for government officials to silence their political opponents by labeling their criticism as seditious. Many of the early critics of the government's war policies in Vietnam did not love their country less by warning it that this war was not in the best interests of the United States—that its $1.5 billion-a-month cost was inflationary; that the deferring of domestic reforms because of the cost of the war was allowing American cities to decay and creating increased tension between black and white Americans; that it had cost 50,000 young people their lives and alienated a large portion of America's young and old; that it was seriously straining America's foreign relations with its traditional allies in Europe; and that it "clouded the hope, once mildly promising, of progress toward a detenté with the Soviet Union."[27] Yet, these people were denounced for their unpopular speech by government officials like H. R. Halderman who stated that such speech was giving "aid and comfort" to Ho Chi Minh and his Communist followers.

The distinction between legitimate criticism of government policies and sedition is not always clear, especially in times of emotion and fear. If the government sits idly by while extremists plot and advocate its overthrow, it may be destroyed and freedom lost. This certainly was one of the serious mistakes made by Weimar officials in Germany when Hitler was making his bid for power. On the other hand, if the government overreacts it may commit suicide by abridging freedom. Indeed, there is some evidence to indicate that one of the strategies of the Communist Party has been to help the United States along the road to suicide.[28]

Moreover, overreaction may abridge legitimate and useful criticism, thereby denying the government and its citizens the opportunity

[26] Pennsylvania v. Nelson, 350 U.S. 497 (1956); Yates v. United States, 354 U.S. 298 (1957); Scales v. United States, 367 U.S. 203 (1961).
[27] Arthur M. Schlesinger, Jr., *The Bitter Heritage* (New York: Fawcett Crest Book, 1967), pp. 63–69. A dramatic example of this occurred in Georgia when the State Legislature refused to give Julian Bond his seat because of his criticism of the war in Vietnam.
[28] This strategy has been well developed in the writings of Regis Debray and Che Gueverra.

to learn and change a foolish course of action. One may learn from personal experience or by watching and listening to others. Learning by experience is often a school of hard knocks, whereas listening and watching, while not necessarily comfortable, can be profitable and less dangerous. As Mark Twain put it:

> We should be careful to get out of an experience only the wisdom that is in it—and stop there; lest we be like the cat that sits down on a hot stove-lid. She will never sit down on a hot stove-lid again—and that is well; but also she may never sit down on a cold one anymore.

In protecting the speech of Communists, the Court was paying the *price* of freedom, which requires that unpopular as well as popular expression be tolerated. To silence Communists at the price of abridging freedom of expression is too high a cost to bear. It should be remembered that the only type of speech that will need the protection of the First Amendment *is* unpopular speech. Justice Robert Jackson summed it up when he explained: "The very purpose of a Bill of Rights was to withdraw certain subjects from the vicissitudes of political controversy, to place them beyond the reach of majorities and officials. . . ."[29] To make "Democracy Safe for the World," to combine majority rule with respect for the rights of the minority, has been the principle aim of American political life. No one more eloquently stated this principle than did Thomas Jefferson in his first inaugural address, when he said:

> All, too, will bear in mind this sacred principle, that though the will of the majority is in all cases to prevail, that will to be rightful must be reasonable; that the minority possess their equal rights, which equal law must protect, and to violate would be oppression.

Here, at least, was one safeguard to alleviate Voltaire's fear of "mobocracy."

Yet, even freedom of expression is not an absolute right. As Holmes observed, "The most stringent protection of free speech would not protect a man in falsely shouting fire in a theatre and causing a panic."[30] The Court has the difficult responsibility of deciding what is to be gained or lost by the regulation of expression. With few guidelines, it must decide how much freedom Americans should be willing to give up in order to have security. "Security," Herbert Agar has said, "in any form, is an enemy of freedom." Yet, we must learn to live with this enemy, "but we should watch him always with a sturdy

---
[29] West Virginia State Board of Education v. Barnette, 319 U.S. 624 (1943).
[30] Schenk v. United States, 247 U.S. 47 (1919).

distrust . . ."[31] The virtue of tolerance can endanger a democracy, and if democracy is to endure, freedom must be prevented from turning sour.

Are we to extend the full toleration of our democracy to those who are bent on replacing constitutional government with tryanny? Since regimentation is a great misfortune, at what point do we tell those who are planning to regiment us to stop talking? At what point should the Weimar Republic have told the Nazis to stop?[32]

The answer to this question is usually broken up from its heroic proportions into bits and pieces in cases like *Schenk, Gitlow,* and *Dennis*. During the postwar period, freedom of speech has also been challenged in the name of "security," by the withholding of information by the government. By withholding facts that are not essential to the security of the nation, the government not only stifles creative dissent, but also denies the citizen the opportunity to vote intelligently. In denying the Nixon Administration the right to restrain the publication of the *Pentagon Papers,* a set of documents which revealed the deception and bureaucratic flimflam involved in the conduct of the war in Vietnam, Justice Black emphasized that

> The word "security" is a broad, vague generality whose contours should not be invoked to abrogate the fundamental law embodied in the First Amendment. The guarding of military and diplomatic secrets at the expense of informed representative government provides no real security for our Republic.[33]

The Split-Level Theory of Speech: Libel, Slander, Obscenity, and Fighting Words

The Court has protected the right of an individual to say something—even something false—as long as what is said does not tend toward incitement to the violent overthrow of the government. A major exception to this developed in the 1950s. Beginning with *Beauharnais v. Illinois,* the Supreme Court ruled that there was a second level of speech, a level completely unprotected by the First Amendment, which included libel, slander, obscenity, and "fighting words."

During the 1930s and 1940s the Nazis had made effective use of systematic defamation and character assassination. These lies,

[31] Agar, *op. cit.,* p. 24.
[32] *Ibid.,* p. 25.
[33] *U.S. Law Week* (June 29, 1971), Section 4.

whether in printed form (libel) or spoken form (slander), had contributed to the massacre of over 6 million Jews in German concentration camps like Dachau and Buchenwald. Many states in the United States reacted to these new circumstances by passing criminal libel laws making it a crime to intentionally defame the character of a race or religion through lies. Illinois was one of the states that adopted a group libel law.

Joseph Beauharnais, a white bigot (there is a substantial difference between defamation of character by truth and by lies or libel), protested against Negroes moving into his all-white community and in the course of his protest defamed the Negroes as a race. Following his conviction in Illinois, he appealed to the Supreme Court to reverse the decision, arguing that his speech may or may not have been popular, but it did not present a "clear and present danger," which was "imminent."

The Court found it difficult to disagree with Beauharnais, but upheld his conviction anyway, insisting that his statement was libelous and not protected by the First Amendment; therefore it was unaffected by the "clear and present danger" test. Justice William O. Douglas dissented, fearing that the *Beauharnais* decision represented "an ominous and alarming trend" for libel can be broadly defined and has historically been a popular device of government officials to prevent criticism and discussion of public issues. One need only recall the famous Zenger trial of 1734 to understand Mr. Douglas' concern, for in that case Governor Cosby of New York, laying down the English principle, "the greater the truth the greater the libel" attempted to silence criticism of his administration. In winning a verdict of "not guilty," Zenger offered the jury the then strange and audacious defense that his speech was protected *because* it was the truth! This landmark decision was subsequently described by Gouverneur Morris as "the morning star of that liberty which subsequently revolutionized America."[34]

Justice Douglas' fear was not without basis as *The New York Times v. Sullivan* (1964) case was to demonstrate. In March 1960 *The New York Times* carried a full-page advertisement on the racial struggle in Montgomery, Alabama and nonviolent demonstrations at a nearby Negro college. The ad read in part:

> In Montgomery, Alabama, after students sang "My Country, 'Tis of Thee" on the State Capitol steps, their leaders were expelled from school, and truckloads of police armed with shotguns and tear-gas

[34] New York Times v. Sullivan, 376 U.S. 254 (1964).

ringed the Alabama State College Campus. When the entire student body protested to state authorities by refusing to reregister, their dining hall was padlocked in an attempt to starve them into submission.

Toward the end of the ad, reference was made to the treatment of Dr. Martin Luther King by the Alabama authorities and by implication Montgomery's police commissioner, L. B. Sullivan.

> Again and again the Southern violators have answered Dr. King's peaceful protests with intimidation and violence. They have bombed his home almost killing his wife and child. They have assaulted his person. They have arrested him seven times—for "speeding," "loitering," and similar "offenses." And now they have charged him with "perjury"—a *felony* under which they could imprison him for ten years . . .[35]

Even though Sullivan was not even mentioned by name in the ad, he claimed that he had been libeled and sued for damages. In collecting damages, the plaintiff must show that the libelous or slanderous speech hurt him in the amount being asked for—and that the speech was delivered with malice. As this is very difficult to do, many lawyers will advise against a suit, noting that libel is like having mud thrown upon your suit. If you try to wipe it off while it is wet and fresh, you will only spread it further. It is better to let time set in to let it dry and then flick it off. Moreover, as Louis Nizer notes, "It is customary for defendants in a libel suit to be contrite" and "to publish some retraction, thus diminishing damages. That is why 6-cent verdicts have so often occurred in libel actions."[36]

When Sullivan demanded a retraction from *The New York Times,* the newspaper responded by saying to Sullivan that they did not know why he felt the ad referred to him. Sullivan then sued *The New York Times* for $500,000 in the Alabama courts—and he received it. It should be noted at this point that there *was* some falsity in the ad, although it was of a minor nature. For example, the Negro students did not sing "My Country, 'Tis of Thee" as stated, but rather sang The National Anthem. Martin Luther King had been arrested four times, not seven, and "not the entire student body, but most of it, had protested the expulsion, not by refusing to register, but by boycotting classes."[37]

If the Supreme Court followed *stare decisis* or precedent, it would appear that the libeler, in this case *The New York Times,* would have

---
[35] *Ibid.*
[36] Louis Nizer, *My Life In Court* (New York: Pyramid, 1961), p. 23.
[37] *N.Y. Times v. Sullivan.*

to pay the penalty. But it was clearly not in the interest of justice nor consistent with the mood of the nation to uphold the claim of Police Commissioner Sullivan.

The Court reversed the judgment without overruling the *Beauharnais* decision, but it significantly modified it. It argued that "debate on public issues should be uninhibited, robust and wide-open, and . . . may well include vehement . . . attacks on government officials." In other words, the speech of *The New York Times* was privileged, even though it contained some falsity, because Sullivan represented the State of Alabama and criticism of the government must be "wide-open" in a free society. In consolation to Sullivan, one might recall the advice given to politicians and government employees by President Truman: "If the kitchen's hot, get out."[38]

Not only is libel outside the protection of the First Amendment, but so are fighting words and obscenity. Fighting words represent a particularly interesting category of speech. What are fighting words? To the man who has no more backbone than a chocolate eclair, few words could induce him to fight. To another person with a more fiery temper, almost anything might be deemed a fighting word, and thus may be made illegal by the various levels of government. To this date no clear definition of fighting words has been given by the Supreme Court, but they are illegal, or at least unprotected by the First Amendment.

Although the punishment of sedition, libel, and fighting words has been justified on the ground that some tangible harm to society may result, there has been no agreement that reading pornography or watching stag films will have such an effect. Indeed, some sociologists have argued that such material may even be healthy for society in that it may prevent a sex deviate from committing his crime by affording to him the opportunity to sublimate his sexual desires by reading pornography or watching "girly" movies. Others have alleged that carving a turkey before the eyes of a starving man will not satiate his appetite. When such material is suppressed, it is usually because many people find it offensive and do not want their children to be exposed to it.

Yet what is obscenity? State laws have banned its publication, sale, or possession, and the national government has banned its

---

[38] The Court has, however, set some limits to the heat in the kitchen. During the 1964 presidential election, Ralph Ginzburg's libelous statements asserting that Barry Goldwater had been judged insane by a large number of psychiatrists cost him $75,000 as "actual malice" was shown. In Curtis Publishing Company v. Butts, 18 L.Ed. 2d 1094 (1967) the ruling was applied to "public figures" like policemen not holding elective office.

shipment in the mails. Violation of these laws may result in a fine and/or imprisonment for the violator, so a definition of obscenity is more than merely an academic question.

The Court reluctantly addressed itself to this question in *Roth v. United States* (1957). Rejecting the British rule of picking out isolated passages of a book and testing it with the most susceptible people in the community, the Court argued that the test must apply to the work as a whole. Obscenity must be a *dominant theme,* in respect to the *average man* in the community, that appeals to his *prurient interest*[39] . . . that is, an "itching" for lust or a shameful interest in sex. Black and Douglas, as usual, dissented, arguing that such material was utterly worthless and therefore protected since it did not present a clear and present danger.

At this point, the obscenity test rested upon the "average man" or "community standards" test. And since the "average man" differed greatly from a Greenwich Village or a Sunset Strip, California setting to a more conservative rural-town setting like Shoshone, Idaho, the definition of obscenity also varied from community to community. In one city *Playboy* might be forbidden, but in other cities it might not only be legal, but considered tame material compared to the rest of the reading or viewing fare.

Several years later, the Court once again applied the test of the *Roth* case, but added that "community standards" meant *national,* not local, standards.[40] Needless to say, this decision could make Greenwich Village or Shoshone, Idaho very unhappy, for the "national average man"—whatever that may be—may not fit either type of community. This case also tried to deal with the sticky question of what to do with such classics as Boccaccio's *Decameron* or Aristophanes' *Lysistrata,* which might appeal to the prurient interest of the average man in some communities.

Do we want to rip out of the marketplace of ideas such works that are considered to be major records of man's history? Obviously not. So the Court embroidered on its "dominant theme" test, noting that a work to be considered obscene had to be "utterly without social importance," thus protecting such classics as the *Decameron* and *Lysistrata,* which had "social importance."

But what if this author wrote an illustrated volume of naked men and women cavorting together in various sexual acts? Would this not have "social importance" as long as the American flag was in the background teaching the values of patriotism?

[39] "Prurient" is defined as "itching; longing; uneasy with desire or longing."
[40] Jacobellis v. Ohio, 378 U.S. 184 (1964).

The "social importance" test did not help much. Justice Potter Stewart summed up the frustration of the Court when he admitted in *Jacobellis v. Ohio* (1964) that the First Amendment forbids "hard core pornography," that he could not define it, "but I know it when I see it." The problem is, of course, that it doesn't help the individual citizen to know that Justice Stewart knows it when he sees it. The individual must know it when *he* sees it or run the risk of fine and/or imprisonment.

Until the late 1960s all of this had been the subject of skits in Rowan and Martin's *Laugh-In* showing the "nine old men" retiring for the evening to view stag films or to read shelves of dirty books —evidence in the current obscenity cases or smug scholarly treatises ridiculing Potter Stewart's "I know it when I see it" logic. However, in 1966, the Court delivered a decision in *Ginzburg v. United States* that stopped the laughter and jogged the security of the complacent.

In the *Ginzburg* case, the Supreme Court affirmed the conviction of Ralph Ginzburg, who was sentenced to five years in a federal penitentiary and fined $28,000 for mailing "obscene" materials like *The Housewife's Handbook on Selective Promiscuity* from places with such suggestive postmarks as Intercourse, Pennsylvania and Middlesex, New Jersey. The Court, in convicting Ginzburg, added a stiff new rule for obscenity cases that may make the conduct of the publisher more important than the content of his publication. Justice William J. Brennan, speaking for the Court, said that

> Where the purveyor's sole emphasis is on the sexually provocative aspects of his publication, that fact may be decisive in the determination of obscenity.[41]

In other words, obscenity may not depend solely on the content of the publication; it may be obscene if it is advertised in such a manner as to cause "titillation" or "excite pleasurably."

Since the *Ginzburg* decision made it possible to prosecute someone for pornography offenses without necessarily proving that the publication met the test of obscenity, a number of well-known works, including the *Bible,* have been challenged for being advertised for "titillation" rather than "intellectual content." Indeed, in 1971 the Post Office ordered the Nashville Bible House to stop sending advertisements for its Family Heritage Bible to a New Yorker who said that they aroused him sexually. From this, one is led to wonder what literature may not be obscene and therefore removed from the marketplace by the government?

[41] Ginzburg v. United States, 383 U.S. 463 (1966).

The Bill of Rights: The Right of Expression   193

In June 1973, the four Nixon appointees joined by Byron White held that while the aforementioned guidelines to measure obscenity were still valid the measurer (judge or jury) could rely on the application of "contemporary community standards" to the disputed material.[42]

While materials involving sex have been removed from the mail for depraving the morals of persons, little governmental or public concern over the effects of the "literature of violence" on the morals or behavior of persons has been demonstrated, at least until the assassinations of President Kennedy, Senator Robert Kennedy, and the Reverend Martin Luther King.

When Postmaster Summerfield removed Aristophanes' *Lysistrata* (written in the fifth century B.C.) from the mail in 1958 for its "depravity," Marya Mannes of the *New York Herald Tribune* raised this poetic question:

> Is your libido, normal mite,
> Roused by the birds and bees?
> If so, Mr. Summerfield is right
> To ban Aristophanes.
>
> For pleasure and wit in amorous play
> Are depraving and profane,
> But never the bloody kill-a-day
> On the pages of Spillane.
>
> Censor the healthy urge of man
> Especially if it's fun,
> But never stop an American
> From making love with a gun.

---

[42] *Miller v. California; Paris Adult Theater # 1 v. Slayton; U.S. v. Orito; Kaplan v. California; U.S. v. 12-200 ft. Reels of Super 8 Millimeter Film;* see *U.S. Law Week*, Vol. 41, p. 4925.

THE TIDES OF JUSTICE:
Due Process of Law

10

The streets of our country are in turmoil. The universities are filled with students rebelling and rioting. Communities are seeking to destroy our country. Russia is threatening us with her might and the Republic is in danger. Yes, danger from within and from without. We need law and order. Yes, without law and order our nation cannot survive. Elect us and we shall restore law and order.

Campaign rhetoric from the 1972 presidential elections? No, a campaign promise made by Adolph Hitler in Hamburg, Germany, during the 1932 elections.[1] Hitler was elected and did keep his pledge to restore law and order. The expansion of German jails into Nazi concentration camps attests to that. For nondemocratic nations, freedom is considered unessential, divisive of national unity, and even a threat to national security. Thus authoritarian governments like Nazi Germany's often institute very efficient law enforcement agencies like the Gestapo, which condemn hundreds of innocent people to jail or the

[1] Saul D. Alinsky, "The Double Revolution," *Civil Rights Digest* (Spring 1971), p. 32.

firing squad if that is what it takes to maintain law and order. No genius is required to acquire law and order by such means. Any police state can do it.

However, for a democratic society, the task is not *merely* to maintain law and order, but rather to maintain it *while* still preserving the freedom and dignity of the individual citizen. Freedom *and* security must be balanced in such a way so as to provide the individual with the maximum amount of both.

Yet this is easier said than done. Rarely is the delicate balance between freedom and security in perfect equilibrium. In time of fear, there is an understandable, yet dangerous, tendency for people to give up freedom for security. It is at just such a time that the balance between freedom and security may radically tilt toward security at any cost.

Many Americans are understandably concerned about their domestic security. Crime rates *have* risen in the past decade. Data concerning "offenses against persons" alone show a 106% increase from 1960 to 1968, and these crimes include the ones that frighten Americans the most: murder, rape, robbery, and aggravated assault.[2] That fear and anger over the law and order issue had rubbed raw the electoral nerve of America was revealed by the Gallup Poll in the spring of 1968. Mr. Gallup indicated that for the first time since he had started polling, the issue of "crime" was ranked by American voters as "the most important domestic problem" in America today.[3]

People afraid of being mugged, disgusted with the student seizure of college buildings, and alarmed over the violence and looting that exploded during the long hot summers of the mid-1960s in Watts, Newark, and Detroit have not been reluctant to place a good deal of the blame on the Warren Court for "coddling criminals" and even on such parts of the Bill of Rights as the Fifth Amendment for providing legal loopholes through which wily criminals can escape. Indeed, as Henry Steele Commager has noted, "The evidence of public opinion is persuasive that a substantial part of the American people no longer know or cherish the Bill of Rights."[4] They are, it would appear, quite prepared to short-circuit the Bill of Rights and use whatever *means* it takes to restore law and order. The danger here is that improper means can invalidate a legitimate *end* as Stalin proved during the 1930s when he tried to industrialize the Soviet Union by means of

[2] Richard M. Scammon and Ben J. Wattenberg, *The Real Majority* (New York: Coward, McCann & Geoghegan, 1971), p. 40.
[3] *Ibid.*, p. 17.
[4] Henry Steele Commager, "Is Freedom Dying In America?," *Look* (July 14, 1970), p. 17.

slave-labor camps. Similarly, Americans could restore law and order by erecting a police state. But the cure for the abscess of crime would certainly be worse than the disease.

Critics of the Bill of Rights are quite correct in their charge that it precludes "efficient law" enforcement. It does not assist the federal or state governments in obtaining easy convictions. Far from it, that part of the Constitution places one obstacle after another in the path of government to prevent easy conviction. Clearly the government might obtain more convictions if it could invade the privacy of the home without search warrants, torture to obtain confessions, eliminate trial by jury, and prohibit the accused person from the right to counsel who, after all, considerably slow up the process of law enforcement by their unending motions and objections. No doubt a few criminals manage to evade justice because of the Bill of Rights. But, so are a good many innocent people spared false imprisonment or even execution by an overzealous government.

The dilemma of the 1780s as well as of the 1970s is to maintain a regime *strong enough* to maintain law and order, yet *not so strong* as to threaten individual liberty. After creating that strong regime, Madison and the Founders attempted to control it by adding a Bill of Rights. They understood that the ultimate exertion of governmental power against an individual would occur when a person was charged with criminal wrongdoing.

In such criminal cases the government (with all of its revenue, investigative agencies, and batteries of lawyers) prosecutes a single individual for an alleged crime. This legal joust for truth is called the Adversary Process, and is sometimes likened to the medieval trial by ordeal between two knights jousting on the field of honor to arrive at truth and justice. Yet, where the two adversaries are not knights, but rather the government and an individual, the joust is hardly a fair one. Whereas the government arrives in regal splendor, armed with its coat of arms, sword, shield—and sometimes mace—its adversary stands shivering on the field of honor clad only in his nightshirt. Clearly, this kind of a contest is weighted in favor of the stronger of the two, who may or may not be correct in bringing criminal charges against an individual.

Thus, the Founders decided to arm the individual against the all-embracing power of the government by adding a Bill of Rights. They decided that since it was impossible to balance perfectly the contest between the government and an individual in criminal proceedings, the contest ought to favor, if anyone, the individual and assume that a citizen is innocent until the government proves guilt "beyond a reasonable doubt." Because history had demonstrated that angels do not govern men, the Founders sought to arm the individual against any whim of government that might unjustly deny him life, liberty, or property. The arsenal included the following rights found in amendments four through eight.

1. To be informed of the specific charges against him to prevent arbitrary arrest. The Constitution guarantees the right to a writ of habeas corpus, which is a court order directing the government to bring the person to court and show cause for his detention.
2. To be brought to trial only after there has been a preliminary hearing (grand jury) to determine if there has been enough evidence presented by the government to justify bringing him to trial.
3. To a speedy and public trial, as well as bail (money posted by a person as the temporary price for his liberty) that is not excessive so that the individual can prepare his case before the trial as well as continue his normal work and family life.
4. To trial by jury.
5. To counsel for help in the preparation of a defense.
6. To the right to cross-examine and challenge witnesses who appear against him.
7. To compel witnesses who might testify in his behalf to appear and testify (subpoena).
8. To the right against self-incrimination.
9. To the right to his property, free from unreasonable search and seizure.
10. To be free from cruel and unusual punishment in the event that he is convicted.

These rights do not make the job of law enforcement any easier. Yet, as Justice William O. Douglas put it, "a degree of inefficiency is a price we necessarily pay for a civilized society."

Still, some may respond that they are law-abiding citizens and therefore have nothing to fear from efficient law enforcement. Like most people they think that they will never be struck by lightning or face criminal prosecution since they have broken no laws. No doubt, Dr. Sam Sheppard must have held these same thoughts himself shortly before lightning struck him and he found himself unjustly put behind prison bars, facing the penalty of death.

If the Bill of Rights had not guaranteed that Sheppard could not be denied his "life, liberty, or property without due process of law," he would never have won a reversal of his conviction and would have faced death in the electric chair. The prospect of such a death forces anyone to a greater appreciation of why the Founders erected a system of justice concerned with protecting the individual from a hasty conviction. The physiological aspects of death in the electric chair are particularly sobering in demonstrating the importance of this point.

The electric current causes instantaneous contraction of all the muscles in the body, resulting in severe contortions of the limbs, fingers, toes, face, and protusion of the eyes. Usually there is a star fracture on the lens of the eye, and in some cases the heart is contracted and in tetanized condition, or even fractured. After death, the temperature of the body rises to a high point; at the site of the leg electrode, a temperature of more than 128 degrees F. has been registered within fifteen minutes. The blood is altered biochemically, becoming very dark and coagulated. There are scientists who claim that electrocution does not kill instantly, and that in some cases it is the autopsy which finally executes the law's edict.[5]

Sheppard did not die such a death, but he did spend twelve years in an Ohio penitentiary. And this happened *with* the protection of the Bill of Rights! What might happen without it?

The Adversary System and the Privilege Against Self-Incrimination

Within the framework of the Constitution, which sets bounds for the Adversary System, three basic questions must be answered to determine whether sanctions or penalties should be applied to a person accused of a crime, or whether that person should be acquitted and cleared of the charges.

1. Did the accused commit the crime?
2. If so, what was his mental condition when the crime was committed? Was he sane or insane?
3. If the accused is guilty and not judged insane, were there any mitigating or extenuating circumstances that might temper the degree and amount of punishment?

[5] Louis Nizer, *The Jury Returns* (Garden City, N.Y.: Doubleday, 1966), p. 119.

To provide answers to these questions, the two adversaries (the government and the defendant) are typically represented by attorneys who are more skilled in the law than they. Each attorney presents the "facts" of his client's case. But what are the "facts"? And how does the system keep these skilled lawyers from hitting below the belt or playing unfairly in an effort to win their case?

The answer to the second question, of course, is that the Adversary System provides an impartial umpire to referee or judge the proceedings—a judge whose knowledge of the law and hopeful fairness will keep the joust for truth from degenerating into a sordid cockfight. Every time a judge overrules or sustains a motion made by one of the adversaries, he is exercising his role in the game of justice.

But what of the first question: what are the facts? Who is to determine one lawyer's "facts" from another lawyer's fiction? Who is to answer the three questions regarding the defendant's guilt, sanity, and whether or not there were mitigating circumstances in the case?

The impartial fact-finder and decision maker who answers these questions may be either a single person (the judge), or a jury, which most often consists of twelve men and women selected from a cross-section of the community at large wherein the crime was committed. The choice rests with the defendant.

In the case of trial by jury, precautions are taken to ensure that the jurors have no preconceived opinions regarding the guilt of the defendant. Each attorney is given the right to interrogate the jurors, who are under oath, to ascertain any possible bias that might be grounds for their dismissal for cause. Additionally, each attorney is ordinarily provided with six to eight preemptory challenges, which may be used to dismiss jurors who have not demonstrated bias through their testimony, but whom the attorney, through investigation or intuition, feels might be prejudicial to his case. By means of this proceeding it is hoped that an impartial jury can be selected.

Once again, the "inefficiency" of law enforcement can be observed. For a conviction to be obtained, all twelve jurors must be convinced that the defendant is not only guilty, but guilty "beyond a reasonable doubt." (However, in 1972, the U.S. Supreme Court ruled in a five to four decision, with all four Nixon appointees in the majority, that the Constitution does not require unanimous jury verdicts in state criminal courts.) This extreme test is the law's safeguard against depriving a citizen of his liberty or life by mistake. Acquittal, by contrast, requires only a simple majority (seven). The failure to reach a decision of guilt or innocence results in a hung jury and the prosecution can reinitiate its case against the accused all over again. This is not a violation of the Fifth Amendment's double-jeopardy clause, which guarantees that no person shall "be subject for the same offence to be twice put in jeopardy of life and limb."[6]

The double-jeopardy provision simply means that when a man has been acquitted of an offense he may never again be retried for that same offense. A retrial after a hung jury is granted on the theory that the first trial was no trial at all since no valid verdict had been reached, and therefore, another jury ought not to be prevented from reaching a proper verdict.

All of these procedures are part of what is termed *due process of law* and is based upon the provisions found in the Fifth and Fourteenth Amendments to the Constitution, which guarantee to every citizen the right to life, liberty, and property. Neither the federal nor the state governments may deny any person of these rights without due process of law.

Because of the rapidity of change in American life, the Supreme Court has not settled upon any precise meaning of "due process of law." In fact, there are two types of due process. The older type, which grew out of our English heritage and the Magna Charta, is called *procedural* due process and is the guarantee to a fair trial. Yet, what good would it be to have a fair trial if the law itself was unfair? There must first be fair law. The guarantee to fair law is called *substantive* due process and is founded upon the same natural-law concepts rooted in the Declaration of Independence. In other words, substantive due process requires that the courts be convinced that the law, not merely the procedures by which the law is enforced, be fair and just.

Procedural due process, to use Daniel Webster's famous definition, requires that the government "hears before it condemns, proceeds upon inquiry, and renders judgment only after a trial." Trial by jury represents an important ingredient of procedural due process and rests squarely upon the principle of popular sovereignty found in the Declaration of Independence.

Elliot Ness may have doggedly tried to enforce a federal law like the Volstead Act, which imposed Prohibition upon a very unhappy American people during the 1920s, but the act generally resulted only in frustration for the national authorities. It must be remembered that a jury consists of the people—the sovereign people—who may either enforce or not enforce a law as they choose. If they find a law like

[6] Bartkus v. Illinois, 359 U.S. 121 (1959).

Prohibition unsatisfactory, as they did, the law will not be enforced and the lawbreaker will go free. After all, what jury would have been willing to put away its primary source of booze during Prohibition!

Because of this very fact, trial by jury is controversial. In a democratic republic the people may not always be right, but they are final. Sometimes this can have alarming consequences, as the murder of Viola Liuzzo in Alabama demonstrates. Mrs. Liuzzo, a civil-rights worker during the 1960s who went into the South for the purpose of helping black Americans register to vote, was gunned down by opponents of her work.[7] J. Edgar Hoover's FBI did its homework and penetrated the band that perpetrated the cowardly deed—the Ku Klux Klan. In spite of the fact that the Klan had wrapped themselves in the American flag as "true" patriots, the FBI had strong reason to suspect that a member of that organization should be charged with murder.

Trial by jury, however, means that the jury shall consist of members of the community wherein the crime was committed. In this case, it consisted of ten individuals who either were at the time or had formerly been Klan members. This jury acquitted Klansman Collie Leroy Wilkins, after only one hour and forty-seven minutes of deliberation, causing many to doubt the virtue of trial by jury. No doubt this controversial aspect of trial by jury has been one of the factors that has made the Supreme Court reluctant to impose it totally upon the state governments via the Fourteenth Amendment. Nonetheless, it must be noted that while trial by jury is a hell of a way to run a railroad, no one has come up with a better way yet.

Equally controversial has been the constitutional protection against self-incrimination afforded to individuals caught up in the Adversary System. Though the Fifth Amendment guarantees that no person "shall be compelled in any criminal case to be a witness against himself," Senators Joseph McCarthy and Estes Kefauver convinced a large segment of the American people that this portion of the Constitution was disreputable. Where there is smoke there is fire. Who would invoke this right to silence unless he had something criminal to hide? And this right of silence does not lend itself to efficient law enforcement. Just what are the values involved in extending the privilege against self-incrimination to individuals being interrogated by the government regarding possible criminal activity?

The origin of this right can be traced to seventeenth-century England and the Court of Star Chamber used by the Tudor and Stuart kings to extract confessions from those who disagreed with their

---

[7] "Juries & Justice in Alabama," *Time* (October 29, 1965), p. 49.

policies. Men were interrogated before these courts regardless of the fact that they had not even been formally charged with a crime. Failure to provide answers or confessions sought by the government inquisitor resulted in torture and cruel punishment for the person being interrogated.

Such had been the fate of John Lilburne in 1673 when he returned from Holland to England, only to find himself accused of sending "factitious and scandalous books" from there to England. For refusing to answer the government's questions, Lilburne was fined, tied to a cart and with his body laid bare was lashed and beaten through the streets of London. At Westminster he was pilloried with his bleeding back bowed to the sun, while his head and arms were shackled in holes in a wooden frame so that he could be held up to further public scorn and abuse. As if this were not enough, he was then put in solitary confinement in Fleet Prison with iron shackles on his hands and legs, and denied anything to eat for ten days.[8] Little wonder that the government was able to obtain so many confessions! Who would not rather provide false testimony and confess to a crime that he did not commit just to avoid this kind of physical pain?

Lest the reader think that Star Chamber methods are a thing of the past or that these practices could not take place in the United States, one needs only to recall the treatment given by Cleveland, Ohio inquisitors to a prominent and wealthy osteopath—Dr. Sam Sheppard. Describing the method of questioning and the *continuous* effect of different teams of police questioning him, Sheppard writes:

> For . . . twelve hours, four teams of detectives questioned me in relays. . . . The method of questioning . . . was consistent with those methods used by police in countries behind the Iron Curtain. I was not beaten and drugs were not administered, but, otherwise, the experience was no different from what has been reported by men subject to Communist methods.
>
> It was mental torture at its worst. Physical beating would have been a pleasure to me in comparison. Hour after hour, they shouted at me, accused me, insulted me and members of my family. They tried to trick me by questioning me about facts they knew were not correct. Each time I told them I didn't kill my wife.[9]

In *My Brother's Keeper,* Dr. Sheppard's brother reveals some of the methods used by the Cleveland police on him to obtain a confession from his brother. A Cleveland detective is speaking:

---

[8] Leonard W. Levy, *Origins of the Fifth Amendment* (London: Oxford University Press, 1971), p. 271.
[9] Dr. Sam Sheppard, *Endure and Conquer* (Cleveland, Ohio: World, 1966), p. 47.

"You know you people are going about this in the wrong way, don't you?" he demanded.

I asked him what he meant.

"Your brother is guilty as hell and you know it," was his next sally.

"I know just the opposite," I told him, "and so do you, Captain Kerr."

"Well, I'm going to tell you something." He leaned over his desk and grimaced at me. "I'm going to tell you something and if you ever tell anyone I said this I will call you a liar. Now then—you see your brother and tell him to confess. God damn it, he can plead insanity or whatever he wants. He will do six months in a hospital and then come out cured. He can return to the practice of medicine and there will be no further difficulty."

"And if he refuses to confess to a crime he didn't commit?"

"Don't give me that crap, Doc," Kerr growled at me, "but if he is silly enough to refuse you can tell him for me that we'll burn him. That's all." [10]

If the individual involved had not been Sam Sheppard, who was wealthy enough to afford the best lawyers, educated enough not to be tricked out of his constitutional rights, and physically strong enough to endure twelve-hour "grillings" by police interrogators, a confession might have come forthwith irrespective of whether or not the person involved had committed a crime. Even with the advantages of wealth, the mere description of "burning" in the electric chair might be enough to extract a confession from anyone. With such a powerful adversary as a state or national government, who wants to take that kind of a chance? The clear intention of the Fifth Amendment's protection against self-incrimination is to protect the individual from having to make this kind of choice.

Self-Incrimination in the Formal Setting: The Courtroom

With two exceptions, every state constitution in the United States contains the privilege against self-incrimination. The two exceptions, Iowa and New Jersey, guarantee that privilege by statute, which could be repealed at any time by a majority decision in their state legislatures. However, because state courts frequently interpret provisions in their constitutions differently from similar provisions found in the U.S. Constitution, the question has arisen as to whether the Fifth Amendment's privilege against self-incrimination is binding upon the states in the same way it is upon the national government. Prior to 1964, the

[10] *Ibid.*, p. 54.

The Tides of Justice: Due Process of Law

Supreme Court had answered no in two famous cases, *Twining v. New Jersey* (1908) and *Adamson v. California* (1947).[11] Finally, in the 1964 decision, *Malloy v. Hogan,* the Supreme Court "incorporated" the protection into the Fourteenth Amendment, thus binding the states to the constitutional interpretations uttered by the Supreme Court.[12]

The Court has enunciated a large body of doctrine that applies to the privilege against self-incrimination in both the formal setting, which would be in the courtroom, and in the informal setting, which would be the police station where a person might be only a suspect rather than someone formally accused of a crime.

In the formal setting there are two types of people who might have need of such a right: the person *accused* of a crime and a *witness* who has been subpoenaed by the court to testify in the case.

In the case of the accused, the scope of the privilege is plenary, that is, he does not even have to take the stand. No questions have to be answered. Moreover, though the Fifth Amendment states that no person shall be "compelled in any criminal case" to be a witness against himself, the Court has long interpreted the protection to extend to civil cases (disputes between *private* parties in such matters as contracts, automobile accidents, and business relations), and in appearances before any group that can compel testimony under oath, such as congressional investigative committees and administrative agencies like the Interstate Commerce Commission.

A witness, by contrast, must answer questions that incriminate others. He may only refuse to answer questions which *tend* to incriminate himself or provide a "link in the chain" of evidence that may be self-incriminating. If such protection were not afforded, instead of being a witness, he might become the accused. It is important to understand the significance of the word "tends" when the statement is made: "I refuse to answer that question on the grounds that it *tends* to incriminate me." This does not mean that it *does* incriminate, but only that answering the question might make one look guilty even if he were not. What if the witness stuttered? Or was not very intelligent? Or simply scared to death of the prosecutor who is skilled in law and asking questions? Conceivably such a person might not want to answer a question, not because he was guilty of any crime, but rather because his answer would tend to make him look guilty even though he was a perfectly law-abiding citizen.

Thus, the privilege of the witness against self-incrimination is protected. But he must answer any question that does not incriminate

[11] Twining v. New Jersey, 211 U.S. 78 (1908); Adamson v. California, 322 U.S. 46 (1947).
[12] Malloy v. Hogan, 378 U.S. 1 (1964).

him. Failure to do so will result in a contempt of court (or Congress) citation, which may be punished by fine and/or imprisonment. Moreover, the witness may be compelled to answer incriminating questions if he is granted immunity from prosecution for any crimes to which his testimony might link him.

In recent years the Supreme Court has placed the witness in a legal dilemma. In *Rogers v. United States* (1951) the Supreme Court laid down its doctrine of "waiver," which stated that if a witness inadvertently answered a question that tended to incriminate him, he waives or loses his right of silence with respect to further questions on the same subject.[13] Hence, if the witness is uncooperative in answering questions, he may find himself cited for contempt. If he is too cooperative, he may lose his privilege against self-incrimination. How is a witness to know when to provide and when to refuse testimony? A lawyer helps, but he may not sit with his client on the witness stand. Consequently, the witness is placed in a dilemma: he is damned if he does and damned if he doesn't.

The consequence of all this has been for the witness to claim his privilege at a very early stage in the proceedings in order to protect himself. The courts have been fairly liberal in permitting the witness to do this. Indeed, during the late 1950s, when Senator John L. McClellan was investigating the alleged criminal activities of Teamster Union president Dave Beck, Beck's son refused to answer a question identifying the Teamster president as his father on the grounds that the question tended to incriminate him. His refusal to testify was accepted as a "link in the chain" of evidence that might have been self-incriminating. Dave Beck was convicted without his testimony.

Self-Incrimination in the Informal Setting: The Police Station

The Fifth Amendment was written in the eighteenth century when the police force was practically nonexistent in America. At that time, the courtroom trial was the critical confrontation between the government and the accused. Mindful of the British Star Chamber, the Founders ringed the trial with safeguards, but what about the rights of a person from the time he is picked up by the police until days or even weeks later, when he is finally brought into the formal court of law? Does the Fifth Amendment and the Bill of Rights follow a citizen into the police station even though he is charged with no crime and is only a suspect in a criminal case? To what extent may a policeman question a suspect before he has been charged and brought into the formal

[13] Rogers v. United States, 340 U.S. 367 (1951); Hoffman v. U.S., 341 U.S. 479 (1951).

setting where his Fifth Amendment privilege against self-incrimination is plenary?

An important source of police investigation comes from interrogating individuals who might have knowledge about particular crimes. At some point in a criminal investigation such a person may be taken to the police station (voluntarily or under arrest) for intense questioning. Not only will the person be asked some general questions, but also some very specific ones, which, if answered, might amount to a confession. In fact, the police frequently endeavor to obtain a confession. Such confessions, police claim, are vital to conviction in 80% of all criminal cases.[14]

Police reliance upon confession is brought about, in part, by a very human urge on their part to make sure that they have not arrested the wrong person. This has led to overreliance on confession in many common-law countries like the United States, and has disposed the police to force confessions from the mouths of their suspects. The framers of the 1872 India Evidence Act in Great Britain put the problem in focus when they observed that, "It is far pleasanter [for the police] to sit comfortably in the shade rubbing pepper into a poor devil's eyes than to go about in the sun hunting up evidence." This raises the question posed by James Madison in *Federalist* #51: How do we permit the law to gather information essential to the maintenance of law and order, yet restrain the law from breaking the law by using Star Chamber tactics to extract confessions?

Beginning with *Brown v. Mississippi* (1936), the Supreme Court has attempted to provide the answer through its interpretation of the Fifth Amendment in relation to what has been termed the *doctrine of coercion.* The case involved extreme police tactics used to obtain confessions from three ignorant Negroes charged with murder.

A deputy sheriff in Mississippi named Dial accused a young, illiterate Negro named Ellington of murder. Upon the denial of the crime by Ellington, Deputy Dial seized him, and with the help of a number of white men, hanged him by the neck with a rope that had been suspended from the limb of a tree. After being let down, Ellington still protested his innocence, so Dial hanged him again. Once more, after dangling with death in mid-air, the Negro was brought down to earth. Again, Dial's suspect refused to accede to his demands for a confession, whereupon he was tied to a tree and savagely whipped. In spite of the intense pain and suffering experienced from rope burns around his neck and a back that had been pummelled red with whiplashes, the young Negro man would not confess.

[14] "Concern About Confessions," *Time* (April 29, 1966), p. 52.

He was released by Deputy Dial, only to be arrested a few days later and taken to jail. On route to the jail, however, Dial stopped and again administered a brutal beating with a steel-studded belt—and he told the suspect that the beating would continue until he confessed. Needless to say, by the time that the deputy delivered his charge to jail, he had his confession.

The other two suspects, Ed Brown and Henry Shields, were also arrested and delivered to the same jail. There they were stripped to the skin and laid over chairs to be lashed with a leather strap with buckles on it until their backs were cut to pieces. They were likewise made by Deputy Dial to understand that the whipping would be continued unless and until they confessed.

On the basis of these confessions, the State of Mississippi conducted a one-day trial that resulted in their conviction and a sentence of death. Aside from the confessions, there was not enough evidence against them to even warrant bringing them to trial; the sole evidence upon which their convictions were obtained was the confessions that had been procured by physical torture.[15]

From the beginning of American history, coerced or forced confessions have been inadmissible as evidence in federal courts because such confessions violate both the privilege against self-incrimination and the due-process clause of the Fifth Amendment. It was not until 1936 in *Brown v. Mississippi* that the Supreme Court applied through the Fourteenth Amendment the same standards to the states. In reversing the convictions of Brown, Ellington, and Shields, the Supreme Court admonished the state governments that "The rack and torture chamber may not be substituted for the witness stand."[16]

From the *Brown* case to the present, the Court has exhibited a dual concern when establishing limits upon the police in obtaining and using such confessions in court. First, it has been concerned about the "trustworthiness" or reliability of such confessions. Since a forced confession is likely to be unreliable evidence given to avoid pain, the Court has tried to take the incentive to torture away from the police by making such evidence inadmissible in court. Second, the Court has been concerned with the undesirability of the state's pursuit of law enforcement by means of the truncheon or rubber hose. The *means* must be compatible with the ends of government, and the *ends* of a democratic government include a commitment to the upholding of the dignity of the individual rather than his debasement.

[15] Brown v. Mississippi, 297 U.S. 278 (1936).
[16] *Ibid.*

Coercion is clearly not a compatible means of obtaining the end of law and order in a democratic society. But what *is* coercion? Since the *Brown* case, the Court has tended to interpret the meaning of coercion broadly, to include not only physical torture, but mental coercion as well. The type of grilling and third-degree tactics so often portrayed in the films of the 1930s and 1940s is no longer constitutional. After all, isn't a spotlight focused upon the eyes of a suspect for a prolonged period of time going to produce, at some point, migraine headaches? Won't the intense questioning of a sleepless suspect by crack teams of detectives, alternating in shifts, break the suspect's will at some point? Torture? Certainly. And not a mark left on the suspect!

In one case, *Leyra v. Denno* (1954), the New York City police picked up a murder suspect and interrogated him at great length. The man was clearly not too bright and complained of headaches. At this point, the police brought in a psychiatrist who wormed his way into the man's confidence and obtained a confession. The confession was later ruled unconstitutional because again the means used by the police constituted a devious kind of coercion. In this decision the Court applied a "subjective test" to its definition of coercion. Whereas in cases like *Brown v. Mississippi* coercion could objectively be demonstrated by simply counting the scars or rope burns, evidence of mental torture has to be subjectively tested in each individual case. Moreover, the Court has indicated that it is willing to consider the capacity of the person being interrogated to withstand coercion. Thus, what might be coercion for one person being interrogated might be acceptable for another.[17]

The coerced-confession doctrine was one of the first limitations placed upon police practices in the states by the Supreme Court, but a parallel development had occurred in the federal courts in the early 1940s and late 1950s. Concern over police lawlessness in attempting to obtain confessions led to the *doctrine of unnecessary delay,* which required that a suspect be brought into the formal setting without "unnecessary delay" so as to minimize the opportunity of the police to use Star Chamber tactics to extract confessions.[18]

One of the problems in a federal system is that there are fifty state governments and one national government, each with their own penal code, courts, and police forces. In federal courts a confession is invalid if it has been coerced. It is *also* invalid if it has been given

---
[17] Leyra v. Denno, 347 U.S. 556 (1954).
[18] McNabb v. U.S., 318 U.S. 322 (1943); Mallory v. U.S., 354 U.S. 449 (1957).

during a period of "unnecessary delay." The Federal Rules of Criminal Procedure require that when a person is arrested by federal authorities he must be taken without "unnecessary delay" before a judge, to be informed of the charges against him, his right to an attorney, and his right against self-incrimination. In *McNabb v. United States* (1944) and *Mallory v. United States* (1957), the Supreme Court held that a violation of this rule by federal officers would make any confession obtained during the "unnecessary delay" inadmissible as evidence in the defendant's trial. What "unnecessary delay" is, however, the Court has yet to define. In one case, all nine of the justices were in disagreement with each other as to what constituted unnecessary delay.

And what about the states? Are they bound by this doctrine, nebulous as it may be? Inasmuch as law-enforcement agencies like the FBI often overlap with state jurisdictions, this is not merely an academic question. A person accused of robbing a Federal Reserve Bank in California can be prosecuted by either the federal or state governments, or both, without violating the prohibition against placing a person in double jeopardy."[19] Ordinarily both will not prosecute, but will agree to allow the level of government that desires to prosecute to do so.

If it is the state that decides to prosecute, does the unnecessary delay doctrine apply? Since the Supreme Court has refused to apply the *McNabb-Mallory* rule to the states, the answer varies and depends upon the will of the states. Some states like California have adopted an unnecessary delay rule and have held that the police may not detain an individual for more than two court days after an arrest. An overwhelming number of states, however, have refused to apply the *McNabb-Mallory* rule to their jurisdictions.

Since the 1930s the Supreme Court has attempted to prevent police lawlessness by forbidding the use of illegally obtained confessions in the courts of law. In 1964 the Court enunciated a new doctrine aimed at the same problem in *Escobedo v. Illinois*. The decision was to bring the wrath of much of America down on the Supreme Court for "coddling criminals."

For decades, police methods of solving crimes have thrived upon the fact that most people are not aware of their constitutional rights. Although the Court has prohibited the use of any confession that has been extracted by the police through physical or mental coercion, and though people do not have to answer a single police question, these facts are generally unknown to the vast majority of arrested

[19] Bartkus v. Illinois, 359 U.S. 121.

Americans who are poor in pocket, mind, and spirit. Ironically, those who *do* know their rights are the big-time, professional criminals who can afford the best attorneys to advise them and be in attendance.

By contrast, 60% of the federal criminal defendants in 1964 were too poor to afford lawyers, and therefore remained ignorant of their constitutional rights. As a result 90% of them pled guilty and were swiftly sentenced without a trial.[20] In effect, they were not convicted by judges and juries, but rather by the police. For them the crucial part of their case was not the trial, but rather their interrogation in the "squeal room," as it is called in many police stations. It was just such a circumstance that led to *Escobedo v. Illinois.*

In January 1960, Danny Escobedo, a twenty-two-year-old Mexican-American laborer, was arrested at 2:30 A.M. by the Chicago police—who had no warrant—for questioning about the murder of his brother-in-law eleven days earlier. Escobedo gave no statement to the police and was released on a writ of habeas corpus obtained by his lawyer after fourteen and one-half hours of questioning.

Eleven days later, the Chicago police rearrested Escobedo and returned him to police headquarters with his hands handcuffed behind his back. No one warned him of his right to silence or counsel. He, nonetheless, asked to see his attorney to find out his rights, but was denied. Concurrently, his attorney, who had found out about his client's arrest, arrived at the Detective Bureau where Escobedo was being kept. He asked to see Escobedo, but was denied. With no lawyer to advise him, Escobedo fell into a well-laid legal trap and confessed. He was convicted and sentenced to twenty years.

In such cases, it is not unusual for a defendant to repudiate his confession, forcing the courts to ascertain the "voluntariness" of the confession. Such was the case with Escobedo. After filing a pauper's appeal (*in forma pauperis*) and spending 4.5 years behind bars, Escobedo succeeded in getting the Supreme Court to reverse his conviction. In so doing, the Court moved the Bill of Rights into the police station and made it clear that criminal prosecutions that began in the "squeal room" required the police to inform the suspect of his right against self-incrimination and to an attorney. Justice Arthur Goldberg ruled for the Court that "when the process shifts from the investigatory to accusatory—when its focus is on the accused and its purpose is to elicit a confession—our adversary system begins to operate, and . . . the accused must be permitted to consult his lawyer."[21]

---

[20] "Concern About Confessions," p. 53.
[21] Escobedo v. Illinois, 378 U.S. 478 (1964).

The *Escobedo* decision, however, raised as many questions as it answered. Is a person entitled to an attorney if he is too poor to retain one? What does it mean to have the opportunity to consult an attorney? May he sit at the side of his client during the interrogation to advise him in respect to every question asked or must advice stop when the interrogation begins?

The answer to the first question came in *Gideon v. Wainwright* (1963) and *Douglas v. California* (1963) when the Court ruled that fundamental procedural fairness requires the states as well as the federal government to provide an attorney for the trial as well as appellate cases if the defendant is too poor to retain one himself.[22]

The second question received its answer in 1966 in *Miranda v. Arizona* when the Court held that no federal or state conviction would be admissible as evidence in court unless the suspect had been told that his lawyer could be present *during* the questioning, that he had the right to remain silent, and that anything that he said might be used against him in court.[23] In *Walder v. U.S.* (1971) Chief Justice Warren Burger, speaking for a 5-4 majority, modified the *Miranda* rule by holding that inadmissible evidence could be used in court to contradict the suspect's on-the-stand testimony.

Unreasonable Searches and Seizures

Under the Fifth Amendment, a person cannot be made to confess or provide incriminating evidence against himself; the Fourth Amendment provides a similar protection for the individual against "unreasonable searches and seizures" by the government, so that people may be "secure in their persons, houses, papers, and effects." Combining the Fourth Amendment protection against unreasonable searches and seizures with the Fifth Amendment safeguard against self-incrimination, the Supreme Court has ruled that illegally obtained evidence by the police in violation of the Fourth Amendment cannot be used as evidence in the courts of law.

Contrary to the impression left by television and motion pictures, neither the FBI nor the local or state police have the right to kick down doors at 2 A.M. and search homes without probable cause and a warrant that stipulates the place to be searched and the object of the search.

This is not to say that some searches are not reasonable without a search warrant. Who would expect the police to return to the police station to obtain a warrant after seeing an individual scampering from

---

[22] Gideon v. Wainwright, 372 U.S. 335 (1963); Douglas v. California, 372 U.S. 535 (1963).
[23] Miranda v. Arizona, 384 U.S. 436 (1966).

a bank with two bags of gold slung over his shoulder and pistols smoking? Or for the police to secure a warrant, no matter how long it took, after hearing screams and bullets ricocheting through a given household?

In "hot pursuit" of armed and dangerous individuals, the police do not need a warrant. With such things as automobiles or boats, the police are not required to obtain a warrant, because evidence might literally flee the scene. However, until 1961, the *states* could and did kick down doors at 2 A.M. without probable cause and without search warrants because the Fourth Amendment did not apply to them until *Mapp v. Ohio* was decided in that year.

That case began in May 1957 when three Cleveland policemen who suspected Miss Dollree Mapp of being involved in the numbers racket went to her home hoping to find tally sheets and other materials used in gambling activities to use as evidence against her. Upon learning that the policemen had no search warrant, Miss Mapp refused to admit them into her home.

The officers then waited outside her home and were joined by four more policemen to keep the house "under surveillance." Three hours later the seven policemen knocked again on the door of Miss Mapp. When she did not come to the door immediately, they broke it down and entered. Again, she demanded to see their search warrant. A scuffle ensued between her and the police and she was finally handcuffed by the police.

The search began. Miss Mapp was physically carried upstairs to her bedroom, where the police ransacked her dresser, drawers, and suitcases. Then the search spread to her child's bedroom, photograph album, personal papers, living room, kitchen, and basement. Unable to find any evidence of any gambling activities, the police seized some papers and photographs which *they* contended were obscene.

She was arrested and charged with violating the Ohio law that made illegal the possession of obscene literature. Upon conviction, Miss Mapp appealed her case to the Supreme Court, arguing that her constitutional rights under the Fourth Amendment had been violated and that her sentence should be set aside.

Agreeing with her, the Court noted that "evidence secured by *official lawlessness*" would be barred from every courtroom—state as well as federal.[24] The decision had been brewing for some time. Almost a decade earlier the Fourth Amendment had been directly applied to the states in *Rochin v. California* (1952). In that case the Court had reversed the conviction of Antonio Rochin who had been

---

[24] Mapp v. Ohio, 367 U.S. 643 (1961).

214 The Republican Experiment: Rights in Conflict

subjected to a gross invasion of his privacy by the police—when his stomach was pumped—as "methods too close to the rack and screw to permit constitutional differentiation."[25]

Other problems have arisen in recent years. The development of a technetronic society—a society shaped culturally, economically, and politically by the impact of technology and electronics—raises new questions regarding the application of the Fourth Amendment. As Alan F. Westin has made frighteningly clear in *Privacy and Freedom,* the individual's right to privacy is now threatened by the widespread governmental use of new electronic tools—listening and watching devices—to monitor the activities of private citizens.

The advances of science and technology have presented new challenges to democracy, and whether the Constitution can adapt to these challenges remains an unsettled question. The federal and state governments have long used wiretapping devices to eavesdrop on people. Does that represent an "unreasonable search and seizure"? In *Olmstead v. United States* (1928) the Supreme Court ruled that since this practice did not result in the actual physical entry by the police into a person's home that it was not prohibited by the Constitution. Justices Holmes and Brandeis vigorously dissented, arguing that the Constitution must adapt to the times and that the "dirty business" of wiretapping had the same effect as physically invading a person's home.[26]

Forty years later the Supreme Court accepted the Holmes–Brandeis position in *Katz v. United States* (1967).[27] However, in spite of the fact that the Court has ruled that evidence obtained by wiretapping would be inadmissible in the courts, it is widely recognized that such practices are commonplace activities of law-enforcement agencies at all levels of government.

Moreover, never before has the government had at its disposal such sophisticated and all-embracing eavesdropping devices. Ranging from radio pills that convert people into walking radio transmitters to infrared photographic surveillance, which permits authorities to literally peer through walls, "it will soon be possible to assert almost continuous surveillance over every citizen and to maintain up-to-date, complete files on the personal behavior of the citizen."[28] What is more, these files will be subject to instantaneous retrieval by the authorities by means of computers.

The pace of change in electronics, optics, and microminiaturization is already so swift that existing surveillance methods like the radio

[25] Rochin v. California, 342 U.S. 165 (1952).
[26] Olmstead v. United States, 277 U.S. 438 (1928).
[27] Katz v. United States, 389 U.S. 347 (1967).
[28] Zbigniew Brzezinski, "America in the Technetronic Age," in George Kateb, ed., *Utopia* (New York: Atherton Press, 1971), p. 137.

pill may yield to "invisible magnetic tattoos" and microminiaturized transmitters the size of a pinhead that may be painlessly implanted under a person's skin, by the end of the century.

Some scholars, such as Jacques Ellul in his book *The Technological Society,* believe that we already live in a nation of one-dimensional men who are secretly controlled by such techniques. Certainly President Nixon's former Attorney General, John Mitchell, has not diminished such fears with his claim to the right to use electronic surveillance on anybody he chooses. Indeed, William Rehnquist, President Nixon's choice of the Supreme Court in 1971, has forwarded views on wiretapping that "Out-Mitchell Mitchell." [29]

Testifying before Senator Sam Ervin's Senate Judiciary subcommittee on constitutional rights, the then Assistant Attorney General Rehnquist argued that the government had a perfect right to engage in the surveillance of any citizen—including congressmen! That the government has already done this has been charged by a host of officially elected representatives ranging from Congressmen John Conyers and Hale Boggs to Senators Birch Bayh and Adlai Stevenson III.

Thus, in spite of a series of Supreme Court decisions that have held that electronic surveillance is a violation of the Fourth Amendment, the Nixon Administration has pursued a vigorous wiretapping policy. This policy, coupled with President Nixon's Omnibus Crime Control Act, which permits wiretapping in the investigation of a long list of specified crimes, has led many important figures to condemn the Nixon anticrime program. Senator Sam Ervin has declaimed the program "as full of unconstitutional, unjust, and unwise, provisions as a mangy hound dog is full of fleas . . . a garbage pail of some of the most repressive, nearsighted, intolerant, unfair, and vindictive legislation that the Senate has ever been presented." [30]

Crime is outrageously high in the United States and the law and order issue is the cutting edge of politics today. When Mr. Nixon, in his Miami acceptance speech of August 1968, spoke of "sirens in the night" and warned that "Time is running out for the merchants of crime and corruption in American society," he sounded a responsive cord to the legitimate concern of the American electorate. The question that remains unanswered, however, is whether effecting a cure to the pestilence of crime through electronic surveillance is better or worse than the disease. The year 1984 is only a decade away. Some argue that the Orwellian nightmare may have already arrived.

[29] TRB, "Rehnquist Holds Views That Out-Mitchell Mitchell," *Los Angeles Times* (November 2, 1971).
[30] *Congressional Quarterly Weekly Report* (June 5, 1970), p. 1497.

THE FIBER OF DEMOCRACY:
Equality in America

... all men are created equal....
—*Declaration of Independence*

... nor [may any State] deny to any person within its jurisdiction the equal protection of the laws.
—*Fourteenth Amendment*

Today, as America approaches the bicentennial commemoration of its Declaration of Independence in 1776, it does so in a more disordered condition than at any time in its history since the Great Depression of the 1930s or possibly even since the Civil War of more than 100 years ago. From California Governor Ronald Reagan's strident statement, "If it's to be a bloodbath, let it be now" to H. Rap Brown's declaration that violence is "as American as cherry pie," both black and white Americans have girded themselves to join battle in the wake of the urban riots of 1965 through 1967.

Three of these riots amounted to major civil convulsions. The 1965 Watts riot in Los Angeles resulted in thirty-four dead with over 1000 more injured in the course of violence, burning, and looting that encompassed over fifty miles of the inner city. The 1967 Newark disturbance caused twenty-three deaths and required more than 4000 policemen and national guardsmen to restore order. The bloodiest of the riots, however, occurred in 1967 in Detroit and left forty-three dead and over 1000 injured.

Many have regarded these events, like the Civil War that preceded them, to be symptomatic of the breakdown of America's democratic process and evidence of the nation's betrayal of its basic philosophy as expressed in the Declaration of Independence that "all men are created equal." We are told by some advocates of civil rights that our present dilemma hinges upon the racism and/or hypocrisy of the Founding Fathers; that the Declaration of Independence is a fraud, which only "by remaining vague . . . could say all men were created equal"; that "unalienable rights never meant Negroes"; and finally that "Nothing was more secure in the new Constitution of the U.S. than Negro slavery."[1]

This opinion is not new. Indeed, one may recall Lincoln's exculpatory letter of April 6, 1859 wherein he dealt with a similar assault on the principles of Jefferson by the proponents of slavery. In that letter, Lincoln wrote:

> The principles of Jefferson are the definitions and axioms of free society. And yet they are denied and evaded, with no small show of success. One dashingly calls them "glittering generalities"; another bluntly calls them "self-evident lies" . . .[2]

Ironically, this view of the Declaration of Independence and our present racial dilemma is one shared by advocates and adversaries of civil rights alike. As in Lincoln's day, it has had "no small show of success" and for that reason deserves consideration.

The American Cosmogony

Following the urban riots of the 1960s, President Lyndon Johnson appointed Governor Otto Kerner of Illinois to investigate what happened, why it happened, and what can be done to prevent such an

---

[1] John Hope Franklin, "The Bitter Years of Slavery," *Life* (November 22, 1968), p. 108; for a rebuttal to Professor Franklin's arguments, see Fred R. Mabbutt, "The Bitter Years Of Slavery: A Response to the Arguments of John Hope Franklin," *University of Houston Forum* (Fall–Winter, 1970), pp. 13–18.
[2] Roy P. Basler, ed., *The Collected Works of Abraham Lincoln* (New Brunswick, N.J.: Rutgers University Press, 1953), Vol. III, p. 375.

occurrence in the future. In the *Report of the National Advisory Commission,* the eleven-member commission called upon history to explain the crisis between black and white. Turning to the Declaration of Independence, they wrote that the statement "all men are created equal" was an expression which "excluded Negroes who were held in bondage, as well as the few who were free men."[3] This is a curious view, certainly one utterly incompatible with the intention of the author of the Declaration of Independence.

Writing twenty-five years after the publication of the Declaration of Independence, Thomas Jefferson made it clear for all to read that *all* men, irrespective of race, were included in the Declaration's famous statement. He said:

> Because Sir Isaac Newton was superior to others in understanding, he was not therefore lord of the person or property of others. On this subject, they are gaining daily in the opinions of nations, and hopeful advances are making towards their [Negro] re-establishment on an equal footing with the other colors of the human family.[4]

When Jefferson wrote of equality in the Declaration of Independence, he understood that all men were not then living in that condition. He simply intended to declare what he considered to be a self-evident truth or what Abraham Lincoln later termed "a standard maxim for free society." In other words, equality was not where America began its existence, but rather represented its *telos* or goal. To expect that this revolution of man's historic condition would be completed at the same moment that it was announced in 1776 is to condemn the men of our founding for not being omnipotent. As long as a large body of Americans refused to consent to the principle of equality, Jefferson could only "declare the right, so that enforcement of it might follow as fast as circumstances should permit." Knowing the proneness of men to sacrifice their principles of justice for economic gain, he "left for them at least one hard nut to crack."[5]

In other words, the declaration of the principle of equality was an act of statesmanship, and statesmanship involves doing as much good as one can get away with. In this sense, statesmanship becomes

---

[3] Otto Kerner and others, *Report of the National Advisory Commission on Civil Disorders* (New York: Bantam Books, 1968), p. 207.
[4] Adrienne Koch and William Peden, eds., *The Life and Selected Writings of Thomas Jefferson* (New York: Modern Library, 1944), p. 595.
[5] Basler, *op. cit.,* Vol. II, p. 405–406.

"removing the greatest amount of evil while disturbing the least amount of prejudice."[6] It is largely a *negative* art involving the destruction of such evils as slavery, oppression, and civil discord.

The statesman's task, as Plato reminded us in *The Republic*, is chiefly that of the nurse or surgeon who has been charged with eliminating the diseases that plague the body politic. In a democratic republic this means that the statesman must instill in the citizenry eager consent to be its best self and make it feel that this is what it wanted all along. Because a democratic republic rests upon popular opinion, the statesman must be a transcendent teacher and take the whole nation to school.[7] One of America's greatest statesmen, Abraham Lincoln, understood this when he observed ". . . he who molds public sentiment goes deeper than he who enacts statutes and pronounces decisions. He makes statutes or decisions possible or impossible to execute."[8]

"Public opinion, on any subject, always has a 'central idea' from which all its minor thoughts radiate." The central idea that accompanied the founding of the United States, from which all minor thoughts radiated, was that all men are created equal.

This teaching was later to be incorporated into the Constitution through the Bill of Rights, and in 1868 through the addition of the Fourteenth Amendment, which extended the protection of rights and "equal protection of the laws" from the national to the state level of government.

To Jefferson, the principle of equality was not only just, but it was in his and every man's *enlightened self-interest* to pursue that justice lest there be "a revolution of the wheel of fortune." In his *Notes on the State of Virginia,* he prophetically warned those who refused to consent to the principle of equality that

> Indeed I tremble for my country when I reflect that God is just; that his justice cannot sleep forever; that considering numbers, nature and natural means only, a revolution of the wheel of fortune, an exchange of situation is among possible events; that it may become probable by supernatural interference! The Almighty has no attribute which can take side with us in such a contest.[9]

---

[6] Morton J. Frisch and Richard G. Stevens, eds., *American Political Thought: The Philosophic Dimensions of American Statesmanship* (New York: Charles Scribner's Sons, 1971), p. 6.
[7] *Ibid.,* p. 20.
[8] Harry V. Jaffa, "Expediency and Morality in The Lincoln–Douglas Debates," *The Anchor Review,* No. 2 (1957), pp. 177–204.
[9] Thomas Jefferson, *Notes on the State of Virginia,* Query XVIII (Chapel Hill: University of North Carolina Press, 1955), p. 163.

Given the ghetto riots of the late 1960s, the ascendance of groups like the Black Muslims, and the Black Panther "shoot-outs" in Chicago, Los Angeles, and Cleveland, no doubt many Americans must have thought that the revolutionary wheel was already spinning. Thus, *undemocratic means*—the conversion of ballots to bullets—toward the democratic end of equality produced more than 150 major riots in American cities between 1965 and 1968.[10]

Equality, however, is not the only principle enunciated in the Declaration of Independence or embodied in the Constitution. Linked to it is the principle that government derives its just powers from "the consent of the governed." The political cornerstone of a democracy is that the people are sovereign. The equality and liberty guaranteed in the Declaration of Independence and Constitution are ultimately in their hands. And because unanimity is impossible in a nation as large as the United States, the pragmatic settlement of majority rule has obtained, as it has in every sizable democracy in the world. As Leslie Lipson has put it, "We count heads in order to avoid breaking them."[11]

During the 1960s, some professed members of the radical left like H. Rap Brown and Jerry Rubin looked to equality as the "true" principle of American democracy and were willing to use undemocratic means, if necessary, to achieve their ends. On the other hand, many conservatives have attached themselves to what *they* consider to be the "true" principle of democracy, namely "consent of the governed" or what, in modern parlance, would be called freedom or liberty. In The words of one conservative writer, Felix Morley, "Democracy, as the word is used in the United States, does not imply equality."[12] Likening equality to Marxian socialism, Morley insists that it spells the death of freedom and that socialism in this country "has been enormously helped by the Jeffersonian half-truth that 'all men are created equal.' "[13]

The sad fact of American history, both past and present, is that a large body of Americans who have professed a love of freedom (at least their own) have refused to consent to their fellow American's

---

[10] Thomas R. Dye, *The Politics of Equality* (Indianapolis: Bobbs-Merrill, 1971), p. 176.
[11] Leslie Lipson, *The Democratic Civilization* (London: Oxford University Press, 1964), p. 551.
[12] Felix Morley, *Freedom and Federalism* (Chicago: Henry Regnery Company, 1959), p. 11. Morley makes a subtle distinction between freedom and liberty, defining the former as "essentially an absence of external restraint," and the latter "as a more positive condition, involving a measure of personal choice which is less inherent in freedom."
[13] *Ibid.*, p. 49.

demands for full equality. And like their counterparts on the radical left, some have not been reluctant to use force to preserve their ideals.

White mobs, whether it be Southern lynching parties or Northern and Western rabble descending upon black ghettos to indiscriminately kill any Negro who happens to cross their path, have punctuated American history with violence.[14] More frequently, however, white majorities have used *democratic means* to arrive at their *undemocratic ends*. By the ballot, they have instituted Jim Crow segregation laws or, more recently, simply refused to consent to the equality demanded by the black majority. A prototype of the withdrawal of consent by a white majority occurred in the 1964 California elections when an overwhelming majority of the voters (4 million to 2 million) approved a state constitutional amendment sponsored by the California Real Estate Association to give absolute freedom to a property owner to discriminate against prospective buyers or renters of his property on any basis, including race.[15] The U.S. Supreme Court subsequently ruled the California amendment unconstitutional in *Reitman v. Mulkev* (1967), since it was in direct conflict with the Fourteenth Amendment's guarantee to any person equal protection of the laws.

No doubt, the long history of the white majority's refusal to consent to the justice of black equality has promoted some Americans—both black and white—to give up the idea of curative political reform in favor of surgical revolution. As one Negro intellectual has put it, the bourgeois–reformist Negroes "clutter up the Negro civil rights movement with their strident protests and really believe that American capitalism is going to *grant* them racial equality. . . ."[16]

The fact that the two democratic principles of liberty and equality found in the Declaration of Independence and the Constitution have not harmonized as well as the Founders had intended accounts for much of the tragedy in American history, as well as for the current politics of confrontation in the United States. Just such a confrontation took place prior to the Civil War when radical spokesmen like William Lloyd Garrison were making demands for full equality, while others like John C. Calhoun were strongly pressing for consent of the governed.

In times of crisis, like the Civil War and the racial strife of our own time, the struggle between the radical advocates of these two principles is magnified and permits the student of society to observe

[14] John Hope Franklin, *From Slavery to Freedom* (New York: Knopf, 1969), pp. 477–497.
[15] For congressional action in the area of open housing, see "Revolution in Civil Rights, 1945–1968," *Congressional Quarterly* (1968), pp. 84–91.
[16] Harold Cruse, found in Lennox S. Hinds, "The Relevance of the Past to the Present: A Political Interpretation," in *Black Life and Culture in the United States* (New York: Thomas Y. Crowell, 1971), p. 365. Italics added.

them with even greater clarity. In this sense, the Civil War "is the most characteristic phenomenon in American politics, not because it represents statistical frequency, but because it represents the innermost character of that politics."[17]

The lessons of history clearly point to the need for statesmanship to harmonize the claims of consent with the claims of equality, and that only when the politics of moderation replaces the politics of confrontation can a wise resolution of this conflict become the basis of public policy.

Intrinsically, the two values of liberty and equality *are* compatible. They are merely two sides of the same coin. Democracy rests upon the recognition of the dignity of the individual and the notion that the state exists for the individual rather than vice versa. The individual's place in society is basically a matter related to liberty, whereas the relationships existing among individuals in groups are essentially the concern of equality.

Thus, liberty is concerned with the *individual,* while equality pertains to the *group.* Yet freedom ends where injury to others begins. Would anyone seriously quarrel with Justice Oliver Wendell Holmes' celebrated opinion, which rejected the freedom to shout falsely "fire!" in a crowded theatre? True liberty is contingent upon the freedom to do as everyone else does as well as upon the acceptance of the responsible use of that freedom. As Harry Jaffa has written, "the great engine of reason and conscience, in a free society, is the awareness that the freedom of each man, and his security from the abuses of power, consists precisely in the recognition that every other man is entitled to the same freedom, and the same security."[18]

Lincoln, of course, demonstrated in his famous debates with Stephen A. Douglas that both liberty and equality are based upon the same principle of enlightened self-interest. His argument is worth recalling:

> If A. can prove, however conclusively, that he may, of right, enslave B.—why may not B. snatch the same argument, and prove equally, that he may enslave A?
> You say A. is white, and B. is black. It is *color,* then; the lighter having the right to rule the darker? Take care. By this rule, you are to be slave to the first man you meet, with a fairer skin than your own.

---

[17] Harry V. Jaffa, *Equality and Liberty* (New York: Oxford University Press, 1965), p. vii; see also Harry V. Jaffa, *Crisis of the House Divided* (Garden City, N.Y.: Doubleday, 1959).

[18] Harry V. Jaffa, " 'Value Consensus' in Democracy: The Issue in the Lincoln—Douglas Debates," *American Political Science Review,* Vol. LII (1958), p. 751.

You do not mean *color* exactly? You mean the whites are *intellectually* the superiors of the blacks; and therefore have the right to enslave them? Take care again. By this rule, you are to be slave to the first man you meet, with an intellect superior to your own.

But, say you, it is a question of *interest;* and, if you can make it your *interest,* you have the right to enslave another. Very well. And if he can make it his interest, he has the right to enslave you.

Accordingly, liberty shades off into equality. With the Negro this is particularly true, since he is free neither to enter nor leave his race. As Professor Leslie Lipson has stated, "the connection between the problems of race relations and the principles of democracy is not primarily an issue of freedom. It is instead an issue of equality."[19] That liberty means nothing without equality was succinctly summed up by one Negro during the 1930s when he asserted that, "The first war was 'bout freedom and the war right after it [against Jim Crow segregation] was equalization."[20]

The Crisis in White over Black

Gross inequalities have always existed in the United States, ranging from the subordination of Negroes and women to the white male population to economic and educational deprivation of America's poor in the form of inadequate health care, housing, education, and unemployment. The broadening of the right to vote, to run for office, to have equal educational and employment opportunities, and to live wherever one chooses not only provides freedom for the individual where it was hitherto absent, but from a group point of view, it also fosters equality.

Yet, as Aristotle pointed out in *The Politics,* equality may take two basic forms, *identical* and *proportional,* and a political regime must choose between them according to the precepts of justice.[21] This is particularly true for a regime dedicated to the proposition that all men are created equal. What kind of equality is implied by that phrase? Identical or proportional?

In the first case equality means just what it says, namely that men are "equal absolutely, and in all respects."[22] The other is an

[19] Leslie Lipson, *op. cit.,* p. 95.
[20] Allen Weinstein and Frank Otto Gatell, eds., *The Segregation Era: 1863-1954* (New York: Oxford University Press, 1970), p. vii.
[21] Ernest Barker, ed., *The Politics of Aristotle* (London, Oxford University Press, 1968), Book V, pp. 204-205.
[22] *Ibid.,* p. 204.

equality based upon the ratio of effort among us, and that is necessarily unequal. The two forms of equality are by no means unrelated, however, identical equality has been the goal in American *political* life, whereas proportional equality has obtained in the *economic* and *social* sphere.

Identical political equality means that every sane adult citizen should have one vote and no more, as well as the same standing before the law. Considering the fact that the first ten amendments were part of the original Constitution and that the Eighteenth and Twenty-first cancel each other (Prohibition), the United States has added only fourteen amendments to its Constitution in the past 185 years. Eight have broadened the scope of suffrage from white males over the age of twenty-one with enough property to meet the state voting requirement to the present condition wherein all citizens over the age of eighteen are entitled to vote irrespective of race, color, previous condition of servitude, sex, property status, or residence in Washington, D.C.

This is not to say that the law has always been respected. All too often white majorities, north and south, east and west, have stood on common ground in denying the Negro political equality. De facto or de jure segregation, it was all the same . . . and behind it stood state enforcement and ultimately white violence. Whereas the South used Jim Crow legislation to require Negroes to use grossly unequal facilities in schools, transportation, housing, and recreation, the rest of the country did the same thing through residential segregation ordinances, restrictive covenants in deeds that forbade the sale of property to Negroes, and discriminatory employment practices. By such means was achieved the institutionalizing of black ghettos, and the cutting off of black America from its more affluent white counterpart. Politically, economic deprivation was effective in all parts of America in deterring the black minority from voting. But when that tactic failed, violence was always a ready alternative.

Violence Southern-style leaned toward lynching, a rather amorphous term that most commonly meant hanging, but which included other illegal acts. Between 1882 and 1946, Southern lynching accounted for no less than 83% of the total of 3425 Negroes murdered during that period.[23]

The rest of the country preferred to express its violence by race riots, though northern white majorities were not exempt from a little lynching of their own. Indeed, only a few months after Negro soldiers returned home from the battlegrounds of World War I after "making

[23] See *1952 Negro Year Book* (Tuskegee, Alabama: Tuskegee Institute, 1952), p. 278.

the world safe for democracy," they found that democracy in America was in itself none too safe for the black American, as approximately twenty-five white-instigated race riots broke out in American urban centers, ushering in "the greatest period of interracial strife the nation had ever witnessed."[24]

In contrast to the racial strife of the late 1960s, which began in the ghetto with blacks rather than as an assault from without, post-World War I race riots saw black Americans making little or no attempts to defend themselves from the white-originated violence directed against any available member of the black community. In the words of one scholar, the

> ... killing of Negroes was indiscriminate. ... Some of those who lost their lives were among the oldest and most respected colored people in the city. Most Negroes in the riot zone made no attempts to defend themselves, and the small number of casualties among the whites clearly showed the one-sidedness of the riot.[25]

American politics has been punctuated with periods of stagnation in the march to redeem the promise of equality in the Declaration of Independence. This was especially true of the era of Jim Crow segregation (1863–1954)[26] when black Americans were denied their identical political equality in voting and holding office through such nefarious devices as white violence, white primaries, racial gerrymandering, poll taxes, and "literacy" tests.

Jim Crow began to wane as a result of the Great Depression in the 1930s and America's resistance to the virulent racism of Nazi Germany during the 1940s. Out of this emerged the welfare state that placed limits upon economic inequality by means of such programs as Social Security, welfare, and the progressive income tax, as well as a renewed commitment to the principle of identical political equality.

One by one the impediments to political equality have been declared unconstitutional by the Supreme Court or prohibited by Congress. Employing the Fourteenth and Fifteenth Amendments, which guarantee equal protection of the law to all Americans and which prohibit the states depriving black Americans of the right to vote,

---

[24] Franklin, *From Slavery to Freedom*, p. 480.
[25] Ellito M. Rudwick, *Race Riot at East St. Louis* (Carbondale, Ill.: Southern Illinois University Press, 1964), p. 53.
[26] C. Vann Woodward notes that this racial caste system was born in the antebellum North and reached an advanced stage before moving South in force after the Civil War. The 1954 Supreme Court ruling in *Brown v. Board of Education* made such a system unconstitutional. See C. Vann Woodward, *The Strange Career of Jim Crow* (New York: Oxford University Press, 1966), p. 17.

the Supreme Court found the Southern white primary unconstitutional in 1944;[27] forbade racial gerrymandering in 1960;[28] and invalidated the use of poll taxes to keep people from voting in 1966.[29] The Voting Rights Act of 1965 mandated that no person may be denied the right to vote because of inability to read or write English if evidence is provided that he has successfully completed the equivalent of a sixth-grade education in an accredited school within the jurisdiction of the United States.

The Voting Rights Act of 1965 was especially significant in reducing the gap between theory and practice, as far as identical political equality is concerned, by preventing Southern whites from refusing to consent to Negro voting. That act provided for direct federal action to help black Americans register and vote, thus avoiding the protracted legal suits that have accompanied Negro efforts to get on the voting rolls when such efforts were handled at the state level by white state officials. The success in providing Southern Negroes with their right to participate equally with white citizens in politics can be seen in the report of the U.S. Commission on Civil Rights.

Moreover, the Court, in its reapportionment decisions of the 1960s, has moved to make each vote carry the same *weight* by eliminating population discrepancies in state and federal legislative districts that underrepresented Americans living in cities in general and black Americans in particular. Although 87% of the black population lived in the rural South in 1900, today about 73% of the 21.5 million black Americans live in metropolitan areas, and almost half of them are outside the South.

This population shift is largely the result of a black migration from the South which reached flood tide during the two world wars when black sharecroppers and tenant farmers were pushed off the land, first by the cotton boll weevil, and, then by the expansion and movement westward of commercial agriculture during and after the 1940s. At the same time that these black Americans were being pushed off the land, they were being pulled into the cities of the North and West by the labor shortages created by both wars. The *American Negro Reference Book* estimates that no less than 3 million black people left the South between 1916 and 1930, and that migration has not abated to the present day. With this exodus the racial problem of the United States changed from a rural "Southern problem" to an urban national concern.

[27] Smith v. Allwright (1944) 321 U.S. 649.
[28] Gomillion v. Lightfoot (1960) 364 U.S. 339.
[29] Harper v. Virginia Board of Education (1966) 338 U.S. 663.

Voting Registration Figures by Race—Eleven Southern States*

SPRING 1968

	Whites Registered	Negroes Registered	% of Voting Age Whites Registered	% of Voting Age Negroes Registered
Alabama	1,212,317	248,432	89.6	51.6
Arkansas	616,000	121,000	72.4	62.8
Florida	2,131,105	299,033	81.4	63.6
Georgia	1,443,730	322,496	80.3	52.6
Louisiana	1,200,517	303,148	93.1	58.9
Mississippi	589,066	181,233	91.5	59.8
North Carolina	1,602,980	277,404	83.0	51.3
South Carolina	731,096	190,017	81.7	51.2
Tennessee	1,434,000	225,000	80.6	71.7
Texas	2,600,000	400,000	53.3	61.6
Virginia	1,140,000	243,000	63.4	55.6
Regional total	14,750,811	2,810,763	76.5	57.2

NOV. 1964

	Negroes Registered	% of Voting Age Negroes Registered
Alabama	111,000	23.0
Arkansas	105,000	54.4
Florida	300,000	63.7
Georgia	270,000	44.0
Louisiana	164,700	32.0
Mississippi	28,500	6.7
North Carolina	258,000	46.8
South Carolina	144,000	38.8
Tennessee	218,000	69.4
Texas	375,000	57.7
Virginia	200,000	45.7
Regional total	2,174,200	43.3

*Source: U.S. Commission on Civil Rights; Voter Education Project of the Southern Regional Council

Not only have Negroes moved into America's metropolitan centers at an unprecedented rate, but the black population has been growing faster than its white counterpart. Thus, while one of every ten Americans was black in 1950, by 1973 one of every eight Americans was a Negro. This statistic, coupled with the exodus of the white population from the cities to the suburbs, shows that the Negro has become more of an urban dweller than the white American. About 73% of all Negroes live in metropolitan areas compared to 70% of whites.[30]

The net result is that Negroes now constitute a disproportionately high percentage of the population in the nation's largest cities. Indeed, a large number of cities during the 1970s will come close to having black majorities, despite the fact that the total Negro percentage of the national population is only about 12%. During this decade, according to the projections of the *Congressional Quarterly*, Negroes will rapidly approach a numerical majority in many of the nation's *largest* cities and already constitute 40% or more of the population in fourteen major cities, including Washington, D.C., Richmond, Gary, Baltimore, Detroit, Newark, St. Louis, New Orleans, and Trenton.[31]

Reflecting these population trends, as well as the "one man, one vote" principle enunciated in the reapportionment cases,[32] is the greater success Negroes have been experiencing in winning political office. By the opening of the decade of the 1970s, not only had Negro suffrage dramatically broadened, but black Americans had served in the Cabinet and on the Supreme Court as well as in the Senate and House of Representatives. Moreover, new black mayors had been elected in many of the nation's largest cities, and an estimated 1860 Negroes were serving as elected government officials throughout the country.[33] This is not to say that Negroes are proportionately represented in public office. They are not. Though they constitute nearly 12% of the population, they hold less than 0.5% of the more than 500,000 elected offices in the country. Nonetheless, the increase in voter registration and turnout, as well as the number of black public officials, is evidence that the United States has again begun to move toward the realization of identical political equality.

Even the economic and social goal of proportional equality is coming closer to approximation. Everyone understands the meaning of this form of equality, for it is the basis of the federal income tax. Instead of the rich and the poor helping to defray the cost of govern-

[30] "Trends in Negro Urban Population," *Revolution in Civil Rights*, pp. 116–119.
[31] *Ibid.*
[32] See Baker v. Carr (1962) 369 U.S. 186; Reynolds v. Sims (1964) 377 U.S. 533; Wesberry v. Sanders (1964) 376 U.S. 1.
[33] "Black Politics: New Way to Overcome," *Newsweek* (June 7, 1971), pp. 30–39. In 1973 Thomas Bradley was elected mayor of Los Angeles, becoming the first black American to be elevated to that position in a major city where the black population was still a minority of the population.

ment by paying an identical per annum tax, each is required to contribute according to his ability on a graduating tax rate as one becomes more wealthy.

Beginning with President Harry S. Truman's Executive Order integrating the armed forces in 1948, 20 million black Americans who had been largely excluded from American society through Jim Crow segregation were started on the road to equal opportunity in education, employment, housing, transportation, and public accommodations.

Richard Wright describes the hopelessness and resignation that characterized the black portion of our population during the Jim Crow period when inequities were so great as to generate nothing but despair. In *Uncle Tom's Children,* he writes:

> My Jim Crow education continued on the next job, which was portering in a clothing store. One morning, while polishing brass out front, the boss and his twenty-year old son got out of their car and half dragged and half kicked a Negro woman into the store. A policeman standing at the corner looked on, twirling his night stick. I watched out of the corner of my eye, never slackening the strokes of my chamois upon the brass. After a few minutes, I heard shrill screams coming from the rear of the store. Later the woman stumbled out, bleeding, crying, and holding her stomach. When she reached the end of the block, the policeman grabbed her and accused her of being drunk. Silently, I watched him throw her into a patrol wagon.
>
> When I went to the rear of the store, the boss and his son were washing their hands at the sink. They were chuckling. The floor was bloody and strewn with wisps of hair and clothing. No doubt I must have appeared pretty shocked, for the boss slapped me reassuringly on the back.
>
> "Boy, that's what we do to niggers when they don't want to pay their bills," he said, laughing.

Later that day, Wright told his fellow Negro porters of the incident. No one seemed surprised, and one injected,

> Huh! Is tha' all they did t' her? Shucks! Man, she's a lucky bitch! . . . Hell, it's a wonder they didn't lay her when they got through.[34]

Richard Wright's Jim Crow education, of course, included much more than this experience. Second-class citizenship and the segregation of white and black people in public and private facilities had been constitutionally sanctioned since 1896 when the Supreme Court upheld such a practice under the "separate but equal" doctrine of

---

[34] Richard Wright, *Uncle Tom's Children* (New York: Harper-Row, 1936).

The Fiber of Democracy: Equality in America   231

Plessy v. Ferguson.[35] Dissenting in that opinion, Associate Justice John Marshall Harlan declared that the Constitution was "color-blind" and that "the thin disguise of equal accommodations will not mislead anyone nor atone for the wrong done this day."

A step was taken toward atonement fifty-eight years later in 1954 when a unanimous Supreme Court knocked down the "separate but equal" doctrine in *Brown v. Board of Education.*[36] Writing the opinion for the Court, Chief Justice Earl Warren wrote that "the doctrine of 'separate but equal' has no place" in American life because "separate educational facilities are inherently unequal."

During that same decade Jim Crow was dealt another blow when the Supreme Court outlawed segregation on interstate motor carriers.[37] In 1960 it completely unhinged Jim Crow in interstate travel by ruling that segregated bus stations, even though not owned by the interstate carrier, also violated the constitutional right to equal protection of the law as guaranteed by the Fourteenth Amendment and implemented by the Interstate Commerce Act.[38]

Even as the gap between American democratic theory and practice was being reduced in these areas, groups like the Congress of Racial Equality (CORE) and the National Association for the Advancement of Colored People (NAACP) were testing Southern compliance to the new Supreme Court rulings. The resistance encountered by the "Freedom Riders" in Montgomery, Alabama in 1961; the murder of NAACP leader Medgar Evers, and the bombing in Birmingham of the Sixteenth Street Baptist Church, in which four Negro girls were killed, both in 1963; the murder of white civil-rights worker Viola Liuzzo by three members of the Ku Klux Klan in 1965, and the 1968 assassination of Nobel laureate Dr. Martin Luther King, the undisputed leader of the nonviolent arm of the Negro movement for equality, demonstrated that Southern white consent to black equality and the death of Jim Crow would not come without agony.

Nonetheless, the black American did make significant gains during the 1950s and the 1960s, albeit most of those victories came in the *cities* of the *South* and affected only the *middle-class* Negro. Largely excluded were the poor Negroes of the North and West, as well as those who remained in the small villages of the South.

Spurred by groups like the NAACP and CORE, as well as stimulated by the realities of cold war politics, which silhouetted the incongruity of America courting new black nations in Africa to prevent them

[35] Plessy v. Ferguson (1896) 163 U.S. 537.
[36] Brown v. Board of Education of Topeka Kansas (1955) 349 U.S. 394.
[37] Henderson v. United States (1950) 339 U.S. 816.
[38] Boynton v. United States (1960).

from turning to Communism, while neglecting its own black population at home, Congress passed a mild Civil Rights Act in 1957. The first such law since 1875, it prohibited interference with the right to vote and created a Commission on Civil Rights to make reports on discrimination and the equal protection of the laws to all American citizens.

On the eve of the commemoration of the Emancipation Centennial in 1963, Birmingham police chief Bull Connor inadvertently stimulated further civil-rights legislation by ruthlessly smashing a nonviolent antisegregation campaign headed by Martin Luther King with clubs, police dogs, and electric cow prodders. A wave of national sympathy and support, heightened by the assassination of President John F. Kennedy in November, led to the passage of the strongest civil rights acts in American history in 1964.

Obtaining consent for the principle of equality that permeates this act involved a bitter struggle in the U.S. Senate in order to end a fifty-seven day Southern filibuster against the bill. On June 10 the Senate succeeded, for the first time in its history, in obtaining the two-thirds vote needed for cloture against a civil rights filibuster. The vote was so close that all 100 senators were present and voting, including the dying California Democrat Clair Engle, who had to be carried to the floor of the Senate after having undergone two brain surgeries for cancer.[39]

Under the provisions of the Civil Rights Act of 1964, Congress prohibited discrimination in public accommodations (restaurants, hotels, theaters, etc.) that are involved in interstate commerce or owned by public authorities. To enforce the law Congress created a Fair Employment Practices Commission (FEPC) and empowered the President to cut off federal funds to programs in which racial discrimination was present.

While these civil rights laws were taking effect in the late 1960s, a wave of ghetto violence spread across the nation. Frustrated by unemployment rates that reached as high as 42% in some cities, by rat-infested and overcrowded housing, and decaying schools, distrusting the police who sometimes used double standards of justice for black and white, and relatively unaffected and unimproved by the civil rights legislation of the 1960s, Northern and Western blacks exploded throughout the country in urban centers from Newark and Harlem to Detroit and Watts. All of the riots were touched off, according to the U.S. Riot Commission Report, by minor incidents involving the police.[40]

[39] "The Congress," *Time* (June 19, 1964), pp. 15–18.
[40] *Report Of The National Advisory Commission On Civil Disorders*, p. 206.

Yet, ironically, the very violence of the 1960s may be indicative of a feeling of hope, generated by progress toward the ideal of equality. Gross inequalities have always existed in the United States. When inequities are most intense, they produce a type of melancholy fatalism borne of despair. Alexis de Tocqueville long ago noted that

> The hatred that men bear to privilege increases in proportion as privileges become fewer and less considerable, so that democratic passions would seem to burn most fiercely just when they have the least fuel.[41]

Crane Brinton's *Anatomy of Revolution* confirmed this observation more recently when he noted that prerevolutionary society is characterized by relative prosperity and growing social equality.[42]

The result of the urban violence, however, was to polarize race relations in the United States. When the civil-rights movement seemed to shift from the nonviolent sit-ins of Martin Luther King to the Black Power movement of Stokely Carmichael and Eldridge Cleaver, fear of urban violence and crime seemed to skyrocket in America.[43]

Although the prospects of a racial revolution in America are very remote,[44] the fear of racial violence played a strong role in the election of Richard Nixon to the Presidency in 1968. Sensing the so-called silent majority's fear of repeated race riots after the violence of the mid-1960s, Nixon defined the social issue of that election by raising the specter of "sirens in the night." Indeed, when President Nixon and Vice President Agnew spoke of the silent majority taking over the country in 1970, public-opinion analyst Lou Harris reported that if such a mythical majority existed, the only glue holding it together was "a common aversion to what is presumably the vocal minority"—the black population, concentrated largely in the South and in the large urban centers, "who had the audacity to say that they wanted 'Equality Now.' "[45]

That aversion has taken many forms, but none more emotional than the storm over busing as a means to integrate public schools.

---

[41] Alexis de Tocqueville, *Democracy in America* (New York: Vintage Books, 1945), Vol. II, p. 312.
[42] Clarence Crane Brinton, *The Anatomy of Revolution* (New York: Vintage Books, 1965), especially Chap. 9.
[43] Richard M. Scammon and Ben J. Wattenberg, *The Real Majority* (New York: Coward, McCann & Geoghegan, 1970), pp. 17, 21, 40–41, 180, 207–208.
[44] Barrington Moore, Jr., "Revolution in America?" *The New York Review* (January 30, 1969), pp. 6–12.
[45] Public address by Louis Harris, Pepperdine College Forum (Los Angeles, California), April 20, 1970.

Although the *Brown* decision dealt squarely with the de jure segregation in the seventeen states that by law required schools to be segregated, it did not deal with segregation resulting from segregated residential patterns, or de facto segregation.

That de jure segregation is widespread has been thoroughly documented by the 1966 Coleman Report (*Equality of Educational Opportunity*) and the Civil Rights Commission's *Racial Isolation in the Public Schools.* The Coleman group, after surveying teachers, administrators, and students in 4000 public schools, found that "Almost 80% of all Negro pupils in the first grade attend schools that are between 90 to 100% Negro. . . . In the South, most students attend schools that are 100% white or Negro. . . ." The study then went on to report that such segregated schools educationally deprived *both* black and white children in America, for evidence suggests that minority children learn faster when there is racial integration of classrooms, and that far from damaging educational opportunity for whites, white pupils have either gained or stayed at about the same level after integration.[46]

Focusing on this problem in 1968, the Supreme Court held that school systems had to convert to unitary, or single systems without racial division, and called for a school system in which there would be no white or black schools, "but just schools." It said, "The burden on a school board today is to come forward with a plan that promises realistically to work, and promises realistically to work *now.*" In 1971, in the *Charlotte-Mecklenburg* case, the Court held unanimously that busing is a proper means of desegregating schools.

It must be emphasized that the Court did *not* order wholesale busing, but rather sanctioned it as *one* reasonable tool. Despite the care with which the Court took in this decision, busing drew a violent reaction during 1970 and 1971 when it began dominating national headlines in the wake of incidents in Lamar, South Carolina; Denver, Colorado; and Pontiac, Michigan where school buses were overturned and burned. Adding fuel to the fire, President Nixon took to national television in 1972 to condemn school busing for having reached massive and unreasonable proportions, and to urge a moratorium on all busing until the passage of his Equal Opportunities Educational Act, which holds multiple attractions for those who would like to dodge school integration. Among other things, the act provides that no busing may be ordered by a court "until it is demonstrated by clear and convincing evidence" that "no other method set out in Section 402

---

[46] James Coleman and others, *Equality of Educational Opportunity* (Washington, D.C.: National Center for Educational Statistics, U.S. Office of Education, 1966).

[of this act] will provide an adequate remedy." One of the methods spelled out in Section 402 is "the construction of new schools," which has led some to fear that Nixon's Equal Opportunities Educational Act would lead back to the "separate but equal" doctrine of the Jim Crow era.[47]

President Nixon's charge that busing has reached a stage of massive proportions does not square with the evidence. His own Secretary of Transportation John A. Volpe, quoting the National Highway Traffic Safety Administration, estimates that less than 1% of the annual increase in busing can be attributed to desegregation.[48] Moreover, school busing did not become a controversial issue in this country until it involved mixing white with black, affluent with poor. As one outraged white parent put it, "As long as we don't have niggers on there, it's not busing. Busing is making white children get on with niggers."[49]

The "massive" busing of children for desegregation purposes that President Nixon declaimed in his 1972 television address clouded more than clarified the issue. The U.S. Commission on Civil Rights itself estimates that the use of this type of school busing accounts for less than 3% of the total busing of children since the *Brown* decision, while the percentage of schoolchildren bused for other purposes has risen almost 45%. All of this points to the inescapable conclusion that busing has historically been regarded by parents as an advantage. It is only when it involves desegregation that it becomes controversial.

In response to the steady increase in enrollments and to school consolidations involving the replacing of the old one- and two-room schools, busing of public-school children has grown rapidly over the years. Since 1921, the number of children transported in school buses has risen from 600,000 to nearly 20,000,000.[50] For almost as long as there has been automotive transportation, American children have been going to school by bus at public expense, and almost always that busing was regarded by the parents involved as an advantage; by means of busing their children may have been able to attend a superior consolidated school, or to take advantage of special classes for gifted or disadvantaged children. Indeed, in the South black children were rarely if ever provided bus transportation, whereas white

[47] I. F. Stone, "Moving the Constitution to the Back of the Bus," *The New York Review* (April 20, 1972), pp. 4–11.
[48] U.S. Commission on Civil Rights, "Your Child and Busing," (Washington, D.C.: U.S. Commission on Civil Rights, May 1972), p. 7.
[49] Neil Maxwell, *The Wall Street Journal* (March 20, 1972).
[50] "Your Child and Busing," p. 7.

children were transported clear across town to their all-white school, with the blessing of their approving parents.[51] As the U.S. Civil Rights Commission put it:

> To grasp the importance of the school bus to American education, one needs only to imagine the national outcry that would result if all bus service for all purposes suddenly were withdrawn. Only when busing is used for desegregation purposes is there bitter complaint.[52]

Conclusion

Thus, busing has served to conceal the real issue. The issue is not the new "yellow peril" in the form of a school bus. Busing of white children to superior schools or for the purpose of segregation has long been a familiar feature of American life. The real issue is whether or not the nation will remain as the U.S. Riot Commission found it in 1968, "two societies, one black, one white—separate and unequal."[53]

To unite the nation will require movement toward the redemption of the promises of liberty and equality as they are found in the Declaration of Independence and the Constitution. That will require enlightened public opinion, one that understands the necessity of fusing, or at least balancing, the principles of liberty with those of equality. The foundation of democratic government rests upon an acceptance of the necessity of a rational society, one equipped with the requisite moral virtue and intelligence to rule itself well. It is for that reason that self-government is best understood as not only government by consent, but also *self-mastery* through bridling one's passion to reason.

As self-mastery is not always in bountiful supply, it is the task of the statesman to elevate and instruct public opinion as behavior good for both the individual and the nation as a whole. To fail in this task is to run the risk that the dangerous gap between two societies—one black, one white—could grow even wider.

[51] *Ibid.*, pp. 7–9; see also "The Agony of Busing Moves North," *Time* (November 15, 1971), pp. 57–64.
[52] "Your Child and Busing," p. 8.
[53] *Report Of The National Advisory Commission On Civil Disorders*, p. 1.

CIVIL RIGHTS IN THE TWENTY-FIRST CENTURY

A monarchy is like a merchantman. You get on board and ride the wind and tide, in safety and elation but by and by, you strike a reef and go down. But democracy is like a raft. You never sink, but, damn it, your feet are always in the water.[1]

So spoke Fisher Ames from the floor of the House of Representatives in 1795 as he viewed with trepidation the new democratic government taking form. He was, of course, wrong. Democracies do sink. But he was most certainly correct in his understanding that "your feet are always in the water" in attempting to make democracy work.

Democracies are constantly being challenged both externally from foreign powers and internally from alienated groups. They have no guardian angels, and must constantly guard against encroachments upon the freedom that has been so hard won.

[1] John D. Hicks, *The Federal Union* (New York: Houghton Mifflin, 1937), Vol. I, p. 217.

Democracy rests upon the recognition of the dignity of the individual, and upon the assumption that men have, or may acquire, sufficient intelligence and honesty to govern themselves. Freedom therefore becomes an essential condition for the development of the individual personality so that it may "translate itself from what it is to what it has the capacity of becoming."[2] In this sense, democratic government is a means toward an end, and that end is freedom. As Herbert Agar has put it, "It is freedom which men have always wanted and upon which they must insist, for without freedom human beings cannot become fully human."[3]

Yet, there is a tendency for every government, democratic or not, to refrain from vigorously promoting the freedom of its citizenry because freedom is a nuisance to the administration of government. Paradoxically, individual freedom may be even more stifled in a democratic state than in an authoritarian one. Remarking on this point while observing *Democracy in America* during the 1830s, Alexis de Tocqueville wrote:

> The authority of the king is purely physical, and it controls the actions of the subject without subduing his private will; but the majority [in a democracy] possesses a power which is physical *and* moral at the same time; it acts upon the will as well as upon the actions of men and it represses not only all contests, but all controversy.[4]

In other words, public opinion in a democracy is so powerful that it literally obliterates the *will* of the individual to exercise his freedom to differ from the popular opinions of the day. Because of this, Tocqueville feared that the ruling majority would attempt to impose conformity upon the individual citizen and that democratic nations would become "nothing better than a flock of timid and industrious animals, of which the government is the shepherd."[5] The fears of Tocqueville have not proved unfounded as Americans approach the twenty-first century.

Freedom and Conformity in the Twenty-First Century

Men who collect together to form a majority do not suddenly become virtuous or change their characters. Moreover, there is no guarantee

---

[2] Herbert Agar, *The Perils of Democracy* (New York: Capricorn Books, 1968), p. 18.
[3] *Ibid.*
[4] Alexis de Tocqueville, *Democracy in America* (New York: Vintage Books, 1945), Vol. I, p. 273.
[5] *Ibid.*

that people living under a democratic form of government will not succumb to folly or hysteria and vote themselves into slavery as did the people of Germany in 1933 when they elevated Adolf Hitler to the position of Chancellor.

Recognizing this, the Founders of this nation added a Bill of Rights to the Constitution—the purpose of which was to protect the freedom of the individual who differs from the popular opinions of the day. They foresaw that the ruling majority might possibly attempt to cloak its self-interest in the flag, and attempt to curtail criticism of its policies by labeling such criticism unpatriotic or even treasonable. "My country right or wrong" is not a form of speech that will have need of the First Amendment's protection of the freedom of speech.

However, individual freedom, though enshrined in such documents as the Bill of Rights, is never secure. Indeed, a Bill of Rights is only parchment and may be repealed or restricted in a democratic system if that is the will of the people. That this is a real possibility in the United States today was recently revealed by a nationwide poll conducted by CBS News, which concluded that a majority of Americans favor conformity over freedom and indicate a willingness to restrict some of the basic freedoms constitutionally guaranteed by the Bill of Rights.[6]

Progress is not a law of nature, and nothing stands still in politics. Slowly, and with many lapses, we have developed the freedom embodied in the Bill of Rights; but we can slump back in a few complacent years to the status of subjects rather than free men.

Adverse public opinion, however, is not the only challenge posed to freedom in the United States. Throughout man's history technological and scientific developments have challenged the delicate balance between freedom and conformity in political systems. These developments may prove to be either a boon or a bane to society, depending on *how* they are applied by man. Yet, one thing is certain: science causes change, and political systems will feel the stress of adjustment. This is not a new phenomenon. Indeed, one need only to recall one of western civilization's "first scientists," Socrates, challenging his political system in Athens by undermining the myth upon which that city-state rested, namely that Zeus was god and the founder of that city. In *The Clouds,* his contemporary Aristophanes, provides posterity with an account of the scientific challenge to the politics of his day.

[6] James Reston, "Washington: Repeal the Bill of Rights?" *The New York Times* (April 18, 1970).

SOCRATES. Zeus! What Zeus! Are you mad? There is no Zeus.
STREPSIADES. What are you saying now? Who causes the rain to fall? Answer me that!
SOCRATES. Why, 'tis these, and I will prove it. Have you ever seen it raining without clouds? Let Zeus then cause rain with a clear sky and without their presence!
STREPSIADES. By Apollo! that is powerfully argued! For my own part, I always thought it was Zeus pissing into a sieve. But tell me, who is it makes the thunder, which I so much dread?
SOCRATES. 'Tis these, when they roll one over the other.
STREPSIADES. But how can that be? You most daring among men!
SOCRATES. Being full of water, and forced to move along, they are of necessity precipitated in rain, being fully distended with moisture from the regions where they have been floating; hence they bump each other heavily and burst with great noise.
STREPSIADES. But it is not Zeus who forces them to move?
SOCRATES. Not at all; 'tis the aerial Vortex.[7]

During the Middle Ages, no doubt the invention of the stirrup, which allowed an armored knight to stay on his mount, lent itself to the principle of political inequality and authoritarianism in much the same fashion that the later developments of gunpowder and the bullet lent themselves to the principle of equality and freedom. The point is simply that scientific-technological change produces political change for better or for worse, and that never before in man's history has there been an era where science has enjoyed so much success. Indeed, one Harvard professor has computed that of all the scientists deemed significant by the world, 90% of them are alive today.[8] It is clear that Americans are living in an age of science, and this cannot but have an effect upon American politics, and, in particular, upon the individual freedoms found in the Bill of Rights.

The question, then, becomes: How will science and technology alter the political landscape in the United States? Will this new technology prove to be our slave or master? The answer seems to be that freedom is being both strengthened and weakened by the new science and technology. This apparent contradiction may be seen if we survey the dimensions of our various freedoms. A selective examination of a few will serve to suggest the nature of this apparent contradiction.

First, it must be noted that the rights we have may include both a *positive* and a *negative* side to them. In the area of the right to speak, for example, we are not only guaranteed the positive exercise of that freedom, but also, in a more limited fashion, its negative coun-

---
[7] Aristophanes, *Complete Plays of Aristophanes* (New York: Simon and Schuster, 1967), p. 282.
[8] Robert Heilbroner, *The Worldly Philosophers* (New York: Simon and Schuster, 1967), p. 282.

terpart, the right to silence.[9] The impact of science and technology is dramatic and has broadened our ability to enjoy this right through such devices as the telephone, telegraph, and television. With the penetration of man into outer-space and the introduction of Telstar devices to broaden our ability to communicate instantly with our foreign neighbors, the expansion of this freedom has been phenomenal.

Yet there is a more sinister side to the use of technology in the area of free speech, for that same technology may be used to stifle speech and to exact conformity to the opinions of the majority that control our government. Consider, for example, the testimony of Dr. Jerome B. Weisner of the Massachusetts Institute of Technology before the 1971 Senate Judiciary Committee investigating the problem of governmental eavesdropping and surveillance of individuals active in American politics.

> Modern information technology provides the potential to add to our general well-being and to enhance human freedom and dignity, if properly used, by extending our muscles, brainpower and material resources, and yet it also threatens to ensnarl us in a social system in which controls could essentially eliminate human freedom and individual dignity.
>
> Improperly exploited computer and communication technology could so markedly restrict the range of individual rights and initiatives that are the hallmark of a free society and the foundations of human dignity as to eliminate meaningful life as we appreciate it. In other words, *1984* could come to pass unnoticed while we applauded our technical achievements. . . .
>
> I suspect that it would be much easier to guard against a malicious oppressor than to avoid being slowly but increasingly dominated by an information Frankenstein of our own creation.[10]

The subject of the Senate inquiry was the ominous invasion of liberty carried on, in the name of constitutionalism and law and order, to equate dissent with lawlessness and nonconformity with treason. Just how far this has gone is hard to say, but one gets an idea when it is discovered that military and civilian authorities have used electronic devices to monitor the activities of such critics as Senator Adlai Stevenson III, Representative Abner Mikva, Federal Appellate Judge Otto Kerner, Reverend Ralph Abernathy, and Louisiana congressman Hale Boggs. This type of military and governmental electronic eavesdropping has, as one judge put it, "a chilling effect" on peaceful

[9] Watkins v. United States, 354 U.S. 178 (1957). The right is, however, a *limited* one and only applies to questions asked by congressional investigative committees which are not pertinent to their work.
[10] *Los Angeles Times* (March 21, 1971).

political activities, and makes it no longer possible to dismiss such works as *1984* and *Brave New World* as mere literary nightmares.[11]

Already the government holds very large dossiers on a major part of the population. Most Americans are unaware of the extent to which governmental agencies are using computers and microfilm to collect information about the activities of private citizens. New York State is developing a statewide police information network, which all authorities agree could be extended across the nation within a very brief period of time.[12] With computers and such scientific innovations as "radio pills," which, when swallowed turn a person into a human broadcasting system, it is quite possible to carry on an almost continuous surveillance over every citizen.

A second freedom that has felt the impact of technology is the right to one's property, which is guaranteed in both the Fifth and Fourteenth Amendments. Again this right has been expanded because of the productive power of technology. America's economic power has produced what John Kenneth Galbraith has called "the affluent society," a society made so rich by technology that one economist has projected that the average income of all families and unattached individuals will be $15,000 a year by the year 2000.[13] Already it is nearing the $10,000 mark.

The United States has emerged as the most prosperous nation on earth, giving more Americans an opportunity to enjoy their Fifth and Fourteenth Amendment protection of property. Since the setback of the Great Depression of the 1930s, Americans have witnessed a steady increase in their production, income, and consumption. Whether one measures the output of industrial and agricultural production, the increase in productivity per man-hour or the wages received for work, the United States either leads its nearest foreign rival or is not far behind. Indeed, Dr. Linus Pauling, a Nobel Prize-winning scientist, estimates that 3 billion poor people living outside the United States have a national income of $200 billion, which is equivalent to the income received by the richest 5% of the American population, and that Americans, who comprise only 6% of the world's population, possess almost two-thirds of the world's wealth.[14] Never before have

---

[11] Mark Arnold, "Fears of Government Snooping to Get New Airing," *The National Observer* (February 22, 1971).

[12] Francois Duchens, ed., *The Endless Crisis* (New York: Simon and Schuster, 1970), pp. 192–198.

[13] Herman P. Miller, *Rich Man, Poor Man* (New York: Thomas Y. Crowell Company, 1971), pp. 240–243.

[14] Linus Pauling, "Table Talk," *The Center Magazine* (Santa Barbara, California: Center for the Study of Democratic Institutions), Vol. I (Sept. 1968), p. 246.

Civil Rights in the Twenty-First Century   243

so many Americans had so much abundance, and never before has the property right been so expanded.

Yet, as the 1964 Report of the Senate Subcommittee on Employment and Manpower noted, this has created a "manpower revolution." Sometime in the 1950s the American economy broke through a technological barrier and introduced automation (i.e. self-correcting machines that feed back information and adjust themselves) and cybernation (i.e. hooking those machines to each other so that they are self-operating), all of which made it possible to expand production of goods while reducing the labor force.

A few examples may serve to demonstrate this point. In 1964, it took only ten men to produce the same number of automobile motor blocks that required 400 men ten years earlier. Two men could make 1000 radios a day, wherein it took 200 men only a few years before. Fourteen men could operate the glassblowing machines used to manufacture 90% of all the light bulbs in the United States.[15] As a result of technological gains, America's agricultural abundance permitted Americans to spend less of their income on food than any other nation in the world, while reducing the rural farming population from 14% to 7%—and it led to a public program of price supports designed to curb production.

This trend illuminates an economic, and by implication political, paradox: the coexistence of prosperity and chronic unemployment. The new technology has drastically reduced the unskilled and semi-skilled industrial jobs, but it has also affected white-collar areas as well. Herbert Simon has observed that by 1985 automation can do away with all middle management.[16] Since middle management is considered the ultimate goal of much of America's middle class, this indeed would have profound results. Other observers, like Ben Seligman, are even gloomier, estimating a job loss of 40,000 a week, or 2 million a year due to automation.[17] At this rate, the work force could be completely abolished by the year 2000. Reacting to this statistic, the national government has emphasized in recent years programs like "manpower retraining" to avoid what former Secretary of Labor Willard Wirtz has termed "dead-end jobs."

While statistics do not show that work as we know it is actually being abolished—employment has, for example, increased in the ter-

---
[15] Michael Harrington, *The Accidental Century* (Baltimore: Penguin Books, 1969), pp. 246–247.
[16] Charles R. Dechert, ed., *The Social Impact of Cybernetics* (New York: Simon and Schuster, 1966), pp. 39–69.
[17] *Ibid.*

tiary or service sector in such areas as teaching and hospital work—they certainly suggest that this is in the realm of possibility in the not-too-distant future. Economists of both liberal and conservative persuasion have advocated a guaranteed minimum income or a negative income tax to establish a minimum income floor for those who lose their jobs to technology. President Nixon's poverty program reflects this concern. In particular, his family assistance plan represents a modified version of the guaranteed income idea. As the President explained it, his family assistance plan would provide a federal foundation "under the income of every American family with dependent children that cannot care for itself." While the bill has not passed the Senate Finance Committee, it is clear from the wide margin of approval given by the House that in time it will pass and thus create a new type of property association or relationship.

In the seventeenth century James Harrington wrote a classic book dealing with the relations between property and power, entitled *The Commonwealth of Oceania*. In that work, Harrington raised one of the oldest problems of government: how can people without property be genuinely free? Echoing this concern, James Madison wrote in *The Federalist*, "Power over a man's support is power over his will." John Adams compressed this into three words: "Power follows property."

In other words, if an increasing number of people are to be on the roll of a government dole, can they use their freedom of speech or assembly, if they are in danger of losing their paychecks should the government disagree? If society becomes split into the highly educated who run the technocracy and the government on the one side, and the passive, consuming mass on the other, can a democracy be maintained? What will replace work for the unemployed? Bread and circuses? Will America face a dictatorship of the technocrats?

These are weighty questions that cannot be easily answered. The discoveries of science are amoral, and they in no way guarantee human progress. How they are used—whether for welfare or warfare—depends solely upon human choice and direction.

A third freedom that has been affected by the impact of science and technology is the guarantee to "life" that may not be denied without "due process of law," i.e. fair law and fair judicial procedures. Science has dramatically broadened this right to life not only by lengthening the lifespan of most Americans, but also by improving the quality of life through the elimination of disease and deformities.

Already some Americans are beginning to talk about their "unalienable right" to such lifesaving devices as kidney machines, and the question has already arisen regarding whether or not a "donor" must consent to give his body organisms after death or whether the state may take them without consent.[18] Indeed, science is challenging the very legal definition of life and death itself as the question emerges as to when a patient is legally dead so that his heart or kidney may be extracted in its best condition for transplantation. On the other side of the coin, artificial insemination has raised the opposite question as to what is legitimate life.[19] As many states do not permit illegitimate children to inherit property, the status of some 10,000 children per year who are conceived by such means is in doubt until the courts come to agreement on a definition of "legitimate" life.

Moreover, science is now beginning to unlock the most fundamental life processes. As Dr. Robert Sisheimer of Caltech has noted: "For the first time in all time, a living creature understands its origin and can undertake to design its future."[20] In the near future, through genetic medicine, science may be able to eliminate genes that may be the cause of such congenital illnesses and deformities as cystic fibrosis, diabetes, mongolism, and hydrocephalus. As man's lifespan lengthens, one may expect new social needs and "rights" in such areas as medical attention, income maintenance, and recreation.

Yet, while there is nothing romantic about a mongoloid child or a disease-ridden body, the use of medical technology to benefit mankind clearly opens the door to the possibility of questionable human engineering. Physicians already see the possibility of artificial involution, i.e. the fertilization in a test tube of eggs, which would then be replanted in the human female uterus. Test-tube babies, once the realm of science fiction, are now not only possible, but even probable.

Indeed, scientists at the National Heart Institute have already experimented with an "artificial womb," and have managed to keep lamb fetuses alive in it for more than two days. Once this apparatus is perfected, the baby hatcheries of *Brave New World* would cease to be myth.

Further, medical researchers have succeeded in reproducing DNA, the chemical substance that carries the human genetic message that determines the sex and makeup of the newborn. Dr. J. B. Gurdon of Britain's Oxford University has used unfertilized eggs to "clone" or reproduce the genetic twin of a tadpole from the original egg.

---

[18] South Africa, for example, has already passed such a law whereby body organisms may be extracted after death with or without the donor's consent. In a country committed to an apartheid policy, only time will tell the consequences.
[19] "The Riddle of Artificial Insemination," *Time* (February 25, 1966), p. 48.
[20] "Man Into Superman," *Time* (April 19, 1971), p. 33.

Scientists are now arguing that one day man may asexually reproduce himself in the same way, creating identical twins "from a test tube full of cells carried through gestation by donor mothers or hatched in an artificial womb."[21] In such an actuality, individual behavior may become far less free and spontaneous, and more subject to deliberate programming. As we become increasingly capable of determining the sex, intelligence, and genetic makeup of our children, there may be a tendency to sacrifice individuality for conformity. Some have argued that television will add to this tendency by reducing within America sectional differences in dress, customs, speech, and values. Such reinforcement of conformity may well produce future problems in the areas of censorship and freedom of speech.

Given the impact of these and other scientific developments, one is led to wonder what traditional rights will be challenged and what new rights or freedoms may emerge.

The Forgotten Ninth Amendment: A New Magna Charta of Freedom?

Some have argued that part of the Constitution contains a "forgotten" but significant new Magna Charta of American freedom that may give to that document the needed elasticity to adjust to the challenges of science and technology. In Bennett R. Patterson's book, *The Forgotten Ninth Amendment,* it is suggested that this amendment represents "a solemn declaration that natural rights are not a fixed category" but rather are "a declaration of the sovereignty and dignity of the individual" and the inherent freedom necessary to maintain that dignity.[22]

Echoing the concern of the Declaration of Independence for the "unalienable rights" of man, the Ninth Amendment reads:

> The enumeration in the Constitution, of certain rights, shall not be construed to deny or disparage others retained by the people.

It is clear from this, and the earlier draft of the Ninth Amendment that James Madison, its author, was not *merely* placing another limitation on the powers of the federal government, but that this amendment was a declaration that inherent human rights are not enumerated.

Since the rights guaranteed under the Ninth Amendment are not enumerated, the only way to discover what they include is by a process

---
[21] *Ibid.,* p. 38.
[22] Roscoe Pound, in Bennett R. Patterson, *The Forgotten Ninth Amendment* (Indianapolis: Bobbs-Merrill, 1955), p. iv.

of elimination of known rights. Not included would be the enumerated powers in the Constitution, those sections like the Bill of Rights and the Fourteenth Amendment that limit the power of the state and federal government, or those that specify the powers remaining to the people. The rights found within the Ninth Amendment would also be conditioned, if not determined, by the developments of science and technology. What, then, is the forecast for the development of new rights for Americans in the twenty-first century, and what may be the future application of the Ninth Amendment?

Forecasting is a dangerous business, and the forecaster has never been a popular figure. Indeed, one may recall that Dante Alighieri reserved the Eighth Circle of his *Inferno* for forecasters for venturing into the future, which belonged to God alone. Their heads twisted completely around, they were unable to see where they were going. No doubt, as Herman Miller has suggested, this is "the reason forecasters to this day continue to have their heads screwed on backward. It is only by looking at the past that they can tell the future."[23]

What, then, is in the past? And what may be in the future?

As we have seen, rights are in flux because of the almost exponential impact of science on law. Until recently, there has been little reason to tap the unenumerated rights guaranteed to Americans under the Ninth Amendment. Indeed, the Ninth Amendment was not even cited by the Supreme Court for 175 years, essentially because the Court was relatively unchallenged by the explosion of knowledge so characteristic of the present; it believed that all basic rights were covered in the first eight amendments.

The only important case yet decided using the Ninth Amendment occurred in 1965 in *Griswold v. Connecticut*.[24] In a 7–2 decision, the Supreme Court overruled an 1879 law forbidding the use of contraceptive devices to prevent birth.

In the *Griswold* case the defendants, cosponsors of a birth-control clinic, cited the First, Fourth, Fifth, Ninth, and Fourteenth Amendments in their charge that the law was an invasion of pirvacy.

In Justice William O. Douglas' majority opinion, the Ninth Amendment was cited. He wrote:

> We deal with a right of privacy older than the Bill of Rights—older than our political parties, older than our school system. Marriage is a coming together for better or for worse, hopefully enduring, and intimate to the degree of being sacred. The association promotes

[23] Miller, *op. cit.*, p. 234.
[24] Griswold v. Connecticut, 381 U.S. 479 (1965); for an earlier analysis of the Ninth Amendment, see Knowlton H. Kelsey, "The Ninth Amendment of the Federal Constitution," *Indiana Law Journal*, Vol. XI (April 1936), p. 319.

a way of life, not causes; a harmony in living, not political faiths; a bilateral loyalty, no commercial or social projects. Yet it is an association for as noble a purpose as any involved in our prior decision.[25]

In a concurring opinion Justices Arthur Goldberg, William Brennan, and then Chief Justice Warren asserted that the Ninth Amendment protects certain fundamental rights not listed in the Bill of Rights including the right to privacy in marriage. Justice Goldberg used Patterson's *The Forgotten Ninth Amendment* to substantiate this claim of marital privacy.[26]

Application of the Ninth Amendment in the future seems to be assured, and there has been much speculation concerning possible areas of use. Patterson feels that the Ninth Amendment includes the Declaration of Independence's guarantee to the rights of life, liberty, and the pursuits of happiness, plus the rights of security, freedom of conscience, freedom of contract, and freedom to engage in a profession, trade, or business.[27] He believes that the Ninth Amendment will guard private or personal rights rather than public or group rights, and that it should be used as a counter to the "general welfare" clause of the Preamble to the Constitution, which states the purpose of the Constitution to be group welfare. If the Ninth Amendment were viewed as protecting public rights, the rights of the individual would be even more obscured than in the past and would be lost in conformity in an essentially egalitarian society.

As Patterson has observed,

> The psychological fact is that to the mass of men, acting as a whole, liberty is primarily the removal of restraint on crowd behavior, and what the crowd calls liberty is not liberty for the individual; it is liberty for the crowd to act without considering the results of their behavior on other people.[28]

Although the Founding Fathers clearly intended the Ninth Amendment to protect the individual from the oppression of an autocratic majority, this amendment may prove equally important in the future in protecting the individual from the pressures of conformity that may attend this age of science. Cases like that of *Loving v. Virginia* (1967), which knocked down state laws forbidding interracial marriages, might

---

[25] *Griswold v. Connecticut*, p. 486.
[26] *Ibid.*, p. 490.
[27] Patterson, *The Forgotten Ninth Amendment*, p. 23.
[28] *Ibid.*, p. 57.
[29] *Ibid.*

Civil Rights in the Twenty-First Century   **249**

well have used the Ninth Amendment rather than the Fourteenth to guarantee "unlisted rights," including the right to choose one's marriage partner.[29]

New rights are on the horizon. Already cases claiming the right to a cloud—a right inconceivable before science made the seeding of rainclouds possible—and the right to leave property to children conceived by artificial insemination are or have been before the courts of law. Here, too, the Ninth Amendment may ease the adjustment of America to the realities of scientific advances.[30] In this modern age of science, the Ninth Amendment may well prove to be a great centurion of traditional as well as new individual freedoms. As one writer put it, "Those who regard the invasion of the individual's privacy . . . as one of the great threats of our time may come to regard" the Ninth Amendment as "the Magna Charta" of our time.[31]

[30] Gordon MacDonald, "Science and Politics of Rainmaking," *Bulletin of the Atomic Scientists,* Vol. XXIV, Number 8 (October, 1968), pp. 8–14.
[31] James D. Carrol, "The Forgotten Amendment," *Nation,* Vol. CCI (September 6, 1965), p. 122.

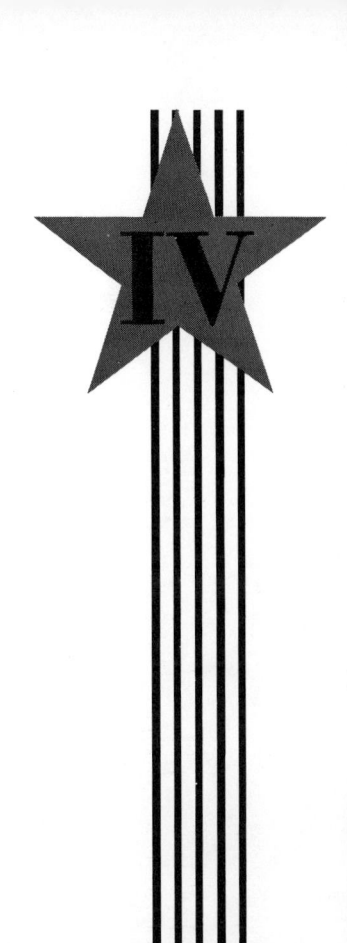

GOVERNING THE REPUBLIC: RESOLUTION OF CONFLICTS

Despite conflicts between individual rights and the social order, discussed in Part III, the United States has succeeded in maintaining viable republican institutions where almost all other ex-colonial nations have signally failed. Although not all events in its 200-year history have demonstrated a consistent application of republican principles, the United States has succeeded in its bold experiment in doing what was hitherto thought impossible: make an independent republic viable at home and influential abroad. In the process, enormous wealth was created.

But perhaps the United States has been too successful. There is danger in success. One hazard is presumptuousness. Bathed in success, people may be tempted to assume that present or future difficulties will automatically resolve themselves merely because difficulties were overcome in the past. Even more perilous is ignorance of the causes of such wellbeing. Anesthetized by unbounded prosperity and freedom many Americans no longer are conscious of the rationale on which the republic rests. If ignorant of these principles, Americans can neither define accurately the problems facing them nor provide appropriate remedies.

In this last Part some of the republican principles discussed earlier will be applied to the peculiar difficulties involved in governing the American republic as it begins its third century as a nation. In the struggle for political power, is James Madison's remedy of multiplying the number of factions in order to prevent any one from seizing political control and advancing its narrow, selfish ends still appropriate today, when the number of interest groups is being merged into huge, ever-increasing organizations of labor, manufacturers, religions, and the bureaucracy of government itself? In arranging foreign policies to preserve the country in the midst of world conflict, is the United States remembered as an ex-colonial nation that has provided the world with a rationale for revolution and popular government? In solving domestic conflicts, is the republican rationale for resolving the tensions between a rich minority and a poor majority still appropriate today when the numbers have been reversed, creating an unprecedented sociology of a prosperous majority and a poor minority?

THE WEB OF POLITICS:
Struggle for Power

Tweedledum and Tweedledee
Agreed to have a battle;
For Tweedledum said Tweedledee
Had spoiled his nice new rattle.

And so it has been that America's version of the famous struggle in Lewis Carroll's *Alice's Adventures in Wonderland* has transpired over the past century through the competition of Republicans and Democrats over the rattle of politics. Ever since Lord James Bryce, in his analysis of the nineteenth-century American commonwealth, first invoked the Tweedledum–Tweedledee analogy to describe the overriding consensus that seems to exist between the Jumbos and Jackasses of American politics, it has been a favorite metaphor used to describe the two-party system.

Segregationists and socialists alike have invoked it to decry what they deem to be the failure of either of the two major parties to provide real alternatives for the electorate in terms of defining the issues or tendering answers to the problems of our time. Thus, by Alabama's Governor George Wallace we are told that there is "not a nickel's worth of difference" between the two major parties. At the other end of the political spectrum, socialist Michael Harrington is seemingly in perfect agreement.

If the critics of the American two-party system are correct in their claim that American politics offers no real choice to the voter, serious questions are raised regarding the health of this democratic republic. If democracy is to exist in fact as well as in name, there must be both conflict and consensus reflected in the politics of the system. Perfect consensus is perfect conformity and the antithesis of freedom. Total conflict or cleavage is civil war, a condition that is at odds with both the freedom and the security of all who are touched by it. Thus, conflict and consensus, freedom and security must coexist in delicate tension with each other if life is to provide freedom without violence and security free of arbitrary constraint.

It is important then to examine the validity of the claim that American political parties have too much *unum* and not enough *pluribus*.

Madisonian Pluralism: Distributive Justice or Upper-Class Accent?

There is nothing intrinsically wrong with consensus. Indeed, every political community, by definition, is established on the ground that its individual members hold certain things in common.

> And a democratic political community would be . . . constituted by the fact that the political things its members hold in common are democratic. The problem of discovering what constitutes a democratic consensus . . . is the problem of what things fellow-citizens in a democracy *must* hold in common, what they *may* hold in common, and what they *may not* hold in common if they are to constitute a democratic political community.[1]

The signal idea upon which this democratic republic was founded was the belief in the proposition that all men are created equal, that all people should not only be equal before the law, but that all people should have an equal right to affect the course of their government. This is certainly an idea that both major parties must and do hold in common, though with varying and regional degrees of enthusiasm.

Political equality is, however, contingent upon the enlightened consent or liberty of the governed, which is and must be the sheet anchor of all democratic regimes. That individual liberty is not always

---

[1] Harry V. Jaffa, " 'Value Consensus' in Democracy: The Issue in the Lincoln–Douglas Debates," *American Political Science Review*, Vol. LII (1958), p. 745.

exercised with enlightenment is an unfortunate truth of history, a truth verified by the violence and mayhem of such groups as the Ku Klux Klan.

Yet, as James Madison put it in *Federalist* #10, to remove the mischiefs posed by such factions as the Ku Klux Klan, the Black Panthers, the John Birch Society, or the Students for a Democratic Society (SDS) by denying people the liberty to join what today are termed *interest groups,* would provide a remedy worse than the disease.

The Madisonian answer to the problem presented by the potential mischiefs of factions, as well as his hope for distributive justice, rested on the establishment of a pluralist society. By extending the geographic sphere of the republic *and* establishing a commercial republic, the size of the country and the division of labor occasioned by capitalism would multiply the number of interest groups to such an extent that no one faction could constitute a majority by itself. Thus, majorities could only come into existence by coalition and compromise, a process that should moderate the ruling majority so that its policies would not be adverse to justice and the general good. The result would be that any party that hoped to obtain a majority would have to appeal for broad support, and in so doing would have to cut across the lines of geography, religion, and class. As this is what both the Republicans and Democrats attempt to do, they must mollify many of the same factions and undertake the same process of compromise. It is little wonder that they emerge as moderate democratic versions of Tweedledum and Tweedledee, especially when compared to such minor parties as George Wallace's American Independent Party or the Socialist Party. Still, it would be unfair and unrealistic to assume that the Republican Tweedledum and the Democratic Tweedledee are carbon copies, or as Senator Barry Goldwater put it in his 1964 presidential campaign, "little echoes" of one another. We shall return to this point later.

There is little contention regarding the virtues of Madisonian pluralism, though there is widespread disagreement regarding its vices. Few would disagree that a pluralistic society "permits citizens to have a variety of loyalties and allegiances, thus preventing the possibility that they might live under a single source of authority."[2] The network of interest groups still provides a relatively powerless citizen with something of a buffer against a powerful and sometimes overbearing state. And probably few would deny the validity of Tocqueville's observation that interest groups sometimes prevent

[2] Andrew Hacker, *The Study of Politics* (New York: McGraw-Hill, 1963), p. 25.

individual citizens from being reduced to a cipher in an egalitarian crowd, and also serve as indispensable teachers of the art of self-government.[3]

None of this, however, proves or disproves the validity of the Madisonian pluralist model's claim to mitigate the mischiefs of faction and provide a measure of distributive justice as far as upholding the Declaration of Independence's promise of the right to the pursuit of happiness.

There is little question that Madison viewed the America of 1787 as a nation of joiners, and assumed that the "latent causes of faction" were "sown in the nature of man." Thus, it was believed that everyone would belong to a number of interest groups (some of them with conflicting interests so that the process of compromise and moderation would take place internally within the individual as well as externally between various interest groups), thereby providing every member of American society with an equal opportunity to influence and be part of the politico–economic decision-making process. Capitalism and American politics alike would witness ambition checking ambition, and private interest thereby converted into public welfare.

All of this was quite plausible in the eighteenth century when none of the frogs in the pond were giant business corporations like General Motors, whose *yearly* world sales total $28.3 billion,[4] making it wealthier than twenty-one states in the Union and more economically powerful than some of the 120-odd nations in the world.[5]

Adolph Berle and Gardiner Means, in their 1932 analysis, *The Modern Corporation and Private Property,* found that one-half of all corporate wealth was concentrated in the hands of just 200 companies. At the rate those 200 business corporations were growing, Berle and Means projected that by 1950 they would control nearly three-quarters of the nation's incorporated wealth. Robert Heilbroner, carrying the calculations even further, noted that if that growth rate continued that "by 1975 or thereabouts" that "the 200 giants would virtually rule the economic life of the nation, not unlike the feudal principalities which once ran the economic life of Europe."[6]

Not only are the frogs bigger in the pond than they were in Madison's day, but the "owners" of the giant corporations neither

---

[3] See Alexis de Tocqueville, *Democracy in America* (New York: Vintage Books, 1945), Vol. I, pp. 198–205.
[4] "Global Companies: Too Big to Handle?," *Newsweek* (November 20, 1972), p. 96.
[5] Robert Heilbroner, *The Worldly Philosophers* (New York: Simon and Schuster, 1968), p. 269.
[6] *Ibid.*

operate their businesses nor exercise much voice in charting the course the corporations will take. Although legal ownership of these giants rests with thousands of stockholders, actual control has drifted into the hands of corporate managers who are "singularly free to pursue whatever ends they desire," as stockholders dutifully authorize them to act in their behalf.

Needless to say, few Americans (to say nothing of foreign nations) belong to any interest groups that can contend with that kind of factional power. And former President Eisenhower's Secretary of Defense notwithstanding, most people do not believe that what is good for General Motors is necessarily good for the nation.

Some scholars, like economist John Kenneth Galbraith, have offered new hope for rescuing Madisonian pluralism from its present business bias in the twentieth-century corporate world. Professor Galbraith has called attention to a new form of competition that may prevent giant businesses from dominating American politics through their economic power. Galbraith grants that the frogs are bigger in the pond of politics, but argues that a new countervailing force exists because giant labor unions like the AFL-CIO are pitted against the corporate giants, making both labor and capital more responsive and responsible to the American people.[7]

The fly in the ointment is that just as 40% of the American people regularly do not vote, a like percentage belong to no interest group and are unrepresented in the politics of pluralism. And certainly a much larger percentage are members of neither a giant corporate interest nor a giant labor interest. Thus, the impact of the 40% who are typically the poor and the powerless, is zero in terms of transferring their interest-group goals into the arena of party politics.

Even those who are not poor or powerless find that, far from profiting from the supposed countervailing competition posed by giant labor and giant business, they are caught in an inflationary prison, walled in by rising labor costs on one side and rising prices on the other. Those who are members of such giant interests as General Motors or the AFL-CIO often find little reason for cheer as they discover through experience the truth of Robert Michels "iron law of oligarchy," which postulates the tendency of leaders of interest groups to dominate rather than represent the views of the rank-and-file membership.[8] In light of this, it is difficult to see how the competition

[7] See John Kenneth Galbraith, *American Capitalism: The Concept of Countervailing Power* (Boston: Houghton Mifflin, 1956), pp. 108-134.
[8] See Robert Michels, *Political Parties: A Sociological Study of Oligarchical Tendencies of Modern Democracy* (New York: The Free Press, 1949).

between private interest groups redounds to the benefit of the public welfare.

The pluralist world is very small and overwhelmingly dominated by the business interests in America. In his celebrated study, *The Semi-Sovereign People,* the late Professor E. E. Schattschneider's analysis of the American *Lobby Index, 1946-1949* revealed not only that two-thirds of the registered interest groups in this country were business organizations, but that even the nonbusiness organizations reflected "an upper-class tendency." It is little wonder that he should conclude that "The flaw in the pluralist heaven is that the heavenly chorus sings with a strong upper-class accent."[9]

Theodore J. Lowi has issued another serious criticism of the justice of Madisonian pluralism in distributing the goods and power of society fairly. He argues that the "pulling and hauling among competing interests" has resulted in a government that operates by fits and starts, a "government that can neither plan nor achieve justice."[10] Not only have special interests like big labor, big business, agribusiness (as corporate farms like to call themselves), and the American Medical Association managed to carve out their own feudal empires in the bureaucracy of government, turning various agencies into their special spokesmen, but they have often worked against each other and the public interest.

Thus, the late Mendel Rivers, chairman of the powerful House Armed Services Committee, became so much the mouthpiece of special interests in the Pentagon and the defense industry that he managed to establish so many military installations in his single congressional district in South Carolina as to warrant a federal payroll of almost $300 million a year. It is hard to believe that such a small area in South Carolina could be under such a heavy military siege to justify such an expenditure.

Agribusinessmen have also captured a large share of the government largesse and have managed to squeeze out of the taxpayer fat federal price supports for *not* planting various crops. Typically one finds congressmen like W. R. Poage chairing such important committees as the House Agriculture Committee, which allots business welfare checks to agribusinessmen like himself. In 1967, Congressman

---

[9] E. E. Schattschneider, *The Semisovereign People: A Realist's View of Democracy in America* (New York: Holt, Rinehart and Winston, 1960), p. 35. Lester W. Milbrath's research in the area of political participation revealed that about one-third of the American adult population is politically apathetic and another 60% merely spectators. Lester W. Milbrath, *Political Participation* (Chicago: Rand McNally, 1965), p. 21.

[10] Theodore J. Lowi, *The End of Liberalism* (New York: W. W. Norton, 1969), p. x.

Poage found it in the "public interest" to allot himself a $285,713,000 welfare check, nearly one third of the total paid to the nation's cotton farmers that year.[11] James Eastland, third-ranking member of the Senate Agriculture and Forestry Committee, receives more than $130,000 annually in welfare (or "subsidy") for his 5800-acre plantation in Mississippi.[12] And so it goes in the politics of special interests.

Even such supposedly humanitarian organizations as the American Medical Association (AMA) provide ample evidence of the advantage of wealth in the upper-class world of Madisonian pluralism. Not only has the AMA coerced physicians to join upon pain of being denied the use of hospital facilities,[13] but it has used the power of the purse to block such governmental programs as Medicare when they seemed to encroach upon AMA members' profits. The attitude of such special interest groups vis-a-vis the public interest was summed up by one physician when he said, "We keep the supply of doctors low and the demand up, and the prices soar. It's as simple as that."[14]

The power that groups like the AMA wield in the pluralist world of politics in America may be illustrated by the Medicare issue, which the AMA doggedly opposed throughout the early 1960s. Though legislation to provide some sort of federal assistance to help the elderly meet the high costs of medical care had been introduced into Congress by the Truman Administration following World War II, the first such bill to attract serious attention in Congress was the Forand Bill in 1957. When the Forand Bill or, as it later became known, Medicare, passed Congress in midsummer 1965, it provided that aged Americans over sixty-five would be entitled to a yearly medical coverage through a broadened Social Security program. Medicare would pay for all but the first $40 of hospital bills for up to sixty days, and sixty days after discharge from the hospital the elderly person would be eligible for another round of the same benefits. For an additional voluntary fee of $3 a month (eased by a 7% increase in old-age pension checks), the elderly would be covered for 80% of their physician's fees after they had paid the first $50.[15]

---

[11] See Robert Sherrill, *Why They Call It Politics* (New York: Harcourt Brace Jovanovich, 1972), Chap. 4. Mr. Sherrill was labeled "a security risk" after embarrassing the special interests and their public spokesmen in the aforementioned book. *Newsweek* (May 8, 1972), p. 17.
[12] Besides Sherrill's *Why They Call It Politics,* see his article in *Playboy* (November 1968) entitled "Instant Electorate," pp. 155 ff.
[13] L. Harmon Zeigler and G. Wayne Peak, *Interest Groups in American Society* (Englewood Cliffs: Prentice-Hall, 1964), pp. 256–258.
[14] *Wall Street Journal* (February 7, 1969), p. 1.
[15] "What Medicare Will Do," *Time* (April 16, 1965), p. 22.

Clearly there was a need for such a program. Poor countries in Western Europe had established some type of health insurance program a full generation earlier, while the wealthier United States had yet to act. In March 1965, just before the passage of the Medicare Bill, the median income of Americans over the age of sixty-five was a mere $1355 a year.[16] At the same time a physician in California was charging a fee of $400–$500 to set a broken thighbone, or more than 37% of the entire yearly income of the elderly for the performance of that one task.[17] Needless to say, the medical problems of the elderly amount to much more than broken thighbones. Not only do they have a higher incidence of illness than the rest of the population, but they are less financially able to meet their rising medical costs because of reduced incomes. It is small wonder that 69% of the American people favored Medicare in a 1962 Gallup Poll.[18]

In spite of the more than two-to-one popularity of the bill among the *unorganized* American public, American physicians managed to block the bill for more than eight years. In the showdown year of 1965, the AMA led *all* interest groups in the nation in its spending to propagandize its interests. Indeed, it outspent the second biggest interest group spender of that year by nearly six to one, $1,155,935 to $175,365.[19] Among the activities indulged in by the AMA to prevent the passage of the Medicare Bill were the following:

1. Issuing misleading statements claiming that the elderly were in "moderately good financial condition, not hardship cases." On the basis of its own Wiggins–Schoeck study the AMA claimed that of the 1500 persons over sixty-five they surveyed that 90% could think of no personal medical needs not already being taken care of. Senator Eugene McCarthy denounced the report in a full speech as a "poor public-opinion poll."
2. Encouragement of physicians to infiltrate interests groups of the elderly to turn them against Medicare.
3. Sponsorship of television programs like "Dr. Kildare" and "Dr. Ben Casey" to manufacture a more favorable public image of the physician.
4. Arrangement by the AMA to have Blue Cross and Blue Shield offer medical and hospital insurance to the elderly, only to

---

[16] U.S. Bureau of the Census, *Statistical Abstract of the United States, 1969*, p. 279.
[17] "What Will the Doctor Charge Under Medicare?," *U.S. News & World Report* (August 16, 1965), p. 53.
[18] Peter A. Corning, *The Evolution of Medicare* (Washington, D.C.: U.S. Government Printing Office, 1969), p. 93.
[19] All these examples are found in Arnold M. Rose, *The Power Structure: Political Process in American Society* (London: Oxford University Press, 1969), pp. 400–455.

later witness these offers withdrawn or the rates drastically raised to such a degree that they were only subscribed to by one-fourth of the elderly. In spite of that the AMA claimed that a majority of the elderly had subscribed.
5. Circulation of a fraudulent phonograph record in 1963 which was shown in court by the AMA to be a recording of a union meeting in Pittsburgh. When the union sued for libel, the AMA settled out of court for $25,000 and a public apology.
6. Misrepresentation of Medicare as socialism and depiction of British national health service program in such an unobjective light that the *British Medical Journal* denounced the AMA's misrepresentation as "vulgar, cheap and nonsense. . . ."[20]

Like most interest groups, once the proposed legislation has become a fait accompli, as did Medicare following the Democratic landslide of 1964, the AMA seemingly pursued a strategy of capturing and controlling the newly created program. Thus, the AMA successfully opposed the 1969 nomination of Dr. John Knowles as Assistant Secretary of Health, Education and Welfare (HEW) for Health and Scientific Affairs. The manifest reason for the AMA's opposition to Dr. Knowles was that President Nixon had not consulted them before announcing his nomination, but many believed that behind this procedural grievance was the AMA's displeasure with the fact that Knowles was "a 'hospital man,' a devotee of public health and . . . likely to be out of touch with the interests of the nation's private practitioners."[21] Far from losing money from Medicare as the AMA once feared, "doctors are getting rich from the program, and one no longer hears the faintest whisper of a suggestion from the AMA that the program be done away with."[22] In 1969 the Senate Finance Committee reported that 4300 or almost one-fourth of America's physicians secured payments of $25,000 or more from Medicare, and that thousands of other physicians had collected like amounts from Medicaid. Sixty-eight had collected $100,000 from Medicare.[23] Moreover, the Treasury Department reported in 1970 that a third of these physicians were underreporting their income from these government programs.[24]

The AMA represents only one of about 2500 formally registered interest or lobby groups in the nation's capitol. The largest of those interest groups is probably the oil industry, which spends millions

[20] *Ibid.*
[21] "Just What the Doctor Ordered," *Newsweek* (July 7, 1969), p. 15. Quoted in Zeigler and Peak, *Interest Groups in American Society*, p. 257.
[22] The point is made by Robert Sherrill in *Why They Call It Politics*, p. 93.
[23] *Ibid.*
[24] *The New York Times* (September 22, 1970), p. 1.

of dollars every year influencing congressmen to vote for oil import quotas and tax breaks. As a consequence an oilman can "freely pocket 27.5% of his total take from gas or oil wells as a 'depletion allowance' before even thinking about calculating his tax." Through this and other tax loopholes, it is small wonder that the files of the Internal Revenue Service recurrently show scores of people who are millionaires or have incomes in the hundreds of thousands of dollars and who pay no income tax at all.[25]

The most effective weapon interest groups wield in lobbying for their interests is filling the campaign purses of candidates who are friendly to their interests. As Representative Chet Holifield (Democrat, California) once put it, without that function "the power of the lobbyist would be practically nil." Thus, the campaign arm of the milk-producers lobby contributed $5000 to the 1970 campaign of the chairman of the House Agriculture Committee, W. R. Poage, who was running *unopposed* in his home state of Texas.

Declared spending is, moreover, a poor index of the influence interest groups try to obtain from our political parties. ITT (International Telephone & Telegraph) did not even appear in the list of top ten spenders for 1971. This is rather amusing considering the fact that that giant corporation was willing to make a *single* donation of $400,000 (which would have placed it second on the lists) to the Republican National Convention for the reelection of Richard Nixon. This was offered at a time when the Republican Administration was dropping an antitrust suit in favor of an out-of-court settlement against ITT.[26] By contrast, Common Cause, a newly formed group dedicated to such public interests as ecology and congressional reform, posted the top spending for interest groups not so much because they outspent the giant corporations as because that they conscientiously filed their spending reports with the government. Typically, the giant economic interests in the country utilize the loopholes in the 1946 lobbying regulation act to avoid filing their reports of spending, labeling their activities as "public information" or "public service" rather than interest-group lobbying.[27]

Not only are large sums of money contributed to finance political campaigns of favored candidates, but interest groups often cover their own bets by contributing to the campaign coffers of *both* Democrats

---

[25] "How to Make Millions and Pay Not a Cent," *Newsweek* (February 24, 1969), p. 69. Over a two year period President Nixon paid less than $2,000 in federal income tax and no state income tax on his income—in excess of one-half million dollars.
[26] "Hearings Bear Down on [Attorney General John] Mitchell, ITT President," *National Observer* (March 25, 1972), p. 4.
[27] Most of the loopholes were made possible by the 1954 Supreme Court decision *United States v. Harris*.

and Republicans, thus ensuring that access to government is to be had no matter which party is in power. This is not only true of business and labor groups, but of organized crime as well. As Alexander Heard has pointed out in his analysis, *The Costs of Democracy,* "the sums involved in organized crime seem to run in the neighborhood of 10% of the national income, and many of the criminal activities may require political protection."[28] The biggest criminal businesses involve the provision of illegal goods like narcotics and illegal services like gambling, both of which seek the protection of politics to proceed uninhibited by the law. Not only does organized crime cover the country like a blanket,[29] but "underworld interests buy their way into political campaigns and gain strategic positions in party organizations."[30] Again, like other wealthy interest-groups, organized crime covers its bet by contributing to the pocketbooks of both major political parties.

All of this tends to point to the conclusion that Professor Schattschneider's simile regarding the upper-class (wealthy) bias of this pluralist system is not too far off the mark. The system tends to favor the organized over the unorganized, the rich over the poor, the producer over the consumer, the powerful over the helpless, and the economic interests over noneconomic interests. Only recently have consumer interests been represented by groups like Nader's Raiders, and ecology and female equality interests championed by groups like Common Cause. The fact that Common Cause led the list for top lobby-group spending in 1971 suggests not only that there is more honesty in its own financial reporting, but that a new ingredient that will represent hitherto unorganized interests may be entering the system.

Politics Among Parties: The Web of American Politics

The fact that both Democrats and Republicans are encircled and infiltrated by these interest groups with their "upper-class accent" in some measure contributes to the Tweedledee–Tweedledum image the parties impart to the public. But other things contribute to it as well.

The brokerage function that major parties must play in order to appeal broadly enough to win a majority of the electoral–college votes during presidential elections every four years forces the national Dem-

[28] Alexander Heard, *The Costs of Democracy* (Chapel Hill, North Carolina: The University of North Carolina Press, 1960), p. 156.
[29] The Kefauver Crime Committee, Hearings, Part 12, p. 548. Quoted in Heard, *Costs of Democracy,* p. 159.
[30] *Ibid.,* p. 154.

ocrats and national Republicans to mediate among interest groups pursuing different, sometimes opposing goals. The result is a program of compromise, with each major party experiencing the same *process* of give-and-take over many of the same issues. The significance of this is that the major national parties manifest themselves as moderate, middle-of-the-road parties with the Democrats listing slightly to the left and the Republicans slightly to the right of center. Thus, no matter who wins the Presidency, among the overwhelming majority of Americans who are either Democrats or Republicans, loss can be accepted or at least borne in the face of electoral defeat.

The real difference between the two national parties is one of tendencies rather than principles. "In most parts of the country," wrote the late Clinton Rossiter, "it comes down to a difference between an urban, working-class, new-stock, union-oriented [Democratic] party with a penchant for reform and spending, and a rural–suburban, middle-class, old-stock, business-oriented [Republican] party with a penchant for the status quo and saving."[31] Yet, the cleavage between these two parties tends to be vertical rather than horizontal. In other words, our party divisions do not follow strictly the strata of class, regional, or religious differentiation, but rather cut deeply through those strata, leaving on either side of the cleavage a similar cross section of the nation. Each party has its own tilt, but neither is captured by a single special interest and both tend to represent a biased but general view of the national interest.[32] The fact that America, today as in its colonial past, tends to be a "middle-class democracy" leaves many of America's non-middle-class poor, ethnics, and students with a feeling that they have no real choice in American politics. This feeling is reflected in the recent mushrooming, left and right, of such third-party movements as Dr. Benjamin Spock's Peace and Freedom Party and George Wallace's American Independent Party.

Philosophically, the two major national parties again overlap, agreeing on principles but reflecting different tendencies. The justification of the nation's existence is expressed in the Declaration of Independence as a commitment to the values of liberty and equality. Both major national parties have remained largely faithful to *both* values, though each party has placed greater stress on *one* of the two values. Thus, the national Republican party has placed greater value on liberty, but has accepted the principle of equality, whereas the national Democratic party has put greater emphasis on equality, while accepting the principle of liberty.

[31] Clinton Rossiter, *Parties and Politics in America* (Ithaca, N.Y.: Cornell University Press, 1962).
[32] *Ibid.*

In this respect, the national Democrats have been the greater champions of such policies as welfare, civil rights, and federal action to put a ceiling and floor over and under the accumulation of wealth. By way of contrast, the Republicans under the leadership of President Richard Nixon have urged greater self-reliance, voluntary solutions to the problems posed by the nation's segregationist past, and state action in areas involving economic opportunity and employment.

Unlike the two major parties, leading minority parties (when not simply a regional or one-issue phenomenon) like Wallace's American Independent Party (A.I.P.) and the Peace and Freedom Party seem to have embraced *part,* but not all of the commitment found in the Declaration of Independence. Thus, when Governor George Wallace defied the Supreme Court's ruling to integrate Alabama's public schools with his rococo statement, "Segregation today, segregation tomorrow, segregation forever," he was pressing for his own liberty even if it meant denying equality to others. At the other end of the political spectrum, left-wing third parties seem inclined toward pressing for the principle of equality in areas like civil rights even at the expense of the liberty of people like Governor Wallace.

EQUALITY	EQUALITY/LIBERTY	LIBERTY/EQUALITY	LIBERTY
Socialists /	Democrats /	Republicans /	A.I.P.

The conflict that takes place among the upper two-thirds of American society is expressed through the two major parties, which on the one hand resemble one another in their consensus in accepting both goals of American political life, but are different on the other hand in that they represent a "democratic translation of the class struggle" regarding who should rule and whose political agenda should become public policy.

The national parties, however, are more illusion than reality. With the exception of four months out of every four years when the Presidency is at stake, they hardly exist in more than name. Because of the impact of federalism, Democrats and Republicans "tend to be stronger at the base of the national parties' pyramids than at their top, and achieve maximum strength only at the bottom."[33] As a result the Republican party of conservative Governor Ronald Reagan bears little resemblance to the Republican party of liberal Governor Nelson Rockefeller of New York. The same holds true for the Democrats, with the gap being even wider, if anything, running the gamut from

[33] Austin Ranney and Willmoore Kendall, *Democracy and the American Party System* (New York: Harcourt Brace, 1956), p. 264.

Governor George Wallace of Alabama to Senator George McGovern of South Dakota.

Nothing better illustrates the gap existing between warring interest groups within each party than the presidential nominating convention held every four years, "the one truly national instrument of American politics [which] is little better than a happy, disorderly conclave of state and local bosses."[34]

Like the pluralist system the National Nominating Conventions reflect special interests which have an "upper-class accent." Unrepresented in the delegates have been the poor, the young, women, ethnic minorities, and as always such unorganized interests as the consumer. Not only have the two national nominating conventions been unrepresentative, but their monstrous size has precluded them from being *deliberative* in the selection of the presidential and vice-presidential nominees.

In the effort to please as many state and local interests as possible, both the Democratic and Republican national nominating conventions have passed the limits of reasonableness. In 1968, for example, the Democrats had a total of 2622 voting delegates with an *additional* 2512 alternates for a grand total of 5134 delegates at the convention. The Republicans had only about half that number, still far too many delegates for deliberation.[35] Both conventions more closely resembled a mob than a deliberative body charged with the somber responsibility of nominating the most powerful executive leader in the free world.

In the wake of the violence that occurred during the 1968 Democratic Convention in Chicago as a result of student protests against the war in Vietnam, the Democratic Party established the Commission on Party Structure and Delegate Selection, headed by South Dakota's Senator George McGovern, for the purpose of making the party more representative of and responsive to all the American people. As a result of the findings of the McGovern Commission, the Democratic Party gave greater representation to the young, the poor, the ethnic minorities, and women in the National Convention of 1972.

It nominated George McGovern for President and Missouri's Senator Thomas Eagleton for Vice President. Eagleton was subsequently dumped from the ticket (a first in American history) for candidly revealing that while he was now well that he had once undergone shock therapy for mental illness. A member of the Kennedy clan, former Peace Corps Director Sargent Shriver, replaced him on the ticket.

[34] Rossiter, *Parties and Politics in America*, p. 16.
[35] Alexander M. Bickel, *Reform and Continuity* (New York: Harper & Row, 1971), p. 77.

The Republican Party by contrast made no reforms in its national nominating convention and perfunctorily nominated President Nixon and Vice President Spiro Agnew for a second term. As in the past, the delegates were recruited from the organized, wealthy interests in the nation.

After waging a noncampaign, and watching Democratic candidates McGovern and Shriver scurry to form an electoral coalition *after* the nominating convention, the Republican ticket of Nixon and Agnew won a second term in a political landslide of earthquake proportions, winning forty-nine of fifty states and swamping the Democratic ticket by 17 million votes.

It was not the campaign that won reelection for Richard Nixon and Spiro Agnew. According to the leading public opinion polls, the Republican candidates had a majority of three to two from the very start of the race. In spite of that, members of President Nixon's executive staff felt the necessity to break into the Democratic headquarters at the Watergate Hotel in Washington, D.C., to obtain the Democratic election strategy. The decisive event of the election occurred in the spring, months before the campaign even began, with Nixon's decision to mine Haiphong harbor in North Vietnam at a time when public-opinion polls showed that his Vietnam policy was in serious trouble with the voters, and the American military situation seemed to be badly deteriorating.

The Vietnam issue was generally conceded to be Senator McGovern's main source of strength, but the Haiphong decision was to rob the Democrats of the viability of the issue. The Nixon confrontation of the North Vietnamese was reminiscent of the Cuban Missile Crisis during the Kennedy administration in that Americans were anxious, wondering how the Chinese and Russians would react.

When the Soviet Union announced that the impending Summit Meeting with the United States would not be terminated on account of the Haiphong decision, and when Nixon was seen wined-and-dined at Soviet banquets in Moscow, public opinion surveys showed that the American public was vastly relieved. Combined with the President's earlier journey to China and the acquiescence of the Chinese to his Haiphong decision, Nixon obtained a great diplomatic victory and managed to convert McGovern's strongest issue into his own source of strength. The final blow to the McGovern campaign came within a week before the final balloting, when Nixon's foreign-policy expert, Dr. Henry Kissinger, announced to the nation that peace was at hand. It came three months later.

The percentage of potential voters who turned out to exercise their franchise was only 56%, the lowest turnout since 1948 when 52% voted in the election of Harry S. Truman. The Republican landslide did not point to the emergence of that party as the new majority party in the United States.

Professors Philip Converse, Angus Campbell, and Warren Miller have developed a useful typology for classifying elections and determining the percentage of voters that each of our national parties may claim. To borrow a simile of Samuel Lubell,[36] if we may term the majority party as the sun party and the minority as the moon party, the stable, long-term partisan dispositions of the American electorate is to make the Democrats the sun by a margin of 53-54% of the popular vote, and relegate the Republicans to the status of the moon by a margin of 46-47% of the vote.[37]

According to Professors Campbell, Converse, and Miller, short-term electoral forces may temporarily offset the long-term partisan dispositions of the American voter, resulting in an *election of deviation* wherein the minority party wins the White House. It is possible, moreover, for the moon to become the sun and the sun to be reduced to the status of the moon. This happens when the moon or minority party is able to attract to its banner on a regular basis some of the interest groups and/or voters who had helped to form the majority coalition of the former sun or majority party. When this happens, it results in an *election of realignment* and is usually reflected in the new sun party's ascendance in not only the White House, but also in Congress as well. Elections of realignment took place in 1800, 1860, and 1932, and President Nixon would have liked to have a fourth such election in 1972. The Democratic Party, the sun party since 1932, would have liked to have seen a *reinstating election* instead.

It is still too early to tell, but the 1972 Republican presidential victory appears to be an election of deviation rather than one of realignment; the Nixon landslide did not extend to Congress or the state level of politics. Lamenting the fact that Nixon's coattails could not pull other Republicans into elective office, one Washington Republican thundered, "Coattails, hell! That guy [Nixon] is wearing a T-shirt, and he's got it tucked into his trousers."[38]

---

[36] Samuel Lubell, *The Future of American Politics* (Garden City, N.Y.: Doubleday Anchor Books, 1956), Chap. 10.
[37] Philip E. Converse, Angus Campbell, Warren E. Miller, and Donald E. Stokes, "Stability and Change in 1960: A Reinstating Election," *American Political Science Review*, Vol. LV, No. 2 (June 1961), pp. 273-280.
[38] "Some Penance, Much Preference," *Time* (November 20, 1972), p. 31.

The hallmark of the 1972 election was split-ticket voting: casting a vote for a Republican President while voting for Democrats running for Congress, state legislatures, and governor. Thus, the Democrats maintained their 3-2 edge in controlling the governors' mansions and remained firmly in control of the Ninety-third Congress, giving it a slightly more liberal tilt than before the election and actually picking up an additional two seats in the Senate.

Congressmen tied to the special interests of their parochial legislative districts and states and receiving little or no campaign money from their own national party feel little pressure to support their party's presidential platform. The fact that Nixon lost control of both houses of Congress to the Democrats, coupled with the weak discipline that characterizes both major parties, indicates that Nixon's political landslide stopped at the edge of Capitol Hill and, as M.I.T. Professor Walter Dean Burnham concludes, was "almost wholly negatively based."[39] Not only had the Nixon Administration failed to end the Vietnam conflict, but it had failed to stem the chronic deterioration in America's competitive position in international trade with the result that the average American was besieged by inflation and a never-ending dollar crisis. The Nixon Administration's electronic surveillance of the 1972 Democratic National Headquarters in the Watergate affair did little to enhance the image of the Republican President in the eyes of most voters and prompted Burnham to conclude that "President Nixon and his closest advisers have the most doubtful relationship to the first principles of a free society of any Administration in living memory."[40]

On the other hand, many Americans did not think that they had much to applaud in the Democratic nomination of Senator George McGovern. To many, he was viewed as a "radical" for advocating economic policies that threatened to transfer income away from 48% of the population (and even more than 48% of the electorate). To others he represented the standard-bearer of further cultural change, busing and amnesty, and antiwar demonstrations.

To such a choice, Americans responded by split-ticket voting or not voting at all. Forty-four percent of the electorate found neither party's candidates attractive enough to bother to vote. Such "unused political potential," E. E. Schattschneider once noted, "is sufficient to blow the United States off the face of the earth."[41] Such a fact

[39] Walter Dean Burnham, "What Started the Landslide," *The National Observer* (November 18, 1972), p. 30.
[40] *Ibid.*
[41] Schattschneider, *op. cit.*, p. 99.

"is by a wide margin the most important feature of the whole system, the key to understanding the composition of American politics."[42]

The typical explanation of such widespread nonparticipation dismisses the nonvoter as a product of ignorance, indifference, and shiftlessness—and this may well be true to some degree. However, voter abstention also reflects the bias of the political system in favor of those who are organized and who have relatively more, rather than relatively less, in its marketplace. As the political agenda is formed by the former, it is not likely that it will include many issues of interest to the 40% who do not vote.

The issuelessness of American politics for a large segment of the American electorate is reflected not only in the noncampaigns of Nixon and McGovern in 1972, but also in the fact that three-quarters (160 Democratic and 140 Republican) of the congressional districts have been gerrymandered so as to make them *safe* for the local sun party in those districts.

The net result is to make it possible for the local sun party to be irresponsible and unresponsive to the voters in that congressional district. It will be elected no matter what. Moreover, the moon party will not be responsive or responsible to the electorate of that congressional district. In safe districts like that of Congressman Poage, the local moon party may not even bother to run a candidate. After all, no matter what it does its candidate will not be elected. Thus, for three-quarters of the House districts, there is no election at all.

Conclusion

There can be no America without pluralism, no pluralism without politics, no politics without parties, and no parties without compromise and moderation among the organized interests represented in the pluralist world. Politics in America, as in all countries, has been more responsive and responsible to the organized and upper-class interests in the country. The result has been policies of neglect as well as policies of special interest.

Our two national parties do represent, though imperfectly, political versions of Tweedledee and Tweedledum in the *best* sense of that simile. There is an overriding consensus between them regarding the just principles of American political life as they are found in the Declaration of Independence, though they differ on the amount of emphasis that is to be placed upon the values of liberty and equality as well as upon the programs of substance necessary to implement those just principles.

[42] *Ibid.*, p. 103.

The Web of Politics: Struggle for Power 271

Such *procedural and teleological consensus* cannot be overestimated in terms of its benefits, for without it political defeat would be intolerable for the losers in American politics. No doubt a large segment of the American public would feel seriously threatened as far as their life, liberty, or property were concerned if either segregationists or Communists were to come to power.

Most people in the United States can accept political defeat because their sense of electoral crisis is lower than in most countries in the world, including Great Britain.[43] At the same time Americans manifest a deep dissatisfaction with the performance of the two major parties in their responsiveness and responsibility to them. Illustrative of this was a 1969 Gallup Poll among college students which revealed that of nine key American institutions ranging from universities and family to business and the police that political parties ranked dead last in terms of student respect.

Both parties are parties of compromise and moderation. In this respect they are also similar, but there are also differences that are important. The Democratic Party remains the party of the Catholic, the ethnic minorities, and the city dweller. Its muscle and sinew remains organized labor. Since World War II the workingman has gained sufficient income and security to adopt middle-class social and political patterns. He has not defected to the Republican Party, which still remains the party of the white, middle-class Protestant and the champion of big business. The net result is that both parties represent the organized middle-class, the Democrats leaning toward the lower middle class and the Republicans gravitating toward the upper middle class and both competing for the center. Both have been effective in using government to attend to the special organized interests they represent.

The fact that almost half (44%) of the American electorate is complacent or apathetic about a presidential election is a statistic of overwhelming significance. As Professor Schattschneider once put it, these nonvoters represent "the soft underbelly of the system" and its "most likely point of subversion."[44] Their nonparticipation represents "the *sickness* of democracy."[45]

One needs to explain the political apathy verging on narcolepsy that exists in America if one is to get to the roots of this sickness. Certainly it should be a question of vital significance to both of the

---

[43] Gabriel A. Almond and Sidney Verba, *The Civic Culture* (Boston: Little, Brown, 1965); see also Robert E. Lane, "The Politics of Consensus in an Age of Affluence," *The American Political Science Review*, Vol. LIX, No. 4, 1964, pp. 874–895.
[44] Schattschneider, *op. cit.*, p. 104.
[45] *Ibid.*

two major parties, for any party that could attract this 44% to their banner would blow its competitor off the political landscape.

One explanation is that such complacency is a product of contentment. In the light of rising crime rates, runaway inflation, decaying cities, and a disastrous war in Vietnam, this explanation is hardly convincing. Even if it were an apathy borne of contentment, it would mean that almost half of the electorate is not involved in and therefore has a low sense of responsibility to the political system.[46]

More likely such apathy is a product of realism, which for some has turned into cynicism and despair. What good does it do to vote for a congressional candidate when one lives in a safe one-party district as three-quarters of the American people do? What good does it do to vote in a presidential race when the political agenda of both parties reflect the influence of the organized interests and one is a member of none? How are the poor in spirit and pocketbook, the diffuse and unorganized interests like the consumer, and the noneconomic interests like the conservationists able to place their interests high on the political agenda of either party? Until these questions are answered American political parties, as well as American democracy itself, faces a crisis of legitimacy.

[46] See Franz Alexander, "Defeatism Concerning Democracy," in *The American Journal of Orthopsychiatry*, Vol. XI (October 1941).

POLITICS OF A MASS SOCIETY

Sir, your people is a great beast.
—*Alexander Hamilton*

Since the days of Alexander Hamilton, and before, the fear of demagogues manipulating the masses has run through the tapestry of literature in Western civilization like a red thread. From Aristotle's *Politics* through Shakespeare's *Coriolanus* and into the twentieth century, scholars as diverse as Jose Ortega y Gasset and Erich Fromm have issued warnings of a specter of the rise of the manipulated mindless masses.[1]

One of the most eloquent statements of alarm came almost a century and a half ago when Alexis de Tocqueville predicted that if despotism were to be established in America that it would assume a different and more extensive character than in tired old Europe. He saw that where the social and political conditions of people were equal, *public opinion* exercised by the mass upon the mind of the individual would coerce him into conformity, even at the expense of freedom. As Tocqueville saw it,

[1] Jose Ortega y Gasset, *The Revolt of the Masses* (New York: W. W. Norton, 1932); Erich Fromm, *Escape From Freedom* (New York: Holt Rinehart & Winston, 1941). Ortega is a classical conservative, while Fromm is a Freudian Marxist. Both, however, express fear of the rise of the mass man.

274 Governing the Republic: Resolution of Conflict

... in a democratic country ... public favor seems as necessary as the air we breathe, and to live at variance with the multitude is, as it were, not to live. The multitude requires no laws to coerce those who do not think like themselves: public disapprobation is enough; a sense of their loneliness and impotence overtakes them and drives them to despair.[2]

What Tocqueville feared is a matter that confronts democratic man every day. Must he conform? Must he submit to the patterns that mold the mass man? Must freedom yield to the silent and not-so-silent majoritarian pressures of conformity that regiment all into contemporary standards of hair length, education, personality adjustment, and political opinions?

Present-day technology has reinforced the already prodigious pressures of conformity that attend everyday life. A new specter has been added to the old, and the American mind is haunted by the fear that science and technology may be leading the nation toward the static conformity of a *1984* or *Brave New World.* Thus, while books written at the turn of the twentieth century like John Fiske's *The Life Everlasting* could confidently make assurances that science and technology would only end in man's increased freedom and ultimate perfection, books written toward the end of that century are alloyed with warnings that technology might add to the already considerable pressures of conformity by integrating American society in such a way as to produce an apathetic and inert mass that might, as Tocqueville had warned, be "reduced to nothing better than a flock of timid and industrious animals, of which the government is the shepherd."[3]

Like the ancient Roman deity Janus, who could don opposite faces, technology has raised the millennial hopes as well as produced the Orwellian fears of thoughtful American scholars. A representative, though by no means exhaustive, list of the hopefuls and harbingers of the future would include the following: Edward Shils (a radical increase in freedom), B. F. Skinner (an opportunity to increase conformity through programed human behavior), Daniel Bell (the end of ideology and the growth of democratic consensus), Erich Fromm (the increase in authoritarian personalities and foundation for totalitarianism), Ben Seligman (widespread unemployment accompanied

---

[2] Alexis de Tocqueville, *Democracy in America* (New York: Vintage Books, 1945), Vol. II, p. 275.
[3] *Ibid.,* p. 337.

by political impotence), and finally Robert Theobald (freedom from economic want accompanied by almost universal leisure).[4]
What is to be made of all of this? Who is to be believed? Why can't the experts get together?

Technology and Democracy

Alvin Toffler has noted that we are presently living in "nothing less than the second great divide in human history, comparable in magnitude only with that first great break in historical continuity, the shift from barbarism to civilization."[5] Not only are 90% of all scientists known to history alive today, but, since technology feeds upon itself, the rate of scientific discovery and technological change is accelerating.

To embroider on one of Toffler's examples, in 6000 B.C. the fastest communication known to man was the camel caravan, which moved at an average speed of 8 mph (miles per hour). Four thousand, four hundred years later—after the chariot had been discovered, the maximum speed increased to 20 mph. More than 3000 years later, in the middle of the eighteenth century, it took Sir Robert Walpole about the same amount of time to travel from London to Rome by carriage and sailing ship as it had taken Julius Caesar to journey from Rome to London using the same modes of transportation.

The velocity of travel began to accelerate in the nineteenth century, with the development of the steam locomotive, which carried man at speeds of 25 mph in 1825 and advanced to 100 mph by the opening of the twentieth century. By the outbreak of World War I, man was no longer earthbound, and on the eve of World War II he was capable of flying at speeds reaching 400 mph. A mere thirty years later American rocket planes were flying at speeds appraching 4000 mph, and astronauts were landing on the moon, transported by space capsules that traveled in excess of 24,200 mph.

Such technological progress has created what is popularly termed a "mass society," a society in which Americans are closer together

[4] See Edward Shils, "The Theory of Mass Society," in *America as a Mass Society;* B. F. Skinner, *Beyond Freedom & Dignity;* Daniel Bell, *The End of Ideology;* Erich Fromm, *Escape From Freedom;* Ben Seligman, in *The Social Impact of Cybernetics;* and Robert Theobald, *The Guaranteed Income.* The entire issues of *The American Scholar* (Spring 1966) and *Daedalus* (Summer 1967) are devoted to a survey of the impacts of technology on American life.
[5] Alvin Toffler, *Future Shock* (New York: Bantam Books, 1971), p. 12.

and their lives are intertwined with one another's. Such a society is a relatively recent phenomenon, for as late as the turn of the twentieth century our population was a *segmented* one with 85 million American citizens living on farms, or in villages or cities that were mere clusters of individuals living quite apart from one another.[6]

By contrast, today is the age of the mass man. Villages still exist, but they are now a part of a single, interrelated whole. During the past half-century the United States has become a national society in the sense that local events may cause a ripple through the rest of the nation. Now everything, from what is consumed and worn to what is read and heard, comes from distant centers in the form of standard brands and nationally syndicated news.

This, of course, has been made possible only because of the wonders of technology. From mass production techniques of automation and cybernation to communication discoveries like radio, television, and jet transportation, technology has integrated American society. Yet, paradoxically, the same forces that have permitted the increase of interpersonal contacts have also separated men, as Tocqueville warned, producing a sense of loneliness and impotence that drives them to despair.

Radio and television have not only broadened the freedom of communication, but have also occupied a large amount of time formerly spent in familial or neighborhood relationships. Moreover, they have also made it much easier to obtain information on what is happening on the other side of the globe, in far-off places like Vietnam or China, than on what is happening in one's own community. Hence, while the *quantity* of human contacts has increased enormously, the *quality* has diminished, depriving many of old-style personal relationships. Technology has produced what David Riesman has termed "the lonely crowd."

At the center of this new mass society stand distant and mammoth enterprises—what Lewis Mumford calls the *megamachine*—that not only provide Americans with an unending supply of information and customer goods, but also, to a considerable extent, manipulate through advertising consumer styles to which Americans seem to conform almost compulsively.

With the spread of television throughout American life to the point where 95% of all of the homes in America have sets, politicians have increasingly used the Madison Avenue advertising techniques to sell themselves to the voters.

---

[6] Social Science Research Council, *The Statistical History of the United States from Colonial Times to the Present* (Stamford, Conn.: Fairfield Publishers, 1965), p. A 1–16.

Politics of a Mass Society **277**

The attitude of Madison Avenue in manipulating the masses toward its standard brands does not omen well for the future of democracy. In fact, at times it more resembles the American perception of the Soviet Union or the nightmare of George Orwell's *1984*. Consider, for example, the January 29, 1960 edition of *Printer's Ink,* "The Weekly Magazine of Advertising and Marketing," which raises the ultimate question of all business broadcasting: "How can the consumer, like Pavlov's dog, be taught the habit of buying a specific brand?" [7]

Such questions have led scholars and laymen alike to wonder whether political candidates can be packaged and sold like a bag of potato chips to a mesmerized mass television audience. In the 1966 gubernatorial election in New York, for example, Governor Nelson Rockefeller, who was trailing badly in the public opinion polls, won reelection with the help of the advertising firm of Jack Tinker & Partners. The approach of that agency to "marketing" its new product was explained by one of its firms members, Myron McDonald:

> The agency I work for, as you know, is a consumer–goods agency. We peddle Alka-Seltzer, Buick automobiles, Coca-Cola, and so forth. Until thirteen or fourteen months ago none of us had any political experience. We looked at the Governor in the only way we knew how to look at him; that is as a consumer product. Now, if you don't like to think of him as Alka-Seltzer, why think of him as a Buick. It's perfectly all right.[8]

More recently, Joe McGinniss' best-selling book, *The Selling of the President 1968,* has alleged that the slick image makers of Madison Avenue took a tired, dull-looking Richard Nixon, whose appearance more resembled that of a used-car salesman than a President, and restyled him into the "new" Nixon, who was then "huckstered" to the mindless masses in a sleek new package that masked the real man. Nixon himself entertains this view in his autobiographical *Six Crises,* when he explains his poor showing in the Kennedy–Nixon television debates of 1960 by noting, "I spent too much time . . . on substance and too little time on appearance. I paid too much attention to what I was going to say and too little on how I would look." [9]

Are we then faced with a new force of conformity that will reduce us to Tocqueville's "flock of timid and industrious animals" to be

[7] Robert Perrucci and Mark Pilisuk, eds.; *The Triple Revolution Emerging* (Boston: Little, Brown, 1971), p. 289.
[8] Public Broadcast Laboratory interview, November 10, 1967; in Milton C. Cummings and David Wise, *Democracy Under Pressure* (New York: Harcourt Brace Jovanovich, 1971), p. 297.
[9] Richard Nixon, *Six Crises* (New York: Doubleday, 1962), p. 341.

herded in whatever direction the image makers choose? Have public relation firms like Spencer & Roberts and Jack Tinker & Partners now entered the political vacuum left by the old big city political machines and bosses as the new manipulators of mass society? Will the same forces that have brought public relations men into politics also push them into the field of political decision making?

In response to these questions it should initially be understood that image making is nothing new to American politics. In this respect, the Log Cabin Campaign of 1840 may be one of the most important elections in our history, for it provided an early prototype for modern day admen with its frothy, hysterical, circus-and-cider campaign. As Professor Thomas A. Bailey has observed, "Setting an evil precedent for noise-and-nonsense tactics, the Whigs were washed into the White House on a tidal wave of hard cider." [10]

William Henry Harrison in that campaign won the Presidency by being depicted as a common man who lived in a log cabin and drank hard cider, when in fact he was born in a manorial mansion into one of Virginia's first families, was college-educated, and a teetotaler. It is difficult to believe that such subterfuge could escape the lenses of television today. Far from pulling the wool over the eyes of the masses, television provides millions of Americans with a more intimate and probing view of its political leaders than ever before.

This is not to say that television huckstering does not exist. It does, and although it is the ultimate indignity to the democratic process, there is no firm evidence to support the idea that the American people conform "like Pavlov's dog" to the hypnotic suggestions of the admen.

Although one can point to the celebrated Lyndon Johnson "Daisy Girl" commercial of the 1964 presidential campaign, which showed a little girl, plucking and counting flower petals amidst the chirping of birds only to be expunged from the screen by a thundering nuclear explosion and the words, "Vote for President Johnson on November 3" to verify the mindless conformity of the masses, one may find elsewhere confirmation of their alertness to political guile.

In the 1966 California gubernatorial campaign, for example, Governor Edmund G. "Pat" Brown made a series of spot political commercials showing Ronald Reagan as being unfit for governor because he had been an actor. Brief film clips of Reagan's rather talentless

[10] Thomas A. Bailey, *Democrats v. Republicans* (New York: Meredith, 1968), p. 53.
[11] Dr. D. Krech, *Government Research Subcommittee of the Senate Government Operations Committee,* in *The New York Times* (April 3, 1968); and Zbigniew Brzezinski, *Between Two Ages* (New York: Viking, 1970), p. 15.

career in show business ended with the assertion that "Ronald Reagan has played many roles. This year he wants to play governor. Are you willing to pay the price of admission?"

In another political announcement, Governor Brown declared, "I'm running against an actor and, of course, you know who shot Lincoln, don't you?" Reagan carried the state with 59% of the vote and pulled the entire slate of Republican candidates into office with him, except for the office of attorney general which was won by the incumbent, Thomas Lynch.

It is not television, but rather the ten-second or one-minute commercial, that is made to order for political chicanery. Not only do these spot commercials menace the underpinnings of the democratic process, but they also nakedly expose political representatives to the power of special interests rather than the common interest. With television commercials costing a candidate as much as $20,000 per *minute,* what candidate can be free of vested interests?

Where television really makes a difference, however, is in the *primary* rather than in the general election itself. With television a politician can become a household word overnight, but this does not guarantee that he will be elected. Before a political campaign even begins, well over 50% of the voters have already made their minds up because they are either regular Democrats or Republicans. Another 35–40% strongly lean toward Democratic or Republican regularity and are extremely hard to convince. This leaves, at best, 10–15% of the electorate to which a television campaign may be effectively directed.

Television is but one of the many factors that provide the key to political success, but it certainly is not the one that produces the much-feared Pavlovian response on the part of the American voting masses. On the whole, in spite of the lack of ethics demonstrated by spot political announcements, television has helped the American people keep better track of their political leaders, and has forced those leaders to be more regionally consistent in their political stance than ever before. To project the words of Finley Peter Dunne into our own times, television (like newspapers before it) has done its part to comfort the afflicted and afflict the comfortable.

The same may not be said of behavioral technology, especially in the field of psychiatry and to some extent education. Man is increasingly acquiring the ability to modify and control human personality as well as affect through drugs man's memory and intelligence. One researcher, speaking of a future only a few decades away, has written, "I foresee the time when we shall have the means and therefore, functioning of all the people through environmental and chemical manipulation of the brain."[11] Scientists envision that not only may behavior succumb to biochemical therapy, but that it may even be controlled by genetically encoding brain cells.

In one famous experiment, Yale physiologist Josè Delgado dramatically demonstrated that electrical impulses could literally control the behavior of a bull bred for fierceness and stop it in midcharge by sending electronic signals into what Delgado thought to be its violence-inhibiting center. Although Delgado does not see an immediate possibility to utilize his discoveries for the remote-control of human behavior, such a possibility has preoccupied the thinking of scholars from Cal Tech's Robert Sinsheiner to Harvard's B. F. Skinner.

Speaking before the seventy-fifth anniversary conference at Cal Tech, Professor Sinsheiner sounded as if scientists had in effect "become both Nature with a capital N and God with a capital G."[12] Sinsheiner alerted the country to the fact that soon science will make viruses, and ultimately living cells that will result in a "second Genesis"; many at the conference wondered whether the "second Genesis" would be as good as the first.

Many people are rightly concerned as to *how* this new behavioral technology will be used. Will it be used to promote the dignity and freedom of man, or will it be used to force him into conformity?

An early answer to this question came during the early 1950s when Robert Lindner warned:

> *You must adjust* . . . This is the creed of the sciences. . . . For psychiatry, psychology, and the medical and social arts that depend upon them have become devil's advocates and sorcerers' apprentices of conformity. . . . Equating protest with madness and nonconformity with neurosis . . . they labor with art and skill to gut the flame that burns eternally at the core of being.[13]

A generation later, Americans have reason to pause and reflect on the implications that Lindner's theory has for the future of democracy. Psychologists like Harvard's B. F. Skinner, for example, have not been unwilling to apply the new behavioral technology to human engineering and biocontrol. In his novel, *Walden II,* the planner of "utopia" reveals his political philosophy when he asserts, "Our members are practically always doing what they want to do, but *we see to it* that they will want to do precisely the things which are best for themselves and for the community."[14]

---

[12] Joseph Wood Krutch, "What the Year 2000 Won't Be Like," *Saturday Review* (January 20, 1968), p. 43.
[13] Robert Lindner, *Must You Conform?* (New York: Grove Press, 1956), pp. 172–173.
[14] Italics added.

Instead of promoting freedom and dignity as personal attributes, Skinner argues that we should adopt the Pavlovian method of conditioned human behavior. Likening man to a lower animal, Skinner urges in his newest volume, *Beyond Freedom & Dignity,* that we utilize the similarities that exist between men and dogs to promote Pavlovian control of man's behavior.

As Pavlov learned how a dog's salivary glands could be made to work in response to the sound of a dinner bell, Skinner reasons that man can be similarly conditioned to conform to predetermined behavioral patterns. In the same way that men have learned to condition rats by environmental manipulation as well as through education (or what Joseph Krutch calls "brainwashing"), so can men regulate the behavior of man. The result of Skinner's behavioral technology—as he himself candidly admits—would require the end of democratic government. Frazier, the utopian planner in *Walden II,* explains, "I deny that freedom exists at all. I must deny it—or my program would be absurd." Thus, behavioral technology à la Skinner points toward a totalitarian state, a Platonic *Republic* wherein the philosophers are king no matter how clumsy they may be philosophically. All this leads one to at least weigh the validity of one political scientist's assessment of such behavioral technology: of the two schools of behavioral technology, one thinks people are like rats; the other thinks rats are like people. In any case both study rats and have spawned a bestial social science.

Behavioral technology has produced other means to force social and political conformity. In contrast to Skinner's proposals, which have produced more *animus* than *communes,* the fields of psychotherapy and drug therapy have obtained greater support and wider currency throughout America. As Joost Meerloo points out in his book, *The Rape of the Mind,* medicine and psychotherapy can be effective instruments of coercion in any system of government, especially when cloaked in the jargon of science.

Whereas Communist or Nazi military aggression against individual liberty is dramatic and therefore highly visible, the all-pervasive pressure to conform in a democracy, assisted by the behavioral sciences, may be insidiously unnoticed. Protest and nonconformity on the part of an individual does not necessarily mean that he is mentally ill, but for those who dare to protest or nonconform, the danger of being labeled neurotic or psychotic is real.

Miltowns! Thorazines! Libriums! Stelazines! All of these have been used to tranquilize man into conformity when the behavioral scientists utter their Commandment, "You Must Adjust." Robert Lindner rightly indicts these technicians for the misuse of their technology. As he puts it, they have undermined liberty as well as the dignity of man with

> . . . their soporifics, their sedatives, their palliative drugs and their opiate dopes. . . . [And] if these do not "cure" him into conformity, do not level him into the mass, there remain in the arsenals of adjustment the ultimate weapons: the little black box for shock "therapy" and the swift and silent knife for psychosurgery. From the skies the lightning and the thunder are stolen to be discharged into the brain. . . . In the convulsion that follows, resistance ebbs and another sheep is added to the flock. Or the scalpel, quiet and sterile, probes with unerring aim toward the target behind the eyes . . . up, down, to one side, then the other . . . and a walking zombie, the penultimate conformist, stands where a man once stood, "cured" of his humanity.[15]

Frontal lobotomies like the one given to McMurphy in Ken Kesey's novel, *One Flew Over The Cuckoo's Nest,* are largely a thing of the past, but mind-control drugs are their replacement. Such drugs are presently very feasible and mass mind experimentation is currently underway. Two pharmaceutical companies have already established laboratories at the state penitentiary in Jackson, Michigan, where prisoners are subjects of experimentation. It is possible that a *repressive* science could create a *soma state* like that of Aldous Huxley's *Brave New World,* unless public awareness of the inherent dangers of misdirected behavioral technology is aroused.

It is needless to say that the traditional liberties that Americans enjoy—freedom of speech, religion, association, and all the rest—would cease to exist in such a circumstance. Moreover, it should never be forgotten that such technology can easily get out of hand, as Goebbels' propaganda machine proved when it applied psychological principles to anesthetize millions of German people into political submission.

Neither should the nation forget that one of the most chilling techniques used by Soviet authorities to this day to suppress dissent is to declare its rebel intellectuals insane (thus avoiding a public trial that might embarrass the state), and confine them indefinitely to mental institutions. Doctors in the West long refused to acknowledge such malpractice in the Soviet Union until books like Valery Tarsis' *Ward Seven* described life in Russian mental institutions so vividly that it could no longer be ignored.

The behavioral technology of psychiatry and psychology may serve democracy by *not* being "valuefree," and by turning itself com-

---
[15] Lindner, *op. cit.,* pp. 173–174.

pletely toward democratic ends. As a democracy begins and ends with the dignity of the individual, these sciences may strengthen the system by freeing man of the growing internal tensions and confusion that are apparently one of the costs to be borne for the comforts provided by other areas of technology.

The internal danger inherent to all democracies—a populace that is apathetic, lax, and possessing automized minds—may be reduced by a behavioral technology that helps men resist on the one hand the total regimentation of their lives, while on the other helping them to maturely *limit* rugged individualism so that society will not be held up to the tyranny of an Al Capone or a jet hijacker.

This should also be the purpose of public education. Thomas Jefferson's conviction that the people could be the centurions of their own liberty rested upon the notion that an enlightened public was possible through the universal extension of education. No doubt this was a major reason why he regarded his founding of the University of Virginia as one of his three greatest achievements and left for us a reminder of his wisdom on his self-composed tombstone inscription, which reads:

> Here was buried Thomas Jefferson,
> author of the Declaration of Independence
> of the statute of Virginia for religious freedom
> and Father of the University of Virginia.

Jefferson's understanding of the political importance of education was not original. Plato, the Roman Catholic Church, the Communist Party, the John Birch Society, the Black Panthers, as well as the American Legion have long understood its political significance, and for that reason have wanted to control it.

In spite of Jefferson's hopes that education would invest the masses with the ability "to know ambition under all its shapes and . . . [help them] exert their natural powers to defeat its purposes," schools in America have fallen far short of providing its future citizens with a training ground for democracy. As Bel Kaufman's novel, *Up the Down Stair Case,* so aptly demonstrates, teaching ideals in elementary and secondary schools are too frequently lost in the pedagogism and trivia in triplicate that is more concerned with checking hall passes and hair lengths than with the teachings of Jefferson or the relevant issues of the day.

Tragically, we are promoting more mindless conformity than intellectual curiosity. As Edgar Friedenberg has observed in *Coming of Age in America,* "Compulsory school attendance functions as a bill of attainder against a particular age group" so that the first thing that children learn in school is that "they do not participate fully in the freedoms guaranteed by the state, and that, therefore, these freedoms do not really partake of the character of inalienable rights."[16]

Rote learning of disconnected and outdated facts pass for knowledge and gum-chewing or talking in class for citizenship. Describing the Boston public schools in a book aptly titled *Death at an Early Age,* Jonathan Kozol reproduces verbatim quotations of the mindless conformity that is produced in far-too-many classrooms.

Q. Did we win the Revolution, Foot?
A. Yes.
Q. Of course we did . . . So then we had to establish a plan of government that was called what?
A. The Constitution.
Q. I'll hit you in the head. (Hands are up.)
A. The Articles of Confederation.
Q. What were they? (Pages flip in the notebook.)
A. Our first plan of government

It is not accidental that Supreme Court Justice William O. Douglas referred to American schools as a "temporary prison" in *McCollum v. Illinois Board of Education;* neither is it accidental that high-school dropouts have often been among the brightest people in the class.

Conformity, rather than independent thought, is more likely to be the end product of American education. One reason for this is that the schools are largely the product of America's nineteenth-century mechanical age, when industrialization required new kinds of skills neither the family nor the church could provide. As Toffler points out, "the whole idea of assembling masses of students (raw material) to be processed by teachers (workers) in a centrally located school (factory) was a stroke of industrial genius."[17]

Reflecting this, classrooms and curricula are still patterned on the old industrial order, with its focus on the specialization or fragmentation of the curriculum. Educators regiment students into assigned seating, move them from place to place at the sound of a bell (factory whistles), and finally zip them into a subject-matter straitjacket whose relevance to their future is unclear and whose linkage to other subjects is purely coincidental.

At the very moment when technology is extending and integrating knowledge through the everyday exposure of millions to television, as well as through computers and data banks, educational structure

---
[16] Edgar Friedenberg, *Coming of Age in America: Growth and Acquiescence* (New York: Vintage, 1965), p. 42.
[17] Toffler, *op. cit.,* p. 400.

and curricula remain fragmented in the milieu of yesterday's industrialism.

In fact, it is the adoption of the mass-production techniques of industry that has stamped so many students into the mold of conformity. Diploma mills crank out high-school graduates on the basis of how they have been socialized, which is the contemporary idiom for conformity. Given the hierarchial structure of education, which is dominated by the big universities, secondary and even elementary schools are locked into a frozen curriculum that is often obsolete because of the rigid university entrance requirements. In fighting to bring about curriculum change, most educators below the college level are frustrated into stalemates and finally into cynicism.

Although it is important to preserve certain aspects of the present curricula and to provide much-needed common reference points between classes, more *pluribus* and less *unum,* more flexibility and less rigidity, more individual development and less group standardization, are needed in our educational schema.

In this respect educational technology has not provided much relief. Precious little has been done with that technology to reduce the regimentation that characterizes the school systems. Beginning with audiovisual aids, educational technology has now produced machines that will grade tests, keep records, process students, and even videotape lectures that may be canned for student consumption.

Instructors and professors who end up in the audiovisual cans may then be beamed by television to thousands of students. While this practice is no doubt reaching a good many people who otherwise would never continue their education, such mass production technology tends to make education even more impersonal and less spontaneous. Imagination and intellectual curiosity are reduced to machine-graded proficiency tests. No doubt such depersonalization through canned educational practices and microphone large-scale lecture classes was among the reasons for University of California students at Berkeley picketing that institution with placards which read: "I am a human being, do not fold, spindle, or mutilate."

American education, from top to bottom, must reorient itself and its technology toward providing the *liberating* experience that is intended by the phrase "liberal education." Confronted as they are with the "Niagara of data" that comes to them via television and the publication of 1000 books per day throughout the world, students must be helped to organize this data and to bring order out of chaos. Fact-factories no longer suffice, nor do educational techniques that smother personal development while fostering conformity.

Essentially this means that the dignity of the individual must become central to the process of education and that students must be provided with the right and opportunity to develop themselves rather than be developed by others. As industrial technology frees us from the drudgery of menial labor, Americans will spend more and more time in school. Already junior colleges have become part of what used to be called the common school. Educational technology must be directed toward the democratic end of promoting freedom "for without freedom human beings cannot become fully human."[18]

Conclusion

Technology does not necessarily have to deprive the individual of his freedom and dignity by reducing him to the level of a compulsive conformist or Pavlovian robot. In fact, technology has historically fostered man's freedom and distinguished him from lower forms of animal life. Certainly there can be no freedom nor human dignity where man labors in the fields like a beast or where he dwells in ignorance and confusion.

Without technology, the masses are condemned to the servile labor and narrow world that characterized antiquity. If history proves anything, it demonstrates that technology is necessary, if not sufficient, to promote the dignity and freedom of the individual.

Yet, technology is Janus-faced and can be the enemy of mankind as well as its friend. It would be folly to ignore the perceptive insights of a Tocqueville or an Orwell and not anticipate the pressures of mass democracy that might produce the mindless conformity that would spell the death of freedom.

The people of the United States must be vigilant so that technology does not miscarry and replace democracy with a technocracy run by a technocratic elite. Without making a plea for a contemporary Luddite movement to eliminate the possible harmful effects of technology by destroying technology, one should not submit blindly to the uncontrolled march of the sciences.

As Professor William Carleton has asked, are we to commit a substantial amount of our resources and scientific brainpower to the development of American technology with virtually no public awareness or discussion and no control over the uses of that technology?

[18] Herbert Agar, *The Perils of Democracy* (New York: Capricorn, 1965), p. 18.

If democracy is to function in our technicalized society, technology must be transplanted into party terms and philosophies and thus made intelligible and meaningful to the voters.[19]

To do less is to invite Frankenstein's monster.

[19] William G. Carleton, "The Century of Technocracy," *The Antioch Review* (Winter 1965-1966), p. 495. For a contrasting point of view, see Melvin Kranzberg, "Technology and Human Values," *Virginia Quarterly Review* (Autumn 1964), pp. 578-592.

FOREIGN POLICY:
Making the World Safe for Democracy

15

[The United States] will recommend the general cause . . . by her example. . . . But she goes not abroad in search of monsters to destroy.
—*John Quincy Adams*

"Our cause has been the cause of all mankind," repeated Lyndon Johnson throughout the presidential campaign of 1964 in an effort to win the election and also to justify his decision, announced after he won, to escalate American involvement in the Vietnam war.[1] Although his campaign rhetoric attempted to convince Americans that he could be trusted to use the enormous power of the Presidency with greater judgment and restraint than his opponent, Barry Goldwater, who openly campaigned for bombing North Vietnam, President Johnson echoed one of the traditional assumptions of American foreign policy. By the phrase, "Our cause has been the cause of all

[1] Walter LaFeber, *America, Russia, and the Cold War, 1945–1971,* 2nd ed. (New York: John Wiley, 1972), p. 246.

mankind," he meant that the liberties Americans enjoyed could also be enjoyed by all men everywhere; because the United States had the good fortune of growing from a handful of isolated colonies to a position of enormous power, its citizens were morally obligated to help others who wanted these same freedoms.

Thomas Jefferson first linked "our cause" with that of mankind in the Declaration of Independence when he submitted the arguments for revolution to a "candid world" to judge whether the rights Americans were claiming in 1776 were in fact not the rights of all people. But Jefferson's "candid world" was eighteenth-century Europe whereas Johnson's was the "Third World" of emerging ex-colonial nations in Africa and Asia. Further, Jefferson was defending Americans' action in their own war of independence whereas Johnson and Goldwater were defending American involvement in the internal affairs of another country. As long as the United States has existed as a nation, Americans have championed the virtues of republican liberty and through foreign policies have sought to encourage its expansion abroad. But the experience in Vietnam has caused a rethinking of this policy. Not until President Johnson linked "our cause" to that portion of mankind living in Vietnam did Americans seriously consider whether "all mankind" had the traditions and the socioeconomic requirements that are essential to make free governments function.

Growth of the Idea of "American Mission" in Foreign Policy

Jefferson's generation was not content with the remarkable achievement of creating a republic for the United States; they also hoped the American experiment would reassure people living abroad that a free government was a practical alternative to their own political system. Just as the Founders studied the histories of ancient Greek and Roman republics to discover how to create the Constitution of 1787, so they hoped other people living in future times would look to the American republic as a guide for themselves. George Washington summed up this belief in his first inaugural address: "The preservation of the sacred fire of liberty and the destiny of the republican model of government are justly considered as deeply, perhaps as finally staked, on the experiment entrusted to the hands of the American people." [2]

[2] Henry Steele Commager, ed., *Documents of American History*, 7th ed. (New York: Appleton-Century-Crofts, 1962), Vol. I, p. 152.

Foreign Policy: Making the World Safe for Democracy

From the start of the nation, its foreign policy has pursued two ends: one is practical and the other is ideal. Not only should foreign relations be conducted to secure economic and political advantages for the security of the United States but these policies should also advance the cause of republicanism as well.

For its first fifty years, the United States was anxious to protect its own existence as a republic, negotiating with European countries when necessary for trade or territorial matters, but remaining neutral in the face of European conflicts. Except for the War of 1812, Americans pursued Washington's advice to avoid foreign "entanglements." This was not a strict isolationist policy because we did negotiate with Europe when necessary but it did suggest a policy of not becoming involved in foreign matters unless American interests were directly at stake.

This primary concern with national survival gave way when President Monroe announced to Congress in 1823 that the United States henceforth would champion republican liberty for the whole Western Hemisphere. Monroe declared the United States would exclude all European powers, and particularly such antirepublican combinations as the "Holy Alliance" of European despots who threatened to reestablish the Spanish monarch's authority in South America, from interfering in the affairs of the American continents. In return Monroe reaffirmed the United States policy of not interfering in European affairs.

When enunciated, the Monroe Doctrine was of little practical effect because the British fleet, not American words, stood in the way of the Holy Alliance's reconquest of South America. In time, however, the pronouncement developed into one of the basic tenets of American policy. By the end of the nineteenth century, the Monroe Doctrine became a combination of political realism, in which the United States' interest and power could enlarge in South America without competition. It also produced republican idealism, whereby the United States assumed it could and should secure freedom for all peoples living in the Americas. In 1813, Jefferson gave one of the earliest expressions to this ideal when he observed that while Europe is "the domicile of despotism, our endeavor should be to make our hemisphere that of freedom."[3] By the end of the nineteenth century the Western Hemisphere had indeed become "our hemisphere." But the difficulties

---

[3] Thomas Jefferson to James Monroe, October 24, 1823, in *The People Shall Judge: Readings in the Formation of American Policy* (Chicago: University of Chicago Press, 1949), 2 vols, Vol. I, p. 508 (2 vols.).

inherent in such an assumption became apparent when the United States attempted to juggle idealism with economic realism in the Spanish–American War (1898).

By 1898 Americans had gone west, settling the continent to the Pacific Ocean. They had joined England, Germany, and Japan in the scramble for colonies, commercial advantages, and spheres of influence all over the world. Soon the United States found itself deeply involved in the domestic as well as foreign matters of the Caribbean and Central American nations. Its policy here was characterized as "dollar diplomacy" in which oil, shipping, mineral, and fruit investors received favorable foreign policies and protection from the Marines, and politicians acquired new military bases to secure the enlarged interests of the United States. At the end of the Spanish–American War, the United States forced Spain to make Cuba independent and then promptly annexed the Philippine islands. Despite opposition to such imperialism by American congressmen, President McKinley thought Americans had a duty to "uplift and Christianize" the Filipinos. Soon the Army was crushing a Philippine insurrection and the United States found itself doing in the Philippines exactly what it had condemned Spain for doing in Cuba. But two-thirds of the Senate supported McKinley's treaty with Spain. Senator Albert Beveridge linked "our cause" to the will of God and suddenly the old idea of "Divine Right of Monarchs" was replaced with "Divine Right of Republics." In justifying American imperialism over the Philippines, Senator Beveridge insisted the Declaration of Independence did not apply to all of mankind. "It was written by men who, for a century and a half, had been experimenting in self-government on this continent, and whose ancestors for hundreds of years before had been gradually developing toward that high and holy estate. The Declaration applies only to people capable of self-government. How dare any man prostitute this expression of the very elect of self-governing peoples to a race of Malay children of barbarism, schooled in Spanish methods and ideas?"[4]

Senator Beveridge identified those who were "capable" of governing themselves with a racist theory that tied Darwinian evolution, Christianity, and national supremacy together. "The nation alone is immortal. The nation alone is sacred," he declared. The question of annexing the Philippine people "is elemental. It is racial. God has not been preparing the English-speaking and Teutonic peoples for a thousand years for nothing but vain and idle self-contemplation and self-admiration. No! He has made us the master organizers of the

[4] *Congressional Record,* 56th Congress, First Session (January 9, 1900), p. 710.

world to establish a system where chaos reigns. He has given us the spirit of progress to overwhelm the forces of reaction throughout the earth. He has made us adept in government that we may administer government among savage and senile peoples. Were it not for such a force as this the world would relapse into barbarism and night. And of all our race He has marked the American people as His chosen nation to finally lead in the regeneration of the world. This is the divine mission of America, and it holds for us all the profit, all the glory, all the happiness possible to man. We are trustees of the world's progress, guardians of its righteous peace. The judgment of the Master is upon us: 'Ye have been faithful over a few things; I will make you ruler over many things.' " [5]

Many Americans were vigorously opposed to this imperialistic interpretation of the American mission. They rejected the presumption of the United States governing a people without the consent of the governed and quoted the Declaration of Independence to show how far the United States had turned from its original principles. They argued that the United States should concentrate on building a free government within its own boundaries, then by example other nations might be prompted toward self-government. But this opinion never dominated American policymakers in the twentieth century. Now that the United States was a world power, opinion was divided over how this power ought to be used in relations with other countries. One view held that the United States ought to follow an active if not aggressive policy of intervening in world affairs; the other view held that the United States should withdraw from world politics, even to the point of isolation, and concentrate on creating an example of republican government at home.

These two opposing views were brought into tension on the eves of our involvement in both world wars. Woodrow Wilson wrestled with these two currents of opinion in shaping American policy with the European belligerents during World War I. To many Americans that war appeared to be just the kind of European "entanglement" Washington wisely warned us to avoid. Despite being reelected on the pledge "He kept us out of war," Wilson came to believe that freedom at home was impossible to preserve unless the world itself was made safe for democracy. In addition to the economic and political arguments raised to justify our participation in World War I, President Wilson also argued that American liberties within the United States were insecure as long as the world environment was hostile to democracy. This interventionalist policy continued after the war, despite an

[5] *Ibid.*, p. 711.

isolationist sentiment, largely because the United States emerged in 1919 as one of the most powerful countries in the world. This division of opinion was even more sharply focused on the eve of World War II, but even before declaring war in 1941 the United States had become the "arsenal of democracy" for the Allies.

The United States became a superpower following World War II not only because the country ushered in the nuclear age in 1945 by developing and using the world's first atom bomb, but because it held economic superiority over the world. Having escaped the bomb devastation that racked Europe and Asia, the American economy was sufficiently strong to help enable Europe and Japan make an extraordinarily rapid recovery. But the rise of totalitarianism from Communism threatened democracy as much as did the recently defeated Fascist and Nazi states. An aggressive expansion of Russian imperialism from 1945-1948 in Poland, Czechoslovakia, Yugoslavia, the Balkan states of Rumania and Bulgaria, together with revolutionary efforts in Greece, prompted President Truman to have the United States intervene in European affairs on an unprecedented scale. The emergence of Chinese Communism almost simultaneously in Asia prompted Truman to respond in Korea in 1950.

The American purpose of preserving free government seemed challenged now on a global basis by the Communist ideology that blatantly announced it would eventually rule the world. President Truman attempted to secure the future of Western Europe for democratic government by massive economic assistance in the Marshall Plan and by military assistance known as the "Truman Doctrine." Through the Marshall Plan sixteen nations of Western Europe, later joined by West Germany, received $15 billion in grants and loans between 1948 and 1952 and by 1951 all participating countries had increased their productive capacities beyond prewar conditions. After the Marshall Plan, the United States developed a series of economic and military programs that have provided over $140 billion in grants and loans to over 100 countries. But more than economic assistance was needed in 1948. In response to the Communist threat in Greece and Turkey, Truman announced his doctrine that the United States would provide military assistance to European nations so they could protect themselves from external attack. After World War II, both Russia and the United States claimed to have a global mission and for the next twenty years world affairs orbited around the policies and suspicions of these two superpowers to produce what became known as the *cold war*.

When Lyndon Johnson declared, in the campaign of 1964, "Our cause has been the cause of all mankind," he accepted the ideal of preserving what George Washington called "the destiny of the republican model of government," and expanding it from the Western Hemisphere (Monroe Doctrine), through Western Europe (Truman Doctrine), to include now all of Southeast Asia as well. What Johnson's policy did not consider, of course, was that the nations emerging in the 1960s had much different traditions from the West and would follow a national transformation peculiar to their own history and therefore different from the democracies of Western Europe or the United States. Free enterprise, for example, which took some 300 years of experience and adjustment to develop in the United States, was not likely to emerge instantly (if ever) in the "Third World" where people were poor and the countries limited in natural resources. But President Johnson assumed, as did Woodrow Wilson, that without "freedom of enterprise there can be no freedom whatsoever." Instead of considering the difficulty of making our economic system work in the "boiler houses" of these emerging nations, Johnson preferred to quote the idealism of Wilson. "Woodrow Wilson once said: 'I hope we shall never forget that we created this nation, not to serve ourselves, but to serve mankind.'"[6]

Despite this high ideal, however, the Allied leaders in South Vietnam, Cambodia, and Laos proved as hostile toward the democratic process, the rights of free speech, free association, and freedom of the press as any of the self-proclaimed antirepublican dictators in history. American policy was in a dilemma. By explaining United States participation in the wars of Southeast Asia in terms of advancing free government, Presidents Johnson and Nixon alike caused Americans to discuss, study, and debate foreign policy assumptions with an intensity and confusion unmatched in history. And Americans remained divided over what the role of the United States' foreign policies ought to be—should it increase its involvement in world affairs, or withdraw to make an honorable example of republican government at home.

Who Makes Foreign Policies?

This question has been the source of anguish for all republics. The purpose of free government is to allow the public an opportunity to determine national policies, and the idea of freedom cannot be complete unless the people can influence the two matters that affect them all—war and peace. Yet the requirements of conducting foreign affairs

[6] LaFeber, *op. cit.*, p. 246.

have always been recognized to proceed from the Executive. He, rather than Congress, has the advantage of secrecy, expedition, and dispatch. The Founding Fathers believed this and so empowered the President. The invention of nuclear weapons has now transformed the power to make war into the power to blow up the world so that with but twenty-three minutes in which to make a decision for national survival, ultimate power in foreign affairs must be placed in one person. But if foreign affairs has become the property of the Executive, what happens to democratic control?

The Constitution provides no final solution. It gives the President power to negotiate with foreign countries and power to defend the United States as Commander in Chief. To Congress the Constitution grants power to make appropriations, regulate foreign commerce, raise and maintain armies, approve treaties and ambassadors, and give advice to the President. But the execution of this power is not clear-cut. In making treaties and declaring war the President and Congress share in what Alexander Hamilton called a "joint possession." Furthermore, the Constitution is silent on such important issues as the recognition of foreign states; who has authority to proclaim neutrality; what the role of Executive agreements is; who controls foreign intelligence, and how this intelligence is to be transformed into wise policy. The Constitution has truly become what Professor Edward Corwin once called "an invitation to struggle for the privilege of directing American foreign policy."[7]

Presidents and Congress have always competed over the conduct of foreign affairs, and the Presidents, often with the help of Congress, have consistently dominated. Congressional authority over treaties, for example, has been circumvented by the use of joint resolutions. Formal treaties require two-thirds of the Senate for approval but two-thirds of the Senate have seldom approved a treaty without making extensive modifications. To get around this potential stumbling block Presidents have asked Congress for a joint resolution rather than a treaty. Such resolutions only require a simple majority of both houses. Texas was annexed in 1845 and Hawaii in 1898 by such means. Lyndon Johnson had a joint resolution prepared for Congress weeks before the Gulf of Tonkin incident; after the reported attack by North Vietnamese boats on American naval ships, and at the moment of public outcry against North Vietnam, Johnson quickly submitted the resolution to Congress. Both houses passed it in 1964, giving Johnson Congress' support to take whatever military action in Vietnam deemed necessary.

[7] Arthur Schlessinger, Jr., "Congress and the Making of American Foreign Policy," *Foreign Affairs* (Oct. 1972), Vol. 51, No. 1, 78–113.

Foreign Policy: Making the World Safe for Democracy 297

In 1970 Congress repealed the Tonkin Gulf Resolution but by then President Nixon interpreted his powers so expansively that he did not bother getting even Congress' token approval for his invasion of Cambodia.

In addition to bypassing Congress in treaty matters, Presidents have successfully dominated Congress in exercising the "war power." When the Seminole Indians raided the United States in 1818, President Monroe did not consult Congress before ordering General Andrew Jackson to pursue the Indians back into the Spanish-owned Floridas, where Jackson fought the Spanish and hanged a few Englishmen. Without congressional approval, Presidents ordered naval attacks on pirates in Sumatra (1832, 1838, 1839), the Fiji Islands (1840, 1855, 1858), and in Africa on six occasions between 1820 and 1859. President Polk contrived an international situation that forced Congress to declare war on Mexico when, in 1846, he sent American forces into disputed lands, which prompted Mexico to attack American "invaders." Congressman Abraham Lincoln of Illinois observed that Polk's invasion of a neighboring state gave the President power to make war at pleasure. "Study to see if you can fix *any limit* to his power in this respect. . . . If, today, he should choose to say he thinks it necessary to invade Canada, to prevent the British from invading us, how could you stop him? You may say to him, 'I see no probability of the British invading us,' but he will say to you, 'Be silent; I see it, if you don't.'"[8] When he became President, however, Lincoln bypassed Congress and assumed more war powers than any of his predecessors.

Presidents did not seek congressional support to use "police action" against Indians, slave traders, pirates, and frontier ruffians because these hostilities were aimed at private groups rather than foreign countries. But by the early twentieth century Presidents began using "police action" against sovereign states as well. Without consulting Congress President McKinley dispatched 5000 American troops to China to help put down the Boxer Rebellion. Later, Presidents Theodore Roosevelt and William Taft sent troops into Caribbean countries and sometimes actually installed new governments without congressional sanction. Franklin D. Roosevelt rushed troops to Greenland and Iceland in 1941 without asking for Congress' approval and brought the nation into an undeclared naval war with Germany by creating the convoy system and ordering the Navy to "shoot-at-sight." Unlike

---

[8] Lincoln to William H. Herndon, Washington, February 15, 1848, in Roy P. Basler, ed., *The Collected Works of Abraham Lincoln* (New Brunswick: Rutgers University Press, 1953), Vol. I, 451, (8 vols).

Presidents Lyndon Johnson and Richard Nixon, however, FDR did not try to stop Congress' constitutional power to participate in the conduct of foreign affairs.

Without congressional approval President Johnson sent over a half-million Americans to Vietnam. And even when he flashed the Tonkin Gulf Resolution as evidence that Congress at least had made a decision in the war, he freely admitted that he did not even need this resolution to justify his action. President Nixon expanded on Johnson's inflated use of presidential authority by asserting that he had authority to invade Cambodia because of his position as Commander in Chief. By sending an invading army into a foreign country without an invitation from the country or the knowledge of Congress, "President Nixon indulged in presidential warmaking beyond a point that even his boldest predecessors could have dreamed of."[9] By 1973 Nixon argued that the invasion of Cambodia and bombing of that country were merely the routine exercise of presidential power. He held that his actions did not need special congressional approval, not even the fig-leaf covering of another Tonkin Gulf Resolution.

Congress' role in foreign affairs is further weakened by the fact that policy must often be made in a crisis situation and only the President can respond quickly enough to meet the exigencies of the moment. Yet if the American people are to have some influence on foreign affairs then Congress, and particularly the Senate, must begin to do more than wail in self pity over its loss of power. It can begin to exercise some of the powers clearly conferred on it, particularly in its power over appropriations.

Administering Foreign Policies

As the chief architect of American foreign policy the President stands in the middle of a worldwide system of embassies, councils, advisors, and agencies that together help formulate and execute policy. In addition Presidents often have special advisors who have sufficient rapport with the President so that they rival the Secretary of State for power and influence. President Nixon, for example, retained Secretary of State Rogers to administer the internal workings of the State Department bureaucracy, while he consulted with Henry Kissinger on all important matters such as negotiating a treaty with North Vietnam to bring a cease-fire in Vietnam and secure the release of American

[9] Schlessinger, *op. cit.*, p. 102.

prisoners of war, arranging summit meetings with China and Russia, and initiating new policies.

Traditionally Presidents reward political friends who have made large campaign contributions with ambassadorships. Under the Johnson Administration, for example, the U.S. ambassador to Sweden was a Texas businessman who was not only inarticulate on foreign policy matters but could barely speak because of his smoking habit. President Nixon's appointment was little better. Some diplomats suggested that had a career man been appointed rather than another heavy campaign contributor the relations between Sweden and the United States would not have strained to the point where Prime Minister Olaf Palme would publicly liken Nixon's bombing of North Vietnam to Nazi attacks in World War II.

In Nixon's first Administration, twenty of the twenty-six European ambassadorial posts went to political appointees. This represents 77% noncareer appointments as compared to 44% in the Eisenhower Administration, 45% for Kennedy, and 56% for Lyndon Johnson.[10] One important consequence is to make Washington, D.C., the center of European communications with the United States government. Because American embassies abroad are bypassed by United States diplomats, foreign ministers also neglect to consult them. European countries have found that they can deal with the United States most effectively by communicating to their ambassador in Washington. Sometimes foreign ministers will tell American embassy officials within their own country of consultations with the United States that the embassy officials never heard about. Foreign nations thus put their best men as ambassadors to Washington while the United States sends campaign contributors to represent the country abroad.

National Security Council (NSC)

Created by Congress in 1947 to aid the President in making decisions involving national security, the NSC represents the highest policy-recommending body in the area of defense. It was the first effort to centralize and systematize the myriad agencies and personalities FDR used during World War II. It includes the President, the vice president, the secretaries of the Departments of State and Defense, and the director of the Office of Emergency Preparedness. The Central Intelligence Agency (CIA) functions under the council. Congress hoped the council would also provide some continuity of policy from one administration to another but its role and use has varied with

[10] *Los Angeles Times* (May 6, 1973), Part I, p. 21.

different Presidents. Some Presidents were critical of Congress for presuming to interfere with a presidential function. Nevertheless, when a crisis does erupt, the President can summon the council into immediate session, and there have both domestic and international experts advise him on the crisis.

Department of State

The State Department is responsible for formulating policies and programs for the United States in its relations with foreign countries and also for conducting the day-to-day relations with them. The secretary of state, who heads the department, is appointed by the President and is the highest-ranking Executive officer next to the President himself. His duties include negotiating treaties, maintaining extensive communications systems with foreign governments and American officials abroad, issuing passports, granting visas, promoting cultural exchanges between countries and planning economic aid programs. To accomplish these responsibilities the department has an annual budget of over $500 million, processes hundreds of memoranda daily, has six assistant secretaries who head six regional bureaus—African, Inter-American, European, Far Eastern, Near Eastern, and South Asian—with forty-one separate country desks and their attendant bureaucracies. Members of the Foreign Service work in American embassies and consulates overseas.

Central Intelligence Agency

The CIA, like the National Security Council, was created by Congress in 1947 to centralize and coordinate the many different agencies that sprung up during the crisis of World War II. The CIA is to work with the National Security Council by supplying the government with military, political, and economic information on other countries so that policies can be made knowledgeably. In addition to its worldwide intelligence-gathering activities the CIA also engages in secret political warfare. During the Eisenhower Administration the CIA became the principal instrument of American intervention overseas. It helped overthrow governments in Iran (1953) and Guatemela (1954), failed in its effort to overthrow the government of Indonesia (1958) but helped install governments in Egypt (1954) and Laos (1959) and organized an expedition of Cuban refugees against Castro's government in 1960. During the second Nixon Administration the CIA appeared to have turned inward to investigate private American citizens despite the provision in the National Security Act stating the CIA "shall have no

Foreign Policy: Making the World Safe for Democracy 301

police subpoena, law enforcement powers, or internal security functions." One of the questions raised by the Senate Select Committee investigating the Watergate Scandals of 1973 was to what extent the CIA had assisted President Nixon's advisors in their personal investigation of Daniel Ellsberg, the man who revealed the content of the Pentagon Papers.

Because of its secrecy, its activities, and its potential as a secret police force within the United States, critics have charged that the CIA has become a government within the government. It has its own funds and personnel, and it can hire its own army to carry out its own foreign policies without the knowledge or approval of elected officials. Because its operations are so secret most congressmen cannot inquire into its activities, its financial status remains unknown since the CIA budget is hidden within the general budget. But the secrecy system that has mushroomed since World War II presents the greatest danger to democratic control of foreign affairs and, as intimated by the "Watergate Scandals" of 1973, it may potentially threaten private citizens as well. For national security purposes Congress has been excluded from the information the President has pouring in constantly from diplomatic, military, and intelligence operations, but not even President Nixon knew that his underlings were using the CIA for their personal use in 1973. Congress could improve the chances for more democratic control in the conduct of foreign policy if it placed itself strategically within the information gathering services of the country.

Additional Instruments in the Conduct of Foreign Policy

One tactic employed by both the Communist and anti-Communist blocs during the cold war has been to engage in a propaganda campaign. Propaganda has been used to achieve ideological conformity among member countries within each bloc, and it has also been used to convert the masses of people *outside* of these blocs to accept either the Communist or anti-Communist way of life. The struggle has involved a competition of ideas between a Communist political-economic system championed by Russia on the one side, and a western-style capitalism and democracy championed by the United States on the other side. In 1953, the United States Information Agency (USIA) was established to operate a global network of communications that would beam American ideas around the world. It was to work closely with the State Department to harmonize its information with current national policy. The USIA's activities include twenty-four hour radio broadcasts in nearly forty languages, television programs, documentaries, newsreels, and millions of pamphlets and bulletins. Operating on the motto "truth is our weapon" the USIA tended to divide the world into two opposing categories. So too did the Communist propaganda effort. In the context of these verbal exchanges the world was pictured as hovering between the forces of good and the forces of evil. As the ideological representative of the United States, the USIA's libraries and information center have often been damaged by anti-American demonstrations in foreign countries.

In addition to supporting communications, Congress created the Agency for International Development (AID) to work with the State Department in directing economic and technical assistance to foreign nations. After its creation in 1961, AID became increasingly important in the United States effort to prevent the spread of Communism in underdeveloped countries. AID was created especially to finance President Kennedy's Alliance for Progress program, for which Congress appropriated $500 million to assist nineteen Latin American countries make their own internal political and economic reforms. AID was the frontline agency in the United States' stepped-up economic offensive to stop the spread of Communism among people who might listen to the ideas of western-democracy if their stomachs were first full of food. Although President Nixon developed new methods for distributing economic assistance, the AID programs were not entirely replaced. In the past they helped finance dams, highways, schools, hospitals, and they also financed the sending of experts in education, medicine, and agriculture to help poor countries use these facilities. Many of these experts were Peace Corps volunteers. Established by President Kennedy in 1962, the Peace Corps brought human resources to bear on some problems of the world. By 1973 twelve other countries had followed America's example and sent their own volunteers abroad to help people.

National Security in the Seventies

For the past twenty-five years the United States and the Soviet Union have seen each other as mortal enemies. Each saw itself as the champion of the forces of light and envisioned the other as being in league with the forces of darkness. Each superpower assumed the other was in complete control of a bloc of dependent nations: The Communist world was supposed to be a monolithic unit of Russia, China, and countries in eastern Europe; the United States was seen uniting Western Europe through the North Atlantic Treaty Organization to do its own bidding. The two superpowers also demanded that the nonaligned nations must choose to join one side or the other. Moreover, both the United States and Russia presumed its respective allies would accept its own political and economic ideas. "Washington supposed that what was then known as the Free World should reshape itself on the American model, while Moscow, [supposed] that the Communist world should reshape itself on the "Russian model." [11] But these assumptions were not entirely accurate. The real world did not develop along these ideological divisions.

Both protagonists are not as monolithic as they once imagined each other to be. There are fractures between the United States and its European allies just as there are fractures within the Communist world. The Common Market presents a new source of economic and political cooperation among Europeans that may challenge, if not replace, Europe's dependence on the United States. The most notable Communist fissure is between Russia and China, particularly along the lengthy border that separates the two countries. Moreover, the great powers can no longer directly control events in the world. There are too many new nations in existence now for either Russia or the United States to control. Membership in the United Nations, for example, jumped from fifty-one countries when the UN was created in 1945, to 132 member countries by 1973. Sixteen of these countries joined the UN from Africa in 1960 alone; seven were added between 1970 and 1973, including the People's Republic of China, which was admitted in October 1971.

Rising nationalism among nations within the Western and also within the Communist blocs helped cause these fractures. Nationalism among the new, underdeveloped countries of the Third World inspired these countries to resist being absorbed in either the orbit of the United States or of the Soviet Union. The contagion of nationalism has been epidemic. Nationalism nursed home-rule demands in Northern Iceland, encouraged the French in Quebec to push for secession from Canada, continues to inspire Palestinian guerrillas to fight Israel, is the seedbed for African warfare among tribes as well as against European colonialism, and within the United States, it finds curious expression in the "mystique" of black power. The effect of nationalism has been even more spectacular among countries within the Communist bloc. Yugoslavia broke away from Communist "truth" in 1948 and nurtured its own heresy. Ten years later China burst forth as a separate Communist nation and in its exuberance challenged Rus-

[11] Arthur Schlessinger, Jr., "The End of the Superpowers," *Harper's Magazine* (March 1969), Vol. 238, No. 1426, p. 45.

sia's influence in Asia and even its leadership of the international Communist movement. And nationalism in Southeast Asia led Vietnamese people to oppose France in its presumption of recolonizing the area after World War II and to oppose the United States in a bitter war that lasted a decade.

Although the United States and Russia still remain the only two powers that have sufficient military means to blow up the world, their power is less effective now in controlling world affairs. The United States and Russia cannot risk using their power to manipulate the new, vulnerable states that have emerged in the past quarter-century because the consequence of miscalculation can be enormous. These nations dispute local, bitter issues that often have nothing to do with cold war allegiances. But the local hostilities can mushroom into a world crisis if one of the superpowers becomes involved. Now the mere possession of power is no longer a guarantee that a nation will realize the achievements of power. The mightiest nations are frustrated because they cannot use the military power they have. To do so would mean either destroying all the people they are supposed to be protecting or engulfing the world in nuclear holocaust.

Even the Strategic Arms Limitation Talks (SALT) between the United States and the Soviet Union point to the frustrations of power as they try to reach an agreement on controlling strategic nuclear weapons, delivery systems, and related weapons. When the talks originally began in Helsinki, Finland in 1969 they were directed toward reaching an agreement to limit or eliminate the costly antiballistic missile (ABM) system, which both countries were in the process of developing. Later discussions covered nuclear testing and multiple independently targeted reentry vehicles (MIRV). President Nixon sought to expand an understanding with Russia in order to reduce the arms race, military research, and expensive development costs. The difficulty of securing an agreement in the field of nuclear weapons is evidenced by the fact that the two powers tentatively agreed that each side should have no more power than the capacity to destroy the other power nine times over again.

The rising nationalism has brought a blaze of barbarism and terrorism that the superpowers are helpless to stop. One nation's freedom fighter is another nation's terrorist. Hijackings and kidnappings for political motives left two American diplomats murdered in the Sudan in 1973; another diplomat was kidnapped in Mexico but released unharmed after the Mexican govenment yielded to the demand and freed thirty imprisoned revolutionaries. General Amin of Uganda proudly accepted the label of a black Hitler after practicing ruthless racism against Asians and Europeans in his country in 1972. The self-inflicted tortures in the Indian subcontinent did not diminish with the creation of Bangladesh. Sectarian violence in Northern Ireland demonstrates the horror of urban warfare by the use of indiscriminate time bombs. Palestinian guerrillas, along with Japanese gunmen, killed twenty-seven travelers at Lod airport in Lebanon in 1972, which was only a prelude to the Munich kidnapping of the Israeli athletes by the Black September group. A group of American strategists, employed to imagine mad situations in order to provide possible alternatives, have been considering the consequences should such a group as the Black Septembers obtain an atomic bomb. But the terrorists invented letter bombs and thus added a more delicate form of terror to their arsenal. Such groups could care less about the ideologies of communism and capitalism as they pursue more immediate and historic hatreds.

A generation has passed since the end of World War II and during the past twenty-five years some of the factors that once dominated foreign policies have gone also, or have been significantly modified by changing circumstances. President Nixon appears to have recognized that foreign policies based merely on ideological conflicts have led to a deadend. In visiting Communist China in 1972 Nixon reversed a generation of foreign policy instantly. He seemed to be moving the nation onto a new course in which the world would be accepted as it is rather than as it ought to be. The Nixon Administration approved China's admission into the United Nations in 1971; in 1973 diplomatic relations were restored between the two countries for the first time in a generation. If those who formulate United States foreign policy recognize that military power alone will not cause the world to follow, perhaps Americans can return to an earlier conception of the way the United States could influence the world. "She will recommend the general cause by the countenance of her voice, and by the benignant sympathy of her example," said John Quincy Adams. "But she goes not abroad in search of monsters to destroy."

PURSUIT OF HAPPINESS:
Resolving Domestic Conflicts

This time like all times is a very good one if one but knows what to do with it.
—*Ralph Waldo Emerson*

Although each generation lives in a world that is different from the past, no generation has experienced a greater acceleration of social and political change than the Americans who lived since the 1950s. The velocity of change produced by this electronic age of television and computers is unprecedented in any country and in any previous period. This momentum of science and technology is marked as much by the leap into space as by research in human genetics. Since Russia launched Sputnik in 1957, men have walked on the moon, sent spacecraft to photograph other planets, and deployed hundreds of military and communication satellites around the earth. Within one generation since the discovery in 1953 of the genetic code (DNA), scientists saw the possibility of producing babies in test tubes and making them carbon copies of selected individuals. By genetic engineering it seemed possible to eliminate hereditary diseases and also control human behavior, intellect, and physical characteristics.

The rapid pace of change since the 1950s has not only created new possibilities and new dangers but has accentuated the gap that always exists between generations so that the experience of parents appears less relevant to the needs of their children. As we move toward the bicentennial of 1976 the political experience of the past appears incapable of providing adequate solutions or guide-lines to the problems of the present.

But we are not as old as the velocity of history would suggest. When we celebrate the 200th anniversary of the Declaration of Independence on July 4, 1976, we will still be a young nation. We are only eight generations removed from the signers of that document; if we count our history by lifetimes of sixty-five years each, then our total experience as a nation is encompassed in three. Supreme Court Justice Oliver Wendell Holmes, who died in 1935 in his ninety-third year, told his secretary, "Always remember that you have spoken to a man who once spoke with a veteran of the American Revolution." Holmes himself was a veteran of the Civil War and on Memorial Day in 1971 there were over 400 other Civil War veterans celebrating their memory of that event. And some of our national ideals are still young. Americans have always believed that government begins with the people for it was for them that government was created to serve. Lincoln's often repeated phrase "government of the people, by the people, for the people" re-echoed the principle that was the foundation of our existence as a nation.

Seldom has the demand to turn the republican ideal into a reality for all Americans been put with greater force than it has by the people who will celebrate this bicentennial. When Jefferson wrote, the United States numbered fewer than 4 million people, but women could not vote, American Indians were regarded as foreign enemies, and black Americans were computed as three-fifths of a human being. Now there are nearly 210 million Americans and every economic and ethnic interest is pressing for its rights. Projections for 1980 estimate that the population will reach 230 million, and by the time students reading this are middle-aged the total may be over 300 million. Half the people that ever lived in the United States are living now and they are insisting that we celebrate the birth of the republic in 1976 not as a historical theory but as a practical reality.

Identifying the public interest and then translating it into action has always been difficult. This is one reason why many of Jefferson's generation advised that a republic be small in size and in population. The problem of turning republican theory into reality is compounded today, not only by the size of the American population but by the fact that the traditional political mechanisms through which different interests participated in government are no longer functioning. Older state and city political machines, farm bureaus, ethnic organizations, unions, and even political party affiliations that once served voters in the past were shattered by the 1970s. Since the introduction of television in the 1950s, Americans have been making political judgments independently of these older organizations; increasingly, people are forming opinions largely on the basis of what they see for themselves on the television screen.

What Worries Americans in the 1970s?

Recent polls of American opinion reveal a dramatic long-term change in the things Americans want their government to do. Public concern about foreign affairs and national defense, uppermost in the mid-1960s, has diminished now, to be replaced by such domestic issues as inflation, crime and violence, rotting cities, pollution, and the energy crisis. In 1964 the Institute for International Research found that the five most prominent concerns in the United States involved foreign affairs: keeping the country out of war, combating Communism, preserving a strong military defense, controlling nuclear weapons, and preserving respect for the United States abroad. Recently the list of worries has changed. In 1972 the Gallup Poll organization found that the only foreign issue that ranked high in their list was the war in Vietnam that had not yet ended. Other surveys of American opinion support the findings by William Watts and Lloyd Free that Americans have turned inward in their concerns and are less bothered by the cold war now than they were a decade ago. Although the polls do not find a public reversion to isolationism, there has been, nevertheless, an easing of the stalwart internationalist consensus that characterized the post-World War II years, with the change presumably attributable in large measure to disillusionment over the war in Vietnam along with growing concern about urgent domestic problems.[1]

One important observation Watts and Free made in the *State of the Nation* (1972) was that Americans made a distinction between their personal future, which they thought would improve, and the future of the nation, about which they had some doubts. When Americans looked into the mirror of their own lives they were reasonably content

[1] William Watts and Lloyd Free, *State of the Nation* (New York: Universe Books, 1973), pp. 34–41.

with their condition and confidently expected that it would improve; when they looked out of their window and beyond their local neighborhood Americans were not happy with what they saw. Not only were the public concerned with inflation, crime, urban conditions, and pollution, but, according to Watts and Free, they were also skeptical about the ability of the government to be of much help in resolving domestic crises.

Inflation

Rising prices, unprecedented trade deficits, devaluation of the dollar, the annual increase in government spending coupled with the inability of the federal government to balance its expenditures with revenue, all contribute to the fact that inflation has become the nation's principal concern since the end of the Vietnam war. Food prices, for example, jumped nearly 43% in the decade 1962–1972; within fourteen months (December 1971 to February 1973) the dollar's value was slashed 17.9%, and the trade deficit for 1972 found foreign imports exceeding American exports by a staggering $6.8 billion. While inflation traditionally accompanies peace treaties at the end of a war, some economists suggested the root of the economic crises of the 1970s went beyond the post-Vietnam problem of adjusting the economy to peace. Ever since the conclusion of World War II, and particularly since the early 1950s the people and the government of the United States have both been living beyond their means. Consumers, businessmen, tourists, and the government combined have spent tens of billions of dollars each year for the past twenty-odd years buying foreign products, building factories in foreign countries, touring the world, pouring out foreign aid, stationing troops around the globe, and waging the costliest and longest war in American history in Vietnam.

As a consequence of this spending there are between $60 billion and $80 billion in greenbacks, no one knows exactly how many, sloshing around the world. Despite such powers as devaluation, trade restrictions, and diplomatic persuasion, the United States government is unable to control this money completely. No handles have been devised yet, for example, to regulate the effects on the American economy of the policies and speculations of multinational companies. Corporations that operate casually across national boundaries, such as General Motors, Exxon, Ford, IMB, ITT, British Petroleum, Volkswagen, and Singer, are defined as "multinational" when (1) their sales exceed $100 million, (2) they operate in at least six countries, and (3) their overseas subsidiaries account for at least 20% of their assets. In 1973 more than 4000 companies qualified as multinational. These global giants have mushroomed since the 1960s, and now control 15% of the gross world product. Some have assets larger than those of the countries in which they operate. Their interests do not necessarily coincide with those of the country in which they operate; because these companies can easily transfer money into different currencies, their actions defy national control. They are a new, independent force in the world without national allegiance to any country. This absence of nationalism, in fact, is their principal characteristic. They invest in countries where taxes and labor costs are lowest and do business in countries where profits are highest. Some experts on international relations predict that future international conflicts may involve these new, uncontrolled giants. The multinational corporations' economic power may be pitted against the political power of nation states either directly as ITT did in undermining Chile's President Salvadore Allende in 1972, or indirectly as they did in 1971 and 1972 when they transfered dollars into foreign currencies and helped create the dollar crisis that resulted in devaluation.[2]

Government spending on domestic and foreign aid programs has not only been the primary stimulant to inflation, but has also locked higher costs into future budgets, in that these new programs and their attendant costs or bureaucracies tend to be self-perpetuating. Consider, for example, the projected future costs of the Vietnam conflict only in terms of the veterans' benefits that will accrue during the lifetime of the veterans, their wives, and their children. Veterans' benefits for the War of 1812 continued to be paid until 1946, 131 years after the war ended; benefits from the Mexican War of 1848 did not fall below $1 million a year until the 1960s; veterans' benefits from the Spanish–American War amounted to $5.3 billion by 1967, a figure that was twelve times the original cost of the war; benefits from World War I are estimated to have peaked forty-nine years after the war, in 1966, while benefits for World War II veterans are estimated to peak around the year 2000; "and dependents of Vietnamese veterans will be drawing benefits until the twenty-second century!"[3] Veterans' benefits are estimated to equal 150% of the war's initial cost; interest rates may "be roughly half again as much as the original cost."[4] Inflationary costs are thus built into yearly budgets regardless

[2] See: Raymond Vernon, *Sovereignty at Bay: The Multinational Spread of United States Enterprise* (New York: Basic Books, 1971) and also Raymond Vernon, *The Economic and Political Consequences of Multinational Enterprise: An Anthology* (Boston: Harvard Business School, 1972).
[3] James L. Clayton, "Vietnam: The 200-Year Mortgage," *The Nation* (May 26, 1969), p. 662.
[4] *Ibid.*

of whether the government is continuing "Great Society" programs for domestic problems, or for foreign policies that necessitate the maintaining of standing armies in scores of foreign bases.

Stemming the tide of rising prices was the principal domestic consideration of President Nixon, and he relentlessly pruned social programs launched by Lyndon Johnson's Great Society. But cutting waste and inefficiency tended to be one-sided, for government pruning did not extend to the military budget: despite about $4 billion saving on Vietnam, the fiscal 1974 defense budget increased $4 billion. To hold down the rate of inflation, Nixon ordered wages and prices frozen and set the rate by which prices could be raised in a series of three phases, which began in 1971. To reduce trade deficits and foreign speculations on the dollar, Nixon provided for the first dollar devaluation in the Smithsonian Agreement of 1971, which he hailed then as "the most significant monetary agreement in the history of the world," and fourteen months later he devalued the dollar an additional 10%. To improve further the American balance of trade, Nixon sought authority to make selective import–export policies on individual nations from a Congress that was more inclined to introduce a series of protectionist bills that would prevent foreign products from entering the competing with home products. Moreover, by relaxing diplomatic relations with China and Russia, Nixon encouraged American trade with the two most powerful Communist countries, which hitherto were almost entirely closed to American markets. When the American rate of inflation is compared with the rates in European countries in the early 1970s, it can be seen that these policies helped stem the tide toward inflation; however, the problem will take more time and effort to resolve because of the rising costs of maintaining existing programs and meeting other domestic problems.

Crime and Violence

Nothing has accelerated faster in the United States in recent years than the number of crimes, particularly violent crimes. The marching rate of crime has created an age of stark, gnawing fear for most Americans living in urban centers. The statistics are mind-numbing: violent crimes increased by more than 90% in the five years between 1967 and 1972; the chances of an American becoming victim of serious crime have tripled since 1960; statistically a black male between the ages of twenty and forty-five had the best chance of being murdered in 1971, since male murder victims outnumbered female murder victims by four to one, and 55% of these victims were black. Juvenile crime escalated 167% in the ten years between 1962 and 1972. Many high-school campuses had become armed camps, and the neighboring streets were turned into bloody battlegrounds. Although the street gangs of the 1950s were revived in the 1970s, the weapons had shifted from tire chains and switchblades to guns; even eight- or nine-year-old children were carrying handguns for their older partners. Crime has become so commonplace in the District of Columbia that the *Washington Post* reserves a special section next to the classified ads to list the serious crimes committed on the previous day. More "respectable" crimes, such as robberies committed by white-collar employees against huge, faceless corporations, have also increased to such an extent that the *Readers Guide to Periodical Literature* now lists white-collar crime as a separate entry.

Rarely in the past has the notion of a person's home being his castle been taken more literally than now, by Americans who install special locks and burglar alarms or move into walled-in communities protected by guards controlling the gates twenty-four hours a day. Such protective measures have been described as the modern equivalent of moats and crocodiles. Although Americans are learning to live with fear, they are also searching for ways violence can be controlled. But suggestions on how the crime rate can be reduced are almost as varied as are the causes offered for why the rate is increasing.

Some suggest Americans have developed a high tolerance to crime after years of becoming conditioned and desensitized to violence on television and movies. News reports turned Vietnam into a living-room war where nightly footage of the latest carnage, atrocities, body counts and napalming were broadcast for a decade. There is evidence that violence in news and other television programing also provides conscious and subconscious motivation to commit violent acts. In 1971 the U.S. Surgeon General reported "the greater the level of exposure to television, the more the child is willing to use violence, to suggest it as a solution to conflict, and to perceive it as effective." Violent words have become so commonplace that even politicians have worked them into their political rhetoric to wage "war" on poverty or "war" on crime or "war" on drugs. Perhaps American muggers and murderers have become as psychologically habituated to violence as have international terrorists. As one Arab observed in Munich in the summer of 1972 after the massacre of the Israeli Olympians, "They have seen death many times until now it is nothing for them to kill. . . ."

Violence is deeper in our culture than the advent of mass communication, notes historian Arthur Schlesinger, Jr. We began our history as a people who killed Indians and enslaved blacks. "No nation, however righteous its professions, could act as we did without burying deep in itself—in its customs, its institutions and its psyche—a propensity toward violence."[5] The National Commission on the Causes and Prevention of Violence supported this observation. According to the commission, violence formed a "seamless web" in some of the noblest chapters of American history: the nation was born in revolutionary violence; the slaves were freed and the Union preserved in civil war; the West was occupied as a result of Indian wars; vigilantes stabilized frontier society; farmers, laborers, and capitalists advanced themselves in violent industrial confrontations; and police violence was used on occasion in the 1960s to preserve law and order. At times illegal violence has been rewarded and glorified. The Ku Klux Klan lynch mobs were celebrated in patriotic parades in the 1920s; Hollywood had so successfully turned Indians into sneaky, violent savages that in the 1930s and 1940s many esteemed the participants of Custer's last stand; and frontier marshals and city gangsters are still glorified.

Psychologists point to modern urbanization as a fertile seedbed for crime. City congestion increases tension, anger, and irritability, and without any open space to retreat to, individuals begin to lash out at each other. Congestion on freeways, subways, and sidewalks also tends to depersonalize and alienate people. Criminals seldom think of their victim as a human being and therefore are not restrained from murdering him. Many policemen argue that the increase in crime is the result of a generation raised on a permissive philosophy. Because parents allowed their children to grow up without respect for authority, some young adults now rebel against the authority of the police officer. Policemen further argue that the absence of death penalties and the existence of permissive courts have made life for a criminal easier.

Most observers do agree, however, that drug addiction is a major cause for the increased crime rate; paralleling violent crime statistics, arrests for drug violations jumped nearly 500% in the five years between 1967 and 1972. Drug usage has a long and varied history in the United States. Opium, for example, was widely sold as a patent medicine in the nineteenth century. The Bayer pharmaceutical company sold its opium compound to relieve coughs under its brand name of "Heroin." Since then the name of Bayer's "miracle drug" has become a household word around the world.[6] Profits from heroin have

[5] *Los Angeles Times* (December 31, 1972), Section B, p. 1.
[6] In 1972 a Senate Subcommittee reported an epidemic of barbiturate use in the United States. An estimated 1 million Americans, mostly between thirty and fifty years old, were hooked on barbiturates because they took too many prescribed pills. The committee further reported that virtually all barbiturates used illegally originated with legitimate drug companies. This supply was filtered down to the illicit market by thefts, forged prescriptions, or careless handling of drugs in the chain of distribution and selling.

been the source of widespread corruption in some police departments, and a recent study of heroin profits within the governments of countries in Southeast Asia reveals that high-ranking members of governments to which the United States was an ally were deeply involved in narcotic traffic. Revenue from drugs was essential to the economic and political survival of some governments in South Vietnam, Laos, Thailand, and Cambodia.[7]

Since crime was on the list of American worries it became a political issue in the presidential campaigns of 1968 and 1972. In reviewing the FBI's annual crime report in 1971, the Nixon Administration was optimistic that a turnaround in the trend was made because the report indicated that crime grew at a slower rate in 1971 than at any time since 1965. But Democrats insisted this interpretation of the FBI report was more subtle than accurate for the report showed that only the number of crimes against property actually went down, whereas violent crimes (murder, rape, assault) increased at a steady rate. However politicians spar over statistics, Americans do not seem to be swayed by simplistic political rhetoric. When Gallup pollsters Watts and Free asked Americans to choose between various possibilities that would reduce crime, they found that 61% opted for a moderate approach that would clean up the social conditions in ghettos that breed drug addicts and criminals.

Rotting Cities and the Welfare Mess

Although a majority of Americans were concerned with the social conditions that make cities breeding ground for crime, the editors of *State of the Nation* found little support in 1972 for expensive new urban renewal programs. In general Americans felt some progress had been made in improving cities—an optimism that is not borne out by the fact that the core of most American cities has deteriorated seriously in recent years. Whether reacting from an illusion of improvement or a disillusionment with enormous expenditures in the 1960s, there was little enthusiasm among most Americans in the early 1970s to support new spending programs for urban renewal. In fact, most Americans seemed to have given up the cities as fit places to live.

One important finding in this survey of American opinion was that a majority yearned to escape urban areas completely, but instead of heading for the suburbs as so many people did in the 1950s, today's city-dwellers prefer to settle in the wide-open spaces of rural America.

[7] See: Alfred W. McCoy, *The Politics of Heroin in Southeast Asia* (New York: Harper and Row, 1972).

Only about one out of every three Americans now live in rural areas, but more than half of those interviewed opted for that environment; a full 70% of black urbanites wanted to move out in 1972. If Americans could afford to follow their preference it appears the population of the cities would be cut in half, that suburban population would remain fairly constant and that rural America would double in population.

These preferences are not difficult to understand. Growth in city crime rate was eight times the rate of increase in the countryside in 1971. The environment is also less healthy. Air is polluted by factory fumes, automobile exhaust, stinking garbage, and even rotting human excrement—found in condemned buildings inhabited by drug addicts in such ghettos as Kelley Street in New York City. Noise levels are much higher and drinking water is less pure than they are in rural America. Ghetto schools contain so many of the problems found in the neighborhood that there is only limited opportunity for educational achievement. While crime increases and the environment deteriorates, the cost for services rise each year, as does the tax rate, but taxable resources steadily decline as more and more businesses move out. Many downtown night clubs, restaurants, theaters, and shops have either shut down or left; a number of major corporations have relocated outside of New York City and older manufacturing districts in almost all cities cannot cope financially with poorer city services, higher taxes, congested transportation and obsolete buildings. In 1969 the Commission on the Causes and Prevention of Violence predicted that within a few years

> . . . central business districts . . . will be largely deserted except for police patrols during night-time hours. High-rise apartment buildings and residential compounds protected by private guards and security devices will be fortified cells for upper-middle and high-income populations. . . . Ownership of guns will be almost universal in the suburbs; homes will be fortified by an array of devices from window grills to electronic surveillance equipment, armed citizen volunteers in cars will supplement inadequate police patrols. . . . Residential neighborhoods in the central city will be unsafe in differing degrees, and the ghetto slum neighborhoods will be places of terror with widespread crime, perhaps entirely out of police control during night-time hours.[8]

If these predictions are being fulfilled rapidly in the 1970s, it is largely because there has been no national urban policy. Efforts by

---

[8] National Commission on the Causes and Prevention of Violence, *Violent Crime, Homicide, Assault, Rape, and Robbery* (Washington, D.C.: U.S. Government Printing Office, 1969).

the federal government to improve conditions "downtown" have not been developed or supported consistently by either the Johnson or Nixon administrations. Johnson's initial program was directed at the physical rebirth of the central city through urban redevelopment projects and public housing, but the chief beneficiaries of the new buildings were real-estate developers, not the poor. The poor, who originally lived in the "redeveloped area," not only were bulldozed out of their homes but forced to relocate elsewhere, as the new homes cost more than they could afford. When it became obvious that the people with low incomes were becoming victims of a program intended for their benefit President Johnson tried to correct the problem by a "Model Cities" approach that required new projects to furnish a master plan that would accommodate all people in the community.

Instead of focusing only on the city, the Nixon Administration looked for a national-growth policy that would encourage Americans to relocate in rural communities. The Nixon Administration also reduced government spending, which either killed or gutted existing urban-renewal programs such as Model Cities, community action, public service employment and college student loans. More than half of the nation's counties lost population in the 1960s and most of these counties were located in a large section of the country stretching south from the Dakotas, across parts of the South and into Appalachia. Unless rural Americans are discouraged from pulling up stakes and moving into the big cities some demographers predict that 60% of the people will live in a few metropolitan clusters by the year 2000, and only 12% will live in communities of fewer than 100,000. Since the location of people is determined by the location of jobs, the Nixon Administration hoped to use promises of federal revenue grants to lure each state into planning new communities of 20,000 to 120,000 population that would be located outside the orbit of large urban centers. This national-growth policy may require more than the $200 million a year Nixon was willing to spend but if the federal, state, county, and municipal governments can coordinate their interests and if the location of new plant sites can be coordinated with the public's interest in quality schools, medical care, proximity of air and road transportation, and environmental protection, then it may be possible for the many current urban-dwellers to exercise their choice and move out of the cities.

Already some private developers have constructed some "New Cities" after the example of European countries, which built planned towns after World War II to retard the shift of population into existing urban centers. Some senators, congressmen, governors and mayors have pressed for more new cities such as Columbia, Maryland and Reston, Virginia; they urge the government to assist in creating 100 new cities of 100,000 population and ten cities with a population of 1 million each, in order to accommodate the anticipated 100 million population increase in the United States by 2000. Some supporters of the new cities hope the idea will stimulate as much popular support for improving life within the United States as did the space program generate support for landing men on the moon. Without national urban planning, they argue, the increase in population will cause existing overcrowded metropolitan areas to spill over to some 18 million acres of land and the United States will repeat the waste, economic inefficiencies, bureaucratic confusions, and disregard for social needs that characterized the urban sprawl of the 1960s.

None of these new cities have been designed to relieve existing cities of their ghetto population. As the chief planner for Columbia, Maryland candidly explained: "Columbia was designed to be attractive to that majority segment of the population which is economically viable in the market. As a venture of private capital, Columbia will be unable to reach and affect some of the gut social problems of American urbanization."[9] The gut social problem is the bottom fifth of American society, which receives 5% of the nation's income and most of the welfare benefits. It is the nation's poor who are leaving the backroads of rural America and moving into the core of the nation's large cities for one primary reason: they have a better chance to eke out an existence there.

"All of our big cities are overcrowded, near bankruptcy; jobs for the unskilled are scarce," commented Congressman Morris K. Udall on the chaos produced by the welfare system. "Yet the welfare system, like a huge magnet, draws millions of poorly trained, poorly educated people off the farms and out of the rural areas of our country and into the already crowded cities. There many of them whether they want to or not, end up on welfare."[10] Not until 1970 when Nixon proposed a guaranteed minimum income and also a Family Assistance Plan, which taken together represented a possible uniform national welfare system, did it seem possible to reverse this economic cause for urban growth. It was a major attempt to reform the current welfare programs, which came into existence as the result of emergency legislation thrown together to meet the temporary crisis of the Great Depression. Instead of disappearing once the economy was completely "restored" the unwanted, unwelcomed, and unplanned system

[9] Edward B. Lambeth, "New Towns: Can They Work?" *The Washington Monthly* (Oct. 1969).
[10] Morris K. Udall, "A Scandal Called Welfare," *The Progressive* (May 1971).

had mutated, over the past forty years, into a bureaucratic quagmire in every state. There are fifty different welfare plans, one for each state, and the multiplicity of programs irritates existing urban problems. Urban growth is encouraged. A deserted mother with three children in Mississippi would receive $840 a year if she tried to keep her family together at home among friends and relatives, but she could receive $2004 in Tucson, Arizona and $4164 if she went north to Newark, New Jersey.

Congressman Udall, himself a liberal Democrat, claimed the Nixon proposal of 1970 "has offered more in the way of fundamental change for the good in the country's well-intentioned, but basically bad, welfare system than we were able to achieve in a decade of New Frontiers and Great Societies." [11] Nixon's proposal would have federalized welfare and thus create one national program, and ended the practice of denying relief to a family with "a man in the house"—a practice that often forces an unemployed or underemployed father to abandon his family so his children can eat. The plan also would have offered welfare recipients a way of escape into the world of work by permitting a person to keep a portion of the welfare check and all one's earnings, until the earnings increased sufficiently to meet one's needs. But these proposals were abandoned in Nixon's second Administration because, explained HEW Secretary Caspar Weinberger, welfare costs had increased beyond the levels the 1970 plans contemplated and "at this point we do not have in place or ready to submit a substitute for that plan." [12]

When questioned about welfare by the Gallup pollsters in mid-1972, those interviewed indicated they did not begrudge assistance for the poor, but they disliked the "free ride" that welfare provided. Based on this sampling the poll suggested that over 80% of Americans preferred that the government train welfare recipients and find them jobs if necessary, even if such a program were more costly than the existing system, rather than continue a system that handed over cash payments with no work requirement. Until the welfare system is reformed so that there are national criteria that are uniform throughout the nation, the poor will continue to be pulled into the decaying cities.

Environment

Americans are now apparently more worried about the environment than they have ever been before, and if recent polls gauge public opinion correctly, then Americans may be willing to make some of

[11] *Ibid.*
[12] *Los Angeles Times* (Feb. 25, 1973), Part VI, p. 7.

the personal sacrifices necessary to stop pollution. To combat the mounting heaps of garbage, for example, Watts and Free found that 80% of the public were willing to support legislation prohibiting throwaway bottles or cans and requiring large-deposit, reusable bottles. As a consequence of affluence, 2% more refuse is added every year, and this, when coupled with a 2% annual population growth, totals to a 4% growth in garbage and garbage disposal every year. Just the number of nonreturnable bottles in 1970 for beer and soft drinks was estimated at 12 billion, or 33 million bottles thrown away every day. Although Americans are aware of the past use of lakes, rivers, land, and oceans as dumps, such dumping continues, since economical ways to dispose of solid wastes have not yet been found. Domestic garbage can still be recycled as it was in the past through such farm animals as chickens and pigs, although the style of doing it is different today. Pigs served residents of New York City as a free sewer system by rooting through the garbage people dumped through their windows every day in the 1830s—the same time the cholera epidemics hit the city. Today pigs are still used to consume domestic garbage, especially discarded food from large institutions like hospitals, but the cost is sometimes prohibitive because of transportation and the requirement by some states that the garbage be cooked first to stop the trichinosis cycle. Among the various methods being tried to recycle paper products, which constitutes the largest percentage of domestic trash, is the use of paper as feed for cattle. Since paper is nearly all cellulose and therefore digestible to ruminants (cattle), paper is being fortified with vitamins and minerals as cattle feed. Thus today's textbook can become tomorrow's steak![13]

Stopping other forms of pollution is less easy. Air pollution, probably our most serious environmental problem, keeps getting worse every year as statistics grimly reveal: deaths from lung cancer rose 250% from 1950 to 1971, and the figure is doubling every ten years; emphysema, which was rare thirty years ago, now kills 25,000 people annually and its incidence in the United States has doubled in the past five years. The primary source of this pollution is the automobile, for a long time our "sacred cow." But the public and the Detroit car manufacturers are being compelled to consider gasoline rationing, not only to meet the clean air demands of the Environmental Protection Agency, but to meet the growing shortage of oil caused by the "energy crisis."

The water supply of every major city is of poor quality. Oil, industrial chemicals, viscera from slaughterhouses, along with effluent from

[13] See: Charles A. Schweighauser, "The Garbage Explosion," *The Nation* (September 22, 1969), pp. 282–283.

public sewers, are all dumped into the rivers and lakes that provide drinking water for most Americans. Along with concern over pure water and air, however, the problem of noise has been added to the list of environmental pollutants that directly affect our lives. Research on the impact of noise on health is fairly recent but it is steadily showing that too much noise disturbs peace of mind, breeds tension and irritability that can lead to ulcers, high blood pressure, heart attack, and nervous breakdown; it can even permanently damage unborn babies. One British study showed that people living near London's Heathrow Airport had a much higher incidence of admission to mental hospitals than similar types of people living in nearby quieter towns.[14] Studies of noise in the United States show that the decibels are doubling every ten years from more trucks, cars, scooters, jackhammers, factory machines, jetliners, and transistor radios. The Noise Control Act of 1972 was introduced by Senator John Tunney (Democrat, California) after he visited private homes near the Los Angeles International Airport and in one home found a boy who had to wear cotton in his ears all the time to keep out the noise. Although passage of the bill was difficult—it nearly fell victim to the formidable array of lobbyists and hostile Senate committee chairmen—the 1972 Act calls for stiffer aircraft noise standards and also the setting of national standards for noise levels of a wide variety of consumer products, including lawnmowers.

Enforcing existing laws is difficult not only in the actual administration of the laws but in meeting the economic problems arising from enforcement. Until Nixon created the Environmental Protection Agency (EPA), the National Oceanic and Atmospheric Administration (NOAA), and the Council on Environmental Quality in 1970 the federal responsibility for environment regulation had been divided into more than thirty government agencies, which shared authority with each other. The EPA has taken over regulation of air pollution, waste disposal, and some radiation and water problems; the NOAA is responsible for long-range research on the atmosphere and marine conditions; and the Council on Environmental Quality functions in a manner similar to the President's Council of Economic Advisers by setting policy and carrying out the provisions of the National Environmental Policy Act of 1970. Despite this reorganization, there are still multiple federal, state, and local regulations that conflict with each other. The absence of any uniform regulations among the states creates conditions in which some companies have a competitive advantage over others located in states requiring strict environmental protection.

[14] *Los Angeles Times* (Nov. 12, 1972), Section C, p. 7.

Yet the fundamental obstacle to removing environmental pollution is the impact of these regulations on the economy. Will Americans be forced someday soon to choose between continuing our industrial growth or having a healthful place to live? How far must the government go in saving the environment when the consequence of this action causes unemployment and plant shutdowns? The country no longer has the abundance of land, air, water, and soil that was essential to economic prosperity, and some observers argue that there must be a rethinking of the concept of economic growth. A growing economy may no longer be consistent with improving the quality of American life, because pollution will also grow, perhaps to intolerable levels within the United States, and international tensions will increase as the gulf widens between poor and rich nations. Other observers look to improved technological innovations as a way out of a collision between pollution and economic growth. These differences of opinion on the impact of pollution on American life nevertheless do point to the problem of the environment as a unique one, and one of the most formidable problems any government has ever been forced to deal with. Perhaps Pogo in the newspaper cartoon strip was right when he said, "We have met the enemy and it is us."

Is Government Capable of Governing?

Since Americans shifted their focus recently away from international difficulties toward such domestic problems as inflation, crime, urbanization, and pollution, they have become more critical in evaluating the performance of government. Often their expectations have not been realized. The one critical domestic problem that seemed to have been reduced in the early 1970s was "the problem of black Americans." This belief was even shared by blacks themselves. A majority of Americans in mid-1972 apparently thought the nation had made adequate progress in reducing previous legal and economic inequities for blacks because they ranked racial problems in second place from the bottom of their nineteen domestic worries, as itemized by Watts and Free in the *State of the Nation*. Only mass transportation aroused less concern. Despite this important improvement in America's social condition, however, the pollsters found a sense of public dissatisfaction with the government as a whole.

Americans seemed particularly critical with the trend in the past generation of increasing government expenditure and governmental size. Government has become the largest employer in society. Costs of government have mounted with new bureaucracies and programs but the problems seemed unresolved. So extensive has the government expanded its power that it now has the ability, which it often uses, to probe into private affairs of citizens on a scale that even a despot living a century ago could not imagine possible. Almost all recent polls of public opinion indicate Americans are making some of the same general observations as did political scientists Peter Drucker some years earlier, i.e. that government is big rather than strong; fat and flabby rather than powerful; inefficient, sometimes administratively incompetent, but always more expensive. For example, the number of agencies concerned with city problems have increased ten times between 1939 and 1969 and the number of papers and reports have multiplied by a factor of thousands. New York social workers spend 70–80% of their time filling out forms for Washington, the state capitol, and the city, leaving only about an hour and a half a day for their clients. The cause for this dilemma is largely the consequence of the numerous bureaucracies with whom social workers must deal. In 1966, for example, there were 170 federal aid programs financed by over 400 separate appropriations, which in turn were administered by twenty-one federal departments aided by 150 bureaus in Washington and over 400 regional offices in New York. Most bureaucracies are now autonomous ends in themselves so that the government is busy "doing" things rather than achieving the purpose of government, i.e. focusing the political energies of society and making fundamental decisions.[15]

Ironically, the government is losing public respect at the very time when a strong, vigorous government is needed. In mid-1972 a majority of Americans rated federal, state, and local governments "fair" to "poor" in terms of justice and honesty; 61% gave low marks on government's efficiency; and 65% were displeased with government's responsiveness to the people. According to *State of the Nation* most Americans wanted a fundamental change in the organization of government. Although the kind of change the public wanted was not clear, the pollsters believed it to be drastic. Thus on the eve of celebrating the 200th anniversary of the Declaration of Independence, Americans seemed to be searching for a new political, social and economic philosophy that would infuse them with new purpose.

Only rarely does a generation live to witness such fundamental change, as did Jefferson's generation in 1776 and apparently will the

---

[15] See: Peter F. Drucker, "The Sickness of Government," in *The Age of Discontinuity* (New York: Harper and Row, 1968).

generation born since the first atomic bomb exploded in 1945. It was about such a generation that Ralph Waldo Emerson wrote: "If there is any period one would desire to be born in—is it not the era of revolution when the old and the new stand side by side and admit of being compared; when all the energies of men are searched by fear and hope; when the historic glories of the old can be compensated by the rich possibilities of the new era? This time like all times is a very good one if one but knows what to do with it."

APPENDICES

THE DECLARATION OF INDEPENDENCE

When, in the course of human events, it becomes necessary for one people to dissolve the political bands which have connected them with another, and to assume, among the powers of the earth, the separate and equal station to which the laws of nature and of nature's God entitle them, a decent respect to the opinions of mankind requires that they should declare the causes which impel them to the separation.

We hold these truths to be self-evident, that all men are created equal; that they are endowed by their Creator with certain unalienable rights; that among these, are life, liberty, and the pursuit of happiness. That, to secure these rights, governments are instituted among men, deriving their just powers from the consent of the governed; that, whenever any form of government becomes destructive of these ends, it is the right of the people to alter or to abolish it, and to institute a new government, laying its foundation on such principles, and organizing its powers in such form, as to them shall seem most likely to effect their safety and happiness. Prudence, indeed, will dictate that governments long established, should not be changed for light and transient causes; and, accordingly, all experience hath shown, that mankind are more disposed to suffer, while evils are sufferable, than to right themselves by abolishing the forms to which they are accustomed. But, when a long train of abuses and usurpations, pursuing invariably the same object, evinces a design to reduce them under absolute despotism, it is their right, it is their duty, to throw off such government and to provide new guards for their future security. Such has been the patient sufferance of these colonies, and such is now the necessity which constrains them to alter their former systems of government. The history of the present King of Great Britain is a history of repeated injuries and usurpations, all having, in direct object, the establishment of an absolute tyranny over these States. To prove this, let facts be submitted to a candid world:—

He has refused his assent to laws the most wholesome and necessary for the public good.

He has forbidden his governors to pass laws of immediate and pressing importance, unless suspended in their operation till his assent should be obtained; and, when so suspended, he has utterly neglected to attend to them.

He has refused to pass other laws for the accommodation of large districts of people, unless those people would relinquish the right of representation in the legislature; a right inestimable to them, and formidable to tyrants only.

He has called together legislative bodies at places unusual, uncomfortable, and distant from the depository of their public records, for the sole purpose of fatiguing them into compliance with his measures.

He has dissolved representative houses repeatedly for opposing, with manly firmness, his invasions on the rights of the people.

He has refused, for a long time after such dissolutions, to cause others to be elected, whereby the legislative powers, incapable of annihilation, have returned to the people at large for their exercise; the state remaining, in the meantime, exposed to all the danger of invasion from without, and convulsions within.

He has endeavored to prevent the population of these States; for that purpose, obstructing the laws for naturalization of foreigners; refusing to pass others to encourage their migration hither, and raising the conditions of new appropriations of lands.

He has obstructed the administration of justice, by refusing his assent to laws for establishing judiciary powers.

He has made judges dependent on his will alone, for the tenure of their offices, and the amount and payment of their salaries.

He has erected a multitude of new offices, and sent hither swarms of officers to harass out people, and eat out their substance.

He has kept among us, in time of peace, standing armies, without the consent of our legislatures.

He has affected to render the military independent of, and superior to, the civil power.

He has combined, with others, to subject us to a jurisdiction foreign to our Constitution, and unacknowledged by our laws; giving his assent to their acts of pretended legislation:

For quartering large bodies of armed troops among us:

For protecting them by a mock trial, from punishment, for any murders which they should commit on the inhabitants of these States:

For cutting off our trade with all parts of the world:

For imposing taxes on us without our consent:

For depriving us, in many cases, of the benefit of trial by jury:

For transporting us beyond seas to be tried for pretended offences:

For abolishing the free system of English laws in a neighboring province, establishing therein an arbitrary government, and enlarging its boundaries, so as to render it at once an example and fit instrument for introducing the same absolute rule into these colonies:

For taking away our charters, abolishing our most valuable laws, and altering, fundamentally, the powers of our governments:

For suspending our own legislatures, and declaring themselves invested with power to legislate for us in all cases whatsoever.

He has abdicated government here, by declaring us out of his protection, and waging war against us.

He has plundered our seas, ravaged our coasts, burnt our towns, and destroyed the lives of our people.

He is, at this time, transporting large armies of foreign mercenaries to complete the works of death, desolation, and tyranny, already begun, with circumstances of cruelty and perfidy scarcely paralleled in the most barbarous ages, and totally unworthy the head of a civilized nation.

He has constrained our fellow citizens, taken captive on the high seas, to bear arms against their country, to become the executioners of their friends, and brethren, or to fall themselves by their hands.

He has excited domestic insurrections amongst us, and has endeavored to bring on the inhabitants of our frontiers, the merciless Indian savages, whose known rule of warfare is an undistinguished destruction of all ages, sexes, and conditions.

In every stage of these oppressions, we have petitioned for redress, in the most humble terms; our repeated petitions have been answered only by repeated injury. A prince, whose character is thus marked by every act which may define a tyrant, is unfit to be the ruler of a free people.

Nor have we been wanting in attention to our British brethren. We have warned them, from time to time, of attempts made by their legislature to extend an unwarrantable jurisdiction over us. We have reminded them of the circumstances of our emigration and settlement here. We have appealed to their native justice and magnanimity, and we have conjured them, by the ties of our common kindred, to disavow these usurpations, which would inevitably interrupt our connections and correspondence. They, too, have been deaf to the voice of justice and consanguinity. We must, therefore, acquiesce in the necessity which denounces our separation, and hold them, as we hold the rest of mankind, enemies in war, in peace, friends.

We, therefore, the representatives of the United States of America, in general Congress assembled, appealing to the Supreme Judge of the world for the rectitude of our intentions, do, in the name, and by the authority of the good people of these colonies, solemnly publish and declare, that these united colonies are, and of right ought to be, free and independent states; that they are absolved from all allegiance to the British Crown, and that all political connection between them and the state of Great Britain is, and ought to be, totally dissolved; and that, as free and independent states, they have full power to levy war, conclude peace, contract alliances, establish commerce, and to do all other acts and things which independent states may of right do. And, for the support of this declaration, with a firm reliance on the protection of Divine Providence, we mutually pledge to each other our lives, our fortunes, and our sacred honor.

THE CONSTITUTION OF THE UNITED STATES OF AMERICA

We the People of the United States, in Order to form a more perfect Union, establish Justice, insure domestic Tranquility, provide for the common defence, promote the general Welfare, and secure the Blessings of Liberty to ourselves and our Posterity, do ordain and establish this Constitution for the United States of America.

Article I

Section 1. All legislative Powers herein granted shall be vested in a Congress of the United States, which shall consist of a Senate and House of Representatives.

Section 2. The House of Representatives shall be composed of Members chosen every second Year by the People of the several States, and the Electors in each State shall have the Qualifications requisite for Electors of the most numerous Branch of the State Legislature.

No Person shall be a Representative who shall not have attained to the age of twenty five Years, and been seven Years a

Citizen of the United States, and who shall not, when elected, be an Inhabitant of that State in which he shall be chosen.

Representatives and direct Taxes shall be apportioned among the several States which may be included within this Union, according to their respective Numbers, which shall be determined by adding to the whole Number of free Persons, including those bound to Service for a Term of Years, and excluding Indians not taxed, three fifths of all other persons.* The actual Enumeration shall be made within three Years after the first Meeting of the Congress of the United States, and within every subsequent Term of ten Years, in such Manner as they shall by Law direct. The Number of Representatives shall not exceed one for every thirty Thousand, but each State shall have at Least one Representative; and until such enumeration shall be made, the State of New Hampshire shall be entitled to chuse three, Massachusetts eight, Rhode-Island and Providence Plantations one, Connecticut five, New-York six, New Jersey four, Pennsylvania eight, Delaware one, Maryland six, Virginia ten, North Caroline five, South Carolina five, and Georgia three.

When vacancies happen in the Representation from any State, the Executive Authority thereof shall issue Writs of Election to fill such Vacancies.

The House of Representatives shall chuse their Speaker and other Officers; and shall have the sole Power of Impeachment.

Section 3. The Senate of the United States shall be composed of two Senators from each State, *chosen by the Legislature thereof,*† for six Years; and each Senator shall have one Vote.

Immediately after they shall be assembled in Consequence of the first Election, they shall be divided as equally as may be into three Classes. The Seats of the Senators of the first Class shall be vacated at the Expiration of the second Year, of the second Class at the Expiration of the fourth Year, and of the third Class at the Expiration of the sixth Year, so that one third may be chosen every second Year; *and if Vacancies happen by Resignation, or otherwise, during the Recess of the Legislature of any State, the Executive thereof may make temporary Appointments until the next Meeting of the Legislature, which shall then fill such Vacancies.**

---

* Italics indicate passages altered by subsequent amendments. This was revised by the Sixteenth (apportionment of taxes) and Fourteenth (determination of persons) Amendments.
† Revised by Seventeenth Amendment.
* Revised by Seventeenth Amendment.

No Persons shall be a Senator who shall not have attained to the Age of thirty Years, and been nine Years a Citizen of the United States, and who shall not, when elected, be an Inhabitant of the State for which he shall be chosen.

The Vice President of the United States shall be President of the Senate, but shall have no Vote, unless they be equally divided.

The Senate shall chuse their other Officers, and also a President pro tempore, in the Absence of the Vice President, or when he shall exercise the Office of President of the United States.

The Senate shall have the sole Power to try all Impeachments. When sitting for that Purpose, they shall be on Oath or Affirmation. When the President of the United States is tried, the Chief Justice shall preside: And no Person shall be convicted without the Concurrence of two thirds of the Members present.

Judgment in Cases of Impeachment shall not extend further than to removal from Office, and disqualification to hold and enjoy any Office of honor, Trust or Profit under the United States; but the Party convicted shall nevertheless be liable and subject to Indictment, Trial, Judgment and Punishment, according to Law.

Section 4. The Times, Places and Manner of holding Elections for Senators and Representatives, shall be prescribed in each State by the Legislature thereof; but the Congress may at any time by Law make or alter such Regulations, except as to the Places of chusing Senators.

The Congress shall assemble at least once in every Year, and such Meeting shall be *on the first Monday in December,*† unless they shall by Law appoint a different Day.

Section 5. Each House shall be the Judge of the Elections, Returns and Qualifications of its own Members, and a Majority of each shall constitute a Quorum to do Business; but a smaller Number may adjourn from day to day, and may be authorized to compel the Attendance of absent Members, in such Manner, and under such Penalties as each House may provide.

Each House may determine the Rules of its Proceedings, punish its Members for disorderly Behavior, and, with the Concurrence of two thirds, expel a Member.

Each House shall keep a Journal of its Proceedings, and from time to time publish the same, excepting such Parts as may in their Judgment require Secrecy; and the Yeas and Nays of the Members of either House on any question shall, at the Desire of one fifth of those Present, be entered on the Journal.

† Revised by Twentieth Amendment.

Neither House, during the Session of Congress, shall, without the Consent of the other, adjourn for more than three days, nor to any other Place than that in which the two Houses shall be sitting.

Section 6. The Senators and Representatives shall receive a Compensation for their Services, to be ascertained by Law, and paid out of the Treasury of the United States. They shall in all Cases, except Treason, Felony and Breach of the Peace, be privileged from Arrest during their Attendance at the Session of their respective Houses, and in going to and returning from the same; and for any Speech or Debate in either House, they shall not be questioned in any other Place.

No Senator or Representative shall, during the Time for which he was elected, be appointed to any civil Office under the Authority of the United States, which shall have been created, or the Emoluments whereof shall have been encreased during such time; and no Person holding any Office under the United States, shall be a Member of either House during his Continuance in Office.

Section 7. All Bills for raising Revenue shall originate in the house of Representatives; but the Senate may propose or concur with Amendments as on other Bills.

Every Bill which shall have passed the House of Representatives and the Senate, shall, before it become a Law, be presented to the President of the United States; if he approves he shall sign it, but if not he shall return it, with his Objections to that House in which it shall have originated, who shall enter the Objections at large on their Journal, and proceed to reconsider it. If after such Reconsideration two thirds of that House shall agree to pass the Bill, it shall be sent, together with the Objections, to the other House, by which it shall likewise be reconsidered, and if approved by two thirds of that House, it shall become a Law. But in all such Cases the Votes of both Houses shall be determined by Yeas and Nays, and the Names of the Persons voting for and against the Bill shall be entered on the Journal of each House respectively. If any Bill shall not be returned by the President within ten Days (Sundays excepted) after it shall have been presented to him, the Same shall be a Law, in like Manner as if he had signed it, unless the Congress by their Adjournment prevent its Return, in which Case it shall not be a Law.

Every Order, Resolution, or Vote to which the Concurrence of the Senate and House of Representatives may be necessary (except on a question of Adjournment) shall be presented to the President of the United States; and before the Same shall take Effect, shall be approved by him, or being disapproved by him, shall be repassed by two thirds of the Senate and House of Representatives, according to the Rules and Limitations prescribed in the Case of a Bill.

Section 8. The Congress shall have Power To lay and collect Taxes, Duties, Imposts and Excises, to pay the Debts and provide for the common Defence and general Welfare of the United States; but all Duties, Imposts and Excises shall be uniform throughout the United States;

To borrow Money on the credit of the United States;

To regulate Commerce with foreign Nations, and among the several States, and with the Indian Tribes;

To establish an uniform Rule of Naturalization, and uniform Laws on the subject of Bankruptcies throughout the United States;

To coin Money, regulate the Value thereof, and of foreign Coin, and fix the Standard of Weights and Measures;

To provide for the Punishment of counterfeiting the Securities and current Coin of the United States;

To establish Post Offices and post Roads;

To promote the Progress of Science and useful Arts, by securing for limited Times to Authors and Inventors the exclusive Right to their respective Writings and Discoveries;

To constitute Tribunals inferior to the Supreme Court;

To define and punish Piracies and Felonies committed on the high Seas, and Offences against the Law of Nations;

To declare War, grant Letters of Marque and Reprisal, and make Rules concerning Captures on Land and Water;

To raise and support Armies, but no Appropriation of Money to that Use shall be for a longer Term than two Years;

To provide and maintain a Navy;

To make Rules for the Government and Regulation of the land and naval Forces;

To provide for calling forth the Militia to execute the Laws of the Union, suppress Insurrections and repel Invasions;

To provide for organizing, arming, and disciplining, the Militia, and for governing such Part of them as may be employed in the Service of the United States, reserving to the States respectively, the Appointment of the Offices, and the Authority of training the Militia according to the discipline prescribed by Congress;

To exercise exclusive Legislation in all Cases whatsoever, over such District (not exceeding ten Miles square) as may, by

Cession of particular States, and the Acceptance of Congress, become the Seat of the Government of the United States, and to exercise like Authority over all Places purchased by the Consent of the Legislature of the State in which the Same shall be, for the Erection of Forts, Magazines, Arsenals, dock-Yards, and other needful Buildings;—And

To make all Laws which shall be necessary and proper for carrying into Execution the foregoing Powers, and all other Powers vested by this Constitution in the Government of the United States, or in any Department or Officer thereof.

Section 9. The Migration or Importation of such Persons as any of the States now existing shall think proper to admit, shall not be prohibited by the Congress prior to the Year one thousand eight hundred and eight, but a Tax or duty may be imposed on such Importation, not exceeding ten dollars for each Person.

The Privilege of the Writ of Habeas Corpus shall not be suspended, unless when in Cases of Rebellion or Invasion the public Safety may require it.

No Bill of Attainder or ex post facto Law shall be passed.

No Capitation, or other direct, Tax shall be laid, unless in Proportion to the Census or Enumeration herein before directed to be taken.*

No Tax or Duty shall be laid on Articles exported from any State.

No Preference shall be given by any Regulation of Commerce or Revenue to the Ports of one State over those of another: nor shall Vessels bound to, or from, one State, be obliged to enter, clear, or pay Duties in another.

No money shall be drawn from the Treasury, but in Consequence of Appropriations made by Law; and a regular Statement and Account of the Receipts and Expenditures of all public Money shall be published from time to time.

No title of Nobility shall be granted by the United States: And no Person holding any Office of Profit or Trust under them, shall, without the Consent of the Congress, accept of any present, Emolument, Office, or Title, of any kind whatever, from any King, Prince, or foreign State.

Section 10. No State shall enter into any Treaty, Alliance, or Confederation; grant Letters of Marque and Reprisal; coin Money; emit Bills of Credit; make any Thing but gold and silver Coin a Tender in Payment of Debts; pass any Bill of

---

* Revised by Sixteenth Amendment.

Attainder, ex post facto Law, or Law impairing the Obligation of Contracts, or Grant any Title of Nobility.

No State shall, without the Consent of the Congress, lay any Imposts or Duties on Imports or Exports, except what may be absolutely necessary for executing its inspection Laws: and the net Produce of all Duties and Imposts, land by any State on Imports or Exports, shall be for the Use of the Treasury of the United States; and all such Laws shall be subject to the Revision and Control of the Congress.

No State shall, without the Consent of Congress, lay any Duty of Tonnage, keep Troops, or Ships of War in time of Peace, enter into any Agreement or Compact with another State, or with a foreign Power, or engage in War, unless actually invaded, or in such imminent Danger as will not admit of delay.

Article II

Section 1. The executive Power shall be vested in a President of the United States of America. *He shall hold his Office during the Term of four Years,*† and, together with the Vice President, chosen for the same Term be elected as follows:

Each State shall appoint, in such Manner as the Legislature thereof may direct, a Number of Electors, equal to the whole Number of Senators and Representatives to which the State may be entitled in the Congress but no Senator or Representative, or Person holding an Office of Trust or Profit under the United States, shall be appointed an Elector.

The Electors shall meet in their respective States, and vote by Ballot for two Persons, of whom one at least shall not be an Inhabitant of the same State with themselves. And they shall make a List of all the Persons voted for, and of the Number of Votes for each; which List they shall sign and certify, and transmit sealed to the Seat of the Government of the United States, directed to the President of the Senate. The President of the Senate shall, in the Presence of the Senate and House of Representatives, open all the Certificates, and the Votes shall then be counted. The Person having the greatest Number of Votes shall be the President, if such Number be a Majority of the whole Number of Electors appointed; and if there be more than one who have such Majority, and have an equal Number of Votes, then the House of Representatives shall immediately chuse by

† See Twenty-second Amendment.

*Ballot one of them for President; and if no Person have a Majority, then from the five highest on the List the said House shall in like Manner chuse the President. But in chusing the President, the Votes shall be taken by States, the Representation from each State having one Vote; A quorum for this purpose shall consist of a Member or Members from two thirds of the States, and a Majority of all the States shall be necessary to a Choice. In every Case, after the Choice of the President, the Person having the greatest Number of Votes of the Electors shall be the Vice President. But if there should remain two or more who have equal Votes, the Senate shall chuse from them by Ballot of the Vice President.**

The Congress may determine the Time of chusing the Electors, and the Day on which they shall give their Votes; which Day shall be the same throughout the United States.

No Person except a natural born Citizen, or a Citizen of the United States, at the time of the Adoption of this Constitution, shall be eligible to the Office of President; neither shall any Person be eligible to that Office who shall not have attained to the Age of thirty five Years, and been fourteen Years a Resident within the United States.

In case of the Removal of the President from Office, or of his Death, Resignation, or Inability to discharge the Powers and Duties of the said Office, the Same shall devolve on the Vice President, and the Congress may by Law provide for the Case of Removal, Death, Resignation or Inability, both of the President and Vice President, declaring what Officer shall then act as President, and such Officer shall act accordingly, until the Disability be removed, or a President shall be elected.†

The President shall, at stated Times, receive for his Services, a Compensation which shall neither be encreased nor diminished during the Period for which he shall have been elected, and he shall not receive within that Period any other Emolument from the United States, or any of them.

Before he enter on the Execution of his Office, he shall take the following Oath of Affirmation:—"I do solemnly swear (or affirm) that I will faithfully execute the Office of President of the United States, and will to the best of my Ability, preserve, protect and defend the Constitution of the United States."

Section 2. The President shall be Commander in Chief of the Army and Navy of the United States, and of the Militia of the

---

* Superseded by Twelfth Amendment.
† Revised by Twenty-fifth Amendment.

several States, when called into the actual service of the United States; he may require the Opinion, in writing, of the principal Officer in each of the executive Departments, upon any Subject relating to the Duties of their respective Offices, and he shall have Power to grant Reprieves and Pardons for Offences against the United States, except in Cases of Impeachment.

He shall have Power, by and with the Advice and Consent of the Senate, to make Treaties, provided two thirds of the Senators present concur; and he shall nominate, and by and with the Advice and Consent of the Senate, shall appoint Ambassadors. and other public Ministers and Consuls, Judges of the supreme Court, and all other Officers of the United States, whose Appointments are not herein otherwise provided for, and which shall be established by Law: but the Congress may by Law vest the Appointment of such inferior Officers, as they think proper, in the President alone, in the Courts of Law, or in the Heads of Departments.

The President shall have Power to fill up all Vacancies that may happen during the Recess of the Senate, by granting Commissions which shall expire at the End of their next Session.

Section 3. He shall from time to time give to the Congress Information of the State of the Union, and recommend to their Consideration such Measures as he shall judge necessary and expedient; he may, on extraordinary Occasions, convene both Houses, or either of them, and in Case of Disagreement between them, with Respect to the Time of Adjournment, he may adjourn them to such Time as he shall think proper; he shall receive Ambassadors and other public Ministers, he shall take Care that the Laws be faithfully executed, and shall Commission all the Officers of the United States.

Section 4. The President, Vice President, and all civil Officers of the United States, shall be recoved from Office on Impeachment for, and Conviction of Treason, Bribery, or other high Crimes and Misdemeanors.

Article III

Section 1. The judicial Power of the United States, shall be vested in one supreme Court and in such inferior Courts as the Congress may from time to time ordain and establish. The Judges, both of the supreme and inferior Courts, shall hold their Offices during good Behavior, and shall, at stated Times, receive for their

Services, a Compensation, which shall not be diminished during their Continuance in Office.

Section 2. The judicial Power shall extend to all Cases, in Law and Equity, arising under this Constitution, the Laws of the United States, and Treaties made, or which shall be made, under their Authority;—to all Cases affecting Ambassadors, other public Ministers and Consuls;—to all Cases of admiralty and maritime Jurisdiction;—to Controversies to which the United States shall be a Party;—to Controversies between two or more States;—*between a State and Citizens of another State*;*—between Citizens of different States;—between Citizens of the same State claiming Lands under Grants of different States, *and between a State or the Citizens thereof, and foreign States, Citizens, or Subjects.**

In all cases affecting Ambassadors, other public Ministers and Consuls, and those in which a State shall be Party, the supreme Court shall have original Jurisdiction. In all the other Cases before mentioned, the supreme Court shall have appellate Jurisdiction, both as to Law and Fact, with such Exceptions, and under such regulations as the Congress shall make.

The Trial of all Crimes, except in Cases of Impeachment, shall be by Jury; and such Trial shall be held in the State where the said Crimes shall have been committed; but when not committed within any State, the Trial shall be at such Place or Places as the Congress may by Law have directed.

Section 3. Treason against the United States, shall consist only in levying War against them, or in adhering to their Enemies, giving them Aid and Comfort. No Person shall be convicted of Treason unless on the Testimony of two Witnesses to the same overt Act, or on Confession in open Court.

The Congress shall have Power to declare the Punishment of Treason, but no Attainder of Treason shall work Corruption of Blood, or Forfeiture except during the Life of the Person attained.

Article IV

Section 1. Full Faith and Credit shall be given in each State to the public Acts, Records and judicial Proceedings of every other State. And the Congress may by general Laws prescribe the

* Revised by Eleventh Amendment.

Manner in which such Acts, Records, and Proceedings shall be proved, and the Effect thereof.

Section 2. The Citizens of each State shall be entitled to all Privileges and Immunities of Citizens in the several States.

A person charged in any State with Treason, Felony, or other Crime, who shall flee from Justice, and be found in another State, shall on Demand of the executive Authority of the State from which he fled, be delivered up, to be removed to the State having Jurisdiction of the Crime.

No person held to Service or Labour in one State, under the Laws therof, escaping into another, shall, in Consequence of any Law or Regulation therein, be discharged from such Service or Labour, but shall be delivered up on Claim of the Party to whom such Service or Labour may be due.*

Section 3. New States may be admitted by the Congress into this Union; but no new State shall be formed or erected within the Jurisdiction of any other State; nor any State be formed by the Junction of two or more States, or Parts of States, without the Consent of the Legislatures of the States concerned as well as of the Congress.

The Congress shall have Power to dispose of and make all needful Rules and Regulations respecting the Territory or other Property belonging to the United States; and nothing in this Constitution shall be so construed as to Prejudice any claims of the United States, or of any particular State.

Section 4. The United States shall guarantee to every State in this Union a Republican Form of Government, and shall protect each of them against Invasion; and on Application of the Legislature, or of the Executive (when the Legislature cannot be convened) against domestic Violence.

Article V

The Congress, whenever two thirds of both Houses shall deem it necessary, shall propose Amendments to this Constitution, or, on the Application of the Legislatures of two thirds of the several States, shall call a Convention for proposing Amendments, which, in either Case, shall be valid to all Intents and Purposes, as Part

---

* Superseded by Thirteenth Amendment.

of this Constitution, when ratified by the Legislatures of three fourths of the several States, or by Conventions in three fourths thereof, as the one or the other Mode of Ratification may be proposed by the Congress; Provided that no Amendment which may be made prior to the Year One thousand eight hundred and eight shall in any Manner affect the first and fourth Clauses in the Ninth Section of the first Article; and that no State, without its Consent, shall be deprived of its equal Suffrage in the Senate.

Article VI

All Debts contracted and Engagements entered into, before the Adoption of this Constitution, shall be as valid against the United States under this Constitution, as under the Confederation.†

This Constitution, and the Laws of the United States which shall be made in Pursuance thereof; and all Treaties made, or which shall be made, under the Authority of the United States, shall be the supreme Law of the Land; and the Judges in every State shall be bound thereby, any Thing in the Constitution or Laws of any State to the Contrary notwithstanding.

The Senators and Representatives before mentioned, and the Members of the several State Legislatures, and all executive and judicial Officers, both of the United States and of the several States, shall be bound by Oath or Affirmation, to support this Constitution; but no religious Test shall ever be required as a Qualification to any Office or public Trust under the United States.

Article VII

The Ratification of the Conventions of nine States, shall be sufficient for the Establishment of this Constitution between the States so ratifying the Same.

Done in Convention by the Unanimous Consent of the States present the Seventeenth Day of September in the Year of our Lord one thousand seven hundred and eighty seven and of the Independence of the United States of America the twelfth. In witness whereof We have hereunto subscribed our Names.

. . .

† See Fourteenth Amendment, Section 4.

ARTICLES IN ADDITION TO, AND AMENDMENT OF, THE CONSTITUTION OF THE UNITED STATES OF AMERICA, PROPOSED BY CONGRESS, AND RATIFIED BY THE SEVERAL STATES, PURSUANT TO THE FIFTH ARTICLE OF THE ORIGINAL CONSTITUTION.

(Ratification of the first ten amendments was completed December 15, 1791.)

Amendment I

Congress shall make no law respecting an establishment of religion, or prohibiting the free exercise thereof; or abridging the freedom of speech, or of the press; or the right of the people peaceably to assemble, and to petition the Government for a redress of grievances.

Amendment II

A well regulated Militia, being necessary to the security of a free State, the right of the people to keep and bear Arms, shall not be infringed.

Amendment III

No Soldier shall, in time of peace be quartered in any house, without the consent of the Owner, nor in time of war, but in a manner to be prescribed by law.

Amendment IV

The right of the people to be secure in their persons, houses, papers, and effects, against unreasonable searches and seizures, shall not be violated, and no Warrants shall issue, but upon probable cause, supported by Oath or affirmation, and particularly describing the place to be searched, and the persons or things to be seized.

Amendment V

No person shall be held to answer for a capital, or other infamous crime, unless on a presentment or indictment of a Grand

Jury, except in cases arising in the land or naval forces, or in the Militia, when in actual service in time of War or public danger; nor shall any person be subject for the same offence to be twice put in jeopardy of life or limb; nor shall he be compelled in any criminal case to be a witness against himself, nor be deprived of life, liberty, or property, without due process of law; nor shall private property be taken for public use, without just compensation.

Amendment VI

In all criminal prosecutions, the accused shall enjoy the right to a speedy and public trial, by an impartial jury of the State and district wherein the crime shall have been committed, which district shall have been previously ascertained by law, and to be informed of the nature and cause of the accusation; to be confronted with the witnesses against him; to have compulsory process for obtaining witnesses in his favor, and to have the Assistance of Counsel for his defence.

Amendment VII

In Suits at common law, where the value in controversy shall exceed twenty dollars, the right of trial by jury shall be preserved, and no fact tried by a jury, shall be otherwise reexamined in any Court of the United States, than according to the rules of the common law.

Amendment VIII

Excessive bail shall not be required, nor excessive fines imposed, nor cruel and unusual punishments inflicted.

Amendment IX

The enumeration in the Constitution, of certain rights, shall not be construed to deny or disparage others retained by the people.

Amendment X

The powers not delegated to the United States by the Constitution, nor prohibited by it to the States, are reserved to the States respectively, or to the people.

Amendment XI (January 8, 1798)

The Judicial power of the United States shall not be construed to extend to any suit in law or equity, commenced or prosecuted against one of the United States by Citizens of another State, or by Citizens or Subjects of any Foreign State.

Amendment XII (September 25, 1804)

The Electors shall meet in their respective states and vote by ballot for President and Vice President, one of whom, at least, shall not be an inhabitant of the same state with themselves; they shall name in their ballots the person voted for as President, and in distinct ballots the person voted for as Vice President, and they shall make distinct lists of all persons voted for as President and of all persons voted for as Vice President, and of the number of votes for each, which lists they shall sign and certify, and transmit sealed to the seat of the government of the United States, directed to the President of the Senate;—The President of the Senate shall, in the presence of Senate and House of Representatives, open all the certificates and the votes shall then be counted;—The person having the greatest number of votes for President, shall be the President, if such number be a majority of the whole number of Electors appointed; and if no person have such majority, then from the persons having the highest numbers not exceeding three on the list of those voted for as President, the House of Representatives shall choose immediately, by ballot, the President. But in choosing the President, the votes shall be taken by states, the representation from each state having one vote; a quorum for this purpose shall consist of a member or members from two-thirds of the states, and a majority of all the states shall be necessary to a choice. And if the House of Representatives shall not choose a President whenever the right of choice shall devolve upon them, *before the fourth day of March next following,** then the Vice President shall act

* Revised by the Twentieth Amendment.

as President, as in the case of the death or other constitutional disability of the President.—The person having the greatest number of votes as Vice President shall be the Vice President, if such number be a majority of the whole number of Electors appointed, and if no person have a majority, then from the two highest numbers on the list, the Senate shall choose the Vice President; a quorum for the purpose shall consist of two-thirds of the whole number of Senators, and a majority of the whole number shall be necessary to a choice. But no person constitutionally ineligible to the office of President shall be eligible to that of Vice President of the United States.

Amendment XIII (December 18, 1865)

Section 1. Neither slavery nor involuntary servitude, except as a punishment for crime whereof the party shall have been duly convicted, shall exist within the United States, or any place subject to their jurisdiction.

Section 2. Congress shall have the power to enforce this article by appropriate legislation.

Amendment XIV (July 28, 1869)

Section 1. All persons born or naturalized in the United States, and subject to the jurisdiction thereof, are citizens of the United States and of the State wherein they reside. No State shall make or enforce any law which shall abridge the privileges or immunities of citizens of the United States; nor shall any State deprive any person of life, liberty, or property, without due process of law; nor deny to any person within its jurisdiction the equal protection of the laws.

Section 2. Representatives shall be apportioned among the several States according to their respective numbers, counting the whole number of persons in each State, excluding Indians not taxed. But when the right to vote at any election for the choice of electors for President and Vice President of the United States, Representatives in Congress, the Executive and Judicial officers of a State, or the members of the Legislature thereof, is denied to any of the male inhabitants of such State, being twenty-one years of age, and citizens of the United States, or in any way abridged, except for participation in rebellion, or other crime, the basis of representation therein shall be reduced in the proportion which the number of such male citizens shall bear to the whole number of male citizens twenty-one years of age in such State.

Section 3. No person shall be a Senator or Representative in Congress, or elector of President and Vice President, or hold any office, civil or military, under the United States, or under any State, who, having previously taken an oath, as a member of Congress, or as an officer of the United States, or as a member of any State legislature, or as an executive or judicial officer of any State, to support the Constitution of the United States, shall have engaged in insurrection or rebellion against the same, or given aid or comfort to the enemies thereof. But Congress may by a vote of two thirds of each House, remove such disability.

Section 4. The validity of the public debt of the United States, authorized by law, including debts incurred for payment of pensions and bounties for services in suppressing insurrection or rebellion; shall not be questioned. But neither the United States nor any State shall assume or pay any debt or obligation incurred in aid of insurrection or rebellion against the United States, or any claim for the loss or emancipation on any slave; but all such debts, obligations, and claims shall be held illegal and void.

Section 5. The Congress shall have power to enforce, by appropriate legislation, the provisions of this article.

Amendment XV (March 30, 1870)

Section 1. The right of citizens of the United States to vote shall not be denied or abridged by the United States or by any State on account of race, color, or previous conditions of servitude.

Section 2. The Congress shall have power to enforce this article by appropriate legislation.

Amendment XVI (February 25, 1913)

The Congress shall have power to lay and collect taxes on incomes, from whatever source derived, without apportionment among the several States, and without regard to any census or enumeration.

Amendment XVII (May 31, 1913)

The Senate of the United States shall be composed of two Senators from each State, elected by the people thereof, for six years; and each Senator shall have one vote. The electors in each State shall have the qualifications requisite for electors of the most numerous branch of the State legislatures.

When vacancies happen in the representation of any State in the Senate, the executive authority of such State shall issue writs of election to fill such vacancies: *Provided,* That the legislature of any State may empower the executive thereof to make temporary appointments until the people fill the vacancies by election as the legislature may direct.

This amendment shall not be so construed as to affect the election or term of any Senator chosen before it becomes valid as part of the Constitution.

Amendment XVIII (January 29, 1919)

Section 1. After one year from the ratification of this article the manufacture, sale, or transportation of intoxicating liquors within, the importation thereof into, or the exportation thereof from the United States and all territory subject to the jurisdiction thereof for beverage purposes is hereby prohibited.

Section 2. The Congress and the several States shall have concurrent power to enforce this article by appropriate legislation.

Section 3. This article shall be inoperative unless it shall have been ratified as an amendment to the Constitution by the legislatures of the several States, as provided in the Constitution within seven years from the date of the submission hereof to the States by the Congress.*

Amendment XIX (August 26, 1920)

The right of citizens of the United States to vote shall not be denied or abridged by the United States or by any State on account of sex.

Congress shall have power to enforce this article by appropriate legislation.

---

* Repealed by the Twenty-first Amendment.

Amendment XX (February 6, 1933)

Section 1. The terms of the President and Vice President shall end at noon on the 20th day of January, and the terms of Senators and Representatives at noon on the 3rd day of January, of the years in which such terms would have ended if this article had not been ratified; and the terms of their successors shall then begin.

Section 2. The Congress shall assemble at least once in every year, and such meeting shall begin at noon on the 3rd day of January, unless they shall by law appoint a different day.

Section 3. If, at the time fixed for the beginning of the term of the President, the President elect shall have died, the Vice President elect shall become President. If a President shall not have been chosen before the time fixed for the beginning of his term, or if the President elect shall have failed to qualify, then the Vice President elect shall act as President until a President shall have qualified; and the Congress may by law provide for the case wherein neither a President elect nor a Vice President elect shall have qualified, declaring who shall then act as President, or the manner in which one who is to act shall be selected, and such person shall act accordingly until a President or Vice President shall have qualified.

Section 4. The Congress may by law provide for the case of the death of any of the persons from whom the House of Representatives may choose a President whenever the right of choice shall have devolved upon them, and for the case of the death of any of the persons from whom the Senate may choose a Vice President whenever the right of choice shall have devolved upon them.

Section 5. Sections 1 and 2 shall take effect on the 15th day of October following the ratification of this article.

Section 6. This article shall be inoperative unless it shall have been ratified as an amendment to the Constitution by the legislatures of three-fourths of the several States within seven years from the date of its submission.

Amendment XXI (December 5, 1933)

Section 1. The eighteenth article of amendment to the Constitution of the United States is hereby repealed.

Section 2. The transportation or importation into any State, Territory, or possession of the United States for delivery or use therein of intoxicating liquors, in violation of the laws thereof, is hereby prohibited.

Section 3. This article shall be inoperative unless it shall have been ratified as an amendment to the Constitution by conventions in the several States, as provided in the Constitution, within seven years from the date of the submission hereof to the States by the Congress.

Amendment XXII (February 26, 1951)

Section 1. No person shall be elected to the office of the President more than twice, and no person who has held the office of President, or acted as President, for more than two years of a term to which some other person was elected President shall be elected to the office of President more than once. But this Article shall not apply to any person holding the office of President when this Article was proposed by the Congress, and shall not prevent any person who may be holding the office of President, or acting as President, during the term within which this Article becomes operative from holding the office of President or acting as President during the remainder of such term.

Section 2. This article shall be inoperative unless it shall have been ratified as an amendment to the Constitution by the legislatures of three-fourths of the several States within seven years from the date of its submission to the States by the Congress.

Amendment XXIII (March 29, 1961)

Section 1. The District constituting the seat of Government of the United States shall appoint in such manner as the Congress may direct:

A number of electors of President and Vice President equal to the whole number of Senators and Representatives in Congress to which the District would be entitled if it were a State, but in no event more than the least populous State; they shall be in addition to those appointed by the States, but they shall be considered, for the purposes of the election of President and Vice President, to be electors appointed by a State; and they shall meet in the District and perform such duties as provided by the twelfth article of amendment.

Section 2. The Congress shall have power to enforce this article by appropriate legislation.

Amendment XXIV (January 23, 1964)

Section 1. The right of citizens of the United States to vote in any primary or other election for President or Vice President, for electors for President or Vice President, or for Senator or Representative in Congress, shall not be denied or abridged by the United States or any state by reason of failure to pay any poll tax or other tax.

Section 2. The Congress shall have the power to enforce this article by appropriate legislation.

Amendment XXV (February 10, 1967)

Section 1. In case of the removal of the President from office or of his death or resignation, the Vice President shall become President.

Section 2. Whenever there is a vacancy in the office of the Vice President, the President shall nominate a Vice President who shall take office upon confirmation by a majority vote of both Houses of Congress.

Section 3. Whenever the President transmits to the President pro tempore of the Senate and the Speaker of the House of Representatives his written declaration that he is unable to discharge the powers and duties of his office, and until he transmits to them a written declaration to the contrary, such powers and duties shall be discharged by the Vice President as Acting President.

Section 4. Whenever the Vice President and a majority of either the principal officers of the executive departments or of such other body as Congress may by law provide, transmit to the President pro tempore of the Senate and the Speaker of the House of Representatives their written declaration that the President is unable to discharge the powers and duties of his office, the Vice President shall immediately assume the powers and duties of the office as Acting President.

Thereafter, when the President transmits to the President pro tempore of the Senate and the Speaker of the House of Representatives his written declaration that no inability exists, he shall resume the powers and duties of his office unless the Vice President and a majority of either the principal officers of the executive departments or of such other body as Congress may by law provide, transmit within four days to the President pro tempore of the Senate and the Speaker of the House of Representatives their written declaration that the President is unable to discharge the powers and duties of his office. Thereupon Congress shall decide the issue, assembling within forty-eight hours for that purpose if not in session. If the Congress, within twenty-one days after receipt of the latter written declaration or, if Congress is not in session, within twenty-one days after Congress is required to assemble, determines by two-thirds vote of both Houses that the President is unable to discharge the powers and duties of his office, the Vice President shall continue to discharge the same as Acting President; otherwise, the President shall resume the powers and duties of his office.

Amendment XXVI (June 30, 1971)

Section 1. The right of citizens of the United States, who are eighteen years of age or older, to vote shall not be denied or abridged by the United States or any state on account of age.
Section 2. The Congress shall have the power to enforce this article by appropriate legislation.

INDEX

Adair, Douglass, 133-136
Adams, John, 111, 114*n*, 125, 133, 244*n*
Adams, John Quincy, 305
Adamson v. *California,* 322 U.S. 46 (1947), 205
Adversary system, 199-202, 211
Advertising. *See* mass media
Advisory Commission on Intergovernmental Relations (1962), 81
Agar, Herbert, 186-187
Agnew, Spiro T., 110, 233, 267; Justice Department Investigation of, 15-16; Watergate, 39, 40*n*
Agriculture, 54, 57; subsidies, 97, 98
Agriculture, Department of, 98
Alliance for Progress, 302
Amendments: eleventh, 147; fifteenth, 226; fifth, 152, 156, 196, 201, 204-208, 212,

Amendments *(continued)*
242; first, 156, 180-181, 186-188, 190, 192; fourteenth, 74, 178, 201-202, 205, 217, 220, 222, 226, 231, 242; fourth, 212-214; nineteenth, 13; ninth, 178, 246-249; sixteenth, 73, 147; tenth, 66, 77, 178; twenty-fifth, 109
American Independent Party, 264-265
American Medical Association (AMA), 259, 260, 261
Anti-Federalist Papers (Dollard), 173
Aristophanes, 239, 240
Aristotle, 52, 139, 224; middle class, 47-48; socioeconomic principles, 99
Articles of Confederation, 65, 112, 159
Ashley, Thomas, 104
Atomic Energy Act, 130
Atwell, William H., 148

Index

Baker v. *Carr,* 369 U.S. 186 (1962), 21, 146
Bay of Pigs. *See* Kennedy
Beauharnair v. *Illinois,* 187, 188, 190
Bender, Paul, 154-155
Beveridge, Albert J., 77, 292, 293
Bill of Rights, 176-182, 196-197, 206, 239; due process clause in, 74, 199; technology, 240
Bitter Cry of the Children, The (Spargo), 74, 75*n*
Black Americans. *See* Negro
Blackman, Harry, 153, 154
Boggs, Hale, 93, 94
Bolling, Richard, 96, 101
Bond, Julian, 110
Boulding, Kenneth, 162
Brandeis, Louis, 74, 179, 214
Bremer, Arthur H., 135
Brennan, William J., 153, 192
Brinkley, David, 123
Brown, Edmund G., 278, 279
Brown, H. Rap, 217
Brown v. *Board of Education,* 347 U.S. 483 (1954), 78, 231
Brown v. *Mississippi* (1936), 207-209
Bryan, William Jennings, 38
Budget Act of 1950, 101, 102
Budget and Accounting Act of 1921, 90, 100
Budget Management, Office of, 90
Bureaucracy, 131, 132, 160-164, 168, 169; public welfare, 166
Burger, Warren, 153, 154
Burke, James A., 94
Business, 256, 257, 310, 311; agribusiness, 258
Busing. *See* Civil Rights
Byrne, Matthew, 7

Cabinet, 120, 131, 160
Calhoun, John C., 71, 72, 222
Cambodia, 102, 298
Campaign Practices Act of 1972, 8
Cardozo, Benjamin N., 180, 182
Carswell, Harold, 124, 144, 153
Central Intelligence Agency (CIA), 128, 299-301; Watergate, 6, 7, 130, 301
Charles (king of England), 48-49, 113
Charlotte-Mecklenburg Case (1971), 234
Chase, Stuart, 139
Checks & balances, 30, 87, 100; on bureaucracies, 169

Child and the State, The (Abbott), 75*n*
Child Labor. *See* employment
China, 297
Chisholm v. *Georgia,* 2 Dallas 419 (1793), 147
Christmas Tree Bill (1966), 95
Churchill, Winston, 39
Cincinnatus, 113
City government, 81, 82
Civil Rights, 73, 77, 225, 227, 231; equality, 222, 230; Viola Luizzo, 202; Poor People's Campaign, 58; school segregation, 67, 78, 119, 148, 233-236, 265; Supreme Court, 149
Civil Rights Act, 232; school segregation, 67
Civil War, 86, 115, 223
Clark, Joseph, 86
Clean Air Act of 1970, 102
Cleveland, Grover, 109*n*
Coming of Age in America (Friedenberg), 283, 284
Commager, Henry Steele, 107, 128, 177, 178; Bill of Rights, 196; Supreme Court, 137, 138
Commission on Party Structure and Delegate Selection, 266
Committee to Reelect the President, 3, 6, 7
Commonwealth of Oceana, The (Harrington) 48, 49
Communism, 177, 184-185, 303
Congress, 66, 85-89, 99, 268, 270; child labor, 76-77; civil rights, 232; finance, 95; foreign policy, 129, 296-298; under Lincoln, 115; ninety-second, 97, 104; powers, 90-91, 102, 112, 122, 127; reform, 103, 106; seniority, 89, 183; and the Supreme Court, 145, 148
Congressional Record, 89, 101, 104
Congressmen, 36, 85, 96
Congress of Racial Equality (CORE), 231
Connally, John, 131
Constitution, 21, 22, 66, 99, 109, 118, 139, 142; and Congress, 85-88, 90; powers, 66, 112-114; power to tax, 86, 91; and the Supreme Court, 145-148
Convention of 1787, 65, 90, 111
Corwin, Edward S., 121, 145, 179
Cox, Harold, 124
Creative Federalism, 78, 79
Crevecoeur, J. Hector St. John de, 41*n*, 61
Crime, 312-316

Cromwell, Oliver, 48-49, 113
Cuban Missile Crisis, 127
Currency. *See* monetary policy

Dahl, Robert, 144
Daley, Richard, 59
Death at an Early Age (Kozol), 284
Declaration of Independence, 9-10, 12-13, 217; popular sovereignty, 201. *See also* Jefferson; Madison
Defense, Department of, 68
Delgado, Jose, 280
Democracy, 139-141, 223
Democratic National Committee, 6
Democratic Party, 255, 264, 271
Dennis v. *United States,* 341 U.S. 494, 184
Depression of 1929, 73, 108, 161; New Deal legislation, 144
Deutscher, Isaac, 184
Diamond, Martin, 140, 152
Dirkson, Everett, 21-22
Dollard, Patrick, 173
Double-jeopardy, 201
Douglas v. *California,* 372 U.S. 535 (1963), 212
Douglas, William O., 153, 155, 156, 188, 198, 284; free speech, 181; privacy, 247
Dred Scott Case, 19 Howard 393 (1857), 147
Drucker, Peter, 169
Due process clause, 199, 201, 208; trial by jury, 200, 202
Dutch Republic, 63, 65

Eagleton, Thomas, 110, 266
Eastland, James, 58, 98, 124
Economics, 51-55, 108; middle class, 59
Education, 56, 67, 78, 176, 283-284; federal control of, 68-70; and technology, 285-286
Eisenhower, Dwight D., 39*n*, 44, 119, 122, 300
Electoral College, 268
Electorate, 270, 271
Electronic Surveillance, 156, 214-215, 241; Watergate, 4, 6, 8
Elementary and Secondary Education Act of 1965, 69
Ellender, Allen, 98
Ellsburg, Daniel, 7, 301. *See also* Pentagon Papers

Emerson, Ralph Waldo, 307, 324
Employment, 56-57, 90, 243; labor laws, 74-77
Endure and Conquer (Sheppard), 203
England: child labor, 75*n*; Civil War (1641-1649), 48-49; *Lusitania,* 37-39; mercantilism, 54-55; Star Chamber, 202-203, 206; taxation, 91
Engle v. *Vitale,* 370 U.S. 421 (1962), 21
Environmental Protection Agency, 102, 320-321
Equality, 219-220, 226, 232; identical political, 225, 229; propositional, 229-230
Equal Opportunities Educational Act, 234, 235
Erlichman, John, 7, 8
Ervin, Sam, 3, 5-6, 8, 155, 215
Escobedo v. *Illinois,* 378 U.S. 478 (1964), 210-212
Espionage Act, 181
Executive power, 71, 86, 111-114; agreements, 129; veto, 124-125; war powers, 115-116

Fair Campaign Practices Committee, The, 5, 232
Federal Bureau of Investigation (FBI), 152, 165, 167, 202, 315; Watergate, 7-8
Federalism, 63-68, 97; national sovereignty, 70-71; urban development, 66-68, 77-78, 81-82
Federalist, The: #51, 83, 84, 140, 141, 145, 170, 207; #47, 163; #78, 148, 151; #10, 139, 143, 171, 255
Federal Office of Education, 67
Federal Power Commission (FPC), 162
Federal Rules of Criminal Procedure, 210
Fenno, Richard F., 131
Finch, Robert, 120
Fisher, Louis, 102
Fisk, Winston, 116
Florence, William G., 168
Foreign Policy, 52, 128, 291, 297, 299, 305; dollar-diplomacy, 292; imperialism, 292-293; isolationism, 293; in Southeast Asia, 295-298
Forgotten Ninth Amendment, The (Patterson), 246, 248, 249*n*
Frady, Marshall, 36
Frank, John P., 149
Frankfurter, Felix, 143

356 Index

Franklin, Benjamin, 53, 106, 177
Frederick II (king of Prussia), 53
Free Enterprise, 97
Freund, Paul, 145, 147
Friedrich, Carl, 170

Galbraith, John Kenneth, 43, 79n
Garrison, William Lloyd, 222
Gibbons v. Ogden, 9 Wheaton (22 U.S.) 1 (p. 24), 145
Gibbons, Sam, 92
Gideon v. Wainwright, 372 U.S. 335 (1963), 212
Gitlow v. New York, 268 U.S. 652 (1925), 182, 183
Goldwater, Barry, 89, 108, 160, 289
Goodwin, Richard, 165
Government, 25, 50, 64, 323
Gray, L. Patrick, III, 7
Griswold v. Connecticut, 381 U.S. 479 (1965), 247
Grodzins, Morton, 69, 160
Guiteau, Charles, 135

Habeas Corpus, Writ of, 115, 198, 211
Haldeman, H. R., 8, 185
Hamilton, Alexander, 134, 140, 148, 151
Hammer v. Dagenhart, 247 U.S. 251 (1918), 76, 77, 146, 147
Hand, Learned, 178, 184
Harding, Warren G., 114n
Harlan, John Marshall, 231
Harrington, James, 48-49, 59, 73, 99
Harris v. New York, 401 U.S. 222 (1971), 155
Harrison, William Henry, 278
Hayes, Rutherford B., 111
Haynsworth, Clement, Jr., 124, 144, 153
Health, Education and Welfare (HEW), 120, 261, 319
Hitler, Adolph, 195
Hoadly, Benjamin, 143
Holden v. Hardy (1898), 74
Holmes, Oliver Wendell, 137, 148, 179, 214, 308; on free speech, 182-183, 186
Homestead Act, 96
Hoover, Herbert, 109, 119; the Hoover Commission, 120
Hoover, J. Edgar, 8, 9
House Agriculture Committee, 98
House Appropriations Committee, 91

House, Colonel, 38, 39, 129
House of Representatives, 34, 35, 88, 100, 101, 126; finance committees, 91, 92
House Ways and Means Committee, 91-95
Hughes, Charles Evans, 143
Hughes Court, 149
Hunt, E. Howard, 7

Interior, Department of, 71, 72, 120
Internal Security Act of 1950, 150
International Development, Agency for (AID), 302
Interstate Commerce Commission (ICC), 167
International Telephone and Telegraph (ITT), 262, 310, 311

Jackson, Andrew, 114, 115, 297
Jackson, Robert H., 149, 186
Jacobellis v. Ohio, 378 U.S. 184 (1964), 191, 192
Joffa, Harry, 223
Japanese-Americans, 142, 150
Jefferson, Thomas, 4, 114, 127, 186, 283, 291; on the Declaration of Independence, 9-12, 111; on equality, 13-14, 140, 219-220; on government, 24, 46, 290
Jennings, Ivor, 177
Jim Crow: education, 230; legislation, 225, 226, 231
John (king of England), 91
Johnson, Lyndon, 69, 92, 109n, 127, 278, 289, 317; on Civil Rights, 218; and Congress, 123-124; Creative Federalism, 78; Vietnam, 39n, 45n, 118, 127, 295-298
Judicial Review, 137-138, 142-144, 147, 150
Jury Returns, The (Nizer), 199n
Justice Department, 162

Katz v. United States, 389 U.S. 347 (1967), 214
Keating-Owen Child Bill, 76
Kennedy, John, 119, 123-124, 135; Bay of Pigs, 39n, 109n, 127
Kennedy, Robert, 160
Keiner, Otto, 218, 219
Key, V. O., Jr., 97
King, Martin Luther, 189, 231-232; the Poor People's Campaign, 58
Kissinger, Henry, 129
Korea, 294
Korematsu v. United States, 323 U.S. 214

Index   357

Korematsu v. *United States (continued)* (1944), 150
Ku Klux Klan, 202, 231

Labor Unions: AFL-CIO, 257
La Follette, Robert, 39
Laird, Melvin, 102
Lansing, Robert M., 38
Lavelle, John D., 127, 128
Law Enforcement, 197, 209
Leach, Richard, 73, 80
Legislative Reorganization Act of 1970, 103
Levy, Leonard, 143, 147
Leyra v. *Denno* 347 U.S. 556 (1954), 209
Lincoln, Abraham, 68, 111, 166, 218, 220; on equality, 219, 223-224; war powers, 115, 116, 297
Lindner, Robert, 280, 282
Lipson, Leslie, 221
Lobbyists, 92, 262
Lockner v. *New York,* 198 U.S. 45 (1906), 74
Locke, John, 10-13, 16
Loving v. *Virginia,* 388 U.S. 1 (1967), 248
Luizzo, Viola, 202, 231
Lusitania, The, 37-39
Luther v. *Borden,* 7 Howard (U.S.) 1 (1894), 146

Mably, Abbè, 52*n*
McAdoo, William, 162
MacArthur, Douglas, 119, 127
McCarthy, Joseph, 150, 177, 202
McClellan, John L., 206
McCloskey, Robert G., 181
McCollum v. *Illinois,* 284
McCulloch v. *Maryland,* 4 Wheaton (U.S.) 316 (1819), 71
McCulloch, William, 105, 106
McGovern, George, 110, 135, 266-269
McGroarity, John Steven, 105
McKinley, William, 282, 297
McNabb-Mallory Rule, 210
McNamara, Robert S., 68, 163
Madison, James, 31-32, 67, 87, 114*n*, 207, 244, 246; on factions, 42, 43, 99; on government, 24, 29, 65-66, 83-84, 139-140, 142, 145, 163, 170-171; pluralism, 255-258
Magna Charta (1215), 91; procedural due process, 201

Majority Rule, 141, 142, 144, 149, 157, 186
Malaysia, 63
Malloy v. *Hogan,* 378 U.S. 1 (1964), 205
Management and Budget, Office of (OMB), 101, 132
Mannes, Marya, 193
Mapp v. *Ohio,* 367 U.S. 643 (1961), 213
Marbury v. *Madison,* 1 Cranch 137 (1803), 142
Marshall, John, 71, 145
Marshall, Thurgood, 124, 153
Mason, Alpheus, 178
Mass Media, 45, 276; and political campaigns, 117, 118, 277, 278
Medicare. *See* American Medical Association
Medicine, 245
Mercantilism, 54; the wage theory, 55
Middle Class, 59
Military Policy, 72, 86, 126, 171, 312
Mill, John Stuart, 176
Mills, C. Wright, 44-45
Mills, Wilbur, 92-94
Minority Rights, 142, 149, 157, 186
Miranda v. *Arizona,* 384 U.S. 436 (1966), 151-155, 212
Mitchell, John, 7, 8, 215
Monetary Policy, 73, 86, 310; the Smithsonian Agreement, 312
Monroe, James, 291, 297
Morley, Felix, 221*n*
Montesquieu de, Baron de la Brède et, 46, 49
Mueller v. *Oregon,* 208 U.S. 412 (1908), 74, 179
Muskie, Edmund S., 63
My Brother's Keeper (Sheppard), 203, 204

Narcotics, 314, 315
National Advisory Commission on Civil Disorders (Kerner Commission), 219, 232, 236
National Association for the Advancement of Colored People (NAACP), 231
National Budget, 101, 102, 132
National Commission on the Causes and Prevention of Violence, 314
National Defense, 126
National Government, 66, 69, 71, 74, 76. *See* urban development
National Nominating Convention, 114, 266
National Security Council, 132, 299, 300
Negroes, 227-231; civil rights, 217, 218, 234-236; discrimination, 60, 67, 77, 148,

Negroes *(continued)*
188, 222; equality, 224, 232-233
Neustadt, Richard, 117, 121-123, 130
New Federalism, 79
New Jersey Plan of Union, 65
Newton, Isaac, 46, 47
New York State: The Ten Hour Act, 74
New York Times, The, 79*n*, 127
New York Times v. *Sullivan,* 376 U.S. 254 (1964), 188-190
Nigeria, 63
Nixon, Richard M., 70, 79, 100, 102, 109, 118, 124, 131, 135, 150, 187, 233, 266-270, 277, 300, 317; on busing, 234, 235; on crime, 155, 215; the executive office, 120, 160; foreign policy, 29, 119, 128-130; and the Supreme Court, 137-138, 144, 153; on Vietnam, 127-128, 298; on Watergate, 6, 8, 39, 40*n*, 301; on welfare, 97, 244, 318-319
Noise Control Act, The, 321
North Atlantic Treaty Organization (NATO), 302, 303
Nuclear Weapons, 108, 116, 127, 294; the cold war, 177; Strategic Arms Limitation Talks (SALT), 304

Obscenity, 190-193
Oil Industry: lobby, 261-262
Olmstead v. *United States,* 277 U.S. 438 (1928), 214
Olney, Richard, 121
Omnibus Crime Control and Safe Streets Act (1968), 155, 215
On Liberty (Mill), 176
Oregon, 74
Organized Crime: Campaign funding, 263
Orwell, George, 138, 139
Oswald, Lee Harvey, 135
Other America: Poverty in the United States, The (Harrington), 59*n*

Packwood, Bob, 100
Padover, Saul K., 127
Palko Test, 183
Passman, Otto, 124
Patman, Wright, 94, 95
Peace Corps, 302
Peace and Freedom Party, 264, 265
Pentagon, The, 128; budget, 102, 103, 117, 258

Pentagon Papers, The, 45, 127, 168, 187
Pierce, Franklin, 111
Piven, Francis Fox, 167
Plessy v. *Ferguson,* 163 U.S. 537 (1896), 231
Plumbers, 7
Pluralism. *See* Madison
Poage, W. R., 98
Poland, Republic of, 63, 65
Polk, James K., 297
Pollution, 121, 320, 321
Pope, Alexander, 47
Potter, David, 50-52, 60
Powell, Lewis, 153, 154
Power, Presidential, 20, 40, 44, 45, 49, 66
Press, Freedom of, 17, 115, 170-171, 180-181. *See* Mass Media
Privacy and Freedom (Westin), 214, 247, 248
Private Property, 242, 245
Prohibition: the Volsted Act, 201, 202
Proxmire, William, 89
Psychiatry. *See* Technology, Behavioral

Race Riots, 217, 225-226, 232-233
Rape of the Mind, The (Meerloo), 281
Rayburn, Sam, 92
Raynal, Abbè, 52
Refuse Act of 1899, 121
Reagan, Ronald, 217, 278-279
Renquist, William, 153-154, 215
Republican Principles, 9
Republicanism, 65, 66, 87
Republican Party, 255, 264, 267, 271
Reuss, Henry, 104
Revenue Act of 1971, 92, 94
Revenue Sharing, 97
Reynolds v. *Sims,* 377 U.S. 533 (1964), 21
Rivers, Mendel, 36
Roberts, Owen, 144
Rochin v. *California,* 342 U.S. 165 (1952), 213, 214
Rodgers, Paul, 102
Rodgers v. *United States,* 340 U.S. 367 (1951), 206
Roosevelt, Franklin D., 73, 109, 116-117, 120, 130-131, 144, 166, 297
Roosevelt, Theodore, 116, 119, 130, 297
Rostow, Eugene, 150
Roth v. *United States,* 354 U.S. 476 (1957), 191
Rourke, Francis E., 171

Index 359

Scales v. *United States,* 367 U.S. 203 (1961), 185
Schenck, Charles T., 182, 183
Schlesinger, Arthur, Jr., 313, 314
School Prayer Amendment, 22
Search Warrant, 212, 213
Second Treatise on Government (Locke), 10
Security Exchange Commission (SEC), 7, 8
Sedition Act, 181
Segregation, 265; de facto, 234; de jure, 225
Senate, 31, 32, 89, 100, 101; Civil Rights filibuster, 233; foreign policy, 129; Judiciary Committee, 58; Seniority system, 33, 89
Senate Finance Committee, 244, 261
Sheppard, Sam, 180-181, 199, 203-204
Sherman Antitrust Act of 1890, 121
Sherrill, Robert, 89, 95, 117, 153*n*
Shriver, Sargent, 266-267
Skinner, B. F., 280-281
Slavery, 13
Smith Act, 184
Smith, Margaret Chase, 124
Soil Bank, 58, 98, 258, 259
Soviet Union, 267, 282, 294; Cold War, 183
Spanish-American War (1898), 292
Spargo, John, 74, 75*n*
Speech, Freedom of, 175-176, 180, 186; the Sedition Act, 181, 185; and Technology, 241
Spirit of Laws (Montesquieu), 49
Spitz, David, 137
Spoils System, 114, 166
Stans, Maurice, 8
Stanton, Tom, 93
State Department, 128, 184, 300
State Government, 66-69, 73, 78-83
State of the Nation (Watts & Free), 309, 322
Stevenson, Adlai, 5
Stewart, Potter, 153, 192
Story, Joseph, 146
Strauss, Leo, 176
Subsidies, 97, 98
Sugar Act Program, 98
Supreme Court, 145-149; appointments, 124, 144; civil rights, 222, 231, 234; legality of confessions, 208, 210, 211; fifteenth amendment, 226; fifth amendment, 152, 156, 196, 201, 204-208, 212; first amendment, 156, 180-182, 186-188, 190-192; fourteenth amendment, 74, 76,

Supreme Court *(continued)* 201-202, 205, 222, 226, 231; fourth amendment, 212-214; gerrymandering, 21, 80, 88; judicial review, 137, 142, 143; labor laws, 74, 76; Nixon Court, 155-157; religion, freedom of, 21; segregation in schools, 67, 78, 119, 148; sociological jurisprudence, 179, 184; tenth amendment, 77; Warren Court, 149, 151-154
Switzerland, Republic of, 65

Taft, William, 297
Tariffs, 58, 92; oil rebate, 94
Taxation, 58, 69, 70, 93, 95; Income tax, 73, 79, 147; Loopholes, 92, 94, 262; power to, 71, 73*n*, 90-91
Technology, 240, 245, 274-276; behavioral, 279-282; and the employment rate, 57, 243
Tocqueville, Alexis de, 233, 238, 273-274
Toffler, Alvin, 275, 284
Tonkin Gulf Resolution, 296-298
Treasury Department, 93, 97, 166, 261
Treaty of Paris, 147
Truman, Harry S., 121-122, 127, 130, 150, 230; the Hoover Commission, 120; the Marshall Plan, 119, 294
Tugwell, Rexford, 22, 23
Tunney, John, 321
Twain, Mark, 186
Twining v. *New Jersey,* 211 U.S. 78 (1908), 205
Two-party System, 253, 254, 263

Udall, Morris K., 318-319
United Nations, 303
United States Information Agency (USIA), 301-302
Urban, 54, 108, 233; crime rate, 213-314; model cities program, 78-82; renewal, 315-317
Utah Labor Laws, 74

Vesco, Robert, 7, 8
Veteran's Administration, 311
Vice President, Office of, 109, 110
Vieg, John, 164
Vietnam, 45, 51, 127-128, 165, 168, 267, 295, 298, 312
Virginia Plan of Union, 65
Voltaire, 175
Voting Registration, 228, 268

Index

Voting Rights Act of 1965, The, 227

Wage Theory. *See* Mercantilism
Wallace, George, 111, 135, 264-265; school segregation, 67
Washington, George, 36, 37, 113, 133-134, 159, 290
Warren, Earl, 231
Watergate Conspiracy, 3-9, 262
Wayne, John, 58
Webster, Daniel, 201
Weems, Mason L., 36-37
Weisner, Jerome B., 241
Welfare, 56, 167, 319; guaranteed annual income, 57, 318; medicare, 259-261
Wesberry v. *Sanders,* 376 U.S. 1 (1964), 21, 80, 88

Westin, Alan F., 214
White, Byron, 153, 193
White, Theodore, 128
Why They Call It Politics (Sherrill), 89*n*
Wilson, Woodrow, 37, 39, 116, 130, 149, 293
Witherspoon, John, 25-27, 85, 87
Women's Suffrage, 13, 34
Wright, Jim, 104
Wright, Richard, 230

Yates v. *United States,* 354 U.S. 298 (1957), 185

Zenger trial of 1734, 188
Ziegler, Ronald, 39-40

About the Authors

FRED R. MABBUTT is chairperson of the department of political science at Santa Ana College. He received his Ph.D. in political science from Claremont Graduate School and University Center. He is coauthor of *Paths to the Present* and has published numerous articles.

GERALD J. GHELFI, professor of history at Santa Ana College, received his Ph.D. from Claremont Graduate School.